J. Peter Bruzzese
Ronald Barrett

Administrator's Guide
to Microsoft®
Office 2007
Servers

- Forms Server 2007
- Groove Server 2007
- Communications Server 2007
- PerformancePoint Server 2007
- Project Portfolio Server 2007
- Project Server 2007
- SharePoint® Server 2007 for Search

 800 East 96th Street, Indianapolis, Indiana 46240 USA

Administrator's Guide to Microsoft® Office 2007 Servers

ISBN-13: 978-0-672-32949-4

ISBN-10: 0-672-32949-2

Library of Congress Cataloging-in-Publication Data:

Bruzzese, J. Peter.

 Administrator's guide to Microsoft Office 2007 servers : Forms Server 2007, Groove Server 2007, Live Communications Server 2007, PerformancePoint Server 2007, Project Portfolio Server 2007, Project Server 2007, SharePoint Server 2007 for Search / J. Peter Bruzzese.

   p. cm.

 ISBN 0-672-32949-2

 1. Client/server computing. 2. Microsoft InfoPath. 3. Microsoft Office live communications server. 4. Microsoft Project. I. Title. II. Title: Microsoft Office 2007 servers.

QA76.9.C55B798 2007

005.4'476—dc22

2007046115

Printed in the United States of America

First Printing December 2007

Trademarks

All terms mentioned in this book that are known to be trademarks or service marks have been appropriately capitalized. Sams Publishing cannot attest to the accuracy of this information. Use of a term in this book should not be regarded as affecting the validity of any trademark or service mark.

Warning and Disclaimer

Every effort has been made to make this book as complete and as accurate as possible, but no warranty or fitness is implied. The information provided is on an "as is" basis.

Bulk Sales

Sams Publishing offers excellent discounts on this book when ordered in quantity for bulk purchases or special sales. For more information, please contact

 U.S. Corporate and Government Sales
 1-800-382-3419
 corpsales@pearsontechgroup.com

For sales outside of the U.S., please contact

 International Sales
 international@pearsoned.com

Associate Publisher
Greg Wiegand

Acquisitions Editor
Loretta Yates

Development Editor
Kevin Howard

Managing Editor
Gina Kanouse

Project Editor
Mandie Frank

Copy Editor
Keith Cline

Senior Indexer
Cheryl Lenser

Proofreader
Leslie Joseph

Technical Editor
Todd Meister

Publishing Coordinator
Cindy Teeters

Book Designer
Gary Adair

Composition
ContentWorks

Safari BOOKS ONLINE ENABLED

The Safari® Enabled icon on the cover of your favorite technology book means the book is available through Safari Bookshelf. When you buy this book, you get free access to the online edition for 45 days. Safari Bookshelf is an electronic reference library that lets you easily search thousands of technical books, find code samples, download chapters, and access technical information whenever and wherever you need it.

To gain 45-day Safari Enabled access to this book:

▶ Go to http://www.samspublishing.com/safarienabled

▶ Complete the brief registration form

▶ Enter the coupon code **QZMP-3HQL-IAVM-WSLV-MPIF**

If you have difficulty registering on Safari Bookshelf or accessing the online edition, please email customer-service@safaribooksonline.com.

Contents at a Glance

Table of Contents

About the Authors

J. Peter Bruzzese is an independent consultant and trainer for a variety of clients, including CBT Nuggets, New Horizons, and ONLC.com. Over the past ten years, Peter has worked for/with Goldman Sachs, CommVault Systems, and Microsoft, to name a few. He focuses on corporate training and has had the privilege of working with some of the best trainers in the business of computer education. In the past, he specialized in Active Directory and Exchange instruction, as well as Certification Training, and he holds the following certifications: from Microsoft (MCSA 2000/2003, MCSE NT/2000/2003, MCT), from Novell (CNA), from Cisco (CCNA), from CIW (CIW Master, CIW Certified Instructor), and from Comptia (A+, Network+, iNET+).

Peter enjoys taking complex technical topics and breaking them down into something easy to understand and enjoyable to learn. This is what he has tried to do in the many books he has authored and coauthored, including his latest, *Tricks of the Vista Masters*.

Peter is also a contributor to *Redmond* magazine, *WindowsITPro* magazine, and several tech sites. He is a speaker for the MCP TechMentor Conferences. He is also the founder of www.clusteringanswers.com, an online forum and blog site for the furtherance of knowledge regarding Microsoft clustering technologies. He has also created a variety of mini-training clips to assist others in learning more about networking, Office 2007, and Vista (www.cliptraining.com). His belief is that short training sessions in a familiar environment yield greater results.

You can catch up with Peter at jpb@cliptraining.com.

Ron Barrett has been a technology professional for 9 years, spending time working in various capacities for several major financial firms and Dot-Coms. Ron has spent the last $6\frac{1}{2}$ years as the Director of Information of Technology for a Financial Service firm in NYC. For the past several years, along with his IT duties, Ron has been a contributing author for technology books. Contributing chapters to such titles as: *Windows 2000 Enterprise Storage Solutions* and *Exam Cram 70-244: Supporting & Maintaining NT Server 4*, as well as being featured as one of the Vista Masters in the book *Tricks of the Windows Vista Masters* and appearing in several industry magazine interviews most notably a featured article in Network World's 2006 Annual Salary Survey issue. Ron is currently coauthoring an untitled Microsoft Group Policy book, and is contributing to an *Administrator's Guide to Office Communications Server 2007*.

About the Contributing Authors

Fred Celsie is the coauthor of the Project Server 2007 portion of our book. Fred is a project manager for OSS, a systems integration company (www.ossatl.com) that is certified in several leading integration software systems for security in access control, CCTV, and intrusion. Fred has also worked on the NASA, Boeing, Lockheed, and BAE sites, as well as for U.S. Secret Services and other large private-sector organizations.

Mihai Marinescu is a Portfolio Management practice expert at Pcubed, with over five years of experience in the field. Prior to Pcubed, Mihai worked for UMT, the company that originally developed Project Portfolio Server before Microsoft acquired it in 2006. During his period at UMT, Mihai worked both as a Product Manager—being involved in the product's overall design—and as a consultant, where his strong background in Portfolio Management and UMT technologies made him a perfect fit as a Management Consultant in UMT North America.

Mauro Cardarelli is the coauthor for the PresentationPoint section. Mauro has over 17 years of experience in designing and building technology solutions for customers representing a wide range of industry verticals. He is a strategic thinker, technology evangelist, effective presenter, and operational manager. In 2006, Mauro founded Jornata, a Boston-based, Microsoft technologies-focused consulting company.

Mart Muller is the coauthor of Chapter 17, "Project Server 2007: Working with Project Professional." Mart is the tech architect at Tam Tam B.V. (www.tamtam.nl). With his expertise in the Office system, his main focus is implementing solutions based on the SharePoint platform. In addition to his SharePoint blog (http://blogs.tamtam.nl/mart), Mart is an active member of the online SharePoint community. You can contact Mart at mart.muller@tamtam.nl.

Xenia Hope Thomas helped round out and add content to some of the chapters throughout this book. Xenia is a graduate of NJIT, with a bachelor of science degree in Professional and Technical Communications, and is currently working at NJIT in the Division of Human Resources as a Web/Communications Specialist.

QuantumPM, LLC is a project, program, and portfolio management product and services firm that helps its clients create pragmatic and valuable solutions to address real world problems. The company combines state-of-the-art tools from Microsoft and other technology leaders, its own expertise, and industry best practices to create solutions that support the way their customers work. QuantumPM products and services include Management Consulting, Technical Consulting, Training, Hosting Services, Earned Value Management, and Business Intelligence solutions.

They are the authors of both *Special Edition Using Microsoft Office Project 2007* (Que Publishing) and *Microsoft Office Project Server 2007 Unleashed* (Sams Publishing), and are the authors of the Project Portfolio Server 2007 chapters of this book. Without their expertise and involvement, this book would never have been completed. Thanks to Rose Blackburn, Tony Blackburn, Oscar Estrada, Jose Levy, Genie Peshkova, and Jamie Wyant.

Dedications

*This book is dedicated to my wife, Jennette, and our brand-new,
bouncing baby boy Lucas.*

—J. Peter Bruzzese

*To my wife, Alicia, who has worked harder than I have on this project, for keeping
our entire family functioning while I worked on this book. Words cannot express
my feelings enough for your loving support. Thank you so much; it could never
have happened without you! To my children, Ronald and Emma, whose smiles
gave me the energy to keep going until 4 a.m. each morning. Daddy loves you
(and go to sleep, I'll see you in the morning; I need to work). A special thanks to
my mom for standing behind me and supporting me through every dream I ever
chased and for keeping the first poem I ever wrote (at 5 years old). A word of
thanks to Tim, who has been my right arm for five years. Thanks for all your
hard work and support. Thank you to coffee, my lone work companion at 2 a.m.
And last, but certainly not least, to Peter: Thank you so much for the chance to
pursue and achieve a lifelong dream of being able to write. Although this is not
the way I pictured it at 5 years old, it has actually been better than I could have
ever imagined … my eternal gratitude.*

—Ronald Barrett

*I'd like to thank my wife, Henna, and daughter, Maegan, and my son, Austin
(who helped with this), and my new baby boy, Liam, for giving me the time to
complete this work.*

—Fred Celsie

*I'd like to acknowledge Scott Jamison, a Microsoft technical specialist, for his
insights and help with Microsoft technology. I'd also like to acknowledge my
customers who have helped me gain the expertise I carry today. They make each
day worth working. And finally, I dedicate this book to my children, Laura and
Brian. I hope this book makes them as proud of me as I am of them.*

—Mauro Cardarelli

*I'd like to thank my parents, sisters, and supportive friends for always believing in
me and backing my decisions no matter how unrealistic they might have seemed
at the time. They have all been my source for inspiration and have given me the
drive, initiative, and motivation to succeed. Without them, nothing would be
possible. I love you guys!*

—Xenia Hope Thomas

Acknowledgments

"All mankind is of one author, and is one volume.... No man is an island, entire of itself...."

—John Donne

Many have discussed and analyzed John Donne's words and interpret them to mean, we are all interconnected. There certainly is more to Donne's profound meditation, however; it struck me as fitting to the theme of this book, in more than one way: These technologies, the ones presented within this book on Office 2007 servers, are all about interconnecting mankind—allowing greater communications and the transfer of ideas and information (or an exchange of humor and camaraderie). They are about collaboration, performing work collectively. Why? Because, no man (or woman, for that matter) is an island; we all *must* work together.

In that same spirit, this book hasn't been prepared solely on my own. I've had a great deal of support from my wife, my family, and my friends. I've felt an extension of that support from people I've never met before: Microsoft developers, who have written blog sites from which I've been able to unlock the secret of these new server technologies; Internet tech experts, who have been willing to share their knowledge at no cost; and finally, several other authors, who assisted me in writing. I want to thank them all for their assistance.

I would also like to thank Melanie Swarner for her input and editing on the PerformancePoint chapters.

The folks at Sams certainly deserve a tremendous amount of praise, for being committed to this book and seeing it through to completion with me. It's been a huge undertaking and I couldn't have done it without them. With special consideration, I want to thank Loretta Yates, my acquisitions editor. We've worked on many projects in the past and this one required a little extra hand holding to make it through. I'd also like to thank my development editor, Kevin Howard, who knew just how to structure this book to make it the most effective for the reader. I also want to thank my technical editor, Todd Meister; this book's project editor, George Nedeff; and my copy editor, Keith Cline, for catching all my typing/grammatical errors. I also want to thank my proofreader, Leslie Joseph, my indexer, Cheryl Lenser, and a special thanks to the cover designer, Gary Adair.

We Want to Hear from You!

As the reader of this book, *you* are our most important critic and commentator. We value your opinion and want to know what we're doing right, what we could do better, what areas you'd like to see us publish in, and any other words of wisdom you're willing to pass our way.

As an associate publisher for Sams Publishing, I welcome your comments. You can email or write me directly to let me know what you did or didn't like about this book—as well as what we can do to make our books better.

Please note that I cannot help you with technical problems related to the topic of this book. We do have a User Services group, however, where I will forward specific technical questions related to the book.

When you write, please be sure to include this book's title and author as well as your name, email address, and phone number. I will carefully review your comments and share them with the author and editors who worked on the book.

Email: feedback@samspublishing.com

Mail: Greg Wiegand
Associate Publisher
Sams Publishing
800 East 96th Street
Indianapolis, IN 46240 USA

Reader Services

Visit our website and register this book at www.informit.com/title/9780672329494 for convenient access to any updates, downloads, or errata that might be available for this book.

Introduction

The Need for Office Servers

Although many might think that recent releases of the Office product line have been lacking in sensational new features, it is clear that the reason for these blasé feature sets is not so much a lack in ingenuity on the part of Microsoft, but rather a natural evolution of a product to its perfection. In truth, how many updates can be provided to Word, Excel, or PowerPoint (the power-trio of the Office suite)? A ceiling had been reached, leaving room for only minor improvements from one version to the next. With industries competing to bring the next level of technology to its users, these new technological advancements that will take place are guaranteed to alter and transform how things are done on a daily basis. So, the question Microsoft had to ask was "where do we, or *can* we, go from here?"

Office 2007 is more than an upgrade in your office applications, more than a new ribbon user interface. Office 2007 represents a new direction by Microsoft that provides enhanced Office user collaboration, automated business processes, management functionality, project analysis, and more.

Microsoft Office SharePoint Server has been improving its functionality since its release in 2001, and the 2007 version offers greater control over documentation shared among Office users. However, in addition to releasing a new version of SharePoint Server, Microsoft has released a group of *new* "Office servers" that enable you to expand the capabilities of Office. By providing the familiar Office interface, Microsoft has decreased users' fear of the unknown, allowing them to feel comfortable quickly with these new servers.

This book, *Administrator's Guide to Microsoft Office 2007 Servers,* introduces you to the new server lineup. This book will help you install each new server and start working with and using it to its greatest potential for your organization.

An Overview of the Office 2007 Servers Lineup

This section offers an overview of each server and explains what each is designed for. Even as Microsoft strives to be cutting edge, each server is built to be cost- and time-efficient. Although some features might be in common from one server to the next, each server works specifically in a way to improve business; each serves a unique purpose and will be a niche in its own market.

Microsoft Office Forms Server 2007

The first of the new servers, Forms Server 2007, works in harmony with SharePoint Services 3.0 to allow users to fill out electronic forms created with the Office InfoPath

2007 application. InfoPath 2007 enables you to easily create electronic forms. In the past, you could fill out these forms with the InfoPath client program (and you still can), but with Forms Server, you can fill out these via a Web browser (any Web browser), and thus cut out all the hassle that once came along with paper forms. Forms Server allows wider use and provides a way to centrally locate, manage, and secure the forms that your organization uses.

All businesses have forms of one type or another. Consider the benefits of being able to easily design those forms in InfoPath and then deploy them through a specialized server. Although you can use SharePoint Server 2007 to host your forms, the Forms Server can function all on its own. It all comes down to cost. A Forms Server is much more cost-effective than a SharePoint Server; so if all you need is to host forms, Microsoft is allowing you to use this one aspect of SharePoint at a cheaper rate.

Forms Server is the next step in electronic forms processes. Forms Server checks for errors, eliminates repetitiveness, and manages data quickly and effectively. It even allows users "on the go" to fill out forms quickly and efficiently right from their mobile and handheld devices. With Office Forms Server, you're your own boss. Create forms just the way you want them, leaving out all the unnecessary. You can also control who has access to create and publish forms. It's a cheaper solution if all you need is a way to supply forms in an electronic format!

Microsoft Office Groove Server 2007

Groove 2007, an excellent tool included in some of the higher-end versions of Office 2007, enables teams to work together in workspaces that go where they go. According to Microsoft, "Teams can work together dynamically—anywhere, anytime, and with anyone—without compromising...."

It might sound similar to SharePoint Server, but Groove allows for a more personal collaboration structure. Documentation is updated immediately among team members when connected to the Groove server. Those team members can work on items and notify each other immediately and safely through always-on encryption of those files. Groove provides tools for more than file sharing; it provides tools for discussions, meetings, and calendars. You can even play a game of chess through Groove. One frustration of modern communication is "tag" inefficiency (caused by playing phone or email tag). Groove Server addresses this frustration with advanced presence awareness, which means that you know when your team members are online.

To make all of this work properly requires Groove Server 2007, which comes in three different flavors: Manager, Relay, and Data Bridge. These three server applications are installed separately and make up Groove Server 2007. The Manager defines workspaces, the Relay controls site traffic, and the Data Bridge connects back to a SharePoint server or possibly SQL servers (or other databases).

To enable various aspects of Groove functionality, you must have the Office Communicator on your clients (along with the Groove client). And, you can make use of SharePoint Server 2007 sites if you have a SharePoint server.

Microsoft Office Live Communications Server 2005/2007

Consider it the "professional of IMs." Live Communications Server enables you to easily locate and communicate with coworkers and business partners in an instant. With Live Communications Server, you can share applications safely; it allows for Voice over IP (VoIP) connectivity, and does all of this in a secure way without going through a virtual private network (VPN). It's an instant messenger server that functions outside the network to allow immediate communications between team members or business associates, allowing for greater effectiveness and higher-level productivity in the workplace.

In addition, Live Communications Server connects in real time and can be accessed from your mobile device, which gives you greater mobility—no more sitting at the desk waiting for a reply to an email or voicemail left days ago.

With Live Communications Server, you can hold voice- and video-enhanced sessions. You can also go from public IM conversations to network-based conference calls (and thus cut back on travel time and cost).

Office Communications Server 2007, the next release, enhances all the features of Live Communications Server and provides a host of newer features, including enterprise voice (as a way of entering the enterprise VoIP market), on-premise Web conferencing, compliance archiving, and call detail records (CDRs).

Microsoft Office PerformancePoint Server 2007

Consider this one the "psychic" of all servers. This server is a performance management (PM) application that allows for score-carding, analysis, planning, forecasting, consolidating, and reporting. You can create plans and detailed budgets for your departments and make consolidated forecasts, all from one centralized location; this functionality enables organizations to glimpse their timeline and compare according to what's been planned.

Like all the other servers, Office PerformancePoint Server is reliable, fast, and user friendly. It saves time and cuts costs. Its functions help to visibly increase performance all around by monitoring progress. This server easily determines problems, compares plans with real-time performance, and allows users to work side by side so that there is nonstop planning and contributing from all.

With Office PerformancePoint Server, the overall outcome of any business can easily be improved; it is perfect for new businesses.

Microsoft Office Project Portfolio Server 2007

The main purpose of the Office Project Portfolio Server is to allow you to see what works best for you and your business or organization. Project Portfolio enables you to create portfolios that revolve around your project(s). Through the portfolio, you have centrally hosted workflows that you can connect to from anywhere in the enterprise through your browsers.

Project Portfolio aids centralized data aggregation that relates to project planning and implementation, thus providing you helpful insight.

Manage … track … view, that's the power behind Project Portfolio Server 2007.

Microsoft Office Project Server 2007

Designed to keep you on the front edge of your project schedule, job costs, and resources, Microsoft Project Server 2007 will help you create effective communication channels and collaboration, and will provide the visibility and insights necessary to make you successful!

Project Server 2007 provides a central cache of information, and thus enables you and your organization to analyze, manage, report, standardize, and centralize resource management. Project Server functionality includes budget and resource tracking and activity plan management. Much like other 2007 servers that work with Office 2007, you can access the data through your browsers. You can also make use of Excel, Visio, and Outlook.

One of the key features of Project Server 2007 is the Cube Building Service, which allows you to use portfolio analyzer cubes for analysis and reporting at a more refined level.

Microsoft Office SharePoint Server 2007 for Search

You might want to deploy a SharePoint server to take advantage of its ability to search through content, but perhaps you are inhibited by the cost of a SharePoint deployment. The SharePoint Server 2007 for Search (MOSS 2007) allows you to build an intranet or Internet search solution immediately, with the possibility of upgrading this in the future to full SharePoint functionality.

MOSS 2007 for Search should prove interesting to organizations that want to implement enterprise search (with the option to upgrade to a portal later) without changing their infrastructure and search implementation. Via protocol handlers, it enables you to search file shares, SharePoint sites, Web sites, Exchange public folders, Lotus Notes databases, and customer repositories.

NOTE

For more information about each of these servers, see the Office 2007 site at http://office.microsoft.com/en-us/products/default.aspx.

That was the 100,000-foot overview. This book provides you with a closer "look" in the following chapters, from which you will gain a better understanding of each of these servers and what they do.

How to Use This Book

This book is not exactly what you might call a "fireside read." You won't be bringing this to any book club meetings. And, although you will find step-by-step instructions through-out this book (especially in the sections that walk you through the install process of these servers), it's not quite a step-by-step book either. It is a resource guide to each of these seven servers. It's primary function is to explain what the servers are used for, which will essentially dispel confusion as to the purpose of these new servers, and explain how to implement them from a practical sense.

Planning and deployment are some of the key discussions for each server, specifically because you can deploy them in stand-alone situations or in server farms (in the server farms to allow for higher availability, load balancing, and failover). This book covers these different scenarios and indicates which caveats you need to be on the lookout for.

To understand each server, you must also understand its configuration and management. This book will help you to understand the extent of control you have as an administrator over the server.

Advanced techniques are also considered for some of these servers. These concepts are beyond the install/configuration process and generally only get talked about on developer blogs; however, this book includes some of those concepts. Of course, you will need to use the Web to go beyond the scope of this book at times; but you will know, to a greater extent, what you are looking for after learning in this book what these servers can do.

With this book, you should first read the overview about each of the servers. By doing so, you can learn what Microsoft has to offer. When you understand the purpose of each server, you can then decide whether your organization might benefit from any of them. Or, if you are a network consultant, you will be able to recommend a variety of options to your clients.

Before deploying any particular server, you should read the chapters relating to that server and establish a deployment plan that meets your requirements. Consider your hardware and software requirements, determine whether you want to perform a stand-alone or farm implementation, establish your SQL back-end server if necessary, and so forth.

Before you install any of these servers in your production environment, you should install it in a test lab. Take the time to see which issues might arise and document those issues for your true deployment; doing so can prove invaluable. Although this book discusses many of the issues we ran into during our own deployment experiences, nothing beats personal experience. So, test *your* deployment first!

We want to hear back from you about your deployment scenarios (some "in-the-trenches" war stories, if you will). Please write and tell us your experiences. Perhaps we will include them in the second edition.

CHAPTER 1

Forms Server 2007: Overview and Installation

Introduction to Forms Server 2007

Forms Server 2007 enables users to fill out InfoPath 2007 forms by using a Web browser (any Web browser or mobile device with a browser) rather than (or in addition to) by using the InfoPath client program. Forms Server enables you to keep your electronic forms centrally located so that forms can be stored, managed, and accessed by your organization. It's an excellent solution to streamline forms-driven business processes.

Some obvious benefits to online forms in general is the fact that input from persons is clear to read, forms can have policies that prevent it from being submitted unless certain fields are filled in (because we all know what it is like to receive a form that is missing the most important portion completed) and the data can be pulled from the form and added to a database automatically... all things that you cannot do with paper-based forms. Having the server in-house gives you more control over these types of forms and allows you to secure the results, add to the growing number of forms your organization might use, and make immediate edits or updates to forms as they evolve.

NOTE

Years back I worked for a company in downtown Manhattan still using paper-based forms (yes... it was the dark ages). They did a company review on paper forms for everyone in the company. I was hired in, along with a team, to work night and day for months in order to transfer the horrible handwriting into a searchable database. It took months, but paid well and included overtime pay and free Italian dinners from the local eatery. How much easier if there was a secure, online form that managers could fill out on all of their employees. But I would have missed out on all that good food.

Through the Forms Server, you can link the data that comes in to back-end systems. This might include a standard database, a customer relationship management (CRM) application, or an enterprise resource planning (ERP) solution.

NOTE

You might find Forms Server 2007 familiar if you have used InfoPath Forms Services, a component of SharePoint Server 2007. The functionality is the same, but Forms Server 2007 is a separate product with a lower price tag than an entire SharePoint server.

One of the real benefits of Forms Server 2007 is the ability to receive form data both inside and outside the firewall. When you publish the forms to the Forms server, the InfoPath templates are converted into Web-enabled forms. Therefore, users can fill out and submit their data without having the InfoPath clients installed on their systems. However, because the templates are created through InfoPath, the same form can be used for in-house InfoPath users *and* for the Web-based forms. This allows you to update the forms and republish all in one movement, saving time and resources, while ensuring uniformity.

Consider some of the standard uses for electronic forms that might really benefit from a dedicated server solution:

▶ Companies that want to use an electronic forms-based performance review can design and implement the form in InfoPath and publish the form to a Forms server.

▶ Submitting your expense reports can be handled electronically through a Forms server.

▶ Government agencies, software companies, and so forth (looking to gather information) can all create online forms that can be filled out through Web browsers.

Installation Prerequisites

Before installing Forms Server on a stand-alone system, you should endeavor to meet a few hardware and software requirements. This section talks you through the configuration of your system; after that, you learn about the installation itself. You can install Forms Server on a stand-alone system or within a server farm environment.

Hardware Requirements

The following hardware requirements are for SharePoint Services 3.0. If your server meets these requirements, Forms Server will function just fine.

The following table shows Microsoft's minimum and recommended requirements for SharePoint Services.

Component	Minimum	Recommended
Processor	2.5GHz	Dual processors (each being 3GHz or faster)
RAM	1GB	2GB
Disk	NTFS partition with 3GB of minimum disk space available	In addition to the minimum, adequate space for all your websites
Drive	CD or DVD	Either CD, DVD, or a local or network accessible drive that contains the source
Display	1024x768	Same or higher
Network	At least 56Kbps connection between client and server	Same or higher

> **NOTE**
>
> For the install, you might not have a CD or DVD, but an .iso file. This has been the new software download option Microsoft gives you off the TechNet site. If so, this is great for testing purposes. Your VM software allows you to mount an .iso file as if it were a real CD in the drive. You just need to alter some configurations settings. To open these on your system, you can use burning software to burn it to a CD or DVD and it will come alive and expand out. Or you can install a third-party program like MagicDisc to mount your iso files: http://www.magiciso.com/tutorials/miso-magicdisc-history.htm.

Software Requirements

The following software requirements are for SharePoint Services 3.0. If your server meets these requirements, Forms Server will function just fine.

Your operating system must be Windows Server 2003 Service Pack 1 or later. It is recommended that you apply all the critical updates to ensure the server is up-to-date.

The server must be a Web server. Note that if you are installing SharePoint Services 3.0 on a Server 2003 Web Edition, you can only perform a Basic installation. The reason is because SQL Server is installed to function as the database back end, but the Web Server version of Server 2003 doesn't allow it. You can, however, install the Windows Internal Database to serve as the back-end database.

The Windows Internal Database is an alternative name for Microsoft SQL Server 2005 Embedded Edition (SSEE). We use the term when referring to applications like Windows

SharePoint Services 3.0 and Windows Server Update Services 3.0, when being installed as a default back-end database.

Your Web server must include the following:

- ► Common Files
- ► WWW
- ► Simple Mail Transfer Protocol (SMTP)

Configuring Your Web Server

You can configure your Web server in a couple of different ways. You can perform the tasks manually by going through your installation of Windows Components. Or, thanks to Microsoft making the configuration easier, you can use the Configure Your Server Wizard.

To install and configure Microsoft Internet Information Services (IIS), follow these steps:

1. Select **Start**, point to **All Programs**, point to **Administrative Tools**, and then select **Configure Your Server Wizard.**

2. On the Welcome to the Configure Your Server Wizard page, click **Next.**

3. On the Preliminary Steps page, click **Next.**

4. On the Server Role page (shown in Figure 1.1), select **Application server (IIS, ASP.NET)**, and then click **Next**. You may be presented with a Role Removal Confirmation screen, depending on what options you choose while here. Now you may notice in Figure 1.1 that there are other roles on this server. This is permissible with a Forms Server, but not necessary for the function of the server and may reduce performance if you have too many roles on one system.

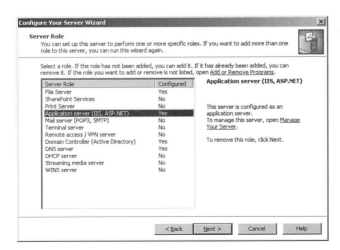

FIGURE 1.1   Configuring your Windows 2003 Server to be a Web server.

5. On the Application Server Options page, click **Next.**

6. On the Summary of Selections page, click **Next.**

7. Click **Finish.**

If you performed an upgrade from IIS 5.0 in Windows 2000 to IIS 6.0, your server might be running in Isolation mode, which you need to turn off. To turn this off, follow these steps:

1. Select **Start,** point to **All Programs,** point to **Administrative Tools,** and then select **Internet Information Services (IIS) Manager.**

2. In the IIS Manager tree, select the plus sign (+) next to the server name, right-click the **Web Sites** folder, and then select **Properties.**

3. In the Web Sites Properties dialog box, select the **Service** tab, shown in Figure 1.2.

4. In the Isolation mode section, clear the **Run WWW service in IIS 5.0 isolation mode** check box, and then click **OK.**

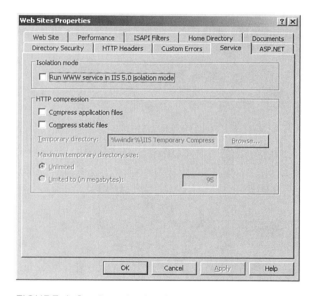

FIGURE 1.2   Deselecting Isolation mode.

Installing the .NET Framework

To install the .NET Framework, you just need to go to the Microsoft Download Center site (http://go.microsoft.com/fwlink/?LinkID=72322&clcid=0x409) and follow the download and install instructions. Note that there are different downloads to choose from depending on whether you are using the x86 or x64 system. With the install of the .NET

Framework, version 3.0, you will also be installing the Windows Workflow Foundation technology, which is required.

Enabling ASP .NET 2.0

When your IIS is up and running, you must enable ASP .NET version 2.0.50727. To do this, follow these steps:

1. Select **Start**, point to **All Programs**, point to **Administrative Tools**, and then select **Internet Information Services (IIS) Manager.**

2. In the IIS Manager tree, select the plus sign (+) next to the server name, and then select the **Web Service Extensions** folder, shown in Figure 1.3.

3. In the details pane, right-click **ASP.NET v2.0.50727**, and then select **Allow.**

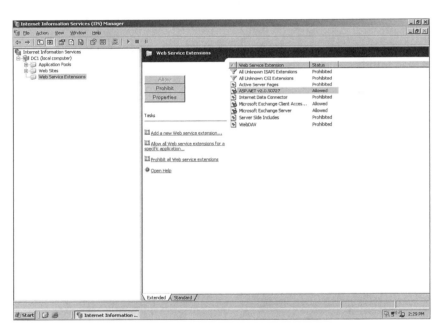

FIGURE 1.3   Enabling ASP .NET 2.0 from your IIS Manager.

Installing Forms Server 2007

After you have met all the prerequisites, the installation is your next step. When installing on a single system, run the Setup program and choose the Basic install option, shown in Figure 1.4. By doing so, you use the default options to install Forms Server and SQL Server 2005 Express Edition.

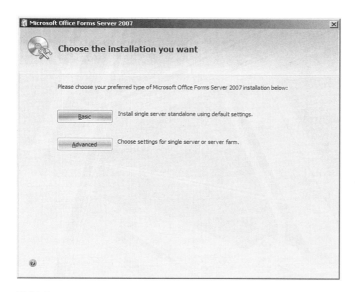

FIGURE 1.4   For the default settings of a stand-alone server, choose Basic installation.

You will be asked for a product key. If you provide a correct one, a green check mark displays; you can then click the **Continue** button.

When you see the Read the Microsoft Software License Terms page, review the terms, and then select the **I accept the terms of this agreement** check box. Then click **Continue**.

On the Choose the installation you want page, select **Basic** to install to the default location. To install to a different location, select **Advanced,** and then on the File Location tab, enter the location you want to install to and complete the installation.

When Setup completes, a dialog box prompts you to complete the configuration of your server. Ensure that the **Run the SharePoint Products and Technologies Configuration Wizard now** check box is selected, as shown in Figure 1.5.

Click **Close** to start the configuration wizard.

> **NOTE**
>
> In the event you don't want to proceed with the configuration wizard, you can deselect the check box; in this case, your system will be on hold for the finalizing of the install. You can always start the Setup again and, after entering your product key, proceed with the SharePoint Products and Technologies Configuration Wizard.

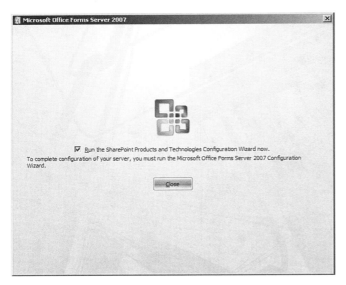

FIGURE 1.5   With the check box on, you will automatically go to the next step through the wizard.

When the SharePoint Products and Technologies Configuration Wizard begins, follow these steps:

1. On the Welcome to SharePoint Products and Technologies page (shown in Figure 1.6), click **Next.**

FIGURE 1.6   The wizard opens with minimal information. Click **Next** to proceed.

2. In the dialog box that notifies you that some services might need to be restarted or reset during configuration, select **Yes** (as shown in Figure 1.7).

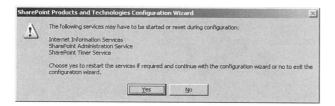

FIGURE 1.7   These services will have to be restarted during the process.

3. You will see the configuration of 10 specific tasks that have to be completed, as shown in Figure 1.8. Doing so might take some time, so you might want to take a break for coffee about now.

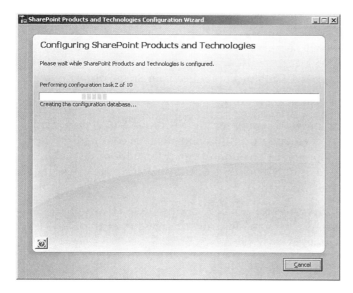

FIGURE 1.8   Configuring SharePoint Products and Technologies.

4. On the Configuration Successful page (shown in Figure 1.9), click **Finish**. At this point, the new SharePoint site opens.

NOTE

At times, you might be prompted for a username and password. If so, check to see whether the SharePoint site is on the list of trusted sites for your browser. You might also see a proxy server error message. If you do, alter your proxy server settings to allow for local addresses to bypass the proxy server.

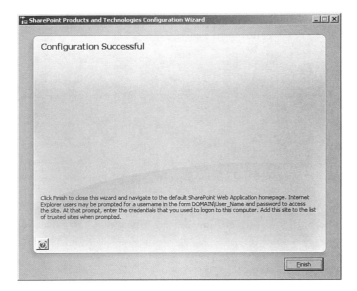

FIGURE 1.9   SharePoint configuration is successful.

When the setup is complete, you can begin adding content to your SharePoint site.

In addition, you might consider the following actions:

▶ Configure your incoming and outgoing email settings. Through SharePoint services, you can configure your email settings to handle emails coming in to save documents and discussions, support the creation of email distribution lists and management, and in the case of outgoing mail, configure alerts to site users and notifications for your site administrators.

▶ You can turn on diagnostic log settings for troubleshooting issues. This would include trace logs, event messaging, User mode error messages, and Customer Experience Improvement Program events.

▶ You can also configure antivirus settings for your sites.

To begin administrating your server, you want to use the Central Administration site. To do this, follow these steps:

1. Select **Start**, point to **All Programs**, point to **Office Forms Server,** and then select **SharePoint 3.0 Central Administration.**

2. On the Central Administration home page (shown in Figure 1.10), under Administrator Tasks, select the task you want to perform. You will be taken to the Administrator Tasks page for that task.

3. On the Administrator Tasks page, next to Action, select the task.

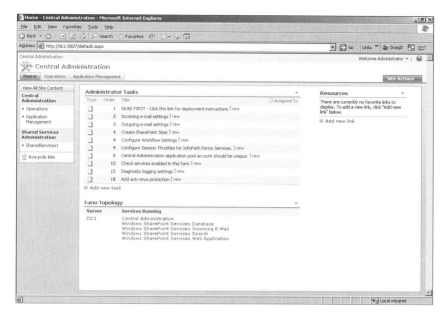

FIGURE 1.10   The Administrator Tasks home page.

TIP

So, as you have just seen, you can quickly and easily set up your first Forms server by setting up your SharePoint Services and installing a stand-alone configuration of Forms Server 2007. This is perfect if your goal is to evaluate Forms Server or deploy it in a small environment. The benefits to you are an easily administrated site, where the installation includes SQL Server 2005 for your back-end database and also the Central Administration tools, along with creating your first SharePoint site collection.

Installing Forms Server 2007 in a Server Farm

A server farm is a collection of two or more servers running the Forms Server application. The main difference between your single-server Forms Server and the farm concept is that you can establish your Forms servers as front-end Web servers, with the back end being your database servers.

You might include clustered database servers, front-end Web servers that are load balanced running IIS with Forms Server 2007, and then perhaps additional servers handling search functionality. The design really depends on the needs of each organization. The reasons for installing Forms Server 2007 as part of a server farm include the following:

▶ You are hosting a large number of sites in your environment.

▶ You want to improve performance by hosting on more than one server.

▶ You want to improve scalability.

▶ Fault tolerance is another major benefit to any load balanced cluster. Losing any single node will not break your overall solution.

How to Deploy Forms Server within a Farm

There are several considerations when installing within a farm, including the following:

▶ You need the proper credentials for each server to perform the installation. For example, you need the Setup user account (to run Setup on each server), the Farm search service account (which is the service account for the SharePoint Services Search service), and the Application pool process account (which is used to access content databases connected to the Web application).

▶ For servers that you will use network load balancing on using Microsoft's NLB service, you need to install the Forms server on the same drive. While the front end can be load balanced, the back-end database servers can be clustered.

▶ All installs of Forms Server must be the same language version within the farm.

▶ When you start the installation, you must choose the **Advanced** option (not the Basic) for a farm implementation.

To prepare all the systems in the farm requires some planning. For example, whereas in the basic stand-alone version of the install an express version of SQL Server is installed (as discussed previously), here you must prepare database servers for your server farm, which requires that you install SQL Server 2005 or SQL Server 2000 (with Service Pack 3a or later). The databases themselves are installed with the installation of Forms Server, but you have to personally install and configure your SQL servers.

One option you need to configure is the surface area settings in SQL Server. To do this, follow these steps:

1. Select **Start**, point to **All Programs**, point to **Microsoft SQL Server 2005**, point to **Configuration Tools**, and then select **SQL Server Surface Area Configuration**.

2. In the SQL Server 2005 Surface Area Configuration dialog box, select **Surface Area Configuration for Services and Connections**.

3. From the tree view, expand the node for your instance of SQL Server, expand the **Database Engine** node, and then select **Remote Connections**.

4. Select **Local and Remote Connections**, select **Using both TCP/IP and named pipes**, and then click **OK**. Note: You may see a message box indicating that the changes will not take effect until the Database Engine service is restarted.

For the front-end installations, the same prerequisites apply as in the Basic install. You need the .NET Framework 3.0 and ASP .NET 2.0 on all servers enabled through the IIS Manager. (You learned earlier in this chapter how to find, install, and enable these features.)

The First Server in the Farm

The first server you install Forms Server 2007 on becomes the establishment of the farm. All other servers are added to the farm. After you have the back-end SQL server configured and ready, and have all the prerequisites installed, kick off the installation of the first Forms server using Setup. Then follow these steps:

1. Review the terms on the Read the Microsoft Software License Terms page, and then select the **I accept the terms of this agreement** check box. Then click **Continue.**

2. From the Choose the installation you want page, select **Advanced.** Remember that the Basic option is only for stand-alone installations.

3. From the Server Type tab (shown in Figure 1.11), select **Web Front End.** The Stand-alone option is for stand-alone installations.

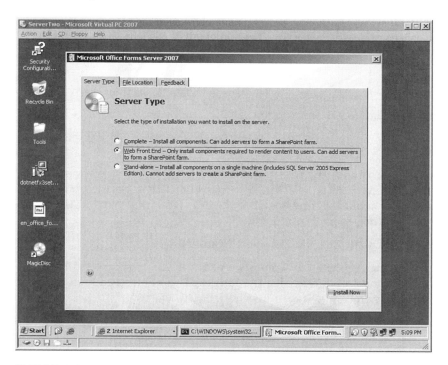

FIGURE 1.11   Setting up your Web front end.

4. In addition, to install your Forms Server 2007 at a custom location, select the **File Location** tab (shown in Figure 1.12), and then type the location name or browse to the location.

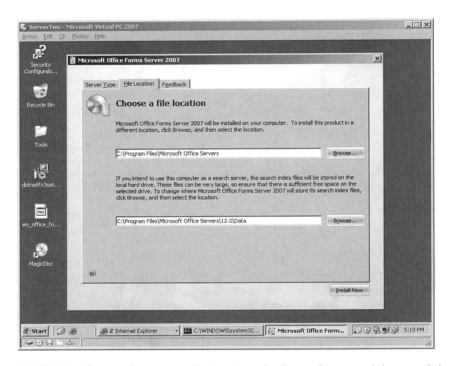

FIGURE 1.12   Configuring the file locations for Forms Server and the search index files.

5. In addition, if you want to participate in the Customer Experience Improvement Program (shown in Figure 1.13), select the **Feedback** tab, and select the option you want. To learn more about the program, click the link. (You must have an Internet connection to view the program information.)

6. After you have chosen all your options, select **Install Now.**

7. When Setup completes, a dialog box displays prompting you to complete the configuration of your server. Ensure that the **Run the SharePoint Products and Technologies Configuration Wizard now** check box is selected.

8. Click **Close** to start the configuration wizard.

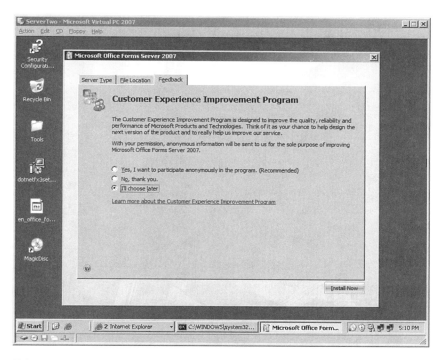

FIGURE 1.13   Determining whether you want to be in the Customer Experience Improvement Program.

At this point, you can work your way through the wizard to set up your server form. To do this, follow these steps:

1. On the Welcome to SharePoint Products and Technologies page (shown in Figure 1.14), click **Next**.

2. Select **Yes** in the dialog box that notifies you that some services might need to be restarted during configuration, as you saw in the Basic installation.

3. On the Connect to a server farm page (shown in Figure 1.15), select **No, I want to create a new server farm**, and then click **Next**. Note that this is because we are working on the first server for the farm. If you were adding servers to the farm, you would select Yes.

4. In the Specify Configuration Database Settings dialog box (shown in Figure 1.16), in the Database server box, type the name of the computer that is running SQL Server. Remember that this should have been established in advance of creating your front-end first server for your farm.

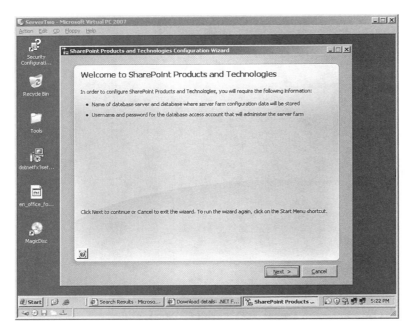

FIGURE 1.14   For a server farm, the Welcome screen reminds you of the information you need to provide for the database back end.

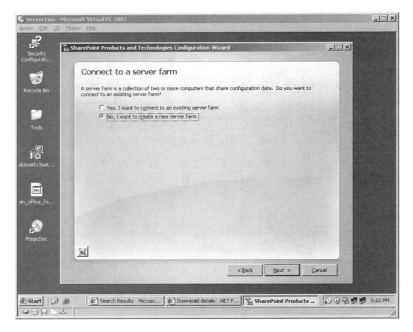

FIGURE 1.15   Creating the first server in the server farm.

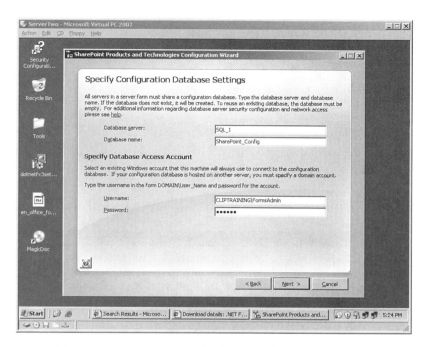

FIGURE 1.16   Connecting to the back-end SQL database.

5. Type a name for your configuration database in the Database name box or use the default database name. The default name is SharePoint_Config.

6. In the User name box, type the username of the Server farm account. (Use the user-name in the format *DOMAIN\username*.) This is the account used to access the SharePoint configuration database. It is also the application pool identity and the account that the SharePoint Services Timer service uses to run.

7. In the Password box, type the user's password, and then click **Next**.

8. On the Configure SharePoint Central Administration Web Application page, select the **Specify port number** check box and type a port number if you want the SharePoint Central Administration Web application to use a specific port; leave the **Specify port number** check box cleared if you do not care which port number the SharePoint Central Administration Web application uses.

9. Within the Configure SharePoint Central Administration Web Application dialog box, you can choose the type of authentication you prefer. You can use the default (which is NTLM authentication) or you can select **Negotiate (Kerberos)** and then click **Next**.

> **TIP**
>
> Microsoft recommends, in the majority of situations, that you use the default NTLM setting. Only use Kerberos if it is supported and functioning well in your environment. For more information about configuring Kerberos for SharePoint Services, go to http://go.microsoft.com/fwlink/?LinkID=76570&clcid=0x409.

10. On the Completing the SharePoint Products and Technologies Configuration Wizard page, click **Next.**

11. On the Configuration Successful page, click **Finish.**

At this point, the SharePoint Central Administration Web site home page will open.

> **NOTE**
>
> At times, you might be prompted for a username and password. If so, check to see whether the SharePoint site is on the list of trusted sites for your browser. You might also see a proxy server error message. If you do, alter your proxy server settings to allow for local addresses to bypass the proxy server.

Adding Servers to Your Farm

Before you begin the configuration of your services and begin the creation of sites, it is recommended that you add your additional Forms servers to the farm. To do this, you run Setup just as you did with the stand-alone install and the first install for the farm.

Then, follow these steps:

1. Review the terms on the Read the Microsoft Software License Terms page, and then select the **I accept the terms of this agreement** check box. Then click **Continue.**

2. On the Choose the installation you want page, select **Advanced.** Remember that the Basic option is only for stand-alone installations.

3. From the Server Type tab, select **Web Front End.** The Stand-alone option is for stand-alone installations.

4. In addition, to install your Forms Server 2007 at a custom location, select the **Data Location** tab, and then type the location name or browse to the location.

5. In addition, if you want to participate in the Customer Experience Improvement Program, select the **Feedback** tab, and then select the option you want. To learn more about the program, click the link. (You must have an Internet connection to view the program information.)

6. After you have chosen all your options, select **Install Now.**

7. When Setup completes, a dialog box displays prompting you to complete the configuration of your server. Ensure that the **Run the SharePoint Products and Technologies Configuration Wizard now** check box is selected.

8. Click **Close** to start the configuration wizard.

At this point, you can work your way through the wizard to set up your server form. To do this, follow these steps:

1. On the Welcome to SharePoint Products and Technologies page, click **Next**.

2. Select **Yes** in the dialog box that notifies you that some services might need to be restarted during configuration, as you saw in the Basic installation.

3. On the Connect to a server farm page, select **Yes, I want to connect to an existing server farm**, and then click **Next**.

4. In the Specify Configuration Database Settings dialog box, within the Database server box, type the name of the system running your SQL server.

5. Select **Retrieve Database Names**, and from the Database name list, choose the name you created when you set up your first server in the farm.

6. For the User name box, use the account you use to connect to the SQL server. (Remember to use the format *DOMAIN\username*.) This has to be the same username you used when configuring the first server in the farm.

7. Type the password in the Password box, and then click **Next**.

8. On the Completing the SharePoint Products and Technologies Configuration Wizard page, click **Next**.

9. On the Configuration Successful page, click **Finish**.

Complete the Configuration of Your Server Farm

After you have established the farm, you need to complete a few additional steps.

To search the content of your servers, you need to start the Windows SharePoint Services Search service on at least one of your servers. To do this, follow these steps:

1. On the SharePoint Central Administration home page, select the **Operations** tab from the top link bar.

2. On the Operations page, in the Topology and Services section, select **Servers in farm**.

3. On the Servers in Farm page, select the server on which you want to start the Windows SharePoint Services Help Search service.

4. Next to Window SharePoint Services Search, click **Start**.

5. Now click the link for Windows SharePoint Services Search on the Services on Server. On the Configure Windows SharePoint Services Search Service Settings

page, in the Service Account section, stipulate the username and password for the user account under which the search service will run.

6. In the Content Access Account section, identify the username and password for the user account that the search service will use to search content. Make sure this account has read access to all the content you want to search. You could leave this blank; if you do so, it will use the same account as the Search service.

7. In the Search database section, you can either accept the default settings or determine a database server name and database name. You can also choose between Windows authentication (selected by default) or SQL authentication. If you choose SQL authentication, you must provide a username and password with access rights to the SQL database.

8. In the Indexing Schedule section, either accept the default settings or specify the schedule that you want the Search service to use when searching content.

9. After you have configured all the settings, click **Start.**

When you have a farm with more than one index server, you should also stop the Central Administration service on all index servers. However, make sure that it continues to run on the server that is hosting the Central Administration site (even if that server is an index server).

To stop the service on an index server, follow these steps:

1. On the Services on Server page, select the index server from the Server drop-down list.

2. Under Select server role to display services you will need to start in the table below, select the **Custom** option.

3. In the table of services, next to Central Administration, in the Action column, click **Stop.**

Forms Server Up and Running: Now What?

Congrats! On getting that Forms Server up and running. In this chapter you learned all the prerequisites to setting up and installing both a single Forms Server and a Server Farm. You are well on your way to in-house online forms. But your next step will be configuring certain features on the server. And then you will need to learn a bit about how to develop forms. True, you might hire a developer to do that, but it's always good to know a little about everything, especially since those developers are going to want to publish content to YOUR server. Show them you know their lingo by learning some InfoPath development in Chapter 3, "Forms Server 2007: Using InfoPath to Create Online Electronic Forms."

But first... Configuration!

CHAPTER 2

Forms Server 2007: Configuration and Advanced Techniques

With the release of Microsoft Office SharePoint Server 2007 (MOSS), and by extension, Forms Server 2007, the new InfoPath Forms Services component was introduced as a means of sharing web-based data entry forms without becoming overly involved in complicated programming. Although the products themselves are separate, the underlying component is the same and the configuration and deployment aspects are the same as well. The component is designed to work with SharePoint Services (the underlying base for both Forms Server and MOSS). By working through the configuration options in Forms Server, as discussed within this chapter, you will be prepared to work with InfoPath Forms Services in SharePoint Server 2007.

This chapter will focus on both the configuration side to Forms server, as well as the deployment of your InfoPath-designed forms.

Deploying Your Forms

After your server (or server farm) is up and running, your next concern is to create and publish your forms to your server. Or, perhaps you already have forms you have been using through InfoPath 2003 (the earlier version of InfoPath 2007, which allowed you to create forms you can fill out through the InfoPath client). These forms could include everything from an in-house review of employees, to vacation time forms, something as common in a business as a form to put in your business expenses, or as "serious" as indicating your choice for this years company outing locations. In every case, you want those forms to be located centrally on your server and accessible to your users.

Putting these forms on the SharePoint Services server was possible in the past, but they were simply viewed as files that have an .xsn extension that users could access through a document library off the server. However, the difference here is that the server has InfoPath Forms Services enabled, which will make the templates we post accessible through a Web browser or in Outlook 2007.

The reason for this is that these forms are called symmetrical forms, because they can be hosted by a browser interface or an Office application. You might wonder how that is possible. The SharePoint server, in running Forms Services, takes the forms and puts them into an ASP .NET framework, which acts as the runtime environment for the form. Simply put, it knows how to mimic the InfoPath environment through the browser. At the same time, the Office applications know how to handle the InfoPath forms' native format. The benefit for an organization is a centralized location for these forms to be edited and managed.

Enable InfoPath Forms Services Functionality

Your first step in deploying your forms is to activate the InfoPath Forms Services support for your Forms server. To do that, follow these steps:

1. Open the SharePoint site you want to enable the service on. If you are doing this for the first time, use the default site that was created when you installed SharePoint Services 3.0. Select **Start**, point to **All Programs**, point to **Office Forms Server,** and then select **SharePoint 3.0 Central Administration.**

2. In the upper-right corner, select **Site Actions** and then **Site Settings.**

3. From Site Collection Administration, select **Site collection features.**

4. From the Site Collection Features area, you need to click the **Activate** button next to the InfoPath Forms Services support heading, shown in Figure 2.1.

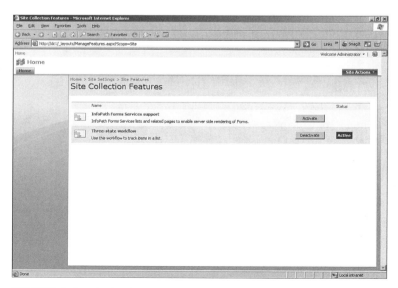

FIGURE 2.1   Activating the InfoPath Forms Services support.

Forms Deployment

When your Forms server is up and running, your goal is to get those forms uploaded to it. There are different forms templates depending on who is responsible for deploying them. You can have user form templates or administrator-approved form templates:

▶ **User form templates.** These can be designed by your forms designer (or anyone who can design a form with InfoPath), who will be given permission to publish his or her forms directly to the document library. This is for forms templates that do not contain managed code and so do not require to be uploaded by an administrator.

▶ **Administrator-approved form templates.** These require additional permission levels from a variety of other roles (designers, farm administrators, site collection administrators, and so forth). These forms can include code.

You can upload a form to the Forms server in several different ways, including the following:

▶ You can publish the form from within the InfoPath template using the Publishing Wizard. This is a great way to upload forms as you create them, but not the easiest way to upload a collection of forms you already have created.

▶ You can upload form templates through the Central Administrator on your Forms server.

▶ You can activate a form to a site collection through the Central Administrator.

Before a form can be deployed in an administrator-approved mode, three steps must be completed. Verify, upload, and then activate. The verification process is done through InfoPath using the Design Checker task pane. This process shows all the information about the form template and can provide errors and informational warnings about the form. Consider the example in Figure 2.2. Note that certain aspects of the form are not healthy for it to be published. You would still be able to publish the form to a SharePoint library, but it would not be functional in a browser because of the features included. To make sure your forms are browser compatible, the Design Checker helps you to eliminate these errors.

> **NOTE**
>
> Before your Design Checker can verify that your form is ready to be uploaded and will be browser ready, you need to change your compatibility settings. This is done through the Design Checker by clicking the hyperlink **Change Compatibility Settings;** then you have to select the check box to **Design a form template that can be opened in a browser or InfoPath.** After you have done this, your Design Checker will immediately show you errors that will not work with the form. After you eliminate the errors, you can use the Publish Wizard.

The next step is the upload (or publishing) step. During the publishing process, you are asked whether you want to enable the form for a browser. You will also be asked whether you want to create a document library, a site content type, or create an administrator-approved document template, as shown in Figure 2.3.

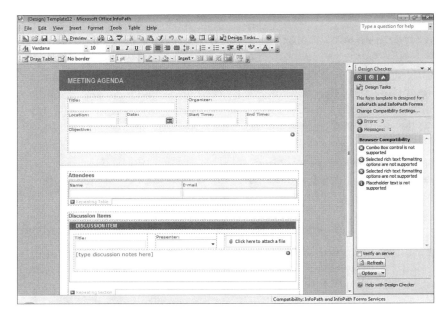

FIGURE 2.2   Using the Design Checker to ensure form verification.

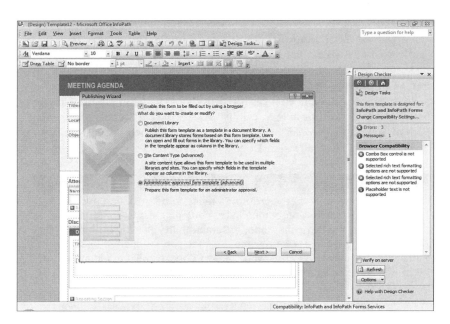

FIGURE 2.3   Uploading, or publishing, your form template.

When a form is uploaded using the administrator-approved method, it must go through the final step in the process: activation. This can be done by either a farm administrator or a site collection administrator. The farm administrator must have site collection administrative permissions on a site collection to be allowed to activate the form template.

Deploy Form Templates to a Central Location

When a user creates and deploys a form to the Forms server, it is all done through the InfoPath 2007 application. When administrators deploy templates, they can use InfoPath, but this is not the best way if you are attempting to deploy more than one form at a time, or if you are attempting to confirm that a set of forms is Web-browser ready. As mentioned previously, in these cases you want to use the Central Administration site from the SharePoint Services system running Forms Server 2007. You can also use the command line to verify and upload form templates.

> **NOTE**
>
> As mentioned previously, you can activate a form through a site collection off the Central Administration site. If you aren't completely familiar with how to do that, open your SharePoint Central Administration tool from your Administrative Tools on your Forms server. Go through the Application Management tab, under the SharePoint Site Management settings, and select **Create site collection.** From here, you can create a site collection for your templates to be centrally located in.

Remembering our three steps to deployment (verify, upload, activate), we are going to look at these in depth from both a command line and the Central Administration console.

Verify Your Forms

Using the Design Checker for each and every form is not the easiest way to verify large groups of forms. You would hope that the forms designer has verified his forms ahead of time; then you only have to upload and activate them. However, in the event you are given forms without verification, you can go about confirming they are ready for the upload stage in two ways.

> **TIP**
>
> If you are an administrator without experience creating forms in InfoPath, you can still practice these steps. Microsoft offers a set of downloadable forms to practice with. These work with their labs and are located at http://msdn2.microsoft.com/en-us/library/bb267337.aspx.

Verifying a Form through the Administration Console

This process is actually connected with the upload process from the console. To verify the form is a fully trusted form template, follow these steps:

1. Select **Start**, select **All Programs**, select **Administrative Tools**, and then select **SharePoint 3.0 Central Administration.**

2. From the top navigation bar, select the **Application Management** tab.

3. On the Application Management page, under InfoPath Forms Services, select **Upload form template.**

4. On the Add Form Template page, select **Browse.**

5. From the Choose file window, browse to the XSN file you want to verify, and then click **Open.**

6. In the Deploy Form Template section, select Verify.

7. In the Report Details section, look for any errors and warnings for the form template.

8. If you did not receive a warning, click **OK** (see Figure 2.4).

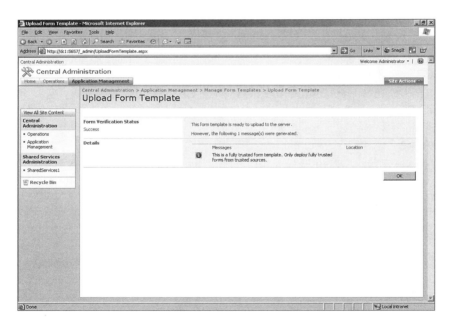

FIGURE 2.4   Verification through the Central Administration site.

Verifying a Form through the Command Line

To perform the same task through the command line, use the stsadm.exe command-line tool. Many administrators have never stumbled upon this tool before, but it offers you all the functionality found through the Central Administration site but with the command-line elasticity most admins need. The tool is located in the C:\Program Files\Common Files\Microsoft shared\Web Server Extensions\12\Bin folder.

TIP

To get the in-depth view of stsadm.exe, read Todd Klindt's article on Microsoft TechNet at www.microsoft.com/technet/technetmag/issues/2007/01/CommandPrompt/default.aspx.

So, to verify your form template through stsadm, you first need to open a command prompt and then change your directory to the Bin folder where stsadm.exe is located. Follow these steps to change your directory, and then initiate the validation:

1. From the command prompt, enter **cd C:\Program Files\common files\Microsoft shared\Web Server Extensions\12\Bin**.

2. Then, at the command prompt, enter **stsadm -o verifyformtemplate -filename** *<full location of the file>*.

The results will be the same as through the Administration site, but it will come back to you in text from the command prompt.

Upload Your Forms

After those forms are verified to work with your Forms server, your next step is to upload them. You can, once again, perform this task both through the Central Administration site or through a command prompt.

Uploading a Form through the Administration Console

Uploading the form follows the same steps as verification. When the verification process is complete, you can upload the form using the Upload option.

Another way to get to the same Upload Form Template site is to go through the Central Administration site, select the **Application Management** tab, and then look under InfoPath Forms Services for Manage Form Templates. You will see all your forms, but you will also see an Upload form template link. If you select this link, you are taken to the Upload page, shown in Figure 2.5.

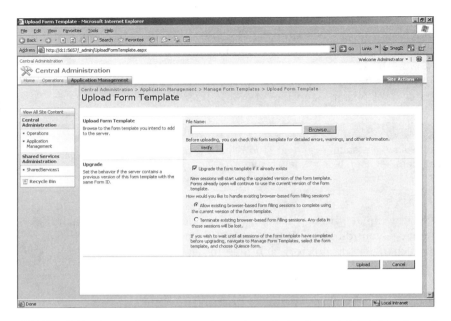

FIGURE 2.5   Uploading form templates through the Central Administration site.

Uploading a Form through the Command Line

Similar to the verification process, you can use the stsadm.exe command to upload the template. From the command line, you need to ensure that you are in the Bin that holds the **stsadm** command. Then type the following from the command line:

```
stsadm -o uploadformtemplate -filename <name of the file>
```

Activate Your Forms

Your forms are verified, they are even uploaded, but they are still not available to users. The administrator (with site collection administration permissions) still needs to activate the forms to a site collection.

To activate a form through the Central Administration site, open the site and go back to the Application Management tab. Then follow these steps:

1. Look for the InfoPath Forms Services section, and select **Manage form templates.**

2. Find the form template you want to activate. When you place your cursor over it, you will see a down arrow. Select this down arrow to see your options.

3. Select the option **Activate to a Site Collection,** as shown in Figure 2.6.

4. From the Activate Form Template page, you can choose to keep the default site collection or change the site collection by selecting the down arrow and choosing **Change Site Collection** from the Activation Location section of the page. Note that you might have to select **Change Web Application** to see the additional site collections you have.

5. When you have the template going into the correct site collection, click **OK**; it will become activated.

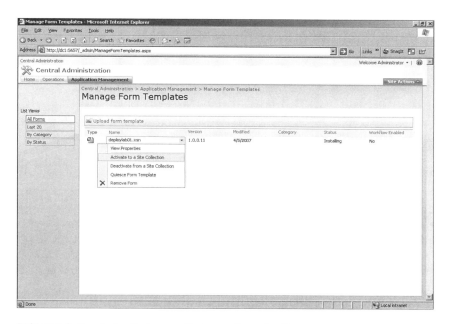

FIGURE 2.6   Activating your site to a site collection.

Verify the Template Is Up and Available for Users

This last step simply involves opening your Web browser (either on the server itself or through another system) and browsing to the location of the site collection. When the default site is up, select **View All Site Content,** and then choose **Form Templates** from the Document Libraries section. It should be there with a little "new" sign tagged to it, as shown in Figure 2.7. If you verified, uploaded, and activated … your form should be fully functional.

FIGURE 2.7   Verify that your site is functional.

Managing Forms Templates

What does it mean to manage forms templates? When you are just getting started, you might have only a handful of templates to worry about. As time goes by and the technology becomes known to departments within your organization, however, you could end up with thousands of forms to worry about. In addition to managing the deployment of your forms (remember, verify, upload, and activate), you have to worry about making sure those forms are available to users, that they are secure, that they are backed up in the event of a problem, and you even need to play a part in the life cycle of those forms because they will change over the course of time.

We've discussed that there are two different types of forms deployment: user approved and administrator approved. Some of the concepts are the same in managing each type of form, but the administrator approved is more complex and involves a larger scale. User-approved forms are only manageable on a stand-alone Forms server and cannot be managed on a farm level.

You can manage your forms templates from the Manage Form Templates page of the SharePoint Central Administration site. The home page for your Central Administration site offers you a list of administrative tasks to perform and attempts to help you get started. You have two other pages that can be very helpful, not only with your Forms server, but in handling your SharePoint Services, too: the Operations page and the Application Management page.

The Operations Page

The Operations page, shown in Figure 2.8, provides you with a list of options to help manage your server.

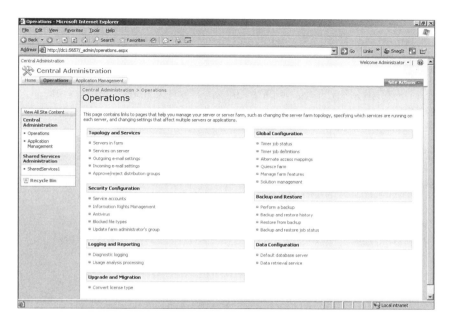

FIGURE 2.8   Managing Your SharePoint Services server.

They include the following:

▶ **Topology and Services.** This grouping allows you to add or remove servers to the server farm. You can configure incoming and outgoing messages for alerts, invitations, and administrator notifications. You can even handle the approval or rejection of distribution groups.

▶ **Security Configuration.** From here, you can alter the service accounts for your Web applications, which are linked to your Web application pools. You can configure Information Rights Management (IRM), which helps protect files from being misused or distributed without permission after they have been downloaded from the server. You can configure antivirus settings. (Remember, however, that you must have an antivirus scanning software installed on all Web servers hosting documents before these settings will take effect.) You can configure blocked file types, which will prevent specific file types from being saved or retrieved from any site on the server. (Note that if a user attempts to retrieve a blocked file type, the user will receive an error.) And, you can add individuals to the Farm Administrators group.

▶ **Logging and Reporting.** From here, you can configure diagnostic logging. You can sign up for the Customer Experience Improvement Program. (You were asked about this when you first installed your SharePoint Services; now you can change your mind.) You can also configure error reports, event throttling, and trace logs. You can also configure usage analysis processing.

▶ **Upgrade and Migration.** From here, you can change the product key for your InfoPath Forms Services.

▶ **Global Configuration.** From here, you can see a list of timer job status and definitions. You can establish alternate access for your sites so that your internal URLs and your public URLs are different. You can "quiesce" your farm to take it offline slowly. And, you can manage the farm features and files.

NOTE

Quiescing a server allows the server to slowly deny access to users (as opposed to harshly taking the server offline). It gradually releases libraries and users and denies new requests to access libraries through the server. This will allow you to take a server offline slowly, as opposed to a harsh snap of connectivity your users might feel if the server were to say, crash. This slowly releases the users and let's you perform administrative tasks smoothly.

▶ **Backup and Restore.** From here, you can back up and restore your server. When you initiate the backup, you have a two-step process, the first of which involves selecting the component you want to back up, as shown in Figure 2.9.

▶ **Data Configuration.** These settings enable you to configure the location of your database. If you are using it as a stand-alone system, you could be using the Express version of SQL on the local system. If you are using a farm configuration, however, you will want to indicate the location of the SQL servers (or other back-end database servers) from within this setting.

The Application Management Page

The Application Management page helps you configure additional settings for applications and components installed on the server or server farm. Most of these settings relate to your SharePoint server itself (arranging site collections and workflow settings, for example). However, there is a section we have already been working with in earlier examples: InfoPath Forms Services. Let's consider some specific uses for this page in managing your Forms server.

TIP

If you want to obtain assistance from the help files for your Forms server, in the upper-right corner of the page, select the blue question mark. Doing so brings up the Office Forms Server 2007 Central Administration Help page.

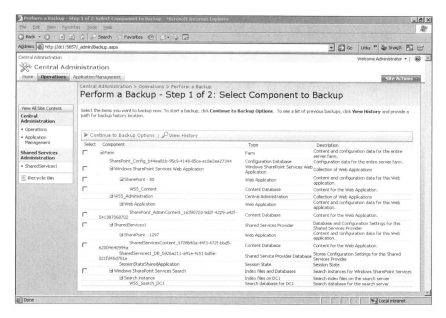

FIGURE 2.9   Selecting components of your SharePoint Services server you want to back up.

There are five different InfoPath Forms Services links, and each helps you manage your forms and the Forms server.

Manage Form Templates

You've seen some of the options included here. You can do the following from this page:

▶ **View form templates.** From the list views, you can choose to view All Forms, Last 20 (which shows the last 20 forms uploaded), By Category (which lists your form templates in a tree view according to their category), and By Status (which lists your form templates by status).

▶ **View form templates' properties.** To view the properties (and provide a category name), select the form and choose **View Properties** from the drop-down menu, as shown in Figure 2.10.

From within the Manage Form Templates page, you can activate or deactivate a template from the site collection. And, you can quiesce a template. We discussed this earlier in terms of the server itself, but you can decide to take a specific form offline by stopping new user connections to the form and slowly releasing the users connected to it. To do this, select the form, and from the drop-down arrow you select **Quiesce Form Template**, which will take you to the Quiesce Form Template page shown in Figure 2.11. You select the time in minutes before the template is fully quiesced, and then select **Start Quiescing.** When the form is quiesced, the status of your form indicates that.

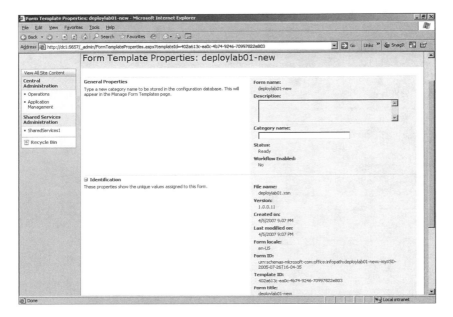

FIGURE 2.10   Viewing your forms' properties.

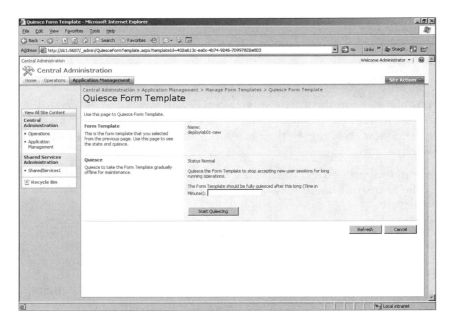

FIGURE 2.11   Viewing the Quiesce Form template.

Configure InfoPath Forms Services

You can configure your Forms server in a variety of ways depending on the needs of your organization. For example, by default, user form templates can be deployed by nonadministrators; however, you can alter this to only allow administrator-approved form templates to be opened by a browser. This is just one of the many options you can configure for your stand-alone server or server farm.

On the Configure InfoPath Forms Services page, shown in Figure 2.12, note that you have a lot of different options at your disposal.

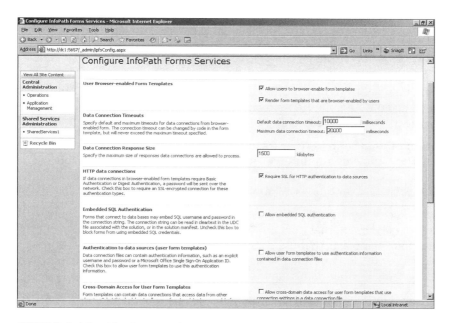

FIGURE 2.12   Viewing your forms' properties.

Let's consider these options one at a time:

► **User Browser-enabled Form Templates.** In this section, you can configure how user form templates are processed by the server, and you are given two options to select/deselect. If you want to continue the default functionality mentioned previously regarding user-deployed form templates, leave the option **Allow users to browser-enable form templates** checked. Otherwise, deselect this option to make forms browser enabled only through administrator-approved methods. The second option, **Render form templates that are browser-enabled by users**, must also be selected to allow form templates to be accessible through a browser, because even though the form may be published to the server and browser enabled, it must be rendered, too.

▶ **Data Connection Timeouts.** This provides a timeout for the connection between a browser and a form. Even though there is a default setting (the default is 10,000 milliseconds), you can use a code within your form template to override this. However, it will not be able to override the maximum data connection timeout (whose default is 20,000).

▶ **Data Connection Response Size.** This establishes a maximum size of responses that data connections are allowed to process. The default is 1500 kilobytes.

▶ **HTTP data connections.** This section contains only one selection box: Require SSL for HTTP authentication to data sources. If you have Secure Sockets Layer (SSL) configured and your browser-enabled forms require Basic or Digest Authentication where a password must be sent over the network, this box ensures that the connection requires an SSL-encrypted connection.

▶ **Embedded SQL Authentication.** This setting, Allow embedded SQL authentication, is for forms that embed the authentication directly within the form itself. This is not allowed by default. Because the username and password are in the connection string in clear text, it can be read easily.

▶ **Authentication of data sources (user form templates).** This setting is for user form templates to "Allow user form templates to use authentication information contained in data connection files." Authentication information might include a username and password, or some other form of authentication.

▶ **Cross-Domain Access for User Form Templates.** At times, a form template might need to access data from another domain. The setting "Allow cross-domain data access for user form templates that use connection settings in a data connection file" is deselected by default but must be selected to allow user form templates to reach for data within another domain.

▶ **Thresholds.** These settings relate to the thresholds on when to end a user session and log error messages. You can configure postbacks per form session and the number of actions per postback. When a form operation exceeds these values, the session is terminated.

▶ **Form Session State.** The session state stores what is called transient data from the filling out of the form. Before the form is complete and submitted, there is data in those fields as the user fills them out during the session between the user and the server. This is the form session state. These options are some of the most important and can cause you to affect the Forms server dramatically. One setting indicates "Active sessions should be terminated after," with a default value of 1,440 minutes (usually plenty of time to fill out any form.) There is also a "Maximum size of form session state" for the amount of session state data (which is data entered into the form that the server will retain up to a point, the default being 4096 kilobytes). In addition, you can configure where the session state data is held, either on the SQL server or with the client computer.

NOTE

How to choose between the session state or the form view? When you choose the session state option, all the sessions are handled on the back end with the SQL server. This uses only a portion of your network bandwidth but can have an impact on your SQL server. When you are using the form view, the sessions are maintained on the client, putting the performance impact off to the client, but each postback to the server will include all the session data (increasing your network traffic). Microsoft recommends to use the forms view in smaller environments to reduce the stress on the SQL server. If you are looking at a larger environment, go with the session state option.

Upload Form Template

We used this part of the Central Administration site to verify and upload our forms templates earlier in this chapter. However, there are additional settings we didn't discuss: the upgrade settings.

At times, you want to upgrade a form that has changed, and you can do this through these settings. The process to upload is the same, but there are a few settings for an upgrade process before you click the **Upload** button.

TIP

If you are going to be upgrading a form that you know is in use, you should quiesce the form first through the Manage Form Templates section discussed earlier. By doing so, you ensure that all users have been gracefully weaned off the form and the form is off limits before you upgrade it. Alternatively, you can choose from one of the two options provided to either allow users to finish filling out the forms they have before upgrading, or terminate users existing sessions and upgrade the form.

Every administrator-approved form template has a uniform resource name (URN) attached to it for identification. So, when you attempt to upload a form, the SharePoint Services server checks to see whether it already exists. If not, it adds the form into the system.

If the server notes that the URN is already registered, it does the following:

▶ If the version you are uploading is an earlier version, it reports an error to let you know it. If you know that you want the earlier version (perhaps there is something with the new version you don't like), you can delete the newer version from the server and upload this version fresh. Or, you can alter the version of the form to a higher URN and then upload it.

▶ If the version you are uploading is the same exact version, you get a warning explaining that you are uploading the same one. You must either choose a different form to upgrade this one or raise the URN on the form and then upload it.

▶ If the version you are uploading is newer, it handles the transition according to the options previously discussed. If you already quiesced the form, it proceeds. If you want to allow users to complete the forms they are working on, the first radio button says "Allow existing browser-based form filling sessions to complete using the current version of the form template." If you want to stop all sessions, the second radio button says "Terminate existing browser-based form filling sessions. Any data in those sessions will be lost."

Manage Data Connection Files

When you select the Manage Data Connection Files option, initially there will be nothing on that page. You need to upload your data connection files to start with. Select the **Upload** option and you will be taken to a page that enables you to select the file, determine a category for it, and choose whether you want it to be accessible through HTTP, as shown in Figure 2.13.

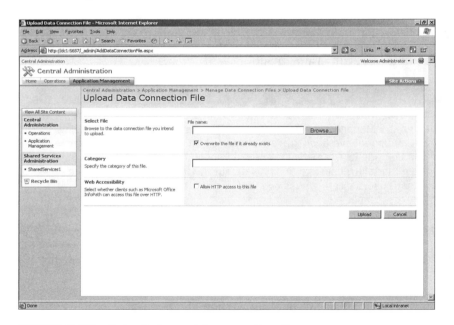

FIGURE 2.13   Uploading your data connection files.

NOTE

You might wonder what a data connection is. This a dynamic link between your form template and a data source that stores or provides data for the template. When you create a template, an automatic data connection is created, called the main data connection. However, you can create and add secondary ones. There are different types of data connections you can use—for example, a database data connection that populates form fields by looking up information in a database after a user has been authenticated. So, if a user has been authenticated, the form can populate fields already in the SQL server for that user. Data connections exist between the form template and an external data source, such as the database (discussed earlier), a Web service, a SharePoint library, or an XML file. These connections are used to query and submit data.

You can read more about data connections in the section "Advanced Techniques with Forms Server 2007."

Manage the Web Service Proxy

Forms Server includes a Web service proxy that will forward Simple Object Access Protocol (SOAP) requests to a Web service to enable authorization for a data query. Basically, the proxy runs under an account trusted by the Web service (and the service will authenticate the account). Based on the identity of the user, the proxy returns the data specific to that user. Enabling the service on the Forms server is the key to the process functioning.

This link off the Application Management page only has two settings with a simple check box for you to enable each:

▶ **Enable the Web service proxy.** This setting, when enabled, will use the proxy for data connections between InfoPath forms and Web services. The data connections must be defined in universal data connection (UDC) files, and they must be enabled to use a proxy.

▶ **Enable the Web service proxy for user forms.** Simply put, this setting, when enabled, will use the proxy for data connections in user forms.

The next step to using the Web service proxy is handled more from a programming perspective through your InfoPath tools. To learn more about advanced server-side authentication for data connection, you can learn a lot from the InfoPath Team Blog. You can find an article relating to this subject at

http://blogs.msdn.com/infopath/archive/2006/07/03/655611.aspx.

Advanced Techniques with Forms Server 2007

As you now know, you can install a server into a stand-alone or farm configuration. You know how to publish your forms as a user of InfoPath, and how to verify, upload, and activate forms under the administrator-approved method. You have seen all the inner SharePoint Services Central Administration screens for tweaking the Forms server to fit your needs (although the standard default settings will usually meet most of your needs). What more could you need to know?

If you are an InfoPath designer, you need to know a great deal more about the programming end of creating forms. Some forms are standard templates that request information that anyone can create with InfoPath. Others are more dynamic in functionality and require programming knowledge. We can be thankful that Microsoft doesn't hide that knowledge from us; you can find a tremendous amount of information from the InfoPath Team Blog, mentioned previously, and from several other great bloggers, such as Mike Ormond (http://blogs.msdn.com/mikeormond/default.aspx).

Where you as an administrator of a forms server need to be educated is in the concepts that your designers might toss your way. An InfoPath forms designer has a tremendous amount of knowledge regarding how his or her forms need to be connected with the back-end database, how to use data connections and Web proxies, and so forth. For example, if you are working on a form that has you put the name of a stock quote in one of the boxes, and then the current price of that stock pops up when you push a button (as shown in Figure 2.14), that is true programming on the side of your forms designer. Unless this is a personal hobby of yours, you won't be as savvy with these concepts. So, this section is going to bring you up to speed so that you will understand what is going on behind the scenes between the forms template and the power within that template.

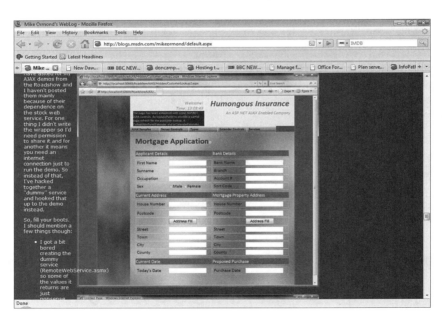

FIGURE 2.14   A great example from Mike Ormond on the power of an InfoPath form.

What Is a Universal Data Connection File?

The UDC file format has been used by FrontPage since Office 2003 to store data connection information used by Web parts. That was UDC version 1. We now have version 2.0 in Office 2007 applications, including InfoPath.

We understand that forms do more than provide a user with information, but dynamic forms can reach out and pull in data from other sources, provided the form template is designed to allow for the proper authentication necessary to pull up certain data. Data connections are used to connect to back-end resources or to cross-domain resources, but sometimes you must use a UDC file. (In actuality, it's impossible to make a cross-domain connection without one.)

> InfoPath has three security modes, which we refer to as restricted (a.k.a. "super-sandbox"), domain, and full-trust. Restricted form templates don't run on the server. Full-trust form templates are allowed to do whatever and consequently need to be administrator approved to run server side. Domain trust form templates constitute the vast majority of form templates in the enterprise, and roughly follow the Internet Explorer security model, which dictates that by default, the user must approve any attempt to access resources that come from a different domain or zone. So, if you have a form template running on http://myserver/, and it tries to connect to a Web service on http://yourserver/, InfoPath will prompt you before trying the connection.

> Works great in InfoPath, but when you run a form in the browser, you may be running server-side business logic. That business logic may want to execute a data query. Because HTTP is a stateless protocol, Forms Services can't halt execution of a server-side process and return to the browser in order to ask you for permission to continue. Additionally, the user in this case may not be the right person to own the decision about whether the cross-domain connection can take place. So, this decision is placed instead in the hands of the server administrator who owns security around the form template. Depending on whether the form is administrator approved or just published to a document library by Joe User, this ownership falls on the farm administrator (I call her Julie) or the site collection administrator (henceforth known as Bob).

> The technology that allows Julie and Bob to determine whether forms can make cross-domain connections involves a system of checks and balances. Central to this system is a data connection settings file in the universal data connection V2 format, called a UDC file. Bob's UDC files live in a special type of document library called a data connection library, or DCL. Julie's UDC files live in the Microsoft Office SharePoint Server configuration database, and are managed via the Manage Data Connection Files page in the Application Management section of SharePoint Central Administration. (I tend to refer to this as "the store.")

NOTE

A DCL is a library that can contain two different types of data connections: Office data connection files and UDC files. Files that are UDC use a .udcx or .xml file extension.

The basic premise behind UDC files is that in InfoPath 2007 your data connection settings can live outside of the form template in one of these files, and both InfoPath and Forms Services will retrieve the current connection settings from this file at runtime before making the connection. The UDC file itself is retrieved from a URL relative to the root of the site collection where the form was opened. This enables lots of cool functionality—for example, you can now share settings across multiple forms and change them once when you move your data source. You can also predeploy test and production versions of your data connection settings to your staging and production environments so that you don't need to update the form template with new data connection settings when you go live.

Why is this more secure? Well, if Bob is a good administrator, he controls access to data connection libraries on his site collection. A DCL requires content approval by default, and while members of the site with Contributor access can write files to the library, nobody but the owner of the file can use the file from InfoPath unless a content approver has approved the file. By default, all members with Designer permissions have the Content Approval right. In short, Bob can set up the site collection such that only people that he designates can approve UDC files. Therefore, forms on Bob's site collection can only make connections outside the farm unless he approves the connection first.

Julie's central store is more secure—only users with access to SharePoint Central Administration can modify those files. Furthermore, by default, only the server object model can access files in the store. In order to make these files accessible to Web clients such as InfoPath, the "Web accessible" flag must be set. Otherwise, the files can be used from browser forms only.

NOTE

The above quote was posted on the InfoPath blog site and has been reprinted with the permission of the team.

As an example of how this would look visually, consider Figure 2.15. This shows how a form template uses a UDC to reach for the data it needs.

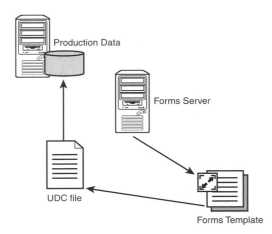

FIGURE 2.15   An example of how a UDC file works.

Where Do UDC Files Come From?

Well, you have to make them. Because they are just XML files that use a namespace and schema, you can use Notepad to create them, or just cut and paste from other examples found on the Web. A sample UDC looks like this:

```
<?MicrosoftWindowsSharePointServices
ContentTypeID="0x010100B4CBD48E029A4ad8B62CB0E41868F2B0"?>
<udc:DataSource MajorVersion="2" MinorVersion="0"
xmlns:udc="http://schemas.microsoft.com/office/infopath/2006/udc">
 <udc:Name/>
 <udc:Description/>
 <udc:Type MajorVersion="2" MinorVersion="0" Type=""/>
 <udc:ConnectionInfo Purpose="" AltDataSource=""/>
</udc:DataSource>
```

Note that the file begins with a processing instruction specifying a ContentTypeId. The purpose of this is to associate the file with the UDC content type. Having the content type identified allows the Name, Title, Description, Type, and Purpose fields to be promoted into columns in the DCL so that the InfoPath designer can see the file.

WARNING

The InfoPath Team pointed out an interesting problem that forms designers should be aware of regarding using InfoPath on a Windows Vista machine. There is a problem with the convert function in the designer (as discussed later in this chapter). They recommend, as a workaround for this issue, that you save the file to the local disk, and then re-upload the file to the library using the SharePoint library upload function.

To learn more about the specific syntax within the UDC file, read the article "The anatomy of a UDC file" from the InfoPath Team Blog, located at http://blogs.msdn.com/ infopath/archive/2006/10/30/the-anatomy-of-a-udc-file.aspx.

Another way to create UDC files is through the InfoPath application. When a forms designer is creating the form and establishing data connections for specific portions of that form, there is an option called Convert.

When you click the **Convert** button and then indicate the path of the DCL you need to place the file in, the UDC file (which will have a .udcx extension) will be created and added to your DCL. The site administrator will still need to set the files status to "approved" for this to work.

We mentioned that the UDC file can be used for authentication purposes. The InfoPath convert feature does not configure authentication options automatically, but it will create an authentication block within the UDC file that is preconfigured to use Office single sign-on (SSO).

NOTE

What is the single sign-on? In Microsoft Office SharePoint Server 2007, SSO authentication allows users to access a variety of system resources without the need to provide authentication more than one time. This is done through a Windows service and a secure credentials database. The SSO settings are managed through the Central Administration application.

You can alter the authentication portion for any number of reasons. For example, you might want to alter the credential type, from NTLM to SQL, Kerberos, CD, Basic, or Digest. The authentication portion is only for forms running in a browser because InfoPath will always ignore the authentication element.

Consider the following UDC addition to make this happen.

```
<udc:Authentication>
  <udc:UseExplicit CredentialType="">
    <udc:UserId/>
    <udc:Password/>
  </udc:UseExplicit>
  <udc:SSO AppId="" CredentialType=""/>
</udc:Authentication>
```

To see the full UDC schema, go to http://blogs.msdn.com/infopath/attachment/877504.ashx.

To learn more about each aspect of the schema, go to http://msdn2.microsoft.com/en-us/library/ms772017.aspx.

Where to Go from Here

Now that you know all there is to know (within reason) about establishing your Forms server, you essentially have three directions to go. You can study up further on SharePoint Services 3.0.

Here are some great sites for SharePoint information:

> The Microsoft SharePoint Products and Technologies Team Blog:
> http://blogs.msdn.com/sharepoint/
>
> A SharePoint Services 3.0 demo site that shows all the great features of SharePoint Services: http://www.wssdemo.com/default.aspx

In addition, you might want to learn more about creating forms with InfoPath 2007. To get started on this, consider the following sites:

The InfoPath 2007 training labs are live on MSDN. There are several labs, with some great examples on how to do everything from publishing a form template to using SharePoint Server workflows. For a good list of the 2007 (as well as the 2003) labs, check out http://blogs.msdn.com/infopath/archive/2007/03/09/infopath-2007-training-labs.aspx.

And for the third direction you might now want to go, you can pursue a greater under-standing of Web server farms using SQL as the back end, or some other type of back-end solution such as a customer relationship management (CRM) solution. There are too many options to list here, but you can study database functionality, Web farm front-end solutions with network load balancing in Windows Server, and more.

2

CHAPTER 3

Forms Server 2007: Using InfoPath to Create Online Electronic Forms

With all the rapid advancements in technology, it's a wonder the world doesn't operate solely on electronic-based applications when it comes to businesses and corporations filling out and filing forms. For a while now, many organizations have been making the transition from paper to computer-based forms; so, it's a no-brainer to see that electronic forms will, in the near future, almost replace paper, becoming a standard method for data submission both within companies and throughout government organizations.

This transition is guaranteed to cut the amount of money and time spent on paper and the excess waste of natural resources (resources until recently destroyed in the process of making paper).

Microsoft Office InfoPath 2007 is the new solution to e-forms. When you think about it, just about everything we do requires us to fill out a form of some sort. A visit to the doctor's office, a trip to the department of motor vehicles, a return in a clothing store—these are just a few of the routine activities that require form filling. And, paradoxically, the data still must be inputted electronically into a database of some kind, for future reference. With an e-form, you can eliminate the input of invalid information caused by human error and the repetition of data within each form.

The real beauty behind InfoPath is that you don't have to be a major developer to produce a professional, high-quality form. In fact, you don't have to be a developer at all; no coding is necessary! This chapter shows you how to make InfoPath work for you. Sooner rather than later, you'll become an InfoPath guru.

Let's begin with an overview of e-forms from the past.

An Overview of E-Form Technology

Maybe you've worked with an e-form before, or maybe you've created one yourself using a program, such as Microsoft Word (see Figure 3.1). The primary purpose behind the development of e-forms was to provide greater ease through the automation of a business process while reducing the inefficiency of paper-based forms.

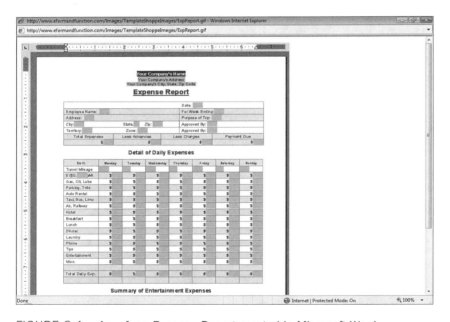

FIGURE 3.1   An e-form Expense Report created in Microsoft Word.

For example, an e-form that requires specific information before it can be submitted is an excellent way to ensure that all necessary parts of the form have been filled out. Nothing's worse than receiving a form and having to send it back because vital information is missing (a waste of valuable time). In addition, easy-to-use drop-down boxes and electronic check boxes make the filling out of a form quick and easy. Finally, typed data is much easier to read and process than handwritten data.

The first e-forms were called print-and-fill (because you printed them out and filled them in). The second generation was fill-and-print (because you filled them in on the computer before printing them). As the Internet became widely used in the late 1990s, Hypertext

Markup Language (HTML) forms developed, keeping pace with IT advances as they were made. Now, in our "modern" times, Extensible Markup Language (XML) is the new standard for e-form technology.

Different Types of Forms

Microsoft isn't the only company racing to provide software that enables users to create e-forms, but they are a pretty big force to reckon with. The following subsections identify some of the different players in the e-form market and the various types of e-forms they provide.

Word Forms

You've already learned about one type of form, the Word form. The basic concept behind a Word form is that you create a document that is partially protected. Parts of the document can be written on, but other parts (the question portions of a form, for example) cannot. You can print out these forms for use as hard-copy forms, or you can send them through email (or make them downloadable from a site or network share) so that those who need to can fill them in. Persons filling out the form can then select the gray areas and fill in the required information, save the form, and send it back to you through email (or print it and mail it back).

Word forms can fill in some information (such as the date) automatically and can include drop-down lists and check boxes to make the filling out of the form easier. Word forms can even perform simple math, to allow the form to handle expenses or purchase orders.

Behind the scenes of a Word form are fields that you can use later to pull the data from a form into another format, such as an Excel spreadsheet, to create a database of information for subsequent automation.

HTML Forms

No doubt you have seen and worked with these before. With an HTML form, as shown in Figure 3.2, you can provide text fields, radio buttons, check boxes, range controls (sliders or knobs), single- or multiple-choice items, required information portions, and more. A user fills out the form and then submits it. You create the Submit button and program it to email the form data back to you through an agent (either a Web server or a mail server).

Standard HTML forms might not suit the style of your Web site. If that's the case, can enhance your Web forms by using Cascading Style Sheets (CSS). Beyond the style itself, one of the biggest frustrations with HTML forms is the layout. Layout (including the grouping of objects, labeling of fields, and so forth) is where most form developers have a problem with HTML forms. JavaScript can also be used with your online forms to enhance their capability. JavaScript (not to be confused with Java) is a smaller language that doesn't create applets or stand-alone applications. You place the JavaScript directly within your HTML page to allow for a greater level of dynamic activity between the client and the form.

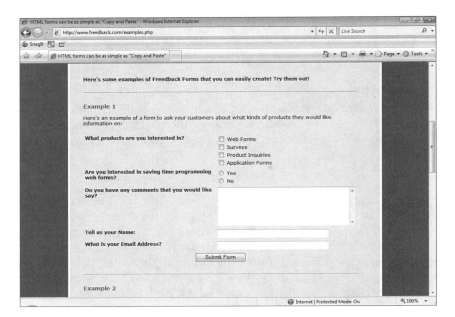

FIGURE 3.2   Working with an online HTML form.

NOTE

For the HTML forms developers reading this, you can find an excellent resource for creating semantic form layout at www.themaninblue.com/writing/perspective/2004/03/24/.

Beyond standard HTML forms, you can use Java to create forms that interact with a Web server using Common Gateway Interface (CGI) standards. Essentially, a Web developer can create a form through HTML that a user fills out from within a browser. The information sent to the CGI application is interpreted, and a dynamic response is sent back to the client. This can allow a form to update dynamically based on the data submitted. Suppose, for example, the user indicates he lives in a specific state or country. That information might alter the offerings provided the user, and the site can update itself based on the back-end CGI.

Adobe Acrobat Forms

Adobe Acrobat PDFs have long held the reputation as a secure and reliable method for distributing documents electronically. In fact, even Microsoft has shown it's acknowledgment by including an add-on to the Office 2007 Suite that allows you to convert your documents to PDF format. In addition, you can use Adobe Acrobat to design, build, and share PDF forms. These forms have been in use for some time now and they can, at times, offer more practical solutions than HTML forms because they can be downloaded and filled out on the personal system.

Some HTML forms take a while to complete. If a connection is lost during that process, the user cannot complete the form. According to Shane Hughes, CEO of Pyxis Consulting,

"… up to 95 percent of users that start a transaction on the Web fail to complete it." Whether that number is accurate to such a high degree or not, it's worth noting that a high percentage of users fail to complete transactions on the Web. So, one of the benefits to a downloadable form, such as a Word form or an Adobe Acrobat form, is that you do not need a connection to fill out the form. PDF forms do not require the always-on connection.

Most PDF forms are created by scanning a standard paper form and using another product, such as Acrobat Distiller (or the PDF Writer or PDF Maker), to convert the scanned form into a PDF. This is a quick way to offer a form from an already created paper version; however, it doesn't provide you with a forward-moving solution for an electronic exchange of data. Most of these forms are called fill-and-print forms; you fill it out, print it, and then mail it in (or scan it and email it).

Acrobat has another form solution called Smart Forms, which does allow you to fill out the form electronically. Much like the Word forms, you have data fields into which you can enter text, as shown in Figure 3.3.

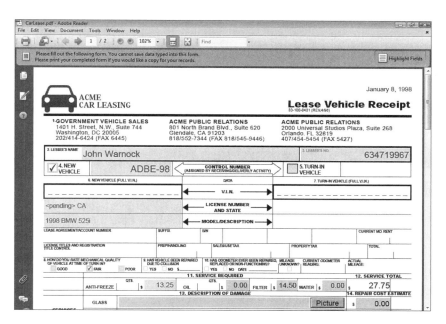

FIGURE 3.3   An Acrobat PDF form.

NOTE

Allowing the submission of forms data to a Web server will require help from your IT department. As the form designer, you can create a Submit button, but your IT department will need to develop a script that accepts the data from your form and then processes it. For example, your IT department could use Microsoft ASP, Macromedia ColdFusion, or Adobe Lifecycle Forms to process your form data.

Other E-Form Solutions

We've only scratched the surface of forms-creation solutions. There are a variety of other solutions, including the following:

▶ **Cardiff LiquidOffice eForms** (www.cardiff.com). Cardiff offers a Web-based form filler that uses XML, HTML, and PDF standards to automate e-forms so that standard Web browsers can be used to fill out forms.

▶ **IBM Workplace Forms** (www-142.ibm.com/software/workplace/products/product5.nsf/wdocs/formsfeatures). IBM bases their forms on open standards and offers dynamic XML forms that self-modify based on user input. IBM enables online and offline access to forms, provides secure transactions, and provides forms in 26 different languages.

▶ **Adobe XML architecture** (www.adobe.com/enterprise/pdfs/xml_whitepaper.pdf). Adobe provides users with a single reusable framework. With the technology and features embedded right into Adobe Acrobat 6.0, form solutions are delivered more quickly and easily. With XML being used as a universal data-integration mechanism, form designing remains simple.

▶ **Palm** (www.palm.com/us/business/solutions/ffa_automation_electronic_forms.html). Palm delivers forms for mobility. These electronic form solutions are made specifically for Palm handheld devices. Working on the road is no longer a problem; you can collect information and send it without the hassle of losing papers in the process. Palm enables you to quickly create forms, collect data, and process information all from the "palm" of your hand.

> **NOTE**
>
> What is an XML e-form? An XML e-form is one that isn't just defined in an XML format; its schema is published, and the template is accessible. Some companies have introduced XML-based forms that they say are based on the standards, but most solutions are proprietary in terms of presentation. So, be careful when a vendor says they support XML for e-forms because their solution might not be compatible with others.

InfoPath 2003

InfoPath was first released with the 2003 Office suite of applications and has since received an upgrade with the Office 2007 suite. Essentially, it is a form-creator application that can be integrated with databases, Web services, XML, or any XML-enabled system.

With InfoPath 2003, you can create your own forms easily and quickly. You can also use one of the 25 predesigned samples. Form solutions are made simple through the use of predefined customer schemas; design what works for you at the moment, eliminating all the extra fields that are not necessary.

Also with InfoPath, changes to forms are made silently and automatically, so the most up-to-date versions are always available. There's no downtime and no wait for maintenance; it's done in an instant.

Within InfoPath, you can establish data validation without programming, so knowing how to code is not necessary. You can also publish your forms to a network, Web server, or SharePoint library.

With InfoPath 2003, data and important information can also be shared whether you're on- or offline. It cuts out the hassle of waiting for paper forms to reach you. With InfoPath you can collect data and act on it right then and there, allowing for improvement of decision making and enhanced team collaboration.

The biggest downside to the InfoPath 2003 product, however, is that you cannot fill out forms from any application. You need to use the InfoPath product to do so. InfoPath 2007 takes care of this problem.

An Overview of InfoPath 2007

With such rapid advances occurring in technology, enhancing, modifying, and updating product capabilities is a must. This latest version of InfoPath offers several improvements and new features over the 2003 version. Included in these new features are the following:

► In addition to creating forms that can be filled out using the InfoPath application, you can create forms that can be filled in by a variety of Web browsers. These forms can be sent through email messages or through mobile devices, as shown in Figure 3.4.

FIGURE 3.4   A variety of methods are used to fill out forms created with InfoPath 2007.

▶ You can convert existing Office documents, such as Word or Excel documents, into InfoPath forms.

▶ You can establish a better level of real-time validation, prepopulated fields, and connections to other sources of information.

▶ You can now spell check your forms and insert formatted text and graphics into certain fields within the form, allowing for greater personalization.

▶ With InfoPath 2007, merging data from multiple forms and exporting data to other programs has been made possible. The functions of several forms can now be established in one single form.

▶ Because InfoPath is based on XML, it makes sharing and repurposing forms more convenient. Mangers, employees, and clients can now use one form to capture the data they need.

▶ InfoPath is no longer required to access and fill in forms, so anyone with access to a browser can now fill out forms with ease; no installing or extra downloading from the Web is necessary.

▶ There is no longer a need for new forms or multiple forms. Forms are easy to modify, and different views can be created for managers, employees, and so on.

▶ By installing an add-in, you can save forms as PDF files, allowing greater management ease.

Getting Started with InfoPath 2007

One of the best things for beginners when first opening an application is the friendly "Getting Started" screen. In the case of InfoPath, we are greeted with more than a "start"; we're greeted with samples to help us in our goal of designing forms. These samples include meeting agendas, expense reports, and other necessary forms.

In case we want to use forms that we don't see immediately, there is a "Form Templates on Office Online" link on the Getting Started page. Just click the link to access a variety of form templates that relate to health care, evaluations, purchase orders, and more.

The key to learning how to develop a form is to start with one already put together so that you can learn from its features. When you open a template (or design your own), you will notice that the form template is a file with an .xsn file extension. These are created in Design mode, but they are deployed as forms in XML.

The template provides tools to add controls, labels, or instructions on filling out the form. In addition, you can configure the look and feel of your form through standard toolbars that allow you to format fonts and other design elements. You also need to determine what will happen when a user completes the form. For example, you must decide and establish policy as to whether the form will be submitted to a database or saved into a folder.

The InfoPath Interface

Because of our experience with other Microsoft applications, the interface for InfoPath won't be so foreign to us. You'll notice a familiar set of menus (including File, Edit, View, and so forth) and familiar toolbars, with the Standard and Formatting toolbars taking center stage in your design of forms. Off to the right is your task pane, where you will find quick links to keep you moving forward in your design process, as shown in Figure 3.5.

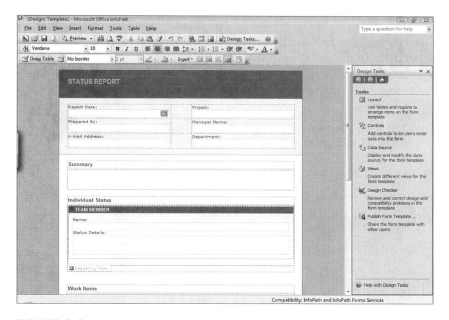

FIGURE 3.5   Your initial view of InfoPath 2007.

You'll notice off the Standard toolbar that you can perform the standard tasks of designing a new form template, opening an existing one, or saving the one you are working on. You can also select the Preview button to see how your form might look in action, or you can select the down-arrow next to the Preview option and choose Preview Settings to see some of the underlying options connected to the form, such as how the form will behave when opened in browser, along with a host of other settings.

> **NOTE**
>
> Preview also has an "Ink Entry mode," where you can fill out a form with a tablet pen (if you have one) and convert the ink into typed text. An Ink Toolbar allows you to change the pen type, ink color, and so forth; alternatively, you can just select Stop Ink Entry to turn this off completely.

To pull back out of Preview, select the **Close Preview** option.

Some of the other options on the Standard toolbar include cut/copy/paste, printing options, spell checker, paintbrush, hyperlinks, layout tables and insert picture buttons, the Design Tasks button (which we discuss shortly), and your little blue circle with a question mark (the Help button). You don't have to wait until you are in a panic before clicking that little button, nor do you need to fear a talking paperclip will come and harass you. That little annoyance has been eliminated from of the 2007 Office suite.

Beneath your Standard toolbar is your Formatting toolbar, which contains formatting elements that you should be familiar with from other Office products (such as font formatting shortcuts, alignment options, bullets and numbering, highlighting tools, and so forth).

Two other common toolbars (you can access through the View menu under the Toolbars heading) are Tables and Task Pane. The Tables toolbar allows you to draw and configure tables, including border options and cell formatting. The Task Pane sits on the right side of your form-creation area and allows you to have additional shortcut links appear based on which task pane is showing.

If you select the down arrow at the top of the task pane's title bar, you can see a list of all the available panes, as shown in Figure 3.6.

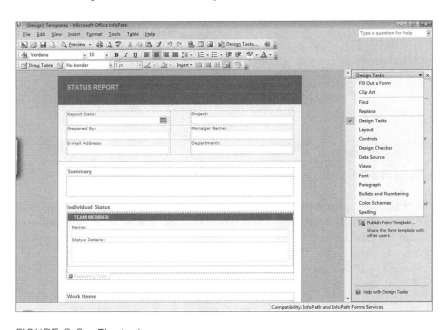

FIGURE 3.6   The task pane menu.

TIP

You can customize your toolbars by selecting Tools, Customize. To view the available options to customize the toolbars and the commands, just drag the commands to the toolbar of your choice.

Creating a New Form

As mentioned previously, the easiest way to design a new form is to start with an existing template and make the changes you need. Delete the unnecessary parts, tweak the necessary ones, and you're all set.

To change an existing form, click the **Customize a Sample** link on the Getting Started pane and choose the sample you want to customize. The form will appear with the Design Tasks pane, available to walk you through any changes you might want to make. Because the form is open in Design mode, you can modify it and then save it as your own.

If you want to start from a blank page, go to the **Design a Form Template** link from the Getting Started screen, and then choose to base the form on either a blank format, a Web service, database, XML or schema, or connection library. One option you might want to select, as shown in Figure 3.7, is the Enable Browser-Compatible Features Only check box.

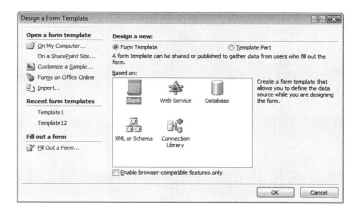

FIGURE 3.7   Creating a new blank form.

The Design Tasks pane offers a variety of options to help you put your form together, including the following:

- ▸ **Layout.** Use tables and regions to arrange items on the form template.

- ▸ **Controls.** Add controls to let users enter data into the form.

- ▸ **Data Source.** Display and modify the data source for the form template.

- ▸ **Views.** Create different views for the form template.

- ▸ **Design Checker.** Review and correct design and compatibility problems in the form template.

- ▸ **Publish Form Template.** Share the form template with other users.

Lay Out the Form

Selecting the Layout option will bring you to a list of layout tables, which are usually easier to work with than creating your own from scratch. You can select a table with title or one/two/three-column tables (all shown in Figure 3.8), or you can create a custom table (by indicating the number of columns and rows you need). Adding text, as in any table, just requires you to place your cursor into the table cell and start typing. All the same formatting options apply that you would use in a Word table, and the toolbars provide all the same features. So, you can really make your forms look perfect.

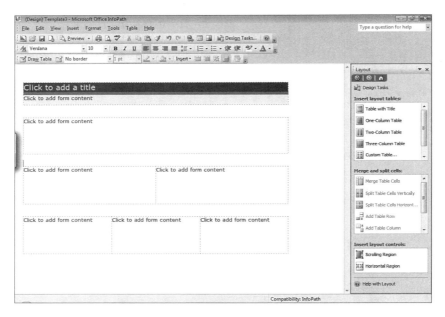

FIGURE 3.8   Layout options for your blank form.

In addition, the Layout task pane gives you options to merge and split cells and tables. And, you can add special layout controls, such as a scrolling region or a horizontal region.

Adding Controls

Some of the coolest parts to any form are the controls you include. These are objects that take your form from simple text boxes (which are also controls) to repeating tables.

To start adding controls, from the Design Tasks pane, click the **Controls** link. The Controls task pane will open. From here, you can play around with many of the options presented. Add a few check boxes and a few radio buttons. Maybe include a date picker (which is another name for a calendar) to the form. Figure 3.9 shows how the standard controls appear.

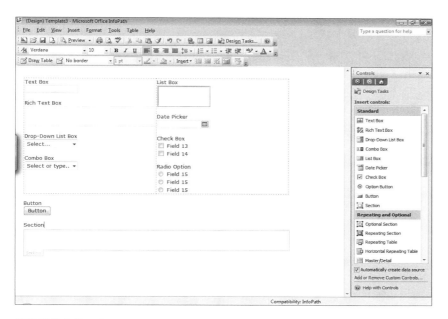

FIGURE 3.9   Control options for your blank form.

To place a control in the form, place your cursor where you want the control, and then select that control from the task pane. To change the label for a control (when it includes a label, it will usually say Field 1, Field 2, and so on), you just select the label and type over the text.

You might notice that each control is different, not only in appearance, but especially in functionality. For example, the text control is clearly going to show up to your user as a location to type text. If you provide the proper instruction to users, they will type the text. However, each of those controls has its own properties that you can configure. To work with these, right-click the added control to display a variety of options, including a Properties option at the bottom of your choices. Select **Properties** and notice that each control has different properties. For example, if you visit the Properties of a List Box screen, you can see that you need to provide those options a user would choose in the box (see Figure 3.10). There are settings for every control. The best way to learn them all is to work with them one at a time.

Another great option that is part of the properties of your controls is the validation setting. If validation is set, users cannot complete the form unless it is filled in completely and properly. You can determine that they must make a selection and then create rules that indicate what a valid response is for that particular control.

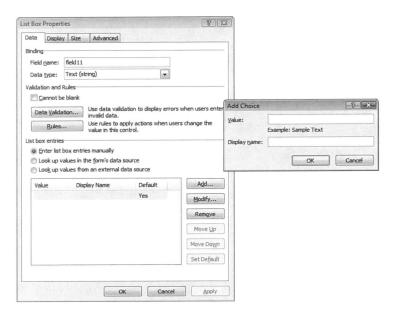

FIGURE 3.10   A list box must have the options added to it through the Properties page.

As you work on a form, you might want to see how it's going to look when it's finished, especially when you are altering the properties of controls and such. To do this, click the **Preview Form** button, mentioned earlier. You will see the form as it will appear to and behave for the user. It's a great way to test the functionality of your form before deployment.

Save or Publish Your Form

When you are satisfied that your form is ready to send to others, you can save it or publish it. (Quick note here: When you go to publish it, if you haven't saved it first, InfoPath will make you do that.) Saving the form is the same as in any other Office application. The InfoPath form template file extension is .xsn. After the form has been saved, you can publish it in a variety of ways, as shown in Figure 3.11. You can publish to a SharePoint server (with or without InfoPath Forms Services running), to a list of email recipients (which requires Outlook 2007 be your default email client), to a network share, or as an installable form template (which requires Visual Studio).

Keep in mind that publishing these forms in any of the methods offered (with the exception of a SharePoint server running InfoPath Forms Services or a Forms Server running InfoPath Forms Services) will require the user to have InfoPath installed to fill out the form.

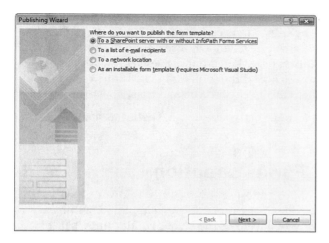

FIGURE 3.11   Publishing a form.

TIP

One concern you might have when sharing your forms with others is whether you want persons to make changes to the form. Generally, a form is open to change, but you can establish protection options. To enable protection, select **Form Options** from the Tools menu, as shown in Figure 3.12. From the Advanced options, select the **Enable Protection** check box. Notice that this will only discourage users from making changes. They can just as easily turn this off and go ahead with any changes if they know how.

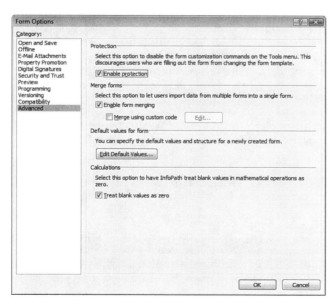

FIGURE 3.12   Enabling protection on a form.

Various problems sometimes arise when you try to publish a form. Most of these issues are basic troubleshooting concerns. If a person can access the form but not open it, ask yourself if that person has the InfoPath client installed. Or, if someone cannot access it, there might be a problem with the location (is it shared out properly?) or with permissions (does the user have the permission to access the form and save it if he or she makes changes?). Usually, with a little standard detective work, you can track down the problem.

If all else fails, however, republish the form to make sure you have the latest copy and a fresh establishment of the form.

Beyond the Basics of Forms Creation

Making forms look professional is an important aspect of InfoPath. InfoPath provides all the tools you need; you just need to master the process. For example, something as simple as changing the background color of a form or the layout width can be part of your formatting.

To change the background color, and other formatting options for the form, you can do one of the following:

▶ You can select Views from the Design Tasks pane, and then click the View Properties button (to change the background and layout).

▶ You can select Background Color from the Format menu.

Both options take you to the same dialog box, which has several tabs for altering the background and layout (through the General tab), for changing text settings for any controls (through the Text Settings tab), for altering the print options (through the Print Settings tab), and for handling the page settings used for printing (through the Page Setup tab).

You can also change the entire color scheme for a form by selecting the Format option and choosing Color Scheme. This is helpful if you are trying to create forms that integrate with a certain theme. Suppose, for example, that the forms are for a school, and you want to incorporate school colors in the forms. Or, perhaps for a company that has a color scheme for their logos and such.

Although you can format text through the View options, you can also perform this task manually by selecting any part of your form and then using the Formatting toolbar to alter fonts, alignment, and so forth.

You can also insert a picture, such as a company logo, to make your forms more company-specific. From the Standard menu, select **Insert Picture**, and then locate the image from your files.

TIP

To make changes to the image you include, select the image and then press **Alt+Enter.** The Format Picture dialog will open. This dialog assists you with text wrapping options, size, and text options.

Security and AutoComplete Settings

You might want to establish several key settings for your forms before deployment (security settings, AutoComplete, and more). To do this, open the form, and then select **Options** from the Tools menu. You will be taken to the Options dialog, as shown in Figure 3.13.

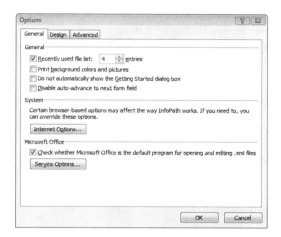

FIGURE 3.13   Working with additional options.

From here, many of the check boxes and settings are self-explanatory. However, if you are on the General tab and click the Internet Options button under the System options settings, you will be taken to the Internet Properties dialog. From here, you can select the Security tab and establish security zone settings. You can also select the Content tab and then click the Settings button under AutoComplete and turn AutoComplete on for forms, as shown in Figure 3.14.

FIGURE 3.14   Turning on AutoComplete.

Repeating Tables and Sections

These are sections that can expand to allow more entries for a form. This type of structure is necessary when you have a form that may require additional entries. For example, if you ask on a form the number of dependants, that number will vary, and so the size of the form will vary, too.

To start, select the **Repeating Section** control from the Controls selections.

After you have the section, you want to add your controls that you need to repeat. The experts recommend that you start by adding a layout table to the section so that you can control its appearance. Then, add the controls to the table's cells.

You can also include repeating sections inside other repeating sections if you like (so that users can add as much information as they need to). You can see in Figure 3.15 that there is a difference between a repeating table and a repeating section. A repeating table is used when you want to repeat data, such as an entry in each row of a table. You fill in the first row, and then click a link that adds another row. A repeating section can be used to repeat an entire portion of information.

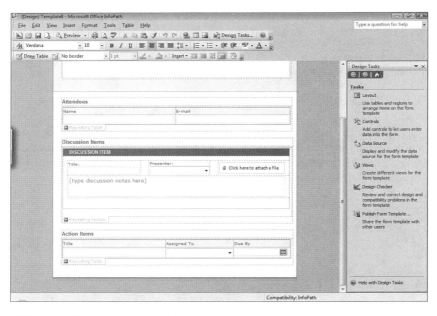

FIGURE 3.15   Repeating tables and sections.

Both repeating tables and repeating sections become connected to groups within the data source. InfoPath will automatically create these groups in the Data Source task pane and will add the fields to correspond to the controls added into the section or table.

You can see how the table and section repetition appears to the end user in Figure 3.16. Notice how the repeating table simply allows you to add more rows to your table, whereas the repeating section allows you to duplicate the entire discussion portion of the form.

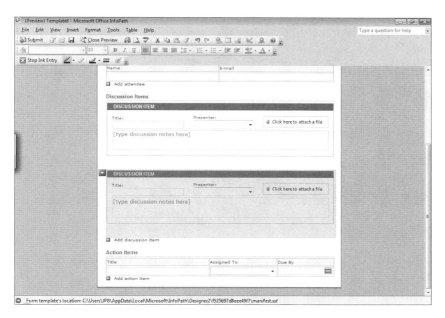

FIGURE 3.16   Repeating tables and sections from the end user's perspective.

By right-clicking the repeating section or table, you can select the option to view the properties behind these controls. On the Data tab of the properties, you can alter the text that is shown to provide direction to the user. For example, instead of saying "Add discussion item," you might want to say "Click here to add additional discussion items." You can make these changes. You can also add rules connected to the selection or make other changes. Keep in mind, however, that some ideas and changes go well beyond the scope of a single chapter. To truly master all the InfoPath settings, you need to do a bit more research.

> **NOTE**
>
> Another type of section control you might want to add is called an *optional section*. This is usually used in case users may want to add comments to a form. The way it works is you add the section through the Controls, provide the text boxes or controls within the form, and then provide instructions, just like with the other types of repeating table/section controls previously discussed. In this case, however, little yellow arrows indicate that users can click the link if they really feel they need to add more information (hence the concept of optional).

Working with Data Sources

When working with a form, you might have different concerns. You have to consider that after that form has been filled in, actual data (important data) must be retained and possibly even relocated into a database. How does an InfoPath form handle all of that?

Open a fresh form that has no controls in it. Select the **Design Tasks** pane, and then click the **Data Source** link. You will see no data sources, because you haven't added any.

By contrast, open one of the existing samples and look at the data sources. You can quickly see the difference; there are already fields included in the Data Source pane, as shown in Figure 3.17.

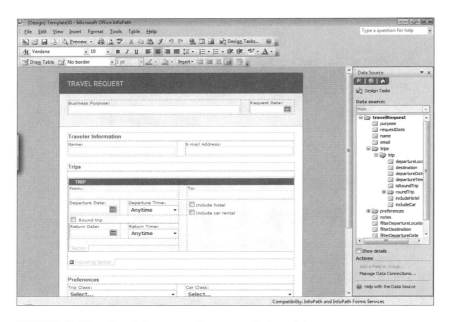

FIGURE 3.17   The data source for a sample template.

Controls, after you include them, are bound to a data source, which is a collection of fields that will now store the data a user will add into the form. The data source is an XML document. You don't have to use this for your data source, but it is the default solution in place. You'll also be able to notice that folders are automatically created for your fields when you add controls (such as repeating tables, sections, or optional sections).

> **NOTE**
>
> If you decide to delete a control from your form, keep in mind that the field will not be deleted automatically. You can do this from within the Data Sources task pane. Right-click the field, and then select **Delete.**

Each time you add a control, it automatically creates an XML field data source. The name it provides is usually not too helpful (examples like Field1, Field2), so you might want to go through and change the names of these fields by going into the properties of your controls and providing a name that is a bit more understandable depending on the control.

From within the Data Source task pane, you can see all your fields, and you can double-click any of these fields to make changes to the properties, including changing the name or the data type (you can select text, numbers, true/false, and so forth) or establishing the requirement that the field not be left blank. You can also establish validation rules through the Validation tab. These rules can make it so that, upon error, the user receives a message to assist.

Populate Controls

You recall that earlier we discussed controls and how some of them require information. For example, you cannot have a drop-down box or a list box that doesn't include the data that a user can select. There are two ways to provide that data. You can manually enter the values (which might be easy if you are only using a few selections) or you can use a secondary data source. A good example of when that might be useful is when you need users to select a state they live in (or perhaps, if you are creating a travel form, to select a destination to go to). This could include a pretty long list of items.

To include the items manually, you insert the control, and then go into the properties of the control and input those values from the Data tab. However, to have it be populated by a secondary data source, you select the option **Look Up Values from an External Data Source**, as shown in Figure 3.18

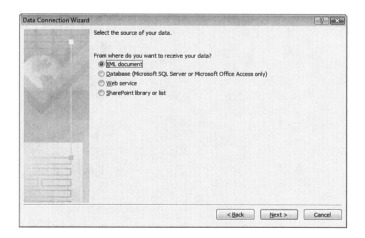

FIGURE 3.18   Using a secondary data source.

When you select the option to add the data source, the Data Connection Wizard appears to walk you through the steps. You need to locate and select the data source. You can use an XML document, a database (SQL or Access only), a Web service, or a SharePoint library or list.

After you have the source selected, you can choose the specific entries you want to use from that source (which may contain more than one field).

Buttons

Adding buttons to your form is one of the more difficult parts to the process. You need to make it so that when a user clicks that button, something happens! What? Well, usually you are hoping to submit data, so a Submit button is one of the more useful types. You could also have a Reset button that returns the form to a blank so that users can start over.

With Submit buttons, you can submit to a database, you can have it sent by email, you can do many different things. To start, insert the Button control and then go into the properties for it. You can change the label to make it more logical (Button is the default; perhaps make it read Submit, for example).

For a simple action, you can change the Action option to Submit, and you will be presented with your submit options, as shown in Figure 3.19. You can configure if you want that form submitted to an email address (or multiple addresses) and the message that will accompany the email. You can also send it to a SharePoint document library, a Web service or server, a hosting environment, or a connection from a data library. You can establish additional rules and code. You can even establish what will occur after the form is submitted. Will the form close? Will it create a blank new form or just stay the same? That's for you to decide.

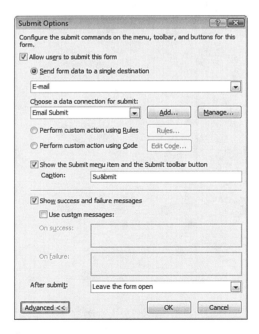

FIGURE 3.19   Creating a Submit button.

In addition to using the Submit action, you can also use the Rules and Custom Code option. From that point, you can alter the codes or rules to perform any number of different tasks, including the following rule options:

- ▶ Show a dialog box message
- ▶ Show a dialog box expression
- ▶ Switch views
- ▶ Set a field's value
- ▶ Query using a data connection
- ▶ Submit using a data connection
- ▶ Open a new form to fill out
- ▶ Close the form

Each of these options has its own set of configuration necessities that you can work through to make your buttons come alive.

Working with Databases

Another way to design forms is to create them so that they pull information from or update information to a database. These databases can only be SQL Server or Access databases. As mentioned earlier, you have an XML data source; but if you decide to use a database, the XML data source will not be created. The fields will not be connected to a data source, but to your database tables.

When you want to create a form based on a preexisting database, select the same **Design a Form Template** we used earlier, but now you select the **Database** option (keeping in mind you can also select Blank, Web Service, XML or Schema, or Connection Library).

You need to provide the wizard with a database you already know exists. When the connection is made between the form and the database, you will be asked which tables you will use. You need to start by selecting the parent table, and then you add others later.

NOTE

You might have many different tables to choose from when configuring your form to work with a database; however, it's recommended that you select the table that has a one-to-many relationship with other tables as the parent table. This is necessary to ensure the form will work properly, especially for submitting data back to the database.

There will be some additional steps to perform to link the database with the form. For example, you need to confirm that the fields are correct that link parent and child tables in your databases. You also want to exclude any fields that you will not be using. This will help to simplify the form. In addition, you can remove fields that aren't supported by InfoPath.

When the wizard completes, you will have a form with two different views. One view is a Query view and allows you to search for data. The other is the Data Entry view. The Data Source pane will show all the fields and will break them up into two different sections: queryFields and dataFields. Keep in mind that you will want to use the right fields in the right view.

After you have the connection made to the database, from the Data Entry view, you will want to add those controls. To do that, right-click a data source field and select the control you need, and it will add it into the form template, with the connection already being established to the database on the back end.

> **NOTE**
>
> To quickly populate the whole form, right-click the dataFields group and choose the option **Section with Controls.** This will populate the form completely with all the fields. Granted, this isn't the prettiest method, but you can go back and really format the whole thing later. You might wonder, how does InfoPath know which control to use? Well, it takes an educated guess based on the data contained in the field and/or the data type from the table structure. Of course, if you have no current data in any of the fields in the database, you are going to have to do all of this manually. If you don't like any of the fields added, you can always change them. Just right-click the field and select **Change To,** and then select the control you want.

Becoming a Forms Master

Quite a number of different InfoPath sites on the Internet can help you to take your knowledge to the next level. The purpose of this part of the book is not to actually make you a master, but to give you enough knowledge of the product so that you have a good understanding to hold your own when discussing matters with a forms developer in your company.

Some great tools can broaden the knowledge you currently have. For example, Microsoft provides free demos and tutorials to help you learn more. Check out http://office. microsoft.com/en-us/infopath/FX100487661033.aspx.

Microsoft will teach you how to convert a Word document into an InfoPath form, how to use InfoPath forms within your Outlook email, and more.

The InfoPath Developer Portal contains quite a bit of in-depth InfoPath information. Located at http://msdn2.microsoft.com/en-us/office/aa905434.aspx, this site can link you to more than developer content and additional training material, too.

The InfoPath Team Blog is an awesome place to connect with some of the best developers of forms. Located at http://blogs.msdn.com/infopath/default.aspx, one of the best things they offer is for you to send them your forms (at ipforms@microsoft.com). They will review them, see the methods you are using to develop your forms. You will be helping them, and they will help you in return.

Last, but certainly not least, Microsoft has created 12 InfoPath Training Labs, and they are on the MSDN site at http://msdn2.microsoft.com/en-us/library/bb251751.aspx.

These new labs will walk you through a real-life scenario, introducing a new InfoPath feature in the process. They include the following:

▶ Lab 1: Publishing an InfoPath 2007 Form Template to a Server Running InfoPath Forms Services

▶ Lab 2: Deploying and Managing InfoPath 2007 Forms

▶ Lab 3: Integrating InfoPath 2007 with the Data Connection Library

▶ Lab 4: Enabling Digital Signatures in InfoPath 2007 Form Templates

▶ Lab 5: Importing Word Forms into InfoPath 2007

▶ Lab 6: Using InfoPath 2007 E-Mail Forms

▶ Lab 7: Restricting Permissions to InfoPath 2007 Forms and Form Templates

▶ Lab 8: Using the InfoPath 2007 Object Model and Visual Studio Tools for Applications

▶ Lab 9: Designing InfoPath 2007 Forms for Mobile Web Browsers

▶ Lab 10: Creating and Inserting InfoPath 2007 Template Parts

▶ Lab 11: Integrating InfoPath 2007 Forms in Web Sites Using Visual Studio

▶ Lab 12: Using SharePoint Server Workflows with InfoPath 2007

Beyond these free tools and blogs, you'll find quite a bit more by searching online for InfoPath 2007 learning. You can also search through books that are being offered on Amazon.com (or some other book site). You'll find that it's slim pickings. You want to purchase only the 2007 version (if that is what you are using) because there are definite changes between it and the 2003 version.

One book you might consider is *Pro InfoPath 2007 (Expert's Voice),* from Philo Janus, a senior technology specialist with Microsoft. Another is *Designing Forms for Microsoft Office InfoPath and Forms Services 2007,* by Scott Roberts (senior development lead on the InfoPath Team at Microsoft) and Hagen Green (software design engineer at Microsoft).

CHAPTER 4

Groove Server 2007: Overview and Installation

To sum up what Groove Server is all about, think collaboration: anywhere, anytime, and with anyone. Consider some of the challenges facing collaboration in our times. Communication tag is all too common these days between email and voicemail and so forth, with costs for communication (long-distance calls, wasted time on phone or email) becoming excessive. More commonly, company team members might be separated by geographical locations, which lead to time zone issues and an inability to know when a colleague might be available. At times, when you collaborate between companies, connecting to each other can be difficult, costing quite a bit for third-party solutions. And, as anyone who has tried to collaborate using email can attest to, versioning issues of documentation are always a concern. Which version is the latest, agreed upon version plagues the dispersed teams of today.

Groove Server is Microsoft's answer to these challenges. In 2005, Microsoft purchased the collaboration software firm Groove Networks Inc. The company was founded by Ray Ozzie, the creator of Lotus Notes, and already had a reputation for excellent peer-to-peer (P2P) software.

Introduction to Groove Server 2007

Without explaining the server side just yet, what the client side of Groove offers is an easy way to create a Groove workspace, which places all the team members and the tools they need in one virtual location. The workspace is initially created by a user who then invites additional Groove users to join the space. Each member of the workspace has access to the space, which is encrypted for security.

> **NOTE**
>
> The Groove client is included with the Enterprise and Ultimate versions of the Office 2007 suite; however, it can also be purchased separately.

A variety of Groove tools can be used within the workspace, including the following: a calendar, discussion, files, forms, InfoPath forms, issue tracking, meetings, Notepad, pictures, SharePoint files, and a sketchpad. You can also request More Tools to see what else you might add to your workspace, as shown in Figure 4.1. More will be added in the future that you can download from the Groove Web site.

FIGURE 4.1   A Groove workspace with the More Tools options showing.

When a Groove workspace is created and other members accept the invitation to be a part of the workspace, both the workspace and the data is stored on each members system, and it is encrypted with keys shared between members. You don't need to worry about encrypting the data on the network side because the client encrypts the data. However, the Groove server keeps each of the team member's data (as well as the workspace, tools, and so forth) in sync even if the member works for a different organization or works remotely. If a member of the group is away for a while (for instance, a vacation) and then reconnects, the member's Groove server will update the team member. The Groove server also handles the issue of data conflict (when two members of a team edit the same information in the workspace at the same time).

Groove Connections Available

As you scan through Microsoft's many new offerings, you see several terms with the same theme, which might confuse you: for instance, Microsoft Office Live Groove, Microsoft Office Groove Enterprise Services, and Microsoft Office Groove Server 2007 (which might include words such as Groove Server Manager, Groove Server Relay, or Groove Server Data Bridge).

Let's clarify each of these offerings:

- ▶ **Microsoft Office Groove 2007.** This is the desktop client. The client will work for a limited time. Microsoft is offering a free trial on their Microsoft Office site for Groove, at http://office.microsoft.com/en-us/groove/FX100487641033.aspx.

- ▶ **Microsoft Office Live Groove.** Essentially, this is the client software with a subscription for the hosted relay infrastructure. No servers are required internally. You need to renew every year, and you get upgrades to new releases as part of the subscription. All users are "unmanaged" and have no Groove Manager support for user account backup/restore (it's not the policy to restore user environments) or user/security policies. To check out the offering and get a free trial, go to http://office.microsoft.com/en-us/officelive/FX101945661033.aspx.

- ▶ **Microsoft Office Groove Enterprise Services.** Buy the client and in addition to the hosted relay (as previously mentioned), you also get hosted Groove Manager, which enables you to have a "Groove domain" with identities managed for your employees by your IT admin and more control via policy over how your employees use Groove. Again, this arrangement offers no on-site infrastructure. The configuration through the Enterprise Services Manager is Web based, and through this tool you can create, configure, and manage user accounts (including backing up the accounts). One of the included features is the Enterprise Services Relay, which is handled through Microsoft, to allow users to keep in sync even when direct client-to-client connectivity isn't possible, or through firewalls. In effect, the relay is necessary when users are not on the same network, or when they are behind firewalls or working offline.

  This purchase is done through a volume license arrangement with your local Microsoft sales representative. It includes no support for auditing, Data Bridge, or directory integration.

- ▶ **Groove Server 2007.** Sometimes you want on-premise servers for your Groove connections. There are three types of servers for Groove (Relay, Manager, and Data Bridge), and each Groove server is deployed separately, with the cost depending on the number of users and the system architecture.

So, what do these offerings all mean? An essential question is this: Do I need the Groove client installed to initiate or be a part of a Groove workspace? The answer is, absolutely! Do you need a Groove server in your organization? Not necessarily. If you have team members who do not require an administrator to manage the accounts, you can have them sign up for Live Groove, for which they pay a yearly fee and they have unmanaged Groove workspace abilities. Alternatively, if you require a bit more control but don't want the in-house infrastructure to support, you can move to the next level with Microsoft Office Groove Enterprise Services, where Microsoft will host your Groove workspaces. And finally, if you want the infrastructure in-house, you need to install your own Groove servers.

> **NOTE**
>
> Knowing this might ease your mind a bit. A Groove workspace can be managed by a Groove server hosted by Microsoft, or it can be hosted by your corporate network. The goal of these chapters is to help you install and configure your corporate Groove servers.

> **TIP**
>
> How do you know when to choose the Enterprise Services hosting option or when to install your own Groove servers in-house? Generally, Microsoft recommends Enterprise Services for more cost-effective, smaller deployments. On the other hand, if you have a larger deployment that requires integration with Active Directory, role-based access control, the need for custom reporting, or in-house security, on-premise Groove Server is the recommended direction.

The Groove Server Line-up

Three main components make up your in-house Groove organization: the Manager, the Relay, and the Data Bridge. Each has its own functionality and set of requirements, but together they enable you to build and optimize your Groove environment.

Let's review what each one does.

The Microsoft Office Groove Server Manager

The Manager contains the Web-based interface that you can use to manage all the user accounts, policy settings, reports, and so forth. The Manager integrates with your Active Directory (or any other Lightweight Directory Access Protocol [LDAP] solution) so that you can add members when you add persons to your domain.

One control you have through the Manager is the ability to determine which tools are available to specific users. You can also control security levels (such as the length of passwords and expiration intervals).

Be default, you cannot view the data passed between members of a workspace from within your Manager. The way Groove is designed, the encryption operates between users of a group. However, you can use an integrated audit service that allows you to audit workspaces that you select if you believe it is necessary.

The Microsoft Office Groove Server Relay

The Groove Server Relay performs the same services discussed previously with regard to the Enterprise Services Relay. These serve the same role, except in the Enterprise Services arrangement, Microsoft maintains these servers; in the in-house Groove setup, you control them. There is a benefit to your control over these servers, as you will soon see.

The Relay server ensures communication and collaboration between members of a workspace when issues potentially impede the process. One of those issues is a network firewall. If two users are members of a workspace within the same subnet (no firewall between), you don't need a server relay. Odds are, users working that close to each other can find other ways to collaborate. The purpose of Groove being "anywhere" collaboration almost heralds the need for a relay in case you have to go through firewalls or deal with users in different subnets. A relay is also necessary because some users may not be online at the same time. The relay keeps the offline user in sync; it waits until that user is online and then transfers the most recent changes to the now-online user.

Relays use a process called fanning out, which optimizes network bandwidth by determining the connection of members, one to the other, and then seeing whether a sizeable document might be handled better through the relay, as opposed to being sent directly from one client to another within the workspace membership list.

One of the benefits to handling your own Relay servers is that you can design your layout to assign specific Relay servers to certain users (based on location and network bandwidth). You can also structure in the design of your deployments multiple Relay servers per user to allow for failover.

The Microsoft Office Groove Server Data Bridge

The Groove Data Bridge server is one aspect not present in the Enterprise Services arrangement. A Data Bridge is used to connect your Groove clients with enterprise databases and applications. For example, a Data Bridge can help to connect your Groove clients with some of your other servers that might handle files or forms. Even better, it can integrate with a SharePoint server or an InfoPath forms server.

Some of the functionality of your Data Bridge server will not be visible immediately upon install. This is because your in-house developers will need to learn to work with it to provide this integration between the data in the workspace and the enterprise systems. What data is pushed to the workspace or pulled into the enterprise system to synchronize the two? All of that must be developed into a solution that works for your organization.

NOTE

Although a Data Bridge server is an important piece to Groove technology, you don't need it to have a fully functional Groove environment. The only two necessary servers are the Manager and Relay. The Data Bridge is for added functionality to your Groove environment.

Installation Prerequisites

The Groove client is a separate discussion, so we won't be pursuing the prerequisites and installation facets here. What we do discuss here is the three main server applications: the Manager, Relay, and Data Bridge. Chapter 5, "Groove Server 2007: Configuration," covers the configuration needs for each of these, whereas here we just discuss the prerequisites and installation.

Prerequisites for the Groove Manager

For each of the server types, this section lists the hardware and software prerequisites. Table 4.1 shows the hardware needed to install the Groove Manager server. Table 4.2 shows the software needed to install the Groove Manager server.

TABLE 4.1   Hardware Prerequisites for the Groove Manager

Component	Requirement
Computer and Processor*	Server computer with 64-bit processor supporting AMD64 or Intel EM64T architectures only; processor speed of 2.0GHz or higher
Memory	2GB RAM, minimum
Hard Disk	40GB RAID disk array
Drive	CD-ROM or DVD drive

* This is an important consideration when you go to install a Groove server. You need to install it on an x64-bit system. If you worked with the beta of Groove Server, which worked on 32-bit systems, this might come as a bit of a surprise.

TIP

If you want to install and test drive Groove Server before deploying it to your main environment, you can try VMWare Workstation 6.0 on your system. However, sorry to tell you, although it has an option for a 64-bit operating system, you have to have a 64-bit processor for it to work. The good news is this: You can run a 64-bit version of Windows 2003 Server x64 Edition on top of your 32-bit XP or Vista OS, on top of your 64-bit processor. So, as long as the underlying processor is 64 bit, the operating system you use to run VMWare doesn't matter.

TABLE 4.2   Software Prerequisites for the Groove Manager

Component	Requirement
Operating System	Microsoft Windows Server 2003 x64 Edition SP1 or later
Web Browser	Internet Explorer 6.0 or later with service packs and JavaScript, cookies, and forms enabled
Additional Installed Components	SQL Server 2000 or later
	IIS 6.0 for Windows Server 2003
	SMTP virtual server
	Microsoft .NET Framework 2.0, including ASP.NET
	LDAP 3.0-based software for directory integration (optional)
Other Systems Required	Groove Relay or Groove Enterprise Services (if you plan to use the Manager to administrate an Enterprise Services arrangement through Microsoft)

Notice that the Groove Manager requires at least one Internet Information Services (IIS) server be configured (to support the Web-based administration site) with a SQL server as the back end for storing data.

Prerequisites for the Groove Relay

Tables 4.3 and 4.4, respectively, list the hardware and software needed to install the Groove Relay server.

TABLE 4.3   Hardware Prerequisites for the Groove Relay

Component	Requirement
Computer and Processor	Server computer with 64-bit processor supporting AMD64 or Intel EM64T instruction set; processor speed of 1.8GHz or higher (AMD) or 2.4GHz or higher (Intel); single-processor, dual-core configuration is supported, dual-processor configuration recommended
Memory	4GB RAM, 8 GB recommended; 8GB or more recommended when supporting large numbers of users
Hard Disk	40GB for system volume, 73GB recommended (for operating system and the Groove Relay application); 250GB for data volume (minimum), 350GB recommended (a local SCSI-attached RAID array with either a RAID5 or RAID10 configuration recommended)
	NTFS required

TABLE 4.4   Software Prerequisites for the Groove Relay

Component	Requirement
Operating System	Microsoft Windows Server 2003 x64 Edition SP1 or later
Web Browser	Internet Explorer 6.0 or later with service packs and JavaScript, cookies, and forms enabled
Other Systems Required	Microsoft Office Groove Server 2007 Groove Manager

Prerequisites for the Groove Data Bridge

Table 4.5 lists the hardware and software needed to install the Groove Data Bridge server.

TABLE 4.5   Hardware and Software Prerequisites for the Groove Data Bridge

Component	Requirement
Computer and Processor	Server computer with 64-bit processor supporting AMD64 or Intel EM64T architectures; processor speed of 3.0GHz or higher
Memory	3GB RAM
Hard Disk	400GB
Operating System	Microsoft Windows Server 2003 x64 Edition SP1 or later

Microsoft provides a set of documents to assist with your deployment of Groove. Perform a search on the download center for the Groove 2007 Planning and Deployment Guide. The guide is filled with worksheets to help you deploy your Groove infrastructure.

Deployment Considerations

Before installing your first Groove server role, you might want to understand a few things about Groove server/client functionality. Knowing these few things will save you time and effort later on (because you will have planned properly).

For example, because Groove uses a variety of protocols to function, you should know which protocols those are, which portions of Groove use which protocol, and how that will affect your network.

Groove Protocols

The key protocol for communication between a Groove client and another client, or a server, is the Simple Symmetric Transmission Protocol (SSTP), which uses port 2492/TCP by default. If the client attempts to communicate with a system and that port is blocked, a Relay server can use port 443/TCP, or SSTP can be encapsulated within HTTP through port 80/TCP. (Keep in mind that this will slow the process down, because of the overhead involved in the encapsulation process.) On the LAN itself, clients use LAN and WAN Device Presence Protocol (DPP), which helps Groove clients to locate one another on the same subnet (through LAN DPP) or over the WAN.

> **NOTE**
>
> A proxy server can be configured in the same way as a firewall. If SSTP cannot go through 2492, you can try sending it through 443. If it is prevented completely, you can have it encapsulated and sent through port 80.

As for the Groove Manager server, HTTP is used to access the administrator site (hosted on the IIS server). Simple Object Access Protocol (SOAP) requests are made over HTTP by clients to the Manager. The Manager also uses SOAP to communicate with the Relay server(s).

The Groove Relay server is quite flexible in its use of protocols. It can use SSTP through port 2492 when clients can communicate through their native protocols, but it can also use other ports to go through firewalls when necessary (or use HTTP).

The Groove Data Bridge also uses SSTP to communicate with Groove clients. It also uses SOAP for interaction with external applications.

Figure 4.2 shows a full picture of each server with the protocols in play.

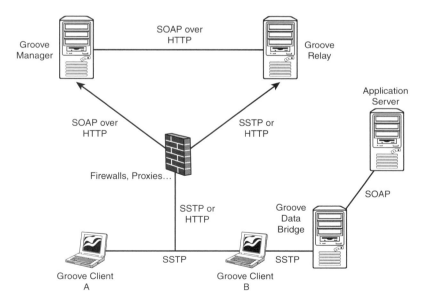

FIGURE 4.2   Groove servers and clients with underlying protocols supported.

NOTE

The deployment guide contains an entire list of all the protocols used within a Groove structure. For example, the IM protocol for instant messaging is used through SSTP. In addition, you can see a list of all the standard ports used for specific protocols and what their functionality is. For example, HTTP over port 8010 is what you use to see the Groove Relay administrative Web page.

Knowing about these protocols and the ports they use is very important in your configuration (of clients, especially). In a domain using Active Directory (especially if your clients are using Windows Vista with both inbound and outbound firewall configurations), you can use Group Policies to confirm ports are open that are required to be open. The standard SSTP port 2492 is an important one for clients to have open both inbound and outbound. So is the LAN DPP port 1211/UDP, both inbound and outbound, to ensure clients can sense other clients. Outbound port 442/TCP is important, as well, to communicate with Relay servers.

The Groove Manager uses SOAP requests from clients (and the Data Bridge server) inbound through port 80. It communicates with the Relay server through outbound ports 8009/TCP. It may also use SMTP through port 25 to send emails to clients, or LDAP protocol port 389/TCP for communicating with an LDAP directory (or Active Directory, which is an LDAP directory [if you remember your AD 101 lessons]).

The Groove Relay would logically require inbound ports 80, 443, and 2492 because clients may be sending a message in through any one of those ports and protocols. It should also be prepared for inbound 8009 for Groove Manager contact and inbound 8010 for the administration site (mentioned earlier). And, 2492 should also be configured for outbound connections so that the Relay can handle the "fanning-out" technique (explained earlier), which will assist with the distribution of larger files between clients by using the Relay server to ensure greater bandwidth connectivity.

Groove Data Bridge servers are easiest to configure. They only require SOAP over port 80 to connect with the Groove Manager server. They also require SOAP over 9080 to be open so that they can receive XML calls from external applications.

How Many Groove Servers Do You Need?

Keeping in mind that the Enterprise Services offered by Microsoft are a valid solution to a smaller deployment plan, you should have a substantial reason for deploying Groove servers in your locale before you even need one server.

Microsoft approximates the number of users supportable by a Groove Manager/IIS front-end server at 20,000 (if installed with the correct requirements outlined in Microsoft documentation). Beyond that, you should add more Manager servers, perhaps load balancing the IIS front-end servers while using the same SQL server on the back end.

> **NOTE**
>
> When installing the Groove Manager server, you can choose to install it as a standard install, or including the Audit feature (which will then allow you to see the data being transferred back and forth within workspaces). Logically, if you enable the Audit feature, you are going to require additional SQL servers because the data is held on the SQL end. Microsoft recommends additional SQL servers for every 1,500 users under the Audit install.

In terms of the Relay server, one of the benefits of having this hosted in-house is that you know exactly how many users are connected to it (as opposed to one hosted by Microsoft, which could be hosting thousands). The recommendation is one Relay for every 18,000 or so users. But, this is not a perfect science, of course. Only you, as the administrator, will know whether the server is being overworked and whether you see a performance decrease. You also know when your users will be online at any given time. For example, if you have 18,000 users all in one location (online at the same time), you will see a greater stress on the Relay server than if those 18,000 are broken up over three shifts and spread out in different locations. Average data being sent by users of Groove (according to a Microsoft benchmark) is 8MB per day. That's about 140GB of data a day, which could put a good amount of stress on the Relay server, too. And, as more users rely on Groove to collaborate, that number will most likely increase.

When considering whether to add more Relay servers, you should also factor in whether you have large clusters of people in separate locations. So, let's say you have 10,000 people (well within the limits of a Relay server), but 5,000 are in Hong Kong and another 5,000 in New York. It would make sense to place Relay servers at each location.

Security Planning

As you learned earlier, you need to open a variety of ports to allow Groove traffic to move easily between clients and clients, and clients and servers (possibly between proxies and firewalls). Port restriction is a very simple form of security between systems over the Internet. Firewalls play a large role in keeping your inner organization safe. Logically, Groove clients and servers require some ports to be open to allow communication, but the overall security for your organization is a company-by-company matter.

Groove clients have their own security through a variety of means. First of all, there exists encryption between every client in the workspace. You can implement password protection on the accounts on the Groove server. And the list goes on with the clients in terms of your ability as a network administrator to protect them through antivirus filtering on the Groove workspaces, version restriction, file-type restrictions, and more.

Having an in-house Groove Manager server also adds control over encryption keys, signature keys, and passwords. You can implement a Public Key Infrastructure (PKI) that provides user authentication within and between domains. Note that PKI support is also available with Groove Enterprise Services; however, this doesn't support third-party PKI support, although your on-premise server can. Through the Groove Manager, you can also configure password policies that include lockout after a certain number of configured attempts, account reset, and use of smartcards.

Security on your Relay servers can be handled by locking down ports other than the ones you need to communicate; however, there are some built-in factors, as well. For example, all Groove clients receive a public key certificate for the Relay server they are configured to use through the Groove Manager. That public key is used between the client and the Relay server to begin the registration of the client with the Relay. When the Relay knows the client, a shared key is created between them (only between the client and the Relay server), and then from that point forward all communication between them is both authenticated and secured. Keep in mind, however, that data routed between the Relay and other clients is encrypted, too, and the Relay server cannot decrypt that information. (I can simply look at the message header information to determine the direction of messages between clients.)

Last, but not least, we have the Data Bridge server. This one is unique because it resides on the LAN and is designed to have all the same security provisions that clients have built in. So, the Groove side to the security is solid, but your concern for security should be on the back-end application connectivity. Groove security doesn't protect the connection between the Data Bridge server and the remote applications. You need to secure that connection in other ways, through IPSec protocols and/or physical protection. For the most part, the rule of thumb with your Data Bridge server is to allow only necessary communication coming in and out of it.

Installing Groove Server 2007

Contrary to this section's heading, you don't just "install" Groove Server 2007 within your organization. You design and deploy it. It's an entity all of its own, and you need to be incredibly prepared if you want it done right. It's not like the old days when you could just install a server into the middle of your organization. As you can understand from what you've already read, you need to do quite a bit of prep work to ensure a solid deployment that is secure and performs well.

Following the guidelines in the deployment guide, combined with the worksheets for deployment, will be helpful to you for a smooth deployment.

However, if your goal is to perform a little testing so that you can get a better hands-on feel for what you will need later on in your real deployment, let's get to it.

The first question people usually ask after all that is said about Groove Server is this: Do I install my Manager servers first? And the answer is no. Microsoft recommends that you start off with your Relay servers and then your Manager(s). If you have any Manager servers with Audit, these should be installed third (noting that you need one normal Manager server in your organization before installing one with the Audit feature enabled). If you need back-end external application connectivity with Groove, you can then install a Data Bridge server. (Note, however, that these aren't necessary unless you have a reason; your Groove structure can function without one.) And then, when the infrastructure is in place, you should install the clients (although many admins may have already deployed the clients when they installed Office 2007 Ultimate or Enterprise on their desktops).

The Groove Relay Install

Keep in mind that you don't have to have the Relay installed first. It's a recommendation, however, that you install and configure your perimeter network infrastructure with your Relay servers before deploying your Manager server into your IIS front end within the perimeter.

> **NOTE**
>
> Even though you might install your Relay server first, you might want to prepare your network for the Grove Manager deployment ahead of time by ensuring your SQL server is ready and the server you install the Manager on is ready with IIS.
>
> You cannot install your Groove Relay server on the same machine as your Groove Manager or Data Bridge. They each require their own server. You also want to make sure you do not have any of the following applications or services running on your Relay before the installation: DNS, WINS, DHCP, IIS, the Groove client (or any part of the Office Suite), SharePoint Server, or any of the other Office servers discussed in this book. The Relay should be a Member server (not a domain controller).

As mentioned in the prerequisites, make sure your Relay server has about 250GB+ of disk space for a production deployment (more is better) in a RAID configuration.

Microsoft lists things you might want to do before you install your Groove Relay server. You can find these at http://download.microsoft.com/download/f/a/d/fadacb68-2569-444c-bb88-5fb3cccced5c/GrooveRelayAdministratorsGuide.pdf.

The recommendations include the following:

> ▶ **Install Terminal Services.** The great thing about Terminal Services for any server is that you can use a remote desktop connection to the server for remote administration.

> ▶ **Install management and monitoring tools.** This would include network monitoring tools you like to work with, which will help you to determine the amount of traffic (and from which protocols) going through your Relay.

> ▶ **Configure the Remote Registry Service.** This will enable you to have remote access to the server's performance counters.

And, the final configuration guidelines include the following:

> ▶ Install the latest service pack and critical updates for your server.

> ▶ Configure your system startup and recovery options to handle a system crash so that a dump file is created.

> ▶ Optimize your system's performance settings by altering your virtual memory to allow for enough space for your page file. (Usually, the default settings are fine.)

▶ On your *internal* network connections (those that connect your Relay server to your private network), configure your network connections to optimize your Relay server's performance. One thing you want to make sure is present and enabled is your Client for Microsoft Networks component. Also, from within your Network properties, enable File and Printer Sharing for Microsoft Networks (don't forget to turn on NetBIOS over TCP/IP through your TCP/IP settings) and the Remote Registry Service (which is optional).

▶ On your *external* network connections (those that connect your Relay server to the outside world), configure your network connections to optimize your Relay server's security. Disable your Client for Microsoft Networks component. Also, from within your Network properties disable File and Printer Sharing for Microsoft Networks (and don't forget to turn off NetBIOS over TCP/IP through your TCP/IP settings).

▶ On one of your network connections, you also want to configure TCP/IP filtering. To do this, go to the network connection you use for external contact, right-click the connection and select Properties. Then, select your Internet Protocol TCP/IP settings and select Properties. From the General tab, click the Advanced button and select the Options tab. On the Options tab, select **Enable TCP/IP Filtering (All adapters),** as shown in Figure 4.3. For TCP, configure port 80 to be permitted (for SSTP connections encapsulated in HTTP). You also want to configure port 2492 for clients to connect to the Relay server and for the server to use the fan-out process for bandwidth performance. Configure port 443 for Groove clients to use SSTP through a firewall. In the event the Manager server will be used to administrate the Relay server, you might want to open port 8009. For UDP ports, select **Permit All.** For IP protocols, allow TCP (6) and UDP (17).

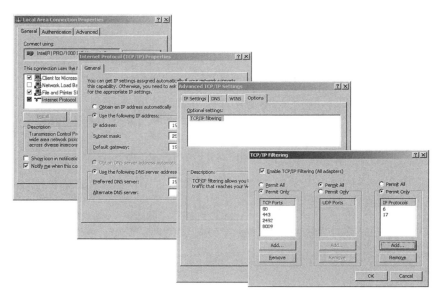

FIGURE 4.3   Configuring your Groove Relay inbound/outbound ports.

Finally, before you actually install the Groove Relay, you might want to confirm the performance viability for your disks on the server. The installation comes with a utility called DBWriteTest.exe that you can run to confirm your disk I/O qualification before you install the Relay. To do this, open a command prompt, navigate to the location of your GRS folder, and enter the following:

Dbwritetest.exe –p [Data Volume Path here]

Here is the output you should see (varies for each system's I/O):

```
d:\grs>dbwritetest -p e:

GrooveDBWrite test Version 1.1

Doing 20000 operations of 1000 bytes each to the e:\GrooveDBWriteTest

70% free disk space, cluster size=4096

Finished 20000 operations 1 to 20000 of size 1000, elapsed time 50.032779 sec,
399.74 operations/sec, 399737.94 bytes/sec
```

Here is what you should be looking for: You want higher than 200,000 bytes per second, and the cluster size must be equal to 4,096. The reasons for this test is to ensure your server can handle the disk traffic for the thousands of users you will have connecting through it. If it can handle 200,000 bytes per second, it can handle roughly 12,000 users. To ensure the throughput values are accurate, you can run the test more than once.

And now, your first step in installing the Groove Relay is to kick off the setup from the CD. The first screen you see asks which Groove server type you want to install, as shown in Figure 4.4. In our case, we would click the link **Office Groove Server 2007 Relay (English)**, and it would take us to the Getting Started page, where we can find more information about our deployment through a collection of links. If we are confident we want to proceed, we select **Run Groove Relay Setup.**

After you put in the product key, you move into the Microsoft Software License Terms, where you select the checkbox to "accept" the terms, and then click **Continue.**

You are given the chance to install the Relay in either a Basic or Advanced way. If you choose Basic, the default settings will apply, including the location of the installation directory under C:\Program Files\Microsoft Office Servers\12.0\Groove\Groove Relay.

FIGURE 4.4   Choosing your Groove Server install type.

Select Advance if you want to configure the following options:

- **File Location.** For the location of the installation directory.

- **Feedback.** To determine whether you want to be part of the Customer Experience Improvement Program. You can say Yes, No, or I'll choose later.

When the installation reaches a certain point, the Groove Relay Server Configuration panel comes up, and you can confirm or alter the settings. The first screen, shown in Figure 4.5, already fills in the default data for the server.

Table 4.6 shows the fields for the server configuration. This isn't just a table to show you the options you can perform; there are steps you *must* perform at each dialog. For example, you need to supply an administrative password and generate your private key and certificate from this dialog before moving on to the next step.

NOTE

You do not want to forget the settings (default or manually configured), so it might be a good idea to keep track of the values entered. For example, you could take screenshots of the dialog screens to help you remember the configuration settings later on.

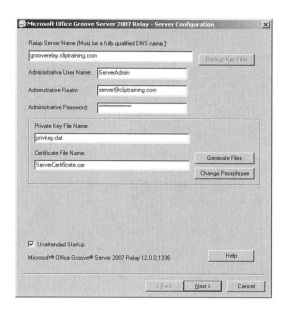

FIGURE 4.5   Configuring your Groove Relay server.

TABLE 4.6   Servers Dialog Box Values

Value	Explanation
Relay Server Name	Default: It takes the name of the server and the domain name. You can use this name or another that is registered with your DNS for this server.
Administrative User Name	Default: ServerAdmin
	This is the name used to access the Groove Relay administration Web site.
Administrative Realm	You can accept the default or change the name to reflect your configuration. You will see this value at the password prompt for the administrative site.
Administrative Password	You have to enter a password of your choosing. Note that you should record this somewhere safe.
Private Key File Name	Default: privkey.dat
	You can accept the default or change it to something else. This is the file that contains the Relay private key.
Certificate File Name	Default: ServerCertificate.cer
	This is the certificate file for the server. Click the **Generate Files** button to actually create the private key and certificate file (which will be given to the clients to allow secure messages through the Relay). Note that you will not be able to generate these files if you haven't supplied an administrative password.
	You need to supply a passphrase next and confirm it. Once supplied, there will be a confirmation that your private key and certificate have been created.

TABLE 4.6   Continued

Value	Explanation
Unattended Startup	This allows the Relay server to restart, without prompting you for a password, in the event the system crashes. A hash of the password is left in the registry for such a purpose; this can come in really handy because if you forget the password, you won't be able to start your Relay server. It is recommended to leave this selected.

The next part of the Relay installation is the SOAP configuration, shown in Figure 4.6. SOAP communication is carried on between the Groove Relay and the Groove Manager servers using port 8009, which we earlier configured to be left open. This dialog contains the settings that the Manager needs to connect to the Relay. In addition to leaving the default names (or editing them), you need to generate keys and export the ID file before moving forward.

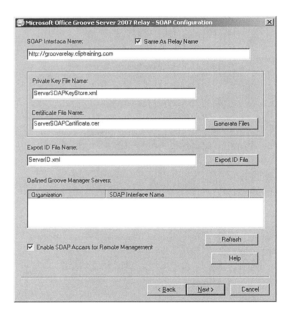

FIGURE 4.6   The SOAP Configuration page.

Table 4.7 shows the fields for SOAP configuration.

TABLE 4.7   SOAP Configuration Dialog Box Values

Value	Explanation
Relay SOAP Interface Name	Can be the same as the Relay name with an http: front end. This is the name that the Groove Manager will use to contact the Groove Relay. You can use a different name than the Relay, but you need to register the name in DNS.
Private Key File Name	Default: ServerSOAPKeyStore.xml
	This key must be generated and is the SOAP interface private key. It will use the same password used from the Server dialog.
Certificate File Name	Default: ServerSOAPCertificate.cer
	This key must be generated, and it contains the SOAP interface public key. The Groove Manager has to provide this certificate when it communicates with the Groove Relay.
Export ID File Name	Default: ServerID.xml
	This file contains the certificates for the Relay server, including the Relay name and public key (which is given to clients that use this server). This file isn't encrypted because it is all the public-side data. You need to select the **Export ID File** to create the file and update the registry located at HKEY_LOCAL_MACHINE\SOFTWARE\Microsoft\Office Server\Groove\Groove Relay\Parameters.
	You need to upload this file to the Manager server to allow communication between the two.

As previously mentioned, to communicate with the Relay, the Groove Manager must have the ID file uploaded. However, the Relay also requires some identity confirmation before communicating with the Manager. The Groove Manager has a registry key file called ManagementServer.reg that you must install on the Relay server in the local registry. We address this subject again later on.

After configuring the keys and exporting the ID file, click **Next.** The Security Configuration dialog box will open. You might be somewhat amused by this screen because it contains just one check box, next to the setting Require Pre-Authentication for Registration (via Groove Manager). The setting is for unmanaged Groove users that Relay communicates with, and the default setting is the most secure, so you can just click **Next** to move forward.

The next dialog is Tuning Configuration, shown in Figure 4.7.

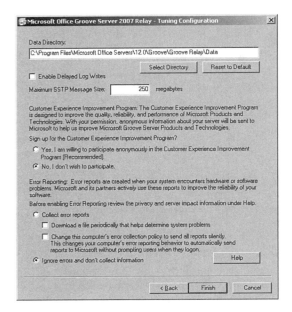

FIGURE 4.7   The Tuning Configuration dialog.

Although you can leave the default settings on your Tuning Configuration dialog for now, you might want to return later to these settings as more users are added to the Groove network. You can enhance performance of your Relay server by making some slight adjustments in log writes and SSTP message size.

The Enable Delayed Log Writes check box is a setting that can assist performance by allowing logs to be written without updating the database automatically. If you understand an Exchange (or any other) transaction log scenario, this will make sense to you. Essentially, when data is sent through the relay, it goes from the system memory into the database; however, transaction logs are also maintained, so updates are written to both the database and to the logs. If you select this option, you prevent the writes from going through until the server has a rest period. The difficulty with this setting is that you can lose data if the server crashes (because perhaps not all writes have been committed to disk). If you are confident that your system is fault tolerant, however, you won't have too much to worry about.

You can also determine a maximum SSTP message size. The default setting is 250MB. The message size relates to client IMs and workspace invitations only. The recommendation for configuring this setting is that you make sure the size is no more than half the memory available on the server. The default should suffice, so we recommend you leave this as is.

You can then decide (again) if you want to enroll in the Customer Experience Improvement Program (or not). And, you can configure error reporting. These reports can be helpful to Microsoft, but it is up to you to decide whether you want to have them collected and sent. You can click the Help button to learn more about error reporting.

Before the install completes, you are given the opportunity to do a backup of Relay registry settings, files, and directories that are important (including the private key, certificate, and ID files). You need to indicate a location for the files. It is best to keep them off the server, in the event the server fails and you need to rebuild it. You can restore the files to the Relay server. Note that if you make any configuration changes or regenerate keys, you should make another backup.

And now, your Groove Relay server should be complete. How can you be sure?

Confirming Your Server Is Functional

After you have installed the server, you still need to start the service. Go to Administrative Tools, select **Services,** and start the Groove Relay service.

When that service starts, you can open the Relay servers administration site by going to your browser and entering **http://127.0.0.1:8010.**

We discuss the management side of your Groove Relay server in Chapter 5.

Making Changes to Your Groove Relay Server

To alter the configuration of any of the Relay settings or to regenerate keys (and then back up those keys), you want to access your Groove Relay settings. To do this, go through your Control Panel and select the **Groove Relay** applet. By doing so, you open the same dialog boxes that you configured when the server was installed.

A Review of Keys Created

Before moving forward into the world of the Groove Manager, let's review the six main files created when we installed the Relay. It is important to understand how these files work in the process. They are, by default, as follows:

▶ **ServerCertificate.xml.** This is the private key file used by the Groove Relay server as the signing key.

▶ **Privkey.dat.** This file contains the private keys given to users so they can authenticate themselves to the Groove Relay when they initially connect and prove that they are legitimate clients.

▶ **ServerCertificate.cer.** This is the certificate file with the public key that allows clients to send data securely through the Groove Relay. It is distributed by the Groove Manager, however.

▶ **ServerID.xml.** This file contains all the important aspects of the Relay that need to be sent over to the Manager server to enable communication between the two servers. Included are the public key (which will be distributed to clients for contact with the Relay server) and the name of the server.

- ▶ **ServerSOAPCertificate.cer.** This file contains the SOAP public key, which is different from the public key that clients use. This key is used by the Manager to send data securely to the Relay.

- ▶ **ServerSOAPKeyStore.xml.** This contains the Relay server's private SOAP key. This key is created during the installation process and then encrypted. It is presented to the Groove Manager when the first connection is made. The SOAP information is also placed in the ServerID.xml file, which is uploaded to the Manager.

So, when a client connects to a Groove Manager server, the client is given the Relay public key and the name of the server (so that the client knows which server to connect to). The client then attempts to register with the Groove Relay. The Relay server responds first by confirming the public key and then providing a private key to the client for future interaction. Make sense yet? It's a little confusing to start with, but it will click.

The SOAP portion is between the Manager and the Relay. The Relay, during install, creates a private key (which says, "I am who I say I am"), and that key is encrypted. When the ServerID.xml file is updated to the Manager, it includes the SOAP information. The Manager makes first contact with the public key as an introduction, and the Relay responds with its private key to prove who it is to the Manager before data is exchanged between them.

The Groove Manager Install

Before you begin the process, remember that you need to have SQL configured on a separate server. In addition, you shouldn't try to install the Groove Manager on a domain controller or even a machine with Groove installed on it. Microsoft recommends you start with a clean Windows 2003 x64 server. You should, however, ensure the system running your Groove Manager server has met all the prerequisites you needed.

NOTE

You want to ensure your SQL server will be able to handle the workload it will be required to perform. Most data from the Groove Manager will be stored in the SQL database (which will include user accounts and certificates). Incoming Groove Manager transmissions will take place over port 1433 (the MS-SQL port), so you want to make sure this is open on the server. The server should also have its own host name registered with the DNS server.

When you install your SQL server, it is very, *very* important that you choose Mixed mode for authentication. If you don't, you might find yourself getting errors on the installation of the Groove Manager and not know why. You can download step-by-step instructions from the Microsoft site to make sure you don't miss an important piece of the puzzle. Mixed mode will allow for SQL authentication on the SQL side and Windows authentication on the IIS side.

When you are looking at your clean server, begin by installing IIS. IIS is such an important part of the process because your Groove administration is going to be done through the Manager Web site hosted on IIS. You can install it through Control Panel (Add and Remove Programs) or by using the Configure Your Server Wizard to install an application server, as we discussed earlier in Chapter 1.

With IIS installed, your next step is to go in through Control Panel (Add and Remove Programs) and install SMTP support. After you have installed this, you will see an added group under your server when you open your IIS Manager, called Default SMTP Virtual Server. You want to configure this so that administrators can send email to Groove clients that contain account configuration codes. To configure these settings, right-click **Default SMTP Virtual Server,** select **Properties**, open the **Deliver** tab, select **Advanced**, and then make sure the fully qualified domain name and the smart host are properly filled in. The FQDN should have the name of your Manager server and its domain included. The smart host should include the name of the true SMTP server for your organization. The SMTP server should be configured so it is not an open relay. Specifically indicate which systems (IP Addresses) are allowed to send mail.

Before the installation, make sure you have the .NET Framework installed (which you can download from Microsoft). If you installed the .NET Framework before you installed IIS, you can either reinstall the .NET Framework or re-register your ASP.NET by performing the following from a command prompt:

C:\WINDOWS\Microsoft.NET\Framework64\v2.0.50727\aspnet_regiis –I

When you are notified that ASP.NET has been installed, go back into your IIS Manager, select **Web Service Extensions**, select **ASP.NET v2.0.50727**, and then click the **Allow** button.

With the entire infrastructure in place, now you are ready to proceed with your installation. Start the Setup process, much like you did with your Groove Relay. This time, select **Office Groove Server 2007 Manager.** You'll be asked to provide the product key. You'll agree to the terms of the license agreement (so far exactly the same as the Relay). And, you will come to the Basic/Advanced installation options. Much like before, if you choose Basic it will install now. If you select Advanced, you will be asked to provide a different file location and asked whether you want to participate in the Customer Experience Improvement Program.

The software installs, and you will then see the Groove Manager Welcome page. Click **Next** and you will be presented with these options: Install Groove Manager or Install Groove Manager with Groove Auditing. Remember that you want to have one standard Manager in place before installing one that handles auditing (and you only want to enable auditing if you truly want to scan the data within workspaces).

Next you are asked all about your SQL configuration (so, I hope you took to heart the need to have that ready to go). Figure 4.8 shows the Groove Manager Database Configuration dialog box.

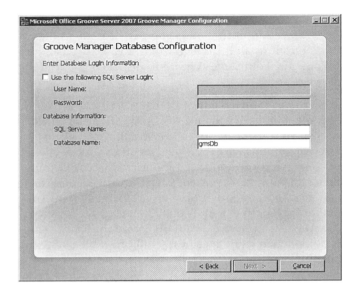

FIGURE 4.8   The Groove Manager Database Configuration dialog box.

You need to provide your Groove Manager the credentials necessary for it to establish a connection with the SQL server. So, you will be allowed to select a SQL login with username and password (if the SQL Server requires distinct authentication; that is, if Windows authentication is not used on the SQL server). Next, you want to provide the SQL server name (or IP address) and the database name. The database will be created on the SQL server (the default name being gmsDb).

> **WARNING**
>
> If you do not register the SQL server with your DNS server, you will never be able to get to the next step in the process. You can spend hours and hours trying to fix the problem (install and uninstall), but it won't find the SQL server. To fix this, you can go back and configure DNS or you can type in the IP address of your SQL Server.

Next you are asked to provide a Groove Manager master password. This password should be the same on all of your front-end Manager servers. After that, the Groove Manager Configuration dialog box displays, as shown in Figure 4.9.

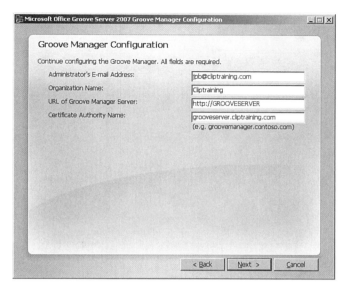

FIGURE 4.9   Groove Manager configuration settings.

You want to insert the administrator's email address and the name of your organization. You can accept the default URL for your Groove Manager server Web tools or you can change this. The default name is that of the IIS machine. If you plan on changing it, use http://hostname (where you use a FQDN for your Groove Manager). This step is important because clients will not be able to access the Manager if the URL is wrong. For your certificate authority name, enter the full name of your Groove Manager (the server, the company, and the domain level).

You are then presented with a configuration summary of your choices. Click **Next**, and the Groove Manager will complete the configuration process.

NOTE

If the process fails somewhere along the way, run the Setup again and remove the installation. Trying to repair the installation will not benefit you; you need to remove it and reinstall.

Confirming the Success of Your Installation

The installation program makes it pretty clear if you have succeeded or failed in your attempt to install Groove Manager. If you are successful, the final screen notifies you, and then you are automatically brought to the Groove Manager administrative Web site, as shown in Figure 4.10.

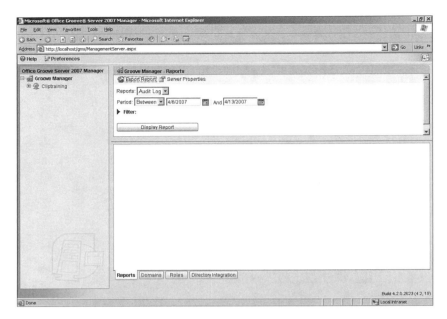

FIGURE 4.10   The Groove Manager administration Web site.

Configuration of your new Groove domain is discussed in the next chapter.

Installation of the Data Bridge

It's important to remember that you don't need to install a Data Bridge at all unless you truly have a need to integrate your Groove structure with other applications and databases within your IT infrastructure, like SQL or a SharePoint Server. Once installed, the Groove Data Bridge acts as a data access tier, with the ability to process XML-based calls from applications. As a network administrator, you won't be responsible to make the programmatic connection between the Data Bridge and the application server; your main responsibility will be to install it and manage it on the server level.

NOTE

If you are a programmer who does need to integrate a Groove Data Bridge into your organization, Microsoft provides some excellent assistance in the Office Groove 2007 Software Development Kit (SDK) (located here: http://www.microsoft.com/downloads/details.aspx?familyid=baa487e9-e1b9-4a10-beea-1fd906b77f92&displaylang=en), including the Groove Web Services Programmer's Guide and the Groove Web Service API Reference.

Unlike the Groove Manager and Relay servers, the Data Bridge has fewer hardware and software prerequisites to install. This is because its primary function is to act as the go-between for the clients.

The installation follows the same pattern as the other two, beginning with the product key, the license agreement, and an option to install Basic or Advanced. And that's it! The install goes through to completion with no additional configuration necessary.

When the installation is complete, follow these steps:

1. Start the configuration application on the Data Bridge by going to All Programs, Microsoft Office Server, and then selecting **Microsoft Office Groove Data Bridge 2007.**

2. The first dialog asks you to select a location for server data. You can keep the default (c:\GDB_Data) or browse for a new location.

3. You will come to the Account Configuration screen, shown in Figure 4.11. From here, select the **Create a new Groove Server Data Bridge** option. If you were restoring a Data Bridge server, you would select the secondary option to restore. Click **Next.**

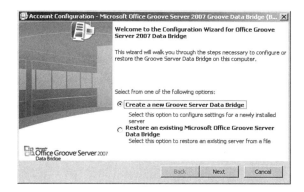

FIGURE 4.11   Configuring a Groove Data Bridge.

4. The next portion of the configuration asks you to provide a server name and password, as shown in Figure 4.12. You can select the Remember password options to have the Data Bridge use the password when operating as an automatic Windows service. You can also configure a backup schedule for your account file. (Note that you can make changes in the schedule at a later time.)

5. Next you are asked for a Web services key of your choosing. This key is needed to allow the Data Bridge to work with Web services. You can choose a string of up to 256 characters. This key will then be given to your developers so that they can develop their programs to access Web services.

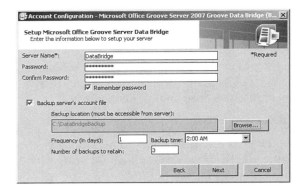

FIGURE 4.12   Providing server information for your Data Bridge server.

6. The next screen is the Setup Identity dialog, shown in Figure 4.13. This identity is necessary for the Data Bridge to work within Groove workspaces. If you want your Data Bridge to be outside of the management realm of the Groove Manager, you can leave the Unmanaged Identity option selected. If you want to have the Data Bridge be a domain member, subject to policies configured by the Manager role, you can select the Managed Identity option. In either case, provide the identity name (up to 256 alphanumeric characters) and an email address.

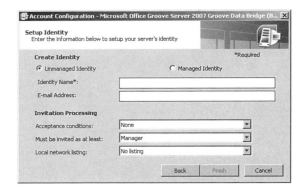

FIGURE 4.13   Configuring your Data Bridge identity.

7. The final step in the identity process is to determine invitation processing. (After all, the primary function of the Data Bridge is to mitigate invitations going to workspaces by accepting or declining them.) These settings can be configured now, or left until later on after the setup is complete. The settings include the following:

   Acceptance Conditions. You can accept all invitations that come in for Groove workspaces. You can accept invitations from server contacts or only from specific users that you choose. Note that for Data Bridges that are managed, you can also accept invitations from users of the same domain (or in trusted domains).

Must be invited as at least. There are three options: Guest, Participant, and Manager. Because the Data Bridge is playing an identity within your workspace, it might require a specific level of strength. You can configure the level that the Data Bridge must be invited in as.

Local network listing. The Data Bridge identity name can be listed in the network listings for your LAN by name only or by full v-card (or not at all, if you choose).

8. When you have completed your setup options, click **Finish**. The Data Bridge will complete the setup and will then take you to the Data Bridge administrative interface.

Are We Grooving Yet?

We aren't "grooving" quite yet. This chapter should have given you an extensive understanding of the need for the Groove client application in the workforce to assist in collaboration (anyplace, anytime, with anyone). The end result: more focus to the work, less to the collaboration … deadlines are met.

We've explored the three Groove server roles: Relay, Manager, Data Bridge. You've seen what they will require from your network, and you might just decide at this point that you like the idea of Live Groove for your users or, if you require a bit more control, Groove Enterprise Services with Microsoft hosting the servers. We walked through the installation of each server together, but there is more to do. For those who need to go forward from here, the next step is configuration and management of those server roles.

CHAPTER 5

Groove Server 2007: Configuration

Now that we have the key infrastructure installed, it's time for us to consider what configuration is necessary on each of our Groove servers and then what we will be required to do for management and maintenance of those servers.

For the most part, the Relay server is configured during the install. The keys need to be uploaded into the Manager for distribution. It's actually the Groove Manager that is going to be the prime focus of this chapter because it's through the administrative site that you handle most of your Groove oversight.

So, let's get Groovin (pun intended).

Working with the Groove Manager Interface

After the installation of your Groove Manager, the administration Web interface will appear. You can close this and return to it again by simply typing in the address to your server in your address bar through your browser.

> **NOTE**
>
> We are going to review all the Groove Manager settings, but if you need to drill down a bit further to understand or implement one of the features we discuss here, take note of the little red question mark that says Help in the top-left corner of the interface. The help files included with the Groove Manager are very detailed in explaining and providing step-by-step instructions on how to perform each task to administer Groove.

When you first look at the interface, shown in Figure 5.1, you'll notice that you are on the Reports tab (by default) for your domain. (Note that this is your Groove domain, not your Active Directory [AD] domain.) On the left side, you see the navigation pane, which shows the domain and the server it's under. You should take note of a link called Server Properties, which will appear along with any of the tabs you select under your Groove Manager. From within this dialog, you can change the email address for administrative email reports in the event of a problem with the server. You can also change the master password (which we established when we first installed the Groove Manager).

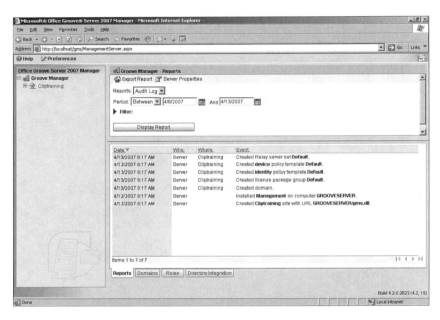

FIGURE 5.1   The Groove Manager administration Web interface showing the Reports tab.

There are four tabs toward the bottom that you can select to take you to a different set of configuration options. Let's discuss each of these tabs in detail.

The Reports Tab

The Groove Manager provides an audit log that you can use to see events that have occurred, such as when a domain is added (or additional users). It will also show you when there is a problem occurring, where the Groove Manager is having difficulty connecting to other servers in the infrastructure that affect the Groove environment.

You can determine the time frame for your display, and the application will go into the audit log and pull up the records for that period. You can also filter through those records by selecting the Filter control and selecting the field you want to filter by. When you are ready to see the results, click the **Display Report** button; all the queried results will appear in middle section.

TIP

In addition to the audit log, you can use Windows Event Viewer to see error reports on your Groove Manager. From the Event Viewer's application log, you should look for Win32 error codes (for codes under 10,000) or Winsock error codes (codes over 10,000). Depending on the type of code you receive (information, error, warning) you can respond accordingly.

The Domains Tab

Groove domains are used within a Groove environment to allow the formation of organizing domains, which enable you to structure your users and apply policies between those domains according to your needs. One important reason to create additional domains is because you can configure different Relay assignments through different domains. The Domains tab shows you each of those domains and the certificate authority (CA) server for that domain.

From the Domains tab, you can select the Add Domain option, shown in Figure 5.2. The initial settings you need to include involve the domain name (including a contact email and an optional description).

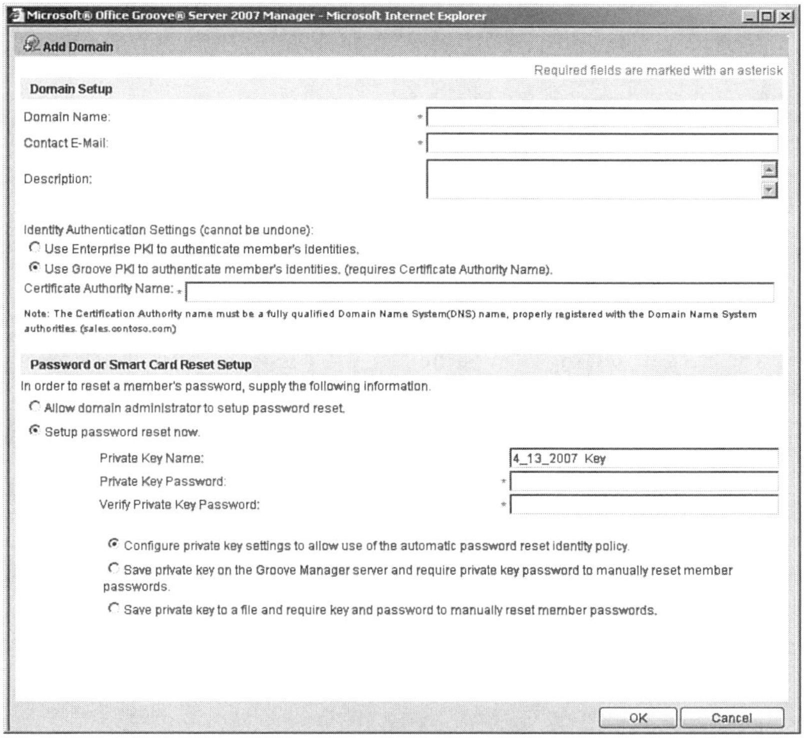

FIGURE 5.2   Adding more domains to your Groove Manager.

Notice that you have to include a Public Key Infrastructure (PKI). This could be an Enterprise PKI that you already have in place for your network, or you can use a Groove PKI. You need to provide the name of the CA. If you are using Enterprise PKI, use the fully qualified domain name (FQDN) for that server. If you use Groove PKI, indicate the name of your Groove Manager, using the FQDN that is registered in DNS.

> **NOTE**
>
> When determining whether to use Groove or Enterprise PKI, consider the structure of your organization and your needs. If you don't currently have a PKI system in place, there is no need to establish one. An Enterprise PKI has its benefits in that it can apply to a variety of applications that require PKI all at one time. The Groove PKI only functions for Groove clients and only for Groove connectivity. One of the benefits of Groove PKI is that you can establish cross-domain certification to make collaboration easier between members of different Groove domains.

Another part of the domain setup is the password or smartcard reset setup. Along with creating a certificate and private key (if you choose the Groove PKI arrangement), a certificate and private key is also created for resetting Groove passwords and smartcard logons. When you configure the domain, the private key is created and saved as an XML file, and the certificate is saved as a CER file.

If you select the option Allow domain administrator to setup password reset, you can proceed with the creation of the domain, but new users will not be allowed to be added until a domain administrator configures these settings.

The default setting is to Setup password reset now. The default private key name is based on the date of its creation. You can leave this or determine your own name. Then determine a password and verify it.

Three radio buttons are located at the bottom of the dialog. You need to select one to determine the private key storage location:

▶ **Configure private key settings to allow use of the automatic password reset identity policy (the default setting).** Saves the key and password with the Groove Manager and would be useful if the Automatic setting is established on the domain's Identity Policy Security page.

▶ **Save private key on Groove Manager and require private key password to manually reset member passwords.** Saves the login reset private key (an XML file) on the Groove Manager.

▶ **Save private key to a file and require key and password to manually reset member passwords.** Lets you browse to a directory on your network where the login reset private key (an XML file) should be saved.

The Roles Tab

From this tab, you can add other administrators to your Groove environment. The primary server administrator can add other admins to handle either the Groove Server Manager or a specific domain scope. Any users added within the roles on the server will now have access to the Web site (although they will only have the amount of administrative power you have configured them to have).

If you do not enable roles, anyone who can access the Groove Manager's site will be able to administer the site. To actually enable the use of roles, you have to go to the Roles tab and select the check box Enable role based access control. After enabling this, you can then select Add Administrator and provide a username for the administrators you configure. Notice in Figure 5.3 that you can add an administrator and determine whether you want him or her to be an administrator for a scope of the Groove Manager (as a server administrator, which allows you to perform all the tasks on the Groove Manager) or for a specific domain.

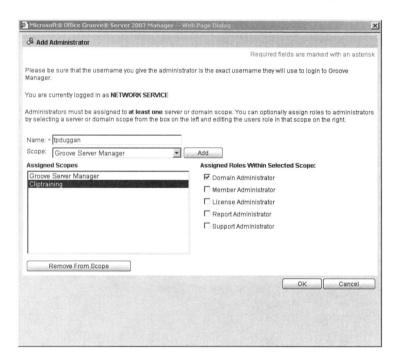

FIGURE 5.3   Adding administrators to your Groove environment.

Then, you can select one of the following roles:

▶ **Domain Administrator.** This role allows complete access to the UI for the domain through the administration site. In addition to access, all tasks associated with administrating a domain can be performed by the one who holds this role.

▶ **Member Administrator.** This role limits the access one has to the UI to the Member portion for the purpose of adding and editing members to the domain.

▶ **License Administrator.** This setting is only necessary if you have Groove clients for Groove 3.1 and earlier. Only allows this individual to handle the assignment and removing of licenses for those older Groove clients.

▶ **Report Administrator.** This role limits the access one has to the UI of the Reports tab for the domain. Only the ability to determine and view specific reports for that domain will be allowed.

▶ **Support Administrator.** This role limits access to only the fields that include user passwords and data recovery, and the one with this role will only be able to perform a reset of passwords or restore backed-up Groove user accounts.

You can create a new administrator and not assign that person a role. In that case, he or she will not be able to access any domain tasks until a role is provided.

Remember that these options do not in any way affect the AD domain structure on any of the permissions.

The Directory Integration Tab

Up until this point, we have discussed Groove servers and performed the installation without addressing the fact that you might have an Active Directory or other Lightweight Directory Access Protocol (LDAP)-based directory server in your organization. You can use this tab to configure your Groove Manager to work with your AD (or other LDAP-based server).

From within the Directory Integration tab, you begin by selecting Add Directory Server and the Server Properties dialog, shown in Figure 5.4. The benefit to configuring this connection between the Groove Manager and the LDAP server is that you can take advantage of the underlying LDAP structure for policies and a possible PKI implementation.

NOTE

Connecting to a directory server within your organization will allow you to pull users into your Groove domains, but you will not be able to use Groove Manager to perform any kind of modifications to the users, other than in terms of Groove. User modifications would still be performed on the LDAP servers.

As you can see from Figure 5.4, depending on your server, you might need to configure a lot of options. As a starting point, however, you need to first choose a directory type (which could be Active Directory, Lotus Domino R5 [or later], Sun ONE, or another generic LDAP server). Give the server a display name and type in the real name of server (as a FQDN). A server port is required and is usually 389, the standard LDAP port (or 636, in some cases).

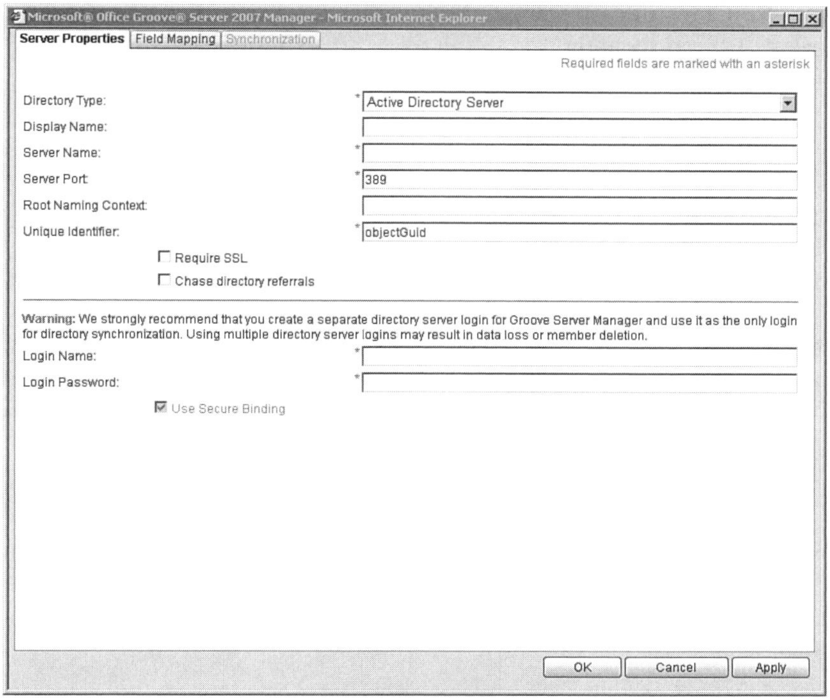

FIGURE 5.4   Defining a directory server.

The preceding options are pretty straightforward (as is the login name and login password to connect to the domain controller, although it is recommended that you create a specific account for the Groove connection), but you might not be as familiar with a few other settings, including the following:

▶ **Root Naming Context.** This field is required for Lotus Domino and Sun ONE but not for AD. The purpose is to provide a search default directory within your directory service hierarchy. An example might be dc=cliptraining,dc=com.

▶ **Unique Identifier.** This is a required field, with the default being objectGUID for AD. (It's different with each server type you select.) This setting is necessary for the Groove server to map users from the directory service over to Groove user lists.

▶ **Require SSL.** Allows the connection to your server to occur more securely through Secure Sock Layers, but only if the directory server is configured to use SSL.

▶ **Chase directory referrals.** This informs the Groove server that you want directory searches to go beyond the one server to other referral servers. This is only possible if the main directory server and referrals use the same username and password to access their directory.

▶ **Use Secure Binding.** Provides an added layer of security to the connection if your LDAP server is configured properly to use it. It allows the Groove server to secure the login information before sending it to the LDAP server.

You might also have noticed that there are two additional tabs for the Directory Integration dialogs. One is called Field Mapping and the other Synchronization (which will be grayed out unless you have a connection to a server.)

Because your servers are LDAP servers at heart (even though they have the names Active Directory, Lotus Domino, and Sun ONE), they share a common schema for the most part. The Groove Manager knows how to map the LDAP schema fields and pull over the information for the users properly. However, if you need to edit the way the fields are mapped, you can use the Field Mapping tab. You can make these changes before or after you import the users (although its recommended you do it beforehand).

Why might you need to do this? Well, it depends on your company and the level of information that might be in your directory service. For example, although the standard fields for users are automatically in the schema (name, telephone, email, and so forth), some fields are missing (such as Social Security Number or any other specialized fields). These can be added to your Groove synchronization, too.

The Synchronization tab is used to schedule the process of connecting and synchronizing to the directory server. You can use a schedule or on-demand synchronization.

Managing Your Groove Domain

Now that you've seen the management features for your Groove Manager, it's time to drill down a little bit into domain management. If you select a domain (it could be any of the new domains you have created or the default one that you created when installing the Groove Manager), you can see several configuration links for that domain within the hierarchy, including Members, Identity Policy Templates, Device Policy Templates, and Relay Server Sets.

Before you can configure a domain and add members, you must make sure the domain properties are set up properly. If you select the Domain Properties option, you will see that it is exactly the same as the dialog you use when you create a new domain. These settings must be established first.

For your primary domain, you can open these settings and add a description, supply the password, and determine the location of your keys. After you have done this, you click **OK,** and you will be able to go forward and add member, policies, and Relay server sets.

You might notice three initial tabs when you select your domain (Reports, E-Mails, and Roles). Let's first consider these:

▶ **Reports.** Like the Reports tab located at the Groove Manager level, these reports can be configured to display all the recorded events of the domain. You can perform more detailed reports than what you saw at the Manager level. The Manager showed you one audit log filter report based on a time criteria or another filter type.

However, at the domain level, you can configure your reports to be based upon member activity or on Groove usage (organized by member, tool, and workspace). Essentially, you can mix and match these reports so that you can see which users are using which tools (or a specific tool) and in which workspaces.

▶ **E-Mails.** Lets you configure one or multiple email contact points for the domain. If an account is configured or restored, an email will be sent to all of the predetermined accounts here. So, this is a good place to configure your domain admin's email account for both configuration and restoration emails.

▶ **Roles.** You configured administrative roles at the Groove Manager level. At that level, you can determine whether you want to create a server manager (with the highest level of authority) or establish administrators over specific domains (and then define those roles a bit further by configuring the administrator as domain, member, license, report or support—to make the responsibilities a bit more granular). Well, you can use the domain-level Roles tab to redefine the roles assigned to administrators within that domain. You select the domain administrators name, and a dialog appears with the five key roles that you can modify.

Domain Properties

To view and change the properties of your domain, select the domain name from the navigation pane of the Administrative UI. The properties will open with three tabs: Domain Settings, Password Settings, and Cross Domain Certification.

Domain Settings

The settings located here are relatively straightforward. You can change the name of the domain, the email account used to contact the administrator, and add or modify the description.

The dialog shows you a notation as to which type of PKI you have chosen (Enterprise or Groove PKI). This is for information purposes only. If Groove PKI was chosen, you will be presented with the name of the CA.

You are asked, "When displaying a member's domain affiliation, show:" You select the radio button for domain only *or* domain and group. This will determine the level of information displayed about a user to other Groove clients. The default is Domain only.

There is a check box to select whether you want to "Support license management for Groove Virtual Office clients version 3.1 and earlier." For more information, see the section "Manage Groove Licenses from Groove 3.1 or Earlier" later in this chapter.

Additional settings include the following:

▶ **Number of days that members can be inactive before being removed from the domain's contact directory** (default is 15). Note that a user is considered inactive when not logged in to Groove.

▶ **Number of days that devices can be inactive before being removed from domain** (default is 90). When the word *device* is used here, it is referring to a system running Groove. That system is registered with the domain and a timestamp is given when the system (device) has Groove running on it and checks in. If Groove isn't running, even if the system (device) is functioning, after the established number of days, it will be removed from the Groove domain. Note that placing a zero in the box will ensure that devices are never removed from the domain.

▶ Under Advanced Settings is a single check box under the heading Domain Migration. To migrate members, go to Members list and select **Migrate Members** from the Manage Members toolbar menu. The check box says, "Enable migration to a new Groove Manager domain. Requires Groove 2007 or later."

Password Settings

From the Password Settings tab, you can change the password/smartcard login reset and data recovery, or change the location of that key. When you first select the Password Settings tab, at the top you will be reminded how you configured the server, (as shown in Figure 5.5).

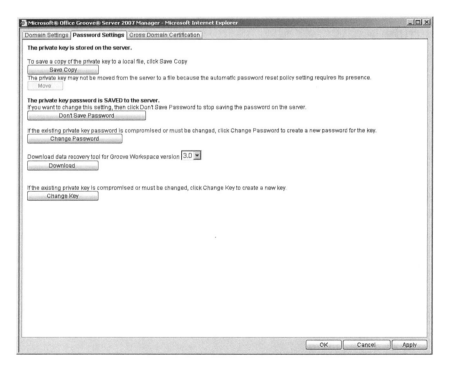

FIGURE 5.5   Changing reset/recovery keys and locations.

You have a variety of options to choose from in dealing with your key. When you configured the key initially when you established the server's private key, you established certain information about the domain. If you want to change that information, here is the location for those changes.

For example, you can click the following buttons to follow these steps:

▶ **Save Copy.** This saves a copy of the private key to a local file. You cannot move the key if the key is stored on the server itself, but you can make this copy.

▶ **Move.** This will be grayed out if you have the password/smartcard key stored on the server because it cannot be moved. If it is stored in a file, you can choose to move the location of that file.

▶ **Save Password on Server.** If you already have the private key stored in a file, you can change this to being stored on the server.

▶ **Don't Save Password.** This enables you to stop the private key from being saved on the server.

▶ **Change Password.** If the private key password is compromised or must be changed, click **Change Password** to provide a new password for the key. This option is only available if the Automatic Password Reset option is set, which causes the password to be saved on the server.

▶ **Download.** Downloads a data-recovery tool for the Groove workspace version. (You select the version from among these options: 3.0, 2.5, 2.1, 2.0.)

▶ **Change Key.** To go beyond changing the password, if you need to change the key itself, you use this option.

Cross-Domain Certification

The Groove Manager let's you configure trusted collaboration between domains (even if those domains are not part of your organization). This isn't possible if you are using an Enterprise PKI as your identity authentication scheme; however, if you are using Groove PKI, you can set up this type of trust between domains.

This requires that administrators of each domain (either in the same organization or separate ones) exchange and cross-register domain certificates. These certificates are like letters of introduction from one to the other using public keys. To perform this cross-domain certification, trust is quite simple. Follow these steps:

1. Both administrators need to go into the properties of the domain and to the Cross Domain Certification tab.

2. They both need to click the **Export Certificate** button, and choose a location for that certificate.

3. Then they need to send the certificate to each other in a safe manner.

4. Finally, from within the same tab, they need to select **Add Certificate** and browse to the correct location for the certificate so that it can be added to the domain trusts.

In this example, we had the trusts going in both directions, but you can configure the trust to only go in one direction. If you want DomainA to trust DomainB, for example, export the key in DomainB and add the certificate in DomainA. This will give DomainA the ability to trust DomainB.

> **NOTE**
>
> It's not imperative that you use a cross-domain trust to make Groove workspace contacts with members outside your organization. It simply affords a higher level of security to use PKI and ensure that persons from other domains (or domains in other organizations) can validate themselves through their PKI. If this isn't enabled between Groove workspace members, the verification of users can take place in other ways.

Members

With all that we have done to plan for and design the infrastructure of a Groove environment, and then deploy and configure those servers, we might have forgotten the single most important piece to Groove: the user. Without Groove clients installed with users collaborating-away on those clients, all our work would be for naught.

When you select the Members option, shown in Figure 5.6, you can see all of your members for that domain. You can see at a glance their status (active, pending, or disabled). You can add members, manage members, or establish Group Properties.

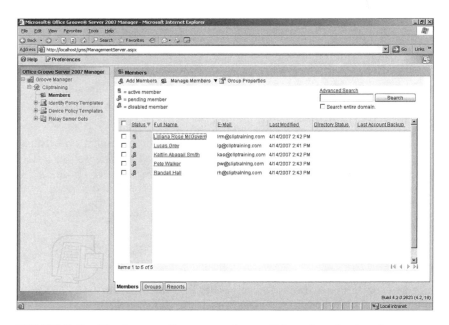

FIGURE 5.6   Viewing your Groove members within a domain at a glance.

Adding New Members

Upon selecting the Add Members option, you are faced with several different options, including the following:

▶ **Add Single Member.** To create a single member

▶ **Add Multiple Members (XML).** To create members using an XML file

▶ **Add Multiple Members (CSV).** To create members using a CSV (comma-separated values) file

▶ **Import Members From a Directory.** To import members from a directory server

> **NOTE**
>
> If you select the XML or CSV options, you are provided with templates that you can use to plug in your users' information. When you complete the template, you can then upload the template to the server.

The easiest solution, logically, is to establish the directory link (discussed earlier) to allow you to import the users and their details into your Groove Manager. If you decide to add users one at a time (which you might do when you are performing tests before a full-scale deployment), select the **Add Single Member** option, and then fill out the information. The information is somewhat simple. You have two required fields: Full Name and E-Mail. Then, you have details of the account such as job title, address, phone, cell, and so forth.

During the addition of new users (in all cases, single, XML, CSV, directory), you have to select an identity policy template and a Relay server set (or leave the setting to the default). We discuss these settings shortly.

Managing Members

Having an account is only the first part of the membership setup. Groove clients still need to connect to your server. To do this, you can automate the process in certain situations through Auto-Account Configuration (discussed in Chapter 6, "Groove Server 2007: Advanced Techniques"). However, the method used if you are not able to automate is to send a Groove account configuration package to your Groove users by email (which explains why email was a requirement when setting up your accounts). The email contains an account code, a managed identity name, and the name of the Groove Manager.

When users receive this code, they can open up their Groove client and input this information into the client. To send this message to a single user or multiple users, you need to select the check box next to the users' names (or select the top check box, which will select all users), and then select **Manage Members.** Select the **Send Groove Account Configuration Code** option, which will bring up the dialog necessary to configure the message users will see, as shown in Figure 5.7.

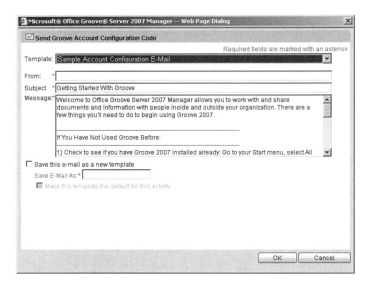

FIGURE 5.7   Configuring the email message for users.

You can choose to use the Sample account template, which will fill in most of the information in the subject and message for you (although you still need to put in your own From line). Or, you can choose No Template (Enter Fields Manually) from the Template options. After typing in your changes (or, if you decided not to use the template, your entire message), you can save the email as a new template for the future (or select to make this template the default for this activity).

When you click OK, the message is sent, and users can start registering their accounts with the server. It's important to mention that you should have Groove 2007 installed on the user's machine before sending the email.

> **NOTE**
>
> What happens when a user receives the email to connect to the Groove world? This actually depends on the client's setup. If they are new to Groove and this is the first time they are opening the Groove client installed on their system, they can open Groove for the first time and walk through the steps necessary. The account configuration code that they received through the email will need to be copied and entered into the wizard. The account configuration server name will need to be added, too, and the client will then connect to the Groove Manager. When that connection is made, the Manager authenticates the user and pushes out authentication information to the user's machine (including identity policies, Relay server assignments, and anything else the client is going to need).
>
> If the user already has a Groove account, however, the user needs to select the Help option and choose Configure Account (and then you will be able to supply the account configuration code and server).

As a side note, if you want to provide a user with the code and server name without sending the email, you could go into the Members section and select a user. Under the Account Information tab, you can take note of the code.

When the account is connected to the Groove Manager, you will have the ability to make edits to the structure of the account. A backup of the account will be made, and now you will be able to select the Restore Account tab to bring the account back in the event the client has a problem later on.

Additional Management Features

The account configuration code is a very important step in the process for accounts. In addition, you have five other options:

► **Move Members.** You can create different groups and move your users to those groups. To create a group, select the **Groups** tab and then **Add Group.** When you create the group, you can give it a name and description. You can also determine an identity policy for the group, a device policy for the group, and a Relay server set. Moving users into those groups will allow those policies to be applied.

► **Disable Members.** This allows you to temporarily disable an account on the Groove Manager, although it has no affect on the users' ability to log in to their domain controllers.

► **Enable Members.** Members that have been disabled can be reenabled with this option.

► **Export Members.** You can export items into XML or CSV files. You can use the file to add members to another domain quickly.

► **Delete Members.** Allows you to remove users from the domain.

Identity Policy Templates

Identity policies control Groove functionality in relation to domain members. These policies are applied to domain groups (which have members inside them). Regardless of where a user goes, whatever machine they are using, the policy will apply to them.

To create a policy is easy. You select **Identity Policy Templates,** and then select **Add Template.** All you have to provide is a name and description. When the policy is created, you then have to configure it. Note that if you select the policy from the list under the Identity Policy Templates, all you will see is the properties of that policy where you can configure the name and description. You need to select the policy from the navigation hierarchy. Then, you will see the policy settings.

There are two tabs: Member Policies and Security Policies.

Identity Policy: Member Policies

Table 5.1 reviews the settings for the Member Policies tab.

TABLE 5.1   Member Policies Tab

Account Backup Policies	Backup account interval in days (default: 4)
Workspace Version Policies	Workspace Acceptance and Restoration Policy: Minimum Workspace Version (default is 2007; other options include Client Default and No Minimum)
	Workspace Creation Policy: Default Workspace Version (only applies if a different minimum workspace version is allowed; options include 2.0, 2.1, 2.5, 3.0, and 2007)
Identity Publishing Policies	Allow publishing of vCard to the Public Groove Directory
Device Management Policies	Check box: Identities may only be used on a managed device in this domain (default: unchecked)
	Check box: Automatically manage devices at account configuration (and account logon for Groove 2007 and later) (default: checked)

Identity Policy: Security Policies

Table 5.2 reviews the settings for the Security Policies tab.

TABLE 5.2   Security Policies Tab

User Verification Policy	Three radio buttons:
	Do not warn or restrict members when communicating with any contacts. (Default: selected)
	Warn member before communicating with contacts that have not been administrator certified or manually verified by the member.
	Only allow members to communicate with administrator-certified contacts.
Password* Reset Policies**	Select automatic password reset to allow users to request and receive a password reset without administrator involvement. (Options include Automatic, Manual password reset [and data recovery], Data recovery, and None.)
Edit Rest Settings (button)	These instructions are shown to members that request a manual password reset and who use Groove 3.0f or later. (Note that you provide the instructions.)
Blocked Files	Check box: Override Groove's default list of blocked files. (Default: deselected)

*Password or Smartcard login certificate reset.

**Requires data-recovery private key password be stored on server in domain properties.

Device Policy Templates

When Groove users connect to the manager, the system they are using is registered, too. These systems (or devices) can also be managed through policy templates if they are registered with the Groove Manager.

How to Register Devices with Groove Manager

The easiest way to register a device is through an identity policy that will set up the registration during the user account registration. You can find the policy setting in Table 5.1. Under the Members Policies, beneath the section for Device Management Policies, you'll see the setting "Automatically manage devices at account configuration (and account logon for Groove 2007 and later)." With this option selected, when users connect to the Groove Manager for the first time, they will be presented with a dialog box that asks them whether they want to have the device managed. When they accept the management, a registry setting is applied to the following key:

HKEY_CURRENT_USER/SOFTWARE/Microsoft/Office/Groove/ManagementDomain

You can go one step further and *ensure* that all devices of each managed Groove identity are managed by selecting the other check box: Identities may only be used on a managed device in this domain. With this selected, the user doesn't have much choice. If users select no to the registering of their device, they will be presented with another message that says they will not be able to configure their Groove account without it. And, this setting will also prevent users from deleting the registry key and thinking this will bring them out from the device policy.

In the event you didn't register the device automatically and now need to do it manually, follow these steps:

1. From within the Groove Manager, open a device policy template within the domain you manage, which will take you to the Account Policies tab, as shown in Figure 5.8.

2. Up at the top of the main window, select the **Download Device Management Key.** You'll be asked to agree to a file download. Agree and save the REG file to a location of your choosing.

3. The key you just saved can be used on any machines you want configured to be managed as part of that domain because all machines will use that same registry key. So, you can deploy that key in whatever way you like, based on your standard methods, or you can move the REG file manually to the client device and open it to install the key.

4. When the key is in place, restart Groove on the client system, and it should automatically come up as managed in the Groove world.

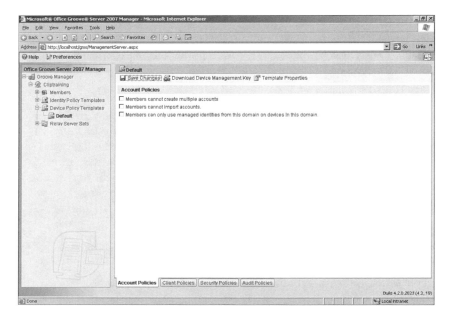

FIGURE 5.8   The Account Policies tab of a device policy template.

Device Policy: Account Policies

Table 5.3 reviews the settings for the Account Policies tab.

TABLE 5.3   Account Policies Tab

Account Policies	Three check boxes (default: none checked):
	Members cannot create multiple accounts.
	Members cannot import accounts.
	Members can only use managed identities from this domain on devices in this domain.

Device Policy: Client Policies

Table 5.4 reviews the settings for the Client Policies tab.

TABLE 5.4   Client Policies Tab

Messenger Integration Policies	Enable/Disable Messenger Integration. (Default: enabled)
	Check box: Allow members to change Messenger integration settings.
Directory Search Policies	Check box: Prevent members from searching for contacts in the public Groove directory.

TABLE 5.4   Continued

Install Policies	Note that install policies apply to Groove 3.1 or earlier. Microsoft Office Groove 2007 and later will be subject to existing Office Update policies.
	Check box: Prevent members from installing any component.
	Check box: Deny installation of self-signed components.
	Check box: Prevent Groove from looking for updates.
	Button: Advanced Install Policies (for more customized policy settings).
Usage Policies	Check box: Prohibit non-Auditable tools.
	Check box: Prohibit use of Groove File Sharing.
	Check box: Prohibit use of forms and forms-based tools (including any InfoPath tools and the Discussion tool released with Groove 2007 and later).
	Check box: Prohibit use of games.
	Note that restricting tool usage can have unintended consequences because of the relationships between Groove tools or Groove tools and third-party tools. See Help for more information.
Bandwidth Policies	Check box: Limit bandwidth to (input number) bits/second. (Minimum: 4,800 bits/second)
	Options: kilobits/second, megabits/second, or percent
	Note that limiting bandwidth could drastically affect the performance of the Groove client.

Device Policy: Security Policies

Table 5.5 reviews the settings for the Security Policies tab.

TABLE 5.5   Security Policies tab

Login Method	Members will log in to Groove using: (Choose one.)
	Passwords
	Smartcards
Password Policies	Passwords must contain at least this many characters. (Default: 4)
	Users cannot repeat previous passwords (number of previous passwords to compare with). (Enter number.)
	Password expires this length of time (in days). (Enter number.)
	Check box: Prevent password memorization.
	Password must contain at least one: (check boxes)
	Alpha character (a,b,c …)
	Numeric character (1,2,3 …)
	Mixed case character (aBc …)
	Punctuation symbol (!,?,$ …)
	Button: Edit Reset Settings (requires Groove 3.0e or earlier).

TABLE 5.5   Continued

Account Lockout Policy	Number of invalid login attempts before account is locked: (Enter number.)
	Maximum duration of lockout (enter number) in seconds. (You can change the setting to minutes, hours, or days.)
	After threshold is reached: (Select one).
	Allow login attempts but repeat maximum duration forever.
	Do not allow any more login attempts (requires password reset to unlock).
Strong Private Key Protection	Check box: Require strong private key protection. (See Microsoft Knowledge Base article 320828.)
Web Service Policies	Check box: Allow direct remote Web services (Groove 3.1 or earlier).

Device Policy: Audit Policies

Table 5.6 reviews the settings for the Audit Policies tab.

TABLE 5.6   Audit Policies tab

Audit Server Policies	Audit Server URL. (Input URL.)
	Upload audit logs every (input number) days. (You can change the setting to minutes or hours.)
	Check box: Disable Groove if auditing fails.
Groove Client Events	Check box: Audit all client events.
	Sub check box: Audit instant messages and invitations.
	Sub check box: Audit login and logoff events.
	Sub check box: Audit contact events.
	Check box: Audit workspace events.
Tool Events	Select one or more of the following:
	Check boxes: Chat, Discussion, Document Review, Files, Forms Tool, Groove File Sharing, InfoPath Tool, SharePoint Mobile Workspaces
	Check box: Audit the contents of files added to tools.

Relay Server Sets

You recall that a Groove Relay server is used to allow communication for Groove clients when direct connectivity isn't possible (either because a firewall is in place, the clients are on different subnets within your organization, or clients are communicating over the Internet). A Groove Relay is established first, and then the connectivity information for that Relay can be provided to the Groove Manager. The Manager then distributes the connection details and keys to contact the Groove Relays.

When a Groove Relay server is registered with the Groove Manager, that server is added to a set. A Relay server set is a group of one or more Relay servers that can be assigned to domain groups or users. If you have one Groove Relay, all users are assigned to use that server and that Relay server set. However, you can provide redundancy to your Groove design (both for load balancing and for fault tolerance to your infrastructure) by adding more Relay servers. These can be placed in the default Relay server set or you can create additional sets and space out the use of the Relay servers.

To start with, you need to add your Groove Relay servers to the Groove Manager.

Adding Relay Servers to the Groove Manager

You recall when you configured your Groove Relay that you needed to configure the Relay to create public/private keys (both for the clients to receive to communicate with the Groove Relay server and for the Manager to use to communicate with the Relay server using SOAP). The Groove Manager needs to be provided with a copy of these keys.

NOTE

Obviously, the registering of your Groove Relay servers is an essential step in the configuration process for your Groove environment. To ensure the process smoothly functions for the download and processing of the keys, make sure you use the 64-bit version of Internet Explorer when you follow these steps, according to Microsoft (http://www.microsoft.com/technet/prodtechnol/office/grooveserver/2007/guide/GMDAG_07.mspx?mfr=true). To start this version, select **Start,** then **Programs,** and then choose **Internet Explorer 64-bit.** If you already have a browser open, you can check the version by selecting the **Help** menu item and selecting **About Internet Explorer.** Most likely, if you don't recall specifically selecting the 64-bit version, you are using 32-bit IE.

To begin the process of adding Relay servers, follow these steps:

1. From the 64-bit version of IE, open the Groove Manager administrative interface. Expand the hierarchy to open the domain you want to add the Relay server to and select the **Relay Server Sets** heading. You should see two tabs: Relay Server Sets, and Relay Servers. If you only see one, you might have selected the Default option beneath the Relay Server Sets heading.

2. Select the **Relay Servers** tab.

3. Toward the top, you can hover your cursor over the Add Relay Server option. You will be presented with two options:

   a. Onsite Relay Server. Used for complete in-house Groove solutions

   b. Hosted Relay Server. Used for Microsoft-hosted Groove under Enterprise Services

4. Select to add an onsite Relay server, and you will see that there are two steps involved in adding the server. The first is to click the button **Download Public Key.** After clicking this button, you need to follow these steps:

   a. Save the Groove Manager public key to a file. The file, by default, is named Groove_Manager_Public_Key.reg.

   b. Move the public key file to the relay server (unless you saved it directly to the server).

   c. On the Relay server, double-click the Groove Manager public key file. This will update the Groove Relay server's registry with the information needed to communicate with the Groove Manager.

5. The Groove Manager still needs to be given the Groove Relay ID file (ServerID.xml), which we created during the installation of the Relay server. (See Chapter 4, "Groove Server 2007: Overview and Installation," for more details about the ServerID.xml file.) Copy this file and move it over to the Groove Manager.

6. From the Add Onsite Relay Server dialog box (shown in Figure 5.9), under Step 2: Import Relay Server Key to Groove Manager, browse to the location of the ServerID.xml. Then click **OK.** And now, your Relay will show up under the Relay Servers tab.

FIGURE 5.9   Configuring Groove Relay and Groove Manager servers.

NOTE

After a Groove device (or user) is configured to be managed under the Groove Manager, the client will check in with the Manager every five hours. To force this to occur immediately (in the event you want specific policies to apply faster to see their effect), you can manually initiate the contact by doing one of the following: Log in to Groove or out of Groove or restart the Groove client completely.

Moving Relay Servers into Relay Sets

By default, all Relay servers you add to your Manager are placed into the default Relay set. As you add more Relay servers, you will want to create additional sets to control your traffic better. Logically, before you can move a Relay server into another Relay server set, you have to create additional sets. To accomplish this, click the **Relay Server Sets** link from the navigation pane in your Groove Manager UI. This will show you the default set that is automatically created when you install Groove Manager. If you want to add new sets, select the **Add Set** option. You will be asked for a name (which is required) and a description (which is not required but can be quite helpful later on when you are attempting to organize multiple sets with tens of Relay servers).

After you have this new Relay server set, select it from the navigation pane. You will see a blank window (because you haven't added any Relay server yet). Hover your cursor over the Add Relay Servers to Set option, and this should show you the list of servers for that entire domain. At any time, you can move one into a new set by creating the new set, going into the set, and on the Relay Servers tab, selecting **Add Relay Servers to Set** and then selecting the Relay server you want to move.

NOTE

When adding a server into a new Relay server set, it's important to note that this doesn't remove that server from the default or any other set. To remove a server from the set, you have to select that set and then choose the **Remove Relay Servers** option. This doesn't delete the Relay server; it only removes it from that particular set. If you do want to delete the Relay server from the domain, you must click the **Relay Server Sets** link, and then go to the Relay Servers tab and select **Delete Relay Servers,** after you have selected the ones you want deleted.

Which Relay Server Does a User Use?

An interesting question. Logically, the Relay server set exists within a domain, and users within that domain are assigned (either individually or through groups they belong to) to use a Relay server set. If there are multiple servers within a set, users are allowed to contact any one of those servers. Users will attempt to contact the first one available starting with the top of the list. What is especially interesting is that you can reorder the list.

Within the Relay server set, there are up and down arrows. You can prioritize the list of servers by moving ones you want used more often up to the top of the list of servers.

Editing Relay Server Properties

You can edit some of the settings for the Relay servers you have configured to work with your Groove Manager (although the major part of the configuration side should be done on the Relay itself). To edit the properties for a Groove Relay through the Manager UI, open the domain Relay server set and then select the **Relay Servers** tab.

Select the Relay server you want to edit. You'll be presented with a dialog box, as shown in Figure 5.10.

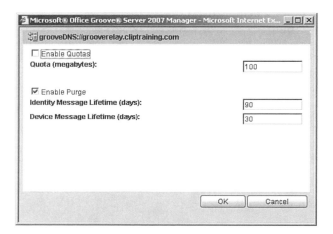

FIGURE 5.10   Editing Relay server Properties.

The following options are available to you:

- ▶ **Enable Quotas.** Select this check box to enable a quota on message queues. Indicate the size of the quota in megabytes that can be stored in the queue for each user. When the queue is filled, the messages are held on the sender's device until the queue frees up. Microsoft says the default is 15MB but ours came up at 100.

- ▶ **Enable Purge.** Allows the Relay to purge messages automatically. There are two subsettings to configure: Identity Message Lifetime (the number of days that identity messages, which include both IM and workspace invitations can stay in the queue; default is 90 days); Device Message Lifetime (the number of days that device messages can stay in the queue; default is 30 days).

Manage Groove Licenses from Groove 3.1 or Earlier

As discussed previously in this chapter, there is a "Support license management for Groove Virtual Office clients version 3.1 and earlier" setting. If you selected this option to turn it on, a new link is placed in your navigation pane called Legacy License Management with a default License Set (although there are no default licenses added).

If you are using Groove clients that are 3.1 or earlier, you have to import Groove licenses into the Manager server for the domain to allow them to work with your modern Groove 2007 users.

Groove license packages (for the earlier versions of Groove) are groupings of Groove tools and the licenses to use them. In earlier versions of Groove, you purchased licenses for your clients. If you want to support legacy Groove clients, you must import those licenses and then assign them to a domain group (or an individual).

To import the licenses, click the new **Legacy License Management** link, and then select the **Licenses** tab. Select **Add License** from the top toolbar. You will be asked to provide the location of the license file. This will pull the license in to the License tab, and then it will be part of the license set for that domain.

TIP

If you are a newcomer to the world of Groove, as many are, you might consider just going forward with an all-Groove 2007 client base. If you are going to continue to manage legacy clients, however, you need more assistance to understand how things used to work in relation to how they work now. The help files from the administrative Web UI can be very helpful. In fact, several appendixes offer suggestions on integration with legacy Groove.

Manage and Monitor Your Groove Relay Server

For the most part, your Groove Relay should be a "set it and forget it" server. In other words, after you configure it, you shouldn't need to hand hold the server and check in on it every day to make sure it is working. There are only a few working parts to the server that you can check to make sure it's working after the install, and you can troubleshoot the server by checking these same features.

NOTE

If you need to alter any of the settings you configured during the installation, back up key files or make changes to your passphrase, or generate new certificate files, go to **Start, Control Panel, Groove Relay,** and you will be presented with the same dialog screens you saw during the installation process in Chapter 4 (Server, SOAP, Security, and Tuning). Refer to Chapter 4 for setting options.

For starters, you can check the Groove Relay service. Select **Start, All Programs,** and then **Administrative Tools, Services.** Scroll down the list of services until you find the Groove Relay service. If it isn't already started, click the **Start** button. (You can also go to a command prompt and enter **net start "Groove Relay".**)

To confirm the Relay is working, open your Internet browser and enter the following:

http://localhost:8010/ or **http://127.0.0.1:8010/**

If your server is up and running, the UI will come up as shown in Figure 5.11.

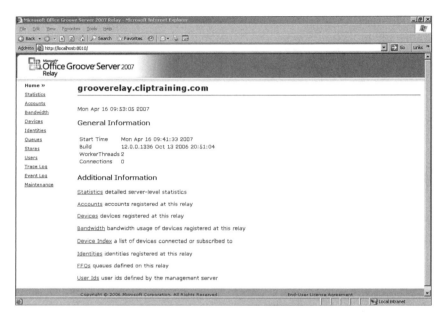

FIGURE 5.11   Groove Relay administrative UI.

> **TIP**
>
> Some have asked, "Can you perform administration through the command line?" Well … there is a **relay** command you can use, but it's doubtful you will find it helpful. It is a throwback to the original creation of Groove. You can see this by navigating to the location of the directory you installed. Relay in on the server from within a command prompt. Type **relay –v** to see version information and **relay –h** for a list of command options.

Administrative Web Pages

The administrative UI has 12 different sites available (with the first one being the home site). Here is a list of the other sites and what they can be used for:

> ▶ **Statistics.** Provides a very detailed list of statistics, including Queue/Store Stats, WorkList Stats, SSTP Commands Received, SSTP Command Sent, SSTP Connect Responses, Summary Connection Table, SSTP Connection Table, Virtual Connection Table, HTTP Connection Table, Admin Service Connection Table, Flow Control

Stats, DPP Counters, and RVP Counters. From this large list of statistics, there is quite a bit you can learn about your server. You will be able to see current connections to the Groove server, the number of queues stored on the server (waiting to be sent to recipients), the number of clients attached to the Relay, and much, much more.

▶ **Accounts.** This page shows you a list of all user accounts that use this server, and you can select one from the list to see detailed information about their connections. Or, you can enter an account URL and click the Lookup button for the detailed information. You can see account information, if the account is locked out or not, security key information, and account quota information.

▶ **Bandwidth.** Shows bandwidth (bytes per second) connectivity between the Groove client and the Relay server over a time interval. There is an option to enter the top number of devices to display (the default is 25) that you can change to indicate another setting. This will display the list of connected devices in descending order of bandwidth usage. There are two groups of statistics (General and Detailed bandwidth usage) that indicate average usage, maximum and minimum usages, and more.

▶ **Devices.** Shows the list of Groove devices that have registered with the Groove Relay. You can select a device from the list or look up a device. The information reported back for a specific device would include the client version of Groove installed, connection success and failure, last known IP address, whether additional user accounts are configured on the one device, and more.

▶ **Identities.** Shows the list of Groove users (not their devices but the users themselves). You will be able to see identity information (such as the account name) and how many messages are queued for that user.

▶ **Queues.** Shows the current number of Groove Relay queues (messages waiting for specific clients). You will be able to see the last time a purge was done. This might lead you to select the Maintenance option and purge the queue.

▶ **Stores.** This shows a subset of queue information for the volume.

▶ **Users.** Shows a list of users (similar to identities).

▶ **Trace Log.** Displays a subset of the Relay's internal trace information.

▶ **Event Log.** Displays the most recent events you can find in the Event Viewer. For more information on the event logs and codes you see, you can view the help files for the administrative UI on the Relay Server.

▶ **Maintenance.** The Maintenance tab enables you to perform several tasks, including the following:

Generate Queue Information Report. The report is written into the Info directory in the Relay Diagnostics/Info subdirectory of the Data\Diagnostics directory. An informational application event log entry confirms when the report is complete.

The report filename is QueueInfo-*yy-mm-dd-hhmmss*.log (where the *yy-mm-dd-hhmmss* portion relates to year, month, day, hours, minutes, and seconds).

Purge all queues to the configured purge interval. This will begin a purge/compress cycle on the entire queue store. A log will be kept at PurgeInfo-*yy-mm-dd-hhmmss*.log (where the *yy-mm-dd-hhmmss* portion relates to year, month, day, hours, minutes, and seconds). The log will show two lines of information for each queue, showing the number of messages and number of bytes before the purge, and then after.

Purge status. You can monitor the current purge/compress activity at any time.

Monitoring Tools in Windows 2003 Server

Several tools included with Windows 2003 Server can help you monitor your Relay server, especially when it comes to disk usage. Daily (or at multiple times during the day) monitoring of the disk usage is a very important task because running out of disk space can be one of the biggest problems a Relay server has to face.

In addition to Event Viewer, you can use Performance Monitor and Task Manager to view important resources. Here is a list of tools and how to use them:

▶ **Task Manager.** Look to the Processes tab to see the relay.exe process to verify that the process is indeed working. You can add more columns to the Process tab, such as I/O Reads/Writes. You can also go to the Performance tab to see how your systems memory and CPU is doing.

▶ **Performance Monitor.** Enables you to view your system in real time (although Task Manager would do that more easily) or establish a running log that will alert you when certain thresholds are reached at your direction. You can select objects to monitor and various counters to track.

▶ **Event Viewer.** As already mentioned, this is an excellent way to see what is happening with your Relay server. You can use the administrative UI to get a view of only those events that relate to your Groove Relay. For more information about the codes, you can use the help files. There is an Appendix A, "Event Log Codes and Messages," to assist in understanding these codes.

▶ **Netstat.** One of the recommendations from Microsoft to test the status of your Relay connections is to use the netstat.exe command. To run the command, open a command prompt and type **netstat -an | more**, and you will see a listing of all the active ports. You want to look for TCP ports 2492, 80, 8010 (for the administration UI), 443, and 8009.

Configure Bandwidth-Usage Statistics

We discussed earlier that through the administration UI on the Relay server, you have the ability to see bandwidth-usage statistics for connections to the server. This is actually enabled on the server by default. However, its important to note that this places a large strain on the server as it tries to perform its true task of serving clients while also taking bandwidth polls. Fortunately, you can turn this feature off ... it just requires a little registry-editing skill.

To disable or reenable bandwidth reporting, follow these steps:

1. Start the Registry Editor (regedit.exe).

2. Navigate in the registry to the following key:

   HKEY_LOCAL_MACHINE\SOFTWARE\Microsoft\Office Server\Groove\Groove Relay\Parameters

3. Add a new **REG_DWORD** key with the value being **ReportBandwidthEnabled.**

4. To disable the bandwidth collection, give the key a value of **0.** To turn it back on, give the key a value of **1.**

5. Restart the server so that it will utilize new registry entries. Note that it doesn't scan the registry for changes the way a server might scan for policy changes.

Changing the Polling Interval

Another idea when it comes to the bandwidth statistic might be to reduce the number of minutes between polling the bandwidth used by clients. The default time is every two minutes. The lower this time, the more accurate the reading; however, it places more stress on the server. The longer this time, the less stress on the server.

To alter the polling interval (lower or higher), follow these steps:

1. Start the Registry Editor (regedit.exe).

2. Navigate in the registry to the following key:

   HKEY_LOCAL_MACHINE\SOFTWARE\Microsoft\Office Server\Groove\Groove Relay\Parameters

3. Add a new **REG_DWORD** key with the value being **BandwidthDataPollInterval.**

4. You can give the key a value from 1 to 30 (representing the number of minutes between polling).

5. Restart the server so that it will utilize new registry entries. Note that it doesn't scan the registry for changes the way a server might scan for policy changes.

Changing the Default Bandwidth Sample Size

Bandwidth sample size involves more statistics that relate to the bandwidth between a device and the Relay server (including an average, minimum, and maximum bandwidth), which is derived at by taking samples every five seconds by default. You can alter the time used to allow more time between samples to increase the performance of the Relay or you can make the number smaller (as low as one second) to get a finer reading (even though this will overburden your server, most likely).

To change the bandwidth sample size, follow these steps:

1. Start the Registry Editor (regedit.exe).

2. Navigate in the registry to the following key:

   HKEY_LOCAL_MACHINE\SOFTWARE\Microsoft\Office Server\Groove\Groove Relay\Parameters

3. Add a new **REG_DWORD** key with the value being **BandwidthSampleSize.**

4. You can give the key a value from 1 to 30 (representing the number of seconds between sample size).

5. Restart the server so that it will utilize new registry entries. Note that it doesn't scan the registry for changes the way a server might scan for policy changes.

Managing Your Groove Data Bridge Server

You recall that your Groove Data Bridge is your go-between within your organization between clients and back-end applications that your developers will introduce. The installation of the Data Bridge is the easiest of the three servers, but you still need to do some management work.

There are different ways to start the Data Bridge. The easiest is to open the administrative interface by selecting Start, All Programs, Microsoft Office Server, and then the Microsoft Office Groove Data Bridge 2007 option. You might be presented with a request for a password, and then your administrative interface will open, as shown in Figure 5.12. Note that you could also open the UI by going through a command line, navigating to the directory for your installation (typically, c:\Program Files\Microsoft Office Servers\12.0\Groove\ Groove Data Bridge\bin), and entering the **grooveeis.exe /cc** command.

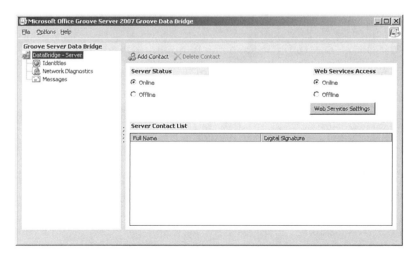

FIGURE 5.12   Groove Relay administrative UI.

Immediately from the UI, you can see whether the server status is online or offline. You can also see whether the Web services access is online. You change the status of each of these by selecting a different setting.

If you want to stop the server from functioning you can do one of the following:

▸ From the Data Bridge UI, select the **File** menu and then **Shutdown Server.**

▸ From Services, select the **Groove Data Bridge Service** and then stop the service.

▸ From the command line, navigate to the directory for your installation and enter `grooveeis.exe /q.`

TIP

Web services allows SOAP requests from external applications using HTTP. To make sure your Web services are functioning, you need to do more than ensure it is online. You need to select **Web Services Settings,** shown in Figure 5.13. From here, you can change the Web services HTTP port (the default is 9080). But, you also must select the "Allow remote web services" check box if you want to allow remote Web service calls from other systems. You can also change the Web services key. This key allows external programmers to access Web services on the server.

FIGURE 5.13   Web Services Settings screen.

Administrative UI Options

When you have the UI open, you can see that there are quite a number of different settings for you to work with. Let's discuss some of these.

Change Server Password:

From the Options menu, you can select the Change Server Password option. You need to provide the old password, provide the new one, and confirm it. This is the password you need to use when opening the Groove Data Bridge administrative interface.

Purging the Web Services Queue

Subscriptions and events may begin to build up on the Data Bridge, although usually Web services has an automatic way of clearing out the queue. If you need to purge the queue manually, however, there is a command line way of doing it. Follow these steps:

1. Stop the Groove Data Bridge service. (You can do this from the Services tool.)

2. From a command prompt, navigate to the proper folder that has the grooveeis.exe tool (typically c:\Program Files\Microsoft Office Servers\12.0\Groove\Groove Data Bridge\bin).

3. Enter the **grooveeis.exe** **/GWSPurge** command.

4. Enter a password if necessary.

5. Restart the Data Bridge server.

TIP

We've mentioned the grooveeis.exe tool several times now. Here is a list of all the options allowed with this command:

/?	Provides help with the command
/c	Closes all server windows
/q	Terminates the Groove Data Bridge processes
/v	Shows the version information for the server
/cc	Launches the administrative interface
/nc	Sets the server to Offline and disables communications
/GWSPurge	Purges the queue for the server

Backup Server Settings

An automatic backup program comes with your Data Bridge. It will back up core account information, server configuration, and a list of workspaces on the server (although it will not include workspace data).

To perform a scheduled (or immediate backup), follow these steps:

1. From the Administrative UI, select the **Options** menu, and choose **Backup Server Settings.** The dialog box shown in Figure 5.14 will appear.

2. The default location for your backup is C:\DataBridgeBackup, although you can Browse to a new location (preferably off-server).

3. You can alter the frequency, time, and number of backups to retain.

4. If you plan on performing maintenance on the server, you can also click the **Backup Now** button to make sure the system has the latest backup before you take it offline.

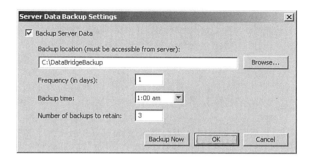

FIGURE 5.14   Backup Settings for your Data Bridge.

TIP

The backup you create will be used in the restore process. When installing the Data Bridge, you are asked whether you want to restore an existing Groove Server Data Bridge. If you say yes, you can navigate to the location of the backed-up files. One of the key questions during the restore process is whether you want to fetch workspaces now or later. The Data Bridge will re-gather workspace connections after it is restored, but this might take a long time. You can decide to do it immediately, or wait until later and choose to fetch these workspaces from the Options menu.

Data Bridge Contacts

Your Groove Data Bridge has its own identity, much like that of Groove users. You can configure which users can see the presence of the Data Bridge, and one way you can do this is by only allowing specific contacts to view the presence. We discuss identities in the next section, but keep in mind that your Data Bridge will have its own identity. It can restrict who can invite it into a session. You can configure contacts that are explicitly allowed to contact the server. Here is how you do that.

For starters, you need a contact card from the Groove user that you want to include. These cards are created by the user themselves, and they have a .vcd extension.

To create a v-card from your Groove client, follow these steps:

1. From within Groove, select **Options**, and then **Contact Manager.**

2. Select the user on the system you want to create the card for and select **Properties.**

3. Click the **Save Contact as File** link, and then save the file using the default .vcd extension.

If you want to just quickly send your contact information through email, select the **Send My Contact via E-Mail** option from within your Groove client under Common Tasks.

After you have the contact v-cards, you need, from within the Data Bridge UI, to select the **Add Contact** option. You will be asked to provide the location of the v-card. After you provide that information, the contact will be added to your contacts list.

Managing Identities

First off, what is a Data Bridge identity? We understand that users have identities, and one Groove user can view and identify another user through these identities to invite others into the workspace. The Data Bridge identity is server based, and it is used to mediate requests that come from users, to other servers. For example, if a Groove client requires something that is located on a back-end SQL server, the client asks the Data Bridge to request that information and present back to the client.

The identities are used to make integration easier with an external application. You can have managed or unmanaged Groove identities. Managed identities come under the control of the Groove Manager.

Creating a Data Bridge Identity

Through the administrative UI, you click the **Identities** link. From within the main window, you can see all your identities. To create a new identity, click the **New Identity** button. The Account Configuration dialog will appear, as shown in Figure 5.15.

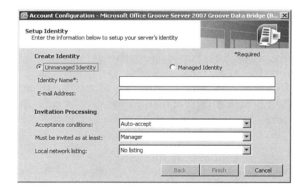

FIGURE 5.15   Set up your identity for the Data Bridge.

Depending on how you need to configure the identities, you might have Web services that can operate through the same identity or you might want to create individual identities for each task. You might have one identity you use to contact the SQL server while another is used to contact a SharePoint server.

From the Setup Identity screen, you can select Unmanaged or Managed, depending on whether you want the identity to come under the policies of the Groove Manager.

If you select Unmanaged, you need to enter an identity name and email address.

If you select Managed, you need to enter a Management server name and activation code. The Management server requires the URL of the company's Groove Manager server. The activation code requires the configuration code you receive when setting up the Groove Data Bridge identity on the Manager.

To acquire this code, you have to prepare the Groove Manager for a Data Bridge identity. It's recommended on the Manager that you create a management group for the identity to go in. This allows you to establish unique policies for the identities within that group without disturbing other user policies. You can add a member to the group by clicking the Add Members link and adding a single member. Enter the name and email of the Groove Data Bridge domain member. After the account has been created, you will want to note the Groove Manager URL and then, notice that the Groove Data Link user is still in Pending mode and note down its account configuration code. This is the code you need to use when configuring the identity.

NOTE

Some of the benefits to having your identity as Managed is that your Data Bridge identity will be easier for users to find because they will be in the managed domain contact list. Managed identity events are recorded by the Groove Manager. User access to those identities can be controlled better. However, they do come under the policies and Relay server assignments from the Manager, just like other users would.

After you have your identity information for your new Data Bridge identity, you need to select invitation processing information. This will determine how the Data Bridge identity will handle requests from others. You can establish acceptance conditions, levels of invitation, and whether the identity should even be listed.

After the identity has been created, it can now be used by clients to access external applications through the Data Bridge. You must inform the developers of these identities so that they can add them to the programmatic needs.

After the creation of an identity, the name will show up under Identities, and you will have four additional links: Workspaces, Archive Schedule, Archive Workspace, and GFS Location. Let's review what each of these is for:

▶ **Workspaces.** Shows you a listing of all the workspaces the Data Bridge is currently invited and connected to.

▶ **Archive Schedule.** You can configure the Data Bridge to periodically back up workspaces that the identity is a member of. To start with, you need to enable the feature, and then set the schedule and location of the archive. There is a check box at the top that enables workspace archiving. There are up to five saved archives before the first one will be replaced by the newest saved archive. The files are GSA (Groove Space Archive) files that you can then back up to another server or to tape. (To learn more about archiving, see the help files on the Data Bridge. From the administrative UI, select **Help**, and then **Data Bridge Help Contents**.)

▶ **Archive Workspace.** This lets you see all the archives and their associated pass-words. You can invite other members to view these archives as a manager, partici-pant, or guest.

▶ **GFS Location.** By default, the location is C:\GFS, and this is where Groove will store GFS workspaces as subfolders. Groove File Sharing (GFS) is supported by Groove 3.1 and later. When a Groove user invites another user to a GFS workspace and that user is using Groove 3.1 or later (which uses the GFS agent), the agent will create a subdirectory here that can allow clients to share files.

Managing Messages

You can send messages from within your Data Bridge to other users, or respond to work-space messages and invitations from the Messages link in the administration UI. The interface is as easy to use as a simple email tool. You can see a list of all your messages in the main window. To respond to a message, you select **Reply.** Additional options, as with any email application, include Reply to All, Forward, and Delete.

In addition to standard mail, instant messages (IMs) appears in the main frame. You can respond to the IMs in the same way you would to mail.

Workspace invitations are also included in the message list. You can open the invitation and view the v-card information of the sender. You can send a reply or simply click the Accept button below the invitation (or the Decline button, if you decline).

Monitoring Your Data Bridge

You can monitor your Data Bridge in a variety of ways, much like your Groove Relay server. You can check the Event Viewer for logs. You can also use Performance Monitor to set objects and counters on the Data Bridge so that you have a good idea on how your server is performing.

> **NOTE**
>
> For a list of event IDs for issues that come up with Web services, server, instant message/invitation, and workspace archiving, view the help files under Monitoring the Groove Data Bridge.

Network Diagnostics

Sometimes you might have specific trouble communicating with Groove users. Click the **Network Diagnostics** link from within your administrative UI to determine the cause of the problem. You can use this tool to identify trends and problems between your Data Bridge and other connections (see Figure 5.16).

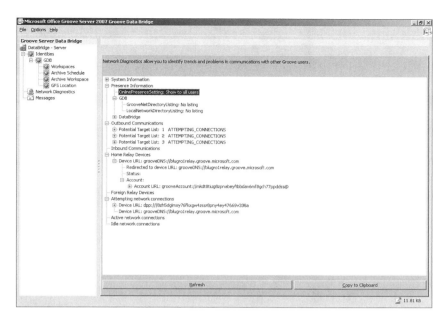

FIGURE 5.16   Using the Network Diagnostics tool.

Establishing Your Groove Environment

In this chapter we've been able to see that a great deal more is involved than simply installing the different Groove elements and walking away. The interaction between Groove clients and the Groove Relay and Manager requires you to walk through the management consoles provided through a browser environment and configure the settings you need.

However, although it requires effort, you've been able to see in this chapter how easy it is to accomplish. The end result will be an environment where your Groove clients will have no problem connecting to their workspace members either within the company or from the outside.

In the next chapter we will take a deeper look at the Groove client and see how much more productive we can be, now that the infrastructure is in place.

CHAPTER 6

Groove Server 2007: Mastering the Groove

There are usually three sides to every deployment: the installation, the configuration, and the client. In the previous two chapters, we discussed the installation and configuration of your Groove Manager, Relay, and Data Bridge servers. In the event you need these servers in-house, you should have no difficulty establishing your server base, ensuring network functionality (by opening the correct ports through firewalls and so forth), or maintaining a connection between your Groove environment and your Active Directory (AD) environment, which are distinct. For most Groove setups, you are complete.

However, there are branches that come off of the base we've given you. This chapter explains how to use your Groove client and what else your Groove structure can be used for, and finishes the discussion about Groove with a solid explanation of how to use the Groove client.

Working with the Groove Client

Some may consider the Groove client to be self-explanatory. They, like all presumptuous software users, will certainly be able to "get it to work," but will most likely be missing out on some of the finer features. But, admins should be up-to-date on what Groove clients can do, and how to do it.

To begin with, let's create our first Groove workspace.

The Groove Launchbar

When you start your computer with Groove 2007 installed, you will see a Groove icon in your taskbar, and the Groove Launchbar (shown in Figure 6.1) will be available by default, although you can alter these startup options. In the event you have disabled your taskbar application icons, which are popular these days, you can always launch Groove through your Programs, under Microsoft Office.

FIGURE 6.1   The Groove client Launchbar.

You can find everything you need to get started with Groove on the Launchbar. You'll notice that you have two tabs, one for Workspaces and one for Contacts. To alter the appearance of your Launchbar, select the **Options** menu and turn off **Tabbed View.** This action stacks both the workspace and contact portions together.

There are different ways to create a new workspace. From the Launchbar, you just click the **New Workspace** link at the top. Or, select the **File** menu and choose **New – Workspace.**

You will be presented with the option to create one of three types of workspaces, as shown in Figure 6.2:

▶ **File Sharing.** This type let's you share the contents of a folder with all computers that you hold a Groove account on or with other users you invite. A file-sharing workspace will appear in your Launchbar under its own heading, to make these workspaces easier to find and sort. If you choose this option, you can select an existing folder for sharing, or create a new folder that can be automatically placed on your desktop (or wherever you choose).

▶ **Standard.** This type let's you work with a Files tool and a Discussion tool. You can add more tools if you like. This is the quickest way to create a functioning workspace. When it is up and running, you can make configuration changes.

▶ **Template.** This custom type let's you choose the initial set of tools within the workspace. Suppose, for example, you just want a workspace for playing chess (yes, an option). You can create one specifically for this purpose and not have to have the Files and Discussion tool in your initial workspace. You can also find other workspaces that you might have saved as templates and use those, with the tools already in place.

NOTE

Because the added documents and such within a workspace are not kept on a server, usually, but within each person's workspace so that he or she can work on individual pieces when not able to connect to a Groove server, that workspace might grow quite large over time. Although no specific size restriction applies to workspaces, it is recommended that you limit your size to 2GB or less. Beyond 2GB and Groove will not even be able to include new invitees to your workspace. To view the size of a workspace, just right-click the workspace from the Launchbar and choose **Properties.** The size is on the General tab.

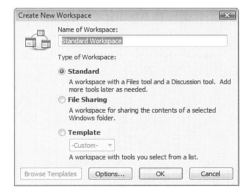

FIGURE 6.2   Choosing your workspace type.

Quick Access to Workspaces

Laurent Kempé, in his blog at http://weblogs.asp.net/lkempe/default.aspx, provides some advice about how to launch a workspace faster than using the Groove Launchbar (upgraded here for Vista):

1. Select the **Start** orb and go to your Documents folder.

2. Create a folder and call it **GWS** (for Groove workspaces), or something of your choosing. In your GWS folder, you might create additional folders to classify your workspaces.

3. Open the Groove Launchbar.

4. Select one workspace and drag it to the folder you just created. Automatically, a shortcut will appear.

5. Continue doing so for all workspaces you want to have access to.

6. Right-click the taskbar and choose in the context menu **Toolbars, New Toolbar.**

7. In the dialog, browse to **Documents, GWS,** and then click **OK.**

You now have a new toolbar called GWS in the window's taskbar that let's you choose a workspace without running the Groove Launchbar.

Working within Your Workspace

A Groove workspace is intuitive and well designed. As you can see from Figure 6.3, you have your workspace members located within a pane on the right, where you can easily add more members to the workspace or chat with existing members. In the Common Tasks pane, you can establish roles, add new tools, send messages, and so forth. And finally, the primary portion of your workspace involves the tools you have available. As you can see from the figure, the default tools provided include the following.

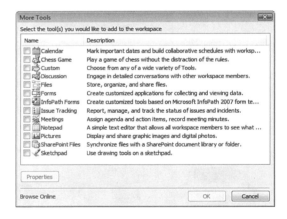

FIGURE 6.3   Choosing your workspace type.

▶ **Calendar.** Mark important dates and build collaborative schedules with workspace members.

▶ **Chess Game.** Play a game of chess without the distraction of the rules.

▶ **Custom.** Choose from any of a wide variety of tools.

▶ **Discussion.** Engage in detailed conversations with other workspace members.

▶ **Files.** Store, organize, and share files.

▶ **Forms.** Create customized applications for collecting and viewing data.

▶ **InfoPath Forms.** Create customized tools based on Microsoft InfoPath 2007 form templates.

▶ **Issue Tracking.** Report, manage, and track the status of issues and incidents.

▶ **Meetings.** Assign agenda and action items, record meeting.

▶ **Notepad.** A simple text editor that allows all workspace members to see what has been typed.

▶ **Pictures.** Display and share graphic images and digital photos.

▶ **SharePoint Files.** Synchronize files with a SharePoint document library or folder.

▶ **Sketchpad.** Use drawing tools on a sketchpad.

To add any of these tools to your workspace select the **Add Tools** option and click the check box next to the tool. You can also click the button in the lower corner of your primary workspace window

NOTE

Many who see the long list of tools available have one question on their mind: How can I create my own custom tool? There are a couple of Groove tools you can use. One is the Groove Forms tool, which developers can use to lay out all the design objects through the Design Sandbox, which provides the environment for tools creation. Another tool you can use is the Groove InfoPath Forms tool. This tool works hand in hand with the InfoPath 2007 tool. Essentially, the InfoPath 2007 tool enables you to define your fields and form layout and then creates an XSN template that can be imported into the Groove InfoPath Forms tool. Then, the developer can add similar features that would be added within the regular Groove Forms tool (such as views and macros).

NOTE

For anyone who is truly looking to build applications for Groove, you should really consider the new Silverlight tools that Microsoft has recently released. You can find one excellent resource, posted by Hugh Pyle, at http://blogs.msdn.com/hughpyle/archive/2007/06/21/silverlight-in-groove.aspx; this will point you in the right direction. He shows you an easy approach, complete with some code examples.

You might find the Discussion tool interesting because of its ability to be modified through the Design Sandbox (see Note). From within the Discussion tool, select the **Designer** menu option and choose **Open Design Sandbox.** This will take you to the settings shown in Figure 6.4, which you can then modify directly.

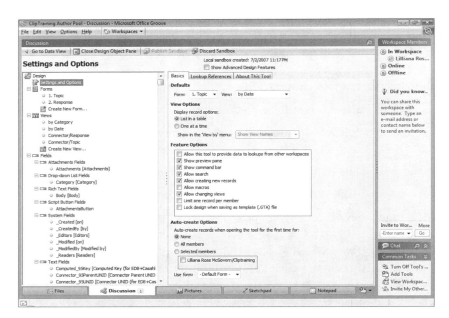

FIGURE 6.4   Working with the Design Sandbox for the Discussion tool.

Sometimes you might add too many tools into your workspace. To remove some of your unnecessary tools, right-click the **Tool** tab at the bottom of your screen and select the **Delete** option. Or, select **Delete Tool** from the File menu.

If you want to quickly enter a workspace from within the tool you need the most, select **File, Save Shortcut to Desktop;** the shortcut will be right on your desktop for quick access to the workspace and the tool.

Managing Workspace Invitees

A workspace is only as useful as the people you've invited into it. Sometimes you only need one other person. Other times, you invite an entire team, or people from other branches (really … whatever is needed at that time).

So, how do you add participants? Well, after you have the workspace established, you want to open the workspace, and from the Workspace Members pane put the name or email address of the recipient of the invitation in the Invite to Workspace box. Note that if you type a name, Groove will look for a Groove contact to send the invitation to. Or, you can just select a contact from the Groove contact list if a name cannot be located. When you find the person, or put in the email address, click **Go** to open the Send Invitation dialog, shown in Figure 6.5.

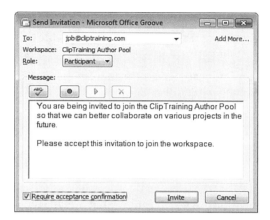

FIGURE 6.5   Sending invitations to join a workspace.

At this point, you need to assign a role to the person (which we discuss shortly). Select a role (Manager, Participant, or Guest), and select the **Require Acceptance Confirmation** check box if you want to be able to confirm the acceptance of the invitation. If you select this option, it is more than just a helpful notice for you (because you would already know whether they accepted the invitation by the fact that they would now be part of the workspace members, even without this option being selected). It is also a security measure because you will now have to accept the recipient's response and confirm the identity of the person. If an invitation is sent through email, it's automatically configured to use the confirmation of acceptance option. The recipient must confirm the invite.

You are also welcome to add a message (perhaps explaining the invitation to the workspace as an "official" invitation). And finally, you click the **Invite** button to send the invitation.

NOTE

Groove sends the invitation to the person(s) using one of the following methods: For Groove contacts, the message goes out as a Groove message. For email addresses, the message goes through Outlook as an email with a file attachment. If you aren't using Outlook, you are informed that Groove cannot send the invitation automatically. You can then copy the invitation and paste it into another email application you have running to send to the user. To do this, don't close the invitation. Instead, just select **File, Copy Invitation to Clipboard**.

The invitation includes instructions for persons with Groove and for those who haven't installed it yet. Those who already have Groove can click a link to open the invitation. Those who don't yet have Groove can click a link that takes them to a Groove download page. After Groove has been installed and is up and running, the invitation will open automatically (or can be reinitiated through the original email received).

Workspace Roles and Permissions

Everyone who participates within a workspace belongs to a role. Each role has specific permissions within the workspace. The roles and their permissions are as follows:

▶ **Manager.** The creator of the workspace is automatically given the manager role. You have permission to change the roles of others, send invitations to others, and so forth.

▶ **Participant.** A participant has permissions to interact within the workspace, invite other members, and add tools to the workspace.

▶ **Guest.** A guest has no additional permissions.

Each tool within the workspace has its own permissions that determine what a manager, participant, or guest can do with the tool. To alter the permissions for a tool, open the **File** menu and select **Properties, Tool.** The Permissions tab will then open, as shown in Figure 6.6. From here, you can select the down arrow under Select a Role to Modify Its Permissions and choose the role. Then, select or deselect various permission settings and apply those settings.

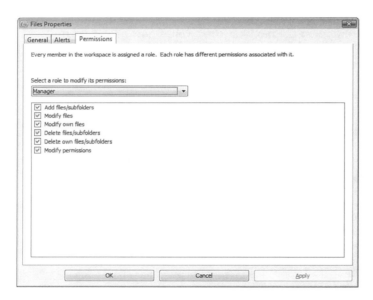

FIGURE 6.6   Modifying tool permissions based on the three built-in roles.

Changing Workspace Settings

Each workspace has its own settings. To see/alter these, open the **File** menu and select **Properties, Workspace.** Or, from the Launchbar, right-click any of the workspaces and select **Properties.** From here, you will see four tabs (General, Alerts, Roles, and Permissions) that relate to the entire workspace.

General Tab
From within the General tab of the workspace properties, you can see the following information:

▸ **Version.** Shows you the version of Groove used when creating the workspace.

▸ **Size.** The current size of the workspace.

▸ **Template.** The version number of the workspace template.

▸ **Created by.** The name of the person who created the workspace.

▸ **Created on.** Displays the date the workspace was created.

▸ **Requirements.** The minimum version of Groove required for access to all workspace and tool features.

▸ **File-sharing properties** (only applies to file-sharing workspaces), the Properties dialog box, and a Folder Info and a Status tab. These tabs provide information about the path of the root folder currently being synchronized, excluded files and file extensions, and the current synchronization status.

You can alter the version requirement, if other versions exist in your environment. You can also add a description about the workspace within the Description text box.

Finally, you can select the check box Download Automatically onto All My Computers. If you select this, the workspace (and its contents) will be downloaded to any computer where you log in to Groove with your account.

Alerts Tab
The Alerts tab, shown in Figure 6.7, allows you to configure Groove to notify you regarding unread information in workspaces or when persons sign in to their Groove workspace.

You can choose from four alert levels, with a reaction and sound you can associate with the alert:

▸ **Off.** Doesn't display an alert for new or modified content

▸ **Medium.** Highlights unread content with an icon

▸ **High.** Display an alert for new or modified content

▸ **Auto.** Similar to High, but auto-dismisses ignored unread alerts

You can select the Notify Me When Any Member Enters This Workspace check box and associate one of the standard sounds available or browse for a sound of your choice.

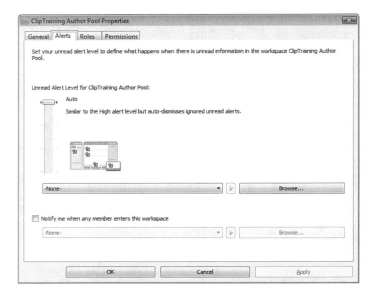

FIGURE 6.7   Working with alerts for your workspace.

Roles Tab

The Roles tab shows you every member in the workspace and the role that each currently holds. You can select a member and change that member's role if you like.

Permissions

Unlike permissions for a specific tool, these permissions relate to the workspace itself. There are five different permissions:

▸ Invite

▸ Uninvite

▸ Add tool

▸ Delete tool

▸ Cancel all outstanding invitations

As discussed previously, the manager role holds all five permissions for the workspace. The participant holds the invite and add tool permissions. The guest holds no permissions. However, you can change that for your workspace by selecting/deselecting the check boxes next to each permission.

The Groove Client Possibilities

This part of the chapter focuses on the workspace world and how to manage some of the features. There is something to be said for each one of the tools at your disposal and how they work. The Groove help files are pretty thorough in their explanations. Logically, you would concur that the Chess tool is not going to be as helpful in business as the Meetings tool, but each tool expands possibilities for your communication and collaboration (some more so than others). Let's consider some of the more robust tools available.

Making Your Meetings Groovy

One of the more impressive Groove tools is the Meetings tool. This tool helps you organize, conduct, and even record meetings for workspace members.

Both managers and participants can create a meeting as follows:

1. Select the **Meetings** tool.

2. In the upper-left corner, select **New Meeting** to start the Meeting Wizard.

3. Enter a subject and start and end times for the meeting.

4. You can add a location, meeting details, and even attachments that may be necessary to read before or during the meeting.

5. Click **OK** to create the meeting.

After the meeting has been established within your workspace tool, you can select that meeting and see five tabs that will help to make that meeting more "groovy," as follows:

- ▶ **Profile.** Contains the start and end dates and time of the meeting, along with the location, attachments, and details.

- ▶ **Attendees.** You can edit the attendees through this tab. By default, any attendee whose role is participant or higher can edit the tab. Just click the **Edit** button and make the changes you want. Attendees are only restricted to members of the workspace. From the Attendees tab, you can select who should attend the meeting, whether they are the chairperson or the minutes taker, and any notes you want to pass on to them.

- ▶ **Agenda.** To construct the agenda for the meeting, click the **New Topic** button and specify the start and end times and the topic and presenter for that portion of the meeting.

- ▶ **Minutes.** During the meeting, the person who is elected to take the minutes can actually use the Minutes tab to work with the agenda and type the notes directly into Groove. Just type the notes for each agenda item as you go. And then, you can save the notes for others to view.

- ▶ **Actions.** Actions are essentially a list of items that must be handled as a result of the meeting. You can establish a priority for the actions and monitor their completion levels.

> **NOTE**
>
> One of the best aspects of the Meetings tool, according to the popular site TheNewPaperClip.com, is the fact that everyone will have the same record of the meeting and its resolutions … immediately after the meeting has concluded. No need to wait for the secretary to complete and edit the notes and send them to all attendees. And, the best part of all of this is that you can invite new persons into the workspace, and they can go back and read the history of previous meetings.

Integrate Groove with SharePoint

At times, envisioning ways to implement new technology is easy. Often, you have a need, and the software fills that need; so, it's a no-brainer. Other times, however, you might already have systems in place (workarounds, if you will) that now hinder your ability to visualize how the new software might benefit you. For example, although you might see the immediate benefit of Groove, especially in working with clients who are outside your corporate structure, you might not see where SharePoint and Groove can work together.

The best Groove site on the Internet these days is, hands down, the Groove Advisor (http://blogs.technet.com/groove/default.aspx), which is one of the MSDN blogs that Microsoft promotes. One scenario presented involves a situation in which a person uses Groove workspaces to communicate with 15 different partners. Essentially, he has 15 different workspaces, 1 for each partner. But, he wants to distribute the same document to all 15 partners. He could just use the workspaces to do this, posting the document to all 15. This would work, and probably is what most of us would do. (Again, it's hard to envision new uses.) But, a question arose: Is there a better, more efficient method?

The solution involves taking those 15 workspaces and connecting them to a single SharePoint document library. The Groove Advisor makes it clear that the partners are not connecting to the SharePoint library; that is your responsibility. "The library basically seeds/feeds the workspace with new documents/content." When changes appear within the workspace, Groove takes over and ensures that the documents are in sync with workspace members.

To accomplish this goal, you need to add the SharePoint files tool to your Groove workspaces and establish synchronization between the tool and the SharePoint library. (Logically, you need the SharePoint library, too.) The user doesn't have to update each client, and only has to keep the one document up-to-date on the SharePoint server.

To configure the SharePoint Files tool within your workspace, follow these steps:

1. Select **Add Tools,** and choose the **SharePoint Files** tool.

2. You will be taken to a welcome screen, as shown in Figure 6.8. It says "This tool allows teams to work together to produce and modify documents in SharePoint libraries. While your team works in Groove, the documents are easily shared and stored in SharePoint through automatic integration." Click the **Setup** button.

3. Either enter the URL or browse to locate the URL for the SharePoint site with the library or folder that you will synchronize.

4. After you've located the library, select **Open.** You will now see the contents of that library from within the SharePoint Files tool.

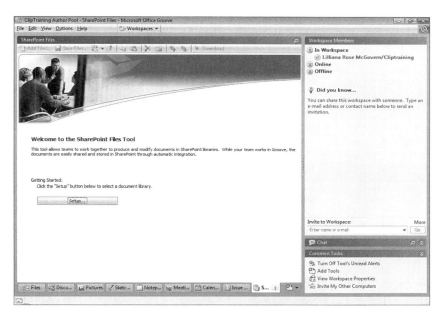

FIGURE 6.8   Setting up your SharePoint Files tool.

After you have the connection made to your SharePoint library, you need to configure the synchronization schedule that will be automatically kept between the files and Groove. To set up a manual or an automatic schedule, follow these steps:

1. Select the **Calendar** icon located in the synchronization bar.

2. Choose **Manually,** if you want to manually synchronize your files, or **Automatically,** if you want the automatic route (which is easier for you). Then, choose the **Every** (so many number of time units).

3. Then click **OK.**

Now, even if you have everything working off a scheduled synchronization, you might need to perform an immediate sync. No problem. Just choose **Edit,** and then select the **Synchronize Now** option. The files are immediately put in sync.

> **NOTE**
>
> Groove and SharePoint security concerns are a big question on many people's minds. Does Groove support SharePoint access control lists (ACLs) in the SharePoint Files tool? Who can edit content in the tool? Who can access the tool? The blog Groove Advisor addresses all of these concerns at http://blogs.technet.com/groove/archive/2007/04/02/groove-security-meet-sharepoint-security.aspx. According to the Advisor, "Groove security and SharePoint security are configured and administered separately and independently." However, within a transaction, a Groove sync request and SharePoint access can conflict. This is because the user who manages the workspace and who has configured the SharePoint connection has one set of credentials on the SharePoint side (at least read access to the content), and that allows the content to be put within the workspace, but users within the workspace can come from anywhere (so they logically have no access to that content). Outside users can modify, delete, and so forth the content based on their Groove permissions, but this means nothing to SharePoint. When the synchronization occurs, it occurs under the ACLs of the original user and modifies the files based on the user who is the synchronizer. For more about the subject, check out the Groove Advisor blog.

Groove Accounts and Identities

To use the Groove client, you need an account. You also need an identity. Although these might seem to be the same thing, they are actually quite different. Let's explore the difference between accounts and identities and explore how to manage them.

Accounts and Identities

The actual account is a file stored on your system that includes the following information, according to Microsoft:

▶ A Groove identity, or more than one identity, along with the private keys that define those identities

▶ Cryptographic information, such as the master key to protect those workspaces

▶ Devices on which you operate Groove

▶ Workspaces that you are included as a member of

▶ Contacts you communicate with and their corresponding information

During the login process, your password or certificate (if you use a certificate) decrypts the account file so that you can assume those identities it contains and access the information within.

An identity, on the other hand, is the "electronic presence" that Groove users need to interact with you. You can only associate identities with one Groove account, although you can have multiple identities linked to that account. And, you can move that account across multiple systems if you like. By default, you are given an identity that just includes your account name. You can leave this or change it to suit your needs. You can also create more than one identity to link to your account.

Now, why would you want more than one identity? Well, with some persons, you might want to be known by your official name, whereas with others you might be more relaxed and want to use a more familiar name. It's all about the persona you want to maintain within the Groove workspace environment.

Each identity you create has a contact file associated with it that will provide others with information about the identity. So, you can give out more or less information regarding yourself depending on the identity you are using and the environment in which you choose to use it. For instance, you might use one identity for a particular business venture that uses the address and contact information for that business, but you might have another identity for your actual place of employment that includes a completely different set of personal information.

To add identities to your Groove world open the preferences either from the Launchbar or from within a workspace. To do so, select **Preferences** from the Options menu. The first tab is the Identities tab. A down arrow lists all your identities. To create a new identity, click the **New Identity** button. You will then see all the information you can enter, as shown in Figure 6.9.

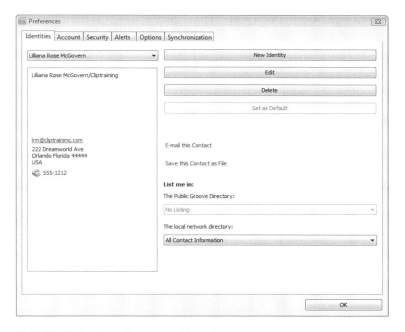

FIGURE 6.9   Creating a new identity.

After you have the information included for the various identities you choose to use, click the **E-Mail This Contact** link to send the identity card to another person's contacts. Alternatively, you can click the **Save This Contact as File** link, to save the identity as a Groove contact file (.vcg extension) that can be sent to others.

Back Up Your Groove Account

You don't want the problem of losing your account in one way or another. The disk could crash, for instance, or you might have a corruption of the files. So, a good backup is always the safest bet.

One easy way to have a secondary copy of your account is to add it to another computer. As mentioned previously, you can use your account (with all your identities) on multiple systems. To do that, you need to add the account to those systems, as follows:

1. From the File menu, select **Use Account on Another Computer**.

2. You will be presented with a set of instructions that explain that first you want to save your account file and then copy it to another computer (see Figure 6.10).

3. Install Groove on the other computer.

4. Close the Account Configuration Wizard when it starts.

5. On the new computer, double-click the file, which should have been copied to the new system. The file will have a .grv extension on it.

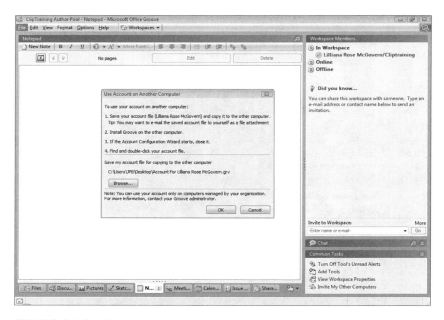

FIGURE 6.10   Backing up and moving your account.

Saving the account doesn't save the data. That data will have to be downloaded again on the new computer, unless you have saved your workspace manually (discussed later). However, one company that is providing a free backup tool for Groove 2007 is ThreeWill (www.threewill.com). It's a command-line based utility for backing up your Groove workspace(s). ThreeWill says, "You can use it to back up your Groove work-space(s) to a particular location. You can use it to back up workspaces by name, or you can back up all of your Groove workspaces at once. The included instructions and online help show how to configure a scheduled automatic backup and how to set other options. Options include the ability to specify the filename and the Groove account to use for the archive, whether to include the members and/or data in the archive, a passphrase to secure the archive, and whether to set the archive as read-only."

If you just want to save your account as a backup copy, follow these steps:

1. Select **Options, Preferences.**

2. Go to the Accounts tab, shown in Figure 6.11.

3. Select **Save.**

4. From the Save Account As dialog, choose the location of the account file.

5. Select **Save.**

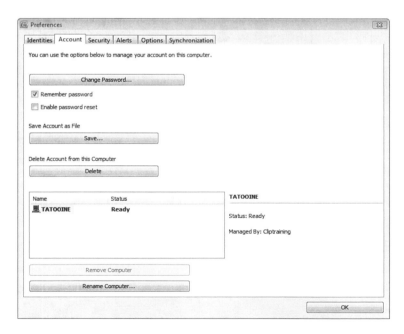

FIGURE 6.11   Saving your account through the preferences.

It is recommended that you save the account information to another location. In the event of a system crash, the account will be safe either on a network server, another system, an external drive, or a USB keychain. (The file isn't very big.)

Note that you can do more than save the account; you have these options, too:

▶ **Change Password.** Select this option to change the password. You have to fill in the Password and Hint fields.

▶ **Remember Password** (check box). Select this option if you want to log in to your account later without having to enter the password again.

▶ **Enable Password Reset** (check box). Select this option if you want to be able to request a new password or smartcard certificate from the administrator of your account.

▶ **Save.** Already discussed above, this option enables you to save the account.

▶ **Delete.** Select this option to delete the account.

▶ **Remove Computer.** This option enables you to you eliminate a system that is handling your account.

▶ **Rename Computer.** With this option, you can you rename the computer account. (Note that this doesn't actually change the name of the actual system.)

NOTE

Microsoft recommends users back up their accounts weekly. A weekly backup is especially important for users who are using Live Groove account configurations for which there is no-behind-the-scenes admin to keep everything safe. If you are using hosted services, however, or if you have established an in-house Groove manager, the admin needs to back up the accounts. In the event of a crash, the user just requests the account backup file from the admin or help desk.

To manually back up or archive your workspace, select **File, Save Workspace As, Archive.** The end result will be a single binary file that includes the workspace data, membership, tools, and more. Keep in mind that this copy will quickly become out-of-date. Microsoft provides a special note in their documentation for restoration issues with the archived copy. They remind us that the copy is not the current workspace (obviously). When the workspace is restored, all the other members will appear as suspended because they don't have this supposed *new* copy of the workspace on their systems (even though, its really the old version).

In addition to ThreeWill, mentioned previously, a couple of other Microsoft partners have workspace archive tools:

▶ **Dicodemy, GForce.Backup** (www.dicodemy.net/ProductsAndServices/ GForceBackup.aspx). GForce.Backup is a personal backup utility for Microsoft Office Groove 2007 that enables users to manage and restore archived workspaces and automatically back up Groove workspaces that have changed, on a user-defined schedule.

▶ **Information Patterns, Toucan Bambuco** (www.infopatterns.com/products/ ToucanBambuco.aspx). Toucan Bambuco is a middleware application that enables you to back up your workspaces by invoking a simple script from the command line or at predefined intervals through the Windows Scheduler.

Groove Security Settings

To configure security settings for a specific identity, select **Preferences** from the Options menu. Then go to the Security tab, shown in Figure 6.12. From here, you can select a down arrow and choose the identity.

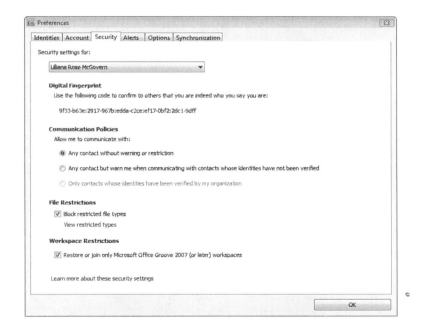

FIGURE 6.12   Security settings.

One item you can see is the digital fingerprint for each identity. These are created when you create the identity. It's a long, random number that is issued automatically. You can use this number to verify other Groove users before accepting them into your workspace.

Under Communication Policies, you have several options, including the following settings under Allow Me to Communicate with:

▶ **Any contact without warning or restriction (default).** No warnings or restrictions will be issued, regardless of the contacts verification status.

▶ **Any contact but warn me when communicating with contacts whose identities have not been verified.** A warning is issued before you contact persons who don't satisfy the requirements. The warning displays in the Contact Verification Alert dialog box, which provides an option for verifying these users.

▶ **Only contacts whose identities have been verified by my organization.** All contacts you interact with must be certified by the Groove admin.

You can select the check box to Block Restricted File Types, and then see the restricted files by clicking the View Restricted Types link. This will show you all the different files that aren't allowed.

Under Workspace Restrictions is another check box: Restore or Join Only Microsoft Office Groove 2007 (or Later) Workspaces. This check box enables you to lock down the ability to join workspaces created with earlier versions of Groove.

The World of Groove Development

As previously discussed, you can make changes to your Groove tools through the various development tools at your immediate disposal. In addition, other solutions are possible—customized solutions you can have your developers focus on. In harmony with that, a great portal is set up on the MSDN sites for developers who need to create solutions for the Groove platform.

Located at http://msdn2.microsoft.com/en-us/office/bb308957.aspx, the site also links to relevant content on TechNet and Office Online, providing easy access to those materials. The available information enables developers new to Groove to build a solid foundation of knowledge before taking Groove deployments to the next level by planning, building, and deploying customized Groove-based solutions.

Tools that you can use to work with Groove development include the following:

▶ **Silverlight and Groove.** Hugh Pyle discusses the possibilities of developing with Silverlight on his blog, at http://blogs.msdn.com/hughpyle/archive/2007/06/21/silverlight-in-groove.aspx.

The concept is simple. Silverlight is a plug-in that allows for vector graphics, animation, storyboards, and more … all using .NET and XAML within a browser. Hugh says, "Groove Forms has a relatively restricted set of user interface capabilities. It's designed for building reasonably straightforward UI for data capture in small teams.

Forms with fields, views with columns, and a Groove workspace for distributed data storage. But many applications would like to go beyond a simple forms-driven UI, and Groove Forms doesn't make that very easy." Using Silverlight in Groove Forms would be a perfect combination, however. Hugh provides some good examples of how this can be done.

▶ **Groove with VSTO.** Another development possibility is brought to us by Paul Stubbs (author of the book *VSTO for Mere Mortals: A VBA Developer's Guide to Microsoft Office Development Using Visual Studio 2005 Tools for Office*) on this blog, at http://blogs.msdn.com/pstubbs/archive/2007/05/21/groove-n-with-vsto.aspx.

He mentions talking directly to the Groove client by using VSTO from an Outlook 2007 add-in. He says, "First start by creating a new C# VSTO Outlook 2007 add-in. The next thing you want to do is create a class library, called GrooveServices, to isolate all of the Groove service code." The rest is on his site to complete the process.

You can find additional resources on the development site, including a grouping of articles from Chris Normal, the development lead on the Groove Team, on how to work with Groove forms and Groove InfoPath forms, and more. So, if you are a Groove developer, or want to learn to become one, this site is a must.

You might also want to download the Groove 2007 Software Development Kit (SDK), which can be found on Microsoft's Web site. The kit includes samples and libraries to help you develop Web services applications for Groove 2007. The SDK includes C# samples and the Web Service Definition Language (WSDL) definitions for the Groove Web services application programming interfaces (APIs). In addition, it provides local copies of the Groove 2007 Web Services Developer Reference Guide and the Groove 2007 Forms Developer Reference Guide.

Another set of tools are Web Helpers for Groove 2007, located at www.codeplex.com/gwsv12helpers, which provide a C# .NET assembly that provides an abstraction layer for Groove 2007 and Groove 3.1 Web services. The abstraction layer provides an easy-to-use API with an object and eventing model, so that custom applications that interface with Groove can be built more quickly.

NOTE

One company that has been developing with Groove in mind is Information Patterns (www.infopatterns.com), with the new Toucan Navigate 2007. This tool blends Microsoft Virtual Earth maps and imagery with geographical information systems (GIS) files and spreadsheets in a desktop application. Now you can easily integrate geospatial information with personal or business data, giving you a competitive advantage in an agile world. And, you can link it to Groove "for a rich geo-collaboration experience" so that you can share your map views with others.

The Ten Habits of Highly Successful Groovers

Mark Ryan (technical specialist, Microsoft Office Groove 2007, Microsoft Business Division) listed his top ten habits for Groove on his blog at http://marktryan.spaces.live.com/blog/:

> I was packing to go to Milan tomorrow and the phone rang - A Microsoft partner, who is rolling out a large deployment of Groove for an Enterprise customer, was calling to see if I had any "Best Practices" in using Groove that I could share. I did so I will now share them with you:
>
> Groove Workspaces are a tremendously powerful tool for supporting collaboration across domains and businesses, but we should be conscious the fact that the tool is as good as it's users and we need to add some "house rules: to make it work effectively. Here are some things to consider:
>
> 1. All members can read everything. If you don't want someone to see something, don't invite them in.
>
> 2. Information Rights Management (IRM) will prevent unauthorized access to documents in Groove; so, if you have a connection to the IRM-issuing AD domain, you can use the document as your rights permit.
>
> 3. Be careful to whom you allow "invite" permissions. If you don't personally know them, think about it!
>
> 4. Groove is a great security and transport container, but its version control is not sophisticated. Make your own folders and copy docs in there for editing, switch on version tracking in Word, for example, and when you are ready the space manager can merge versions using Word.
>
> 5. Talk to each other—phone, email, IM, and Groove messages are great ways to agree who should be doing what—it's more human and very democratic to discuss how revisions should be made.
>
> 6. If you don't want a doc to sync, put it in a new folder and turn off "synchronization" RH click the folder and click Properties tab, click the **Synchronization** tab, and set to **Manual.** When you're ready to share, switch it back to **Automatic.**
>
> 7. Try and invite your membership in before adding too much content; this makes the joining process quicker for the members. Then add your content a little at a time. Groove has excellent compression algorithms which work best on smaller chunks. As Groove is going to attempt to serialize the data into 1MB chunks anyway, you may as well help the process.
>
> 8. As the workspace manager, it's your "private club," so why not use the Notepad tool to create a "Welcome" or "About" page where you can outline the do's and don'ts, working practices, and maybe some useful links. This is a good way to induct new members into the workspace.

9. Remember F7 checks spelling! Make yourself look good!

10. Pressing the "Shift" twice in quick succession invokes the Send Groove Message dialog, even if Groove is running in the background.

NOTE

To Groove with the best of them, you need to find others who are groovy, just like yourself. One great location is a Groove user group at http://grooveuser.org/default.aspx. Its stated goal is to allow you to "Share your Groove Experiences, learn from Groove experts and novices, and let your voice be heard in Microsoft and beyond." It's a great location for both novices and experts to bond.

Groove in a Nutshell

These past few chapters might have been a real eye-opener. So many new technologies came out this year, and they were all lumped under one grouping, and so it might be easy to miss the benefits of Groove. Chapter 4, "Groove Server 2007: Overview and Installation," introduced you to the necessary infrastructure that is already in place to allow you to communicate and collaborate with anyone, anywhere. That chapter explained the installation process, in case you decide there is a need for an in-house Groove environment.

Chapter 5, "Groove Server 2007: Configuration," moved forward into a discussion about the three main Groove servers: Manager, Relay, and Data Bridge. This information is helpful even if you decide to have your Groove services hosted by Microsoft, because you can still "manage" the environment through the Web console provided to you.

Finally, in this chapter, we have discussed the client. It's the most essential piece to the puzzle (at least from an end user's perspective). This chapter has shown you the behind-the-scenes side to the client, because although you can figure out a program pretty quickly, the deeper features take time to learn. This chapter should save you that time.

CHAPTER 7

Live Communications Server 2005: Overview, Installation, and Configuration

Instant messaging (IM) has grown up. No longer is it the idle pastime of teenagers and shut-ins. What was once a home-user technology has invaded the workplace and has become a *viable* productivity tool. That LCS 2005, as a topic, has been included in this book on Office Servers provides good evidence of this fact. But just as IM has grown up, so has Microsoft's second incarnation of LCS.

> **NOTE**
>
> At the time of this writing, Microsoft is in beta for its third generation of communications servers, named Office Communications Server 2007. In Chapter 8, "Live Communications Server 2005/2007: Management of LCS 2005 and Overview of OCS 2007," we look at some of the enhancements to come in this future release.

Introduction to Live Communications Server (LCS) 2005

For the purposes of this book, we discuss LCS 2005 with Service Pack 1 (SP1). This version builds on the features already included in 2005. So, what are those new features? I consider a few to be "key" features that warrant either an upgrade or (if you do not have it in place yet) a deployment of LCS. To begin, LCS 2005 now supports connectivity to three major public IM service providers (MSN, AOL, and Yahoo!) in both the Standard (up to 15,000 users) and Enterprise Editions (up to 125,000 users).

TIP

This public connectivity does require separate client access licenses (CALs) for access to public IM service providers.

This major new feature builds on that collaborative relationship and takes it beyond just intraoffice, intradomain, and intraforest levels and allows for connectivity with outside resources—all while providing secure communications to such resources.

The new version also allows for linking to your corporate phone system (PBX) or the Public Switched Telephone Network (PSTN), integration with Exchange Server free/busy and out-of-office information, and multiple-party application and data sharing. To see a full list of all the new features, go to http://office.microsoft.com/en-us/communicationsserver/HA102026891033.aspx.

Features such as SPIM (unsolicited commercial instant messages) filters and enhanced federation have been improved to allow greater control and require less configuration and overhead to maintain.

Not to be forgotten in the newest release is the availability of Office Communicator 2005, which is available in three different versions: the full client, Web, or Mobile. We discuss the enhanced features of these clients later on in this chapter.

TIP

You can still use Windows Messenger 5.1, but many of the enhanced features in Communicator will not be available to the Windows 5.1 client.

By now you may be saying, "This is nice, but why does my organization need LCS 2005? I can just use public IM and get the same advantages." Many feel the same way, and in their environment that might be the correct decision (to just use public IM). But, let's do a quick overview of the product to show you why it is not just an expensive toy.

Overview of LCS

Let's look at five ways in which LCS can enhance your environment:

▶ LCS enables collaboration in real time with both internal and external users. Think of the early days of the telephone before call waiting, answering machines, and administrative assistants, a time when people picked up the phone and communicated immediately. Real-time presence is an integral part of this Microsoft offering. Although instant communication and file sharing is nothing new to IM clients, what is in this offering is the ability to securely collaborate in real time via instant messaging, video, or phone conferencing with users (internal and external), partners, customers, and suppliers; that's something a public IM solution cannot provide your organization.

▶ LCS enables remote users to work from wherever they are without the need for a VPN or other remote-services solution. Encrypted IM sessions allow for application sharing and for audio and video communication at the touch of a button. Integration with Microsoft Office products and other applications is what makes LCS more than just IM software.

▶ LCS enhances security and administration by allowing users to authenticate via Kerberos and NT LAN Manager (NTLM) for single sign-on authentication with Active Directory. Administration through Active Directory and common administrative tools such as Windows Management Instrumentation (WMI), Microsoft Management Console (MMC), and Microsoft Operations Manager (MOM) make administration both familiar and simple while consolidating administrative overhead.

▶ LCS, a fully scalable enterprise-level solution, enables you to build next-generation applications and enables the sharing of current line-of-business applications simply by providing high availability and increased productivity through the use of real-time collaboration.

TIP

You can find a list of some of the current Microsoft software that works with LCS 2005 in the technical document "Microsoft Office Live Communications Server 2005 with Service Pack 1 Feature Guide," at www.microsoft.com/technet/prodtechnol/office/livecomm/library/featureguide/lcsfea_1.mspx.

▶ LCS integrates Microsoft Office Communicator 2005 clients. Microsoft Office Communicator 2005 extends the real-time presence with such features as corporate phone system integration (PBX), the ability to move multisession IMs to a conference call over PSTN. 1:1 voice and video collaboration, and the ability to view Exchange free/busy and out-of-office messages.

With LCS, users can now communicate and collaborate regardless of organizational boundaries, geographic location, or time zones. As you can understand, this is a product worth paying attention to; so, let's take a look at what it takes to prepare your environment for LCS.

Preparing for Installation of LCS 2005

This section examines the steps necessary to prepare Active Directory and your server for the installation of LCS 2005. Preparing your environment is actually the more involved part of installing LCS 2005. So, we will spend more time on this than the actual file installation. You need to complete each of these steps in the proper order to successfully deploy LCS.

TIP

This chapter covers the planning and deployment of LCS 2005. If you want to work with a preinstalled and configured version of LCS, you can install Virtual PC 2007 (free from Microsoft) and download the Virtual Hard Disk (VHD) solution. Microsoft offers LCS and Exchange 2007 within the same vhd so you have to select the Exchange 2007 vhd. You can find VHD solutions at www.microsoft.com/technet/try/vhd/default.mspx.

Your preparation for installation requires the completion of five steps (with some additional considerations for certain topologies), as follows:

1. Confirm network readiness.

2. Run Prep Schema.

3. Run Prep Forest.

4. Run Prep Domain.

5. Run Domain Add to the Forest Root.

For an in-depth look at the preparation process, consider the following link: http://www.microsoft.com/technet/prodtechnol/office/livecomm/library/prepad/lcspad_4.mspx.

Confirm Network Readiness

Before installing LCS 2005, make sure your infrastructure meets Microsoft's minimum prerequisites, which are as follows:

▶ Domain controllers running Windows Server 2000 with SP4 or Windows Server 2003

▶ Global catalog servers running Windows Server 2000 with SP4 or Windows Server 2003

▶ A minimum of one global catalog deployed in the forest root

▶ For optimal performance, global catalogs present in each LCS domain

Run Prep Schema

Preparing your schema will add 12 new classes and 52 new attributes to the Active Directory schema. To prepare the schema you have to be a member of the Schema Administrators group and have local administration logon rights on the system handling the schema master role.

NOTE

LCS 2003 added 5 new classes and 34 new attributes to the Active Directory schema. LCS 2005 builds on these with the addition of 7 new classes and 18 new attributes.

This step is required in an LCS deployment to allow LCS 2005 to be added to the schema and needs to be run once in an Active Directory forest. To view the extensions that will be modified you can open the LCS2005.ldf file, which should be located in the \Setup\I386 folder on the CD. Keep in mind that these extensions will be replicated across all your child domains so there will be an impact on your network bandwidth. So choose a time when network utilization is not going to be an issue.

Run Prep Forest

This step creates objects and attributes for LCS, such as the RTC Service under the systems container and configuration-naming context. Prep Forest creates the LCS objects and attributes required for the deployment and operation of LCS in an Active Directory environment. These objects are required by Active Directory because most of the management of users in LCS 2005 takes place in Active Directory. Through Active Directory, users can be individually enabled and configured for LCS. (We look at managing an LCS infrastructure in Chapter 8.)

Prep Forest is also required and run once in an Active Directory forest. To do so, you must be part of either the Enterprise Administrator or Domain Administrator group in the forest root domain.

Run Prep Domain

Prep Domain creates the global groups needed to operate LCS, such as RTCDomainServerAdmins and RTCDomainUserAdmins, and adds the security permissions in the domain, which are needed to deploy and administer LCS (again, because much of the administration of LCS takes place in the Active Directory domain).

Prep Domain is required and needs to run once; it also needs to be run in each domain where you plan to deploy LCS. This requires Domain Administrator permissions in each domain where Prep Domain is to be run.

Run Domain Add to the Forest Root

Domain Add to the Forest Root grants permission to the added child domain(s) to access the LCS objects stored at the forest root. It must be run for every child domain that will have an LCS deployed.

If the LCS is being deployed at the forest root, this step is unnecessary and unavailable in the setup. This step requires Domain Administrator permissions in order to grant permissions in the domain.

Additional Steps for Complex Topologies

Complex domain topologies require a few different considerations, depending on the level of administrative control granted or denied from one domain to the next. Therefore, the following additional preparation might be required prior to installing LCS 2005.

Cross-Domain Scenarios

User-only domains, cross-domain searches, and cross-domain administration scenarios might require the following steps:

1. Run Prep Domain and Domain Add (to enable users in the user-only domain to manage LCS settings for users hosted in a different domain).

2. Assign the administrator of one domain the proper permissions to administer the LCS in a second domain.

3. Run Domain Add to grant permission for one domain to access the accounts that are enabled for LCS in another domain.

Preparing Locked-Down Active Directory

Permission inheritance is often disabled, and access control entries (ACEs) are removed. Steps are necessary in this scenario to assign the proper permissions to the objects and containers in the forest root and other domains.

Deployment Methods

LCS offers two methods of deployment for both the preparation and installation of LCS 2005. You can run the LCS deployment tool (Setup.exe). The deployment tool provides you with wizards that walk you through the preparation and install of LCS.

Another method of deployment is via the command-line tool (LCScmd.exe primarily). This method is particularly useful in large environments where you might need to deploy LCS remotely to several servers in a multiple-domain environment (especially if you must run Domain Add to the forest root).

The LCS deployment tool provides an intuitive interface to guide you through the setup of LCS. Taking the user through the sequence of steps, LCS provides explanations of each task, permissions required, and setup wizards for each task. The deployment tools check the status of LCS in three ways:

▶ Has the task already been completed? If a particular task has been completed, a check mark next to that task indicates completion.

▶ Have the prerequisites been met for each step? (That is, SQL Server 2000 SP3a [or higher] needs to be installed before running Domain Add to the Forest Root.)

▶ Which tasks are required (or not) based on your deployment topology?

We concentrate on the wizard-based install method. For a moment, however, let's take some time to explore briefly the LCS command-line installation tools. As you might have already guessed, this is a command-line utility that can perform all the functions of Setup.exe without the interactive GUI/wizard-based screens.

The LCS command-line utilities consist of six separate utilities for installing and managing LCS 2005. When would this be beneficial? As stated earlier, LCScmd is beneficial when you need to perform install tasks remotely. LCScmd enables you to run all tasks for installation except for MSI commands.

Administrators can also run commands in batch, performing multiple tasks by using an XML file.

The command-line utilities provide verbose logging and error events that assist in troubleshooting. And, tasks can be performed by LCScmd both during and after setup, giving you greater flexibility to perform tasks in your environment.

> **NOTE**
>
> You can find more information about using LCScmd.exe at www.microsoft.com/technet/prodtechnol/office/livecomm/library/deploycommandline/lcscml_1.mspx.

Deploying LCS 2005

Select one of the following depending on the version of LCS 2005 you are deploying:

▶ For the Standard Edition, click **Standard Edition Server.** This version provides all you need to use LCS; however, the Enterprise Edition provides for more functionality and high-availability solutions.

▶ For the Enterprise Edition, click **Enterprise Pool.** (The Enterprise Edition is deployed for this setup example.) Note that the Enterprise Edition is used for a larger organization, to provide scalability with LCS running on front-end systems in a "pool," offering client connections, presence, and real-time communication (such as IM). The LCS back end would run SQL Server 2000 SP3a or later, which can be clustered for high availability.

> **NOTE**
>
> When the front-end Enterprise Edition LCS server and the back-end SQL database are used, this is called a pool. So, even if there is only one front-end server in the pool, it's still called a pool. We discuss the configuration of pools in further detail later in this chapter.

Setup.exe brings up the first deployment tool splash screen, shown in Figure 7.1. On this screen, you can choose the server roles you want to deploy. Although in this chapter we go with the Enterprise Pool option, the four different options are as follows:

▶ **Enterprise Pool.** Enables end users for LCS

▶ **Proxy.** Enables various forwarding and application proxy scenarios

▶ **Access Proxy.** Enables federation and outside-user scenarios

▶ **Archiving Service.** Enables IM archiving

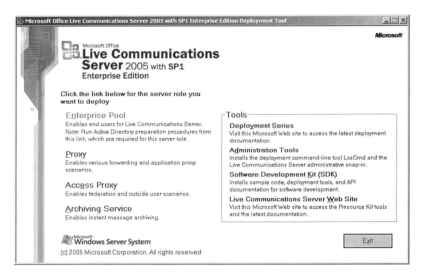

FIGURE 7.1   Selecting your server role.

After choosing the server role to install, you have two options: Prep Schema and Install Files for (Standard or Enterprise) Edition Server (as shown in Figure 7.2).

FIGURE 7.2   The deployment phases and the appropriate credentials needed to initiate these.

> **CAUTION**
>
> You can install the files at any time, because the install copies files to the local hard drive only. However, the prep steps must still be followed in order to have a functioning LCS.

Preparing the Schema

First you need to run the Prep Schema tool. Keep in mind that this requires Schema Admin and administrator credentials on the Schema Master. To begin the process of installation, follow these steps:

1. From the Deployment Tool screen, click **Prep Schema** to launch the Prep Schema Wizard. A screen will appear, as shown in Figure 7.3. This screen explains the purpose of the wizard and provides information about where to find out more about the schema extensions to be added to Active Directory.

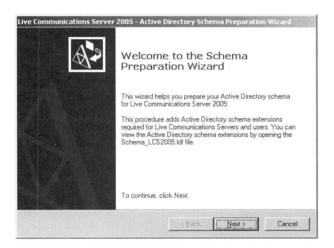

FIGURE 7.3   The first screen in the Prep Schema Wizard.

2. Click **Next.** Doing so takes you to the Specify Directory Location of Schema Files screen, as shown in Figure 7.4. You are asked to specify the location of the schema files. Default assumes the schema files (.ldf) are in the same directory as the setup files, although you can alter the location by selecting the radio button Specify schema files directory location and browsing to the new location. Establish the location (or leave the default), and then click **Next.**

3. In the Ready to Prepare Active Directory Schema window, you can review the Prep Schema settings and go back to make changes if necessary, as shown in Figure 7.5. Your schema files will be uploaded into Active Directory.

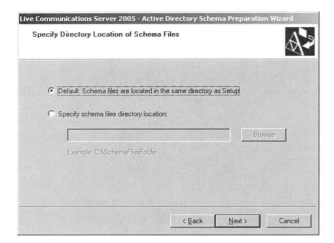

FIGURE 7.4   The Specify Directory Location of Schema Files screen.

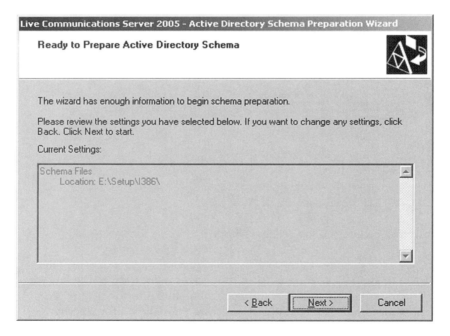

FIGURE 7.5   The Ready to Prepare Active Directory Schema screen.

4. After the Schema Prep has completed installation, you can click Finish or, if you want to see the details, click the View Log button. View Log takes you to an XML file showing the success or failure of the Prep Schema task; expand the Execute action to check that all items have completed successfully.

5. Click **Finish** to return to the deployment tool screen.

NOTE

Before you move on to the Prep Forest step, Active Directory replication must complete after you run Prep Schema. You can wait for Active Directory replication to complete or force replication with all domain controllers listed in Active Directory Site & Services. You can also force replication from the Windows 2003 Server resource tool kit (using Active Directory Replication Monitor, REPLMON).

Preparing the Forest

To perform the Prep Forest step requires either Enterprise Administrator or Domain Administrator credentials for the forest root domain.

CAUTION

If Active Directory has not completed replicating changes made by Prep Schema, you will receive an error message. You can wait for replication to complete or force replication in Active Directory Sites & Services.

1. To begin the process, click the deployment tool splash screen and choose **Prep Forest** to launch the Prep Forest Wizard. The welcome page will now appear (see Figure 7.6). Click **Next.**

FIGURE 7.6   The Forest Preparation Wizard start screen.

2. Figure 7.7 shows the Ready to Run Forest Preparation page. Review your settings, and then click **Next** to start installation. In this step, objects needed for management and operation are added to the forest root. These objects include creating the pools container and LCS users property set and user search property set.

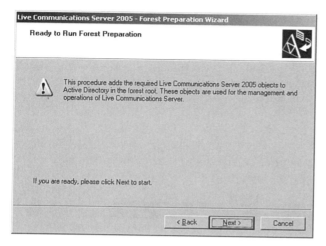

FIGURE 7.7   LCS 2005 objects will be added to the top of the forest root in the Prep Forest task.

After Prep Forest has completed, you can click View Log to see the objects that were added to Active Directory and to check which items might have had a failure.

> **CAUTION**
>
> If Active Directory has not completed replicating changes made by Prep Schema, you will receive an error message when you try to perform the Prep Forest. You can wait for replication to complete or force replication in Active Directory Sites & Services.

Preparing the Domain

The last two tasks (Prep Domain and Domain Add to Forest Root) can be run from any computer in the domain where LCS 2005 is being deployed. Prep Domain requires Domain Administrator credentials and can be run from any server in the domain.

1. Click **Prep Domain** on the deployment page to launch the Prep Domain Wizard. The Welcome to the Domain Preparation Wizard page will display.

2. You don't have any configuration options. This task adds global groups and creates ACEs. These groups allow LCS to create service accounts in Active Directory. To proceed with the preparation, click **Next**.

3. After the Domain Prep has completed installation, you can check the log file to see the results of the Domain Prep. Expand the **Execute** action to check that all items have completed successfully, and then click **Finish**.

CAUTION

If Active Directory has not completed replicating changes made by Prep Schema, you will receive an error message when you perform the Prep Domain. You can wait for replication to complete or force replication in Active Directory Sites & Services.

Running Domain Add to Forest Root

Now let's run Domain Add to Forest Root.

The following procedure is required for any domain outside the forest root where LCSs or pools will be deployed. The procedure grants permissions for this domain, its pools, servers, and administrators to Active Directory objects stored in the forest root domain and used by LCS 2005.

If you use Setup.exe to run this procedure, you must run Domain Add to Forest Root from a server in this domain using an account with Domain Administrator or Enterprise Administrator credentials in the forest root domain. You can also use the command-line tool to run this procedure from any server in the forest.

Domain Add to the Forest Root can only be run from a child domain.

NOTE

This step is not necessary if you are deploying LCS in the forest root; this would be the case in a single-forest, single-domain topology.

1. On the Welcome to the Root Domain Add Wizard page, click **Next** to continue.

2. On the Ready to Root Domain Add page, review your current settings before clicking **Next** to start the procedure.

3. On the Root Domain Add Wizard has completed page, click **View Log**. Under the Action column, expand **Domain Add to the Forest Root.** Look for <Success> Execution Result at the end of each task to verify Domain Add to the Forest Root completed successfully. Close the log when you have finished. Click **Finish.**

NOTE

In a complex domain topology, a cross-domain/locked-down Active Directory scenario might be present. For such cases, you can find additional information about how to deploy these strategies at www.microsoft.com/technet/prodtechnol/office/livecomm/default.mspx.

Determining Which Version You Need to Install

Preparation of your environment is completed. However, before you install LCS, you need to consider which version you will use.

Standard Edition

For Standard Edition installs, LCS uses a Microsoft SQL Desktop Engine (MSDE) as the database for all communications. The Standard Edition supports up to 15,000 users, which would support even most enterprise environments. The Enterprise Edition supports up to 125,000 users and gives the added reliability some organizations might need. (Microsoft recommends the Standard Edition for organizations with fewer than 20,000 users. Products such as Access Proxy and Director work in the Standard Edition.) However, the needs of your environment might make it necessary for you to upgrade from the Standard Edition to the Enterprise Edition.

Enterprise Edition

Made up of an enterprise pool, also known as a two-tier approach, the Enterprise Edition consists of two components:

▶ An LCS back-end database (using Microsoft SQL Server 2000 SP3a or later) providing shared storage and enabling the LCS database to be part of an active-passive cluster for high availability.

▶ LCS Enterprise Edition servers connected to the back-end database. These servers distribute client requests across the "pool" of servers, creating redundancy and scalability. These Enterprise Edition server pools require a load balancer when you deploy an enterprise pool to distribute client requests.

The addition of a SQL server and load-balancing server as separate components makes it necessary for smaller environments to "count the cost." But again, depending on the deployment, the benefits might far outweigh such costs. Enterprise pools enable you to provide clustering, high availability, and disaster recovery to your environment. For organizations with multiple locations, roles can be created to distribute the workload and create an efficient, effective LCS topology. For our discussion, we will configure this server with Enterprise Edition. (However, we do highlight the steps applicable to Standard Edition throughout the rest of the installation process.)

NOTE

Standard Edition users can skip this section and move on to the "Installing LCS 2005 Files" section.

Creating/Updating Enterprise Pools

Now that we have prepared our environment and decided which version we will install, let's begin the installation of LCS 2005. To start, we return to view our deployment tool screen in Figure 7.8.

FIGURE 7.8   The deployment tool screen shows the tasks that have been completed in the preparation phase of deployment.

Notice the check marks on all the prep tools. At this point, we will install Enterprise Edition. We have already set up our SQL server and created a new instance (LCS_RARE). Now we create our Enterprise Edition pool.

IMPORTANT

Before creating your enterprise pool, ensure that no applications are currently using ports 5060 and 5061. You can do this using a common port check tool (because these are the ports used to send SIP communications). You must also make sure that you have created a Domain Name System (DNS) record for your enterprise pool through your DNS Manager.

1. Click **Create/Upgrade Enterprise Edition Pool.** When the Enterprise Pool Wizard welcome page displays, click **Next.**

2. The Create Enterprise Pool Wizard will appear, as shown in Figure 7.9. You need to enter a pool name, the fully qualified domain name (FQDN) where the pool will reside (RARETCH.COM), the back-end database (SQL server; for example, RARE-SQL), and the SQL server instance (database; for example, LCS_RARE). Then, click **Next.**

IMPORTANT

You should create the SQL instance on the back-end SQL server, not the server that will act as the front-end LCS.

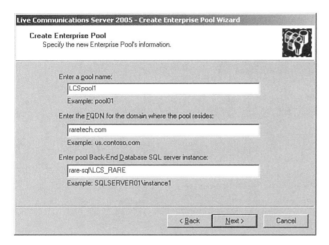

FIGURE 7.9   The pool name, FQDN, SQL server name, and SQL server instance are needed to create or modify an enterprise pool.

3. The next wizard screen is the option for using the existing database screen. By default, the existing SQL instances detected are used. If you want to replace the database, check the box and then click **Next.**

4. The Ready to Create Enterprise Pools screen will display. Before clicking **Next,** review the settings here to make sure this is the enterprise pool you want to join.

5. The Choose Destination Locations screen will display. Here, you can select the location of the database and transaction logs. Choose the location of the LCS database and transaction logs for your back-end database, as shown in Figure 7.10 (Note that UNC paths are being used because this folder is on the back-end database server, which is on a different system in this case. If the back-end database is the local server you can select the buttons 'Local server directory' and it would place the database and transaction logs locally. You can also split up the database and transaction logs to improve recovery and performance).

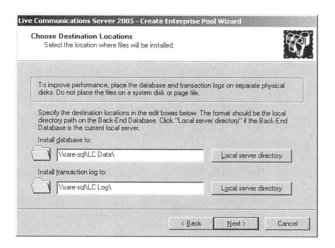

FIGURE 7.10   The Choose Destination Locations screen.

NOTE

To improve performance, the database and transaction logs should reside in separate physical disks. Neither should be placed on the same physical disk as the system disk or page file.

You have now been added to the enterprise pool. We are ready at this point to install the files for LCS 2005.

Installing LCS 2005 Files

You are now ready to install the files for LCS. Installation requires local Administrator credentials and needs to be run locally on the server. Click to install files for Enterprise Edition server or Standard Edition server (if this is what you are installing) from the deployment tools screen.

1. On the Welcome to the Setup Wizard for Microsoft Office Live Communications Server 2005 splash, click **Next** (see Figure 7.11).

2. Accept the terms on the license agreement page and click **Next.** On the customer information page, enter a username organization. Under the product key, enter the 25-character product key. Then, click **Next.**

3. Next is the Choose Destination Location screen. Here you can change the location of your LCS files. The next screen shows the current installation settings and gives you a chance to go back and make changes. At the completion of the install of the LCS files, you are prompted to activate the product.

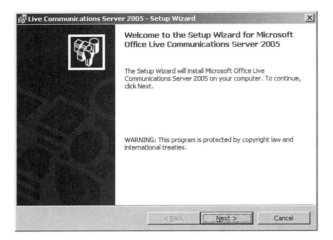

FIGURE 7.11   Wizard for LCS 2005 files installation.

NOTE

You must activate LCS to complete the installation of the product.

4. After clicking **Yes** to activation, you are asked to choose an enterprise pool. After choosing the pool you want to join, click **Next.** You can now see the Select Service Account screen (see Figure 7.12). You can now choose a password for the LCService account or you can you choose an alternative account. (LCService is the default account used; it is recommended for ease of administration and troubleshooting purposes that you continue with the default account.)

FIGURE 7.12   The Select Service Account screen.

> **CAUTION**
>
> By default, this account is set to have its password expire after 14 days; after which time time-based servers will stop, and a new password will have to be chosen and the service restarted. You can change this default in Active Directory's Users and Computers.

5. Next is the option to Enable Archiving Agent, as shown in Figure 7.13. This requires Microsoft Message Queuing Service be installed on the enterprise server.

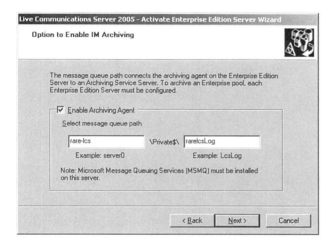

FIGURE 7.13   The Option to Enable IM Archiving screen.

> **CAUTION**
>
> If this is an initial deployment, this step will fail because no Archiving Service servers exist in the enterprise pool yet. So, this step should be performed after the Archiving Service has been installed. We discuss the installation of the Archiving Service as a server role. Therefore, we will not enable the archiving agent in the initial setup.

6. The next screen that appears is Ready to Activate. Here you can review your information and go back and make changes if necessary. If this is okay as it is, click **Next.**

7. The next screen in the setup wizard is the Start Service option. By default, this box is checked. If Active Directory has not replicated, however, the activation will complete, but the service will not be started. You'll need to start the service after Active Directory has finished its replication. Or, replication can be forced by one of the two methods mentioned earlier in this chapter.

This completes the installation of LCS 2005. Next, we look at how to configure LCS roles. Before we do so, however, let's take a moment to consider certificates and their role in LCS. Certificates are used for federation between partners, remote access, server connections using Transport Layer Security (TLS) and Mutual TLS (MTLS), and client connections via TLS. LCS 2005 with SP1 has simplified security certificates, making it no longer necessary to have client-side certificates. Web server certificates are now sufficient in your LCS environment. For more information about certificates in an LCS topology, see the Microsoft article at www.microsoft.com/technet/prodtechnol/office/livecomm/library/deployee/lcsdee_7.mspx.

Configuring LCS 2005 Server Roles

LCS is made up of multiple roles. Each role serves a different function in the LCS architecture. The roles are as follows:

- ► Standard server
- ► Enterprise Edition server
- ► Access proxy
- ► Director
- ► Proxy
- ► Archiving Service

All LCS environments must contain one of the first two server roles because these handle the front-end operations. The remaining four server roles work in conjunction with the front-end LCSs. The remaining four roles can be configured in either the Standard or Enterprise Edition. Each of these remaining four roles can also be configured in an array for load balancing and redundancy.

Review of Each Role

Let's do a quick review of these roles, and then we will go through the configuration of each.

Standard Edition

The Standard Edition server role is a self-contained IM presence server for small to mid-size locations. Standard server offers most of the features as Enterprise Edition without the use of a separate back-end database server.

Enterprise Edition

The Enterprise Edition server role is for environments with more than 12,000 users, or where multiple front-end servers are required. Enterprise Edition offers scalability and high availability. Enterprise Edition is part of an enterprise pool consisting of at least one back-end database and one Enterprise Edition server.

Access Proxy

The access proxy role is used to allow remote users to connect to internal LCSs—to assist with federation of SIP communications between domains, partners, and customers and with the connection to public IM services (with a separate license). This server role is designed to connect the external and internal edge networks. This role can be deployed with either Standard or Enterprise Edition.

> **NOTE**
>
> Although it can be deployed in Enterprise Edition, keep in mind that access proxy does require a Standard Edition license because it only manages SIP domains and does not interact with Active Directory or manage user authentication.

Directory

Active Directory can be a special configuration of Standard or Enterprise Edition Server and functions as a means of authenticating or authorizing remote clients, without being used to house specific users. So, users will connect from outside the firewall by using an Access Proxy. The Access Proxy doesn't communicate with Active Directory and cannot authenticate users, but Directors can. So the director will authenticate and connect users to their home server.

Proxy

LCS 2005 Proxy provides a platform for developing applications and customizing deployment. You can configure static routing rules or develop more complex rules with MSPL (Microsoft SIP Processing Language) or C++ or C#.

Archiving Service

This service contains an archive of IM conversations or usage data if configured for archiving. You need to enable archiving (which we saw earlier in the configuration portion) on all LCS servers that are hosting users you want to have information archived on. The purpose of this type of service is to allow a company to conform to corporate or government policies requiring retention of IM communications.

Configuring Access Proxy

First, a DNS SRV and a record must be created for the access proxy. And, a certificate must be created and associated with each DNS name that is created. Next, configure the internal and external edges of the access proxy as follows:

- ▶ To configure the external edge network, ensure that the adapters have static IP addresses assigned. Then, open the LCS management console. Right-click **Microsoft Office Live Communications Server 2005** and go to the Properties box. Open the **Public** tab and select the public (or external) IP address to be used from the list of available adapters. Click the **Select Certificate** tab and choose the certificate you want to use, and then click **OK.** You can also add another listening port here. Port

5061 is standard for SIP over TLS and is the only port that can be used for federation traffic.

If you are using federation with other enterprises or remote offices, select the **Allow server connections for federation or branch office** check box. If you are enabling direct client connections, select the **Allow client connections for remote access.** Then, click **OK.**

▶ To configure the internal edge network, right-click **Microsoft Office Live Communications Server 2005** and go to the Properties box. Open the **Private** tab and select the private (internal) IP address to be used from the list of available adapters. Click the **Select Certificate** tab and choose the certificate you want to use, and then click **OK.** Port 5061 is standard for SIP over TLS and is the only port that can be used for federation traffic.

Each access proxy deployed maintains an internal SIP domains list authorized to route traffic to it, and a list of internal SIP servers authorized to connect to it. To configure this list, right-click **Microsoft Office Live Communications Server 2005** and go to the Properties box. Click the **Internal** tab, and Under Internal SIP domains supported by Live Communications servers in your organization, click **Add Domains** and add the internal LCS domains.

Also, check the internal servers authorized to connect to this access proxy server and add each internal server that will send SIP traffic to the access proxy. In a large environment with multiple federate partners and a large number of users, you should consider deploying an access proxy array. For information about deploying access proxy arrays, go to www.microsoft.com/technet/prodtechnol/office/livecomm/library/deployap/lcsdea_1.mspx.

We now need to configure the internal next-hop server (or director) role.

Configuring the Director

You can deploy the director role with either Standard or Enterprise Edition. The director does not host users. The director role is used to authenticate and route remote clients (from your organization) to their home server. The director is used in conjunction with the access proxy because access proxy does not authenticate with Active Directory.

Configuring the Director (Internal Next-Hop Server)

In the LCS Properties box, click the **Internal** tab. For the next-hop internal address, enter the FQDN for the next-hop server if this is a single-director environment. If a director array is deployed, enter the FQDN of the load balancer to which the array is attached. If no director is deployed, enter the FQDN of the LCS or load balancer to which you want to send traffic.

Configuring Proxy

The proxy role can be deployed two ways: as a forwarding proxy, which is used in remote sites to connect users through an access proxy to LCSs in a central location; or as an application proxy.

As an application proxy, you can host applications that do not require user registration or authentication. Proxy also let's you customize and develop applications using Microsoft SIP Processing Language (MSPL) or using common programming languages such as C++ or C#. Like access proxy, although proxy is available in Enterprise Edition, it requires a Standard Edition license.

First, install and activate the proxy for LCS 2005. All proxy servers require certificates and MTLS connections. To configure certificates for use with a proxy that is joined to the domain, follow these steps:

1. Download and install the certification path.

2. Request and install the certificate request.

To configure certificates for use with a proxy not joined to a domain, follow these steps:

1. Duplicate the Web server template to ensure that you can export the key.

2. Configure the certificate.

Now you need to configure the MTLS. To do so, follow these steps:

1. Open the computer management console and expand the Services and Application tree.

2. Highlight and right-click **Microsoft Live Communications Server 2005**, and then click **Properties.**

3. On the General tab, click **Add.**

4. Here you add a listening port. Choose whether to listen on all IP addresses or a specific address. The transport type should be TLS. Check the box for **Mutual TLS**, and change the port number to 5061 (for SIP communications). And, select the certificate to use for incoming communications.

Archiving Service

The Archiving Service role uses a SQL database to archive user messages for users configured for archiving. Archiving can be done at the organizational or individual level, and the Archiving Service can also be configured to archive communications between federated partners and to track data usage.

Archiving is a useful tool for companies in need of IM retention policies based on corporate or government governance. This server role has extensive setup configuration parameters, so we will look a little more in depth at this role.

Installing and Configuring Archiving Service

Open the LCS deployment tool (Setup.exe) and click **Archiving Service.** Then choose to install the files for Archiving Service. A welcome screen will display. Click **Next.** Accept the license agreement, and then click **Next.** The IM Archiving Service Options Wizard will open, as shown in Figure 7.14.

NOTE

You need to install MSMQ (Microsoft Message Queue) services. A great link in TechNet to understand further the concepts involved is: http://www.microsoft.com/technet/archive/winntas/proddocs/ntmsgqmn/msmqad02.mspx?mfr=true.

You can add MSMQ from Add/Remove Programs, through Add/Remove Windows Components. Select the Application Server options and click Details. Then locate the Message Queuing option and select the checkbox for it. Finally select OK, then Next, and finally Finish.

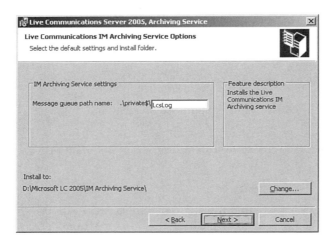

FIGURE 7.14   Here you chose the message queue path name and the location of the Archive Service files.

You will be prompted to activate the Archiving Service. Click **Yes.** You will be asked to select a service account, as shown in Figure 7.15. If this is the first installation of LCS, you can create a new account; otherwise, you may choose to create a new account or use an existing account.

NOTE

The default account name is LCArchivingService. It is recommended that you leave the default name (especially in a new deployment) for the sake of ease of administration and troubleshooting.

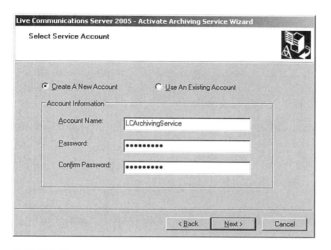

FIGURE 7.15   Select the service account for LCS archiving.

Next you select the SQL server instance for the archiving database, as shown in Figure 7.16. This is the same SQL instance created for the installation of the enterprise pool.

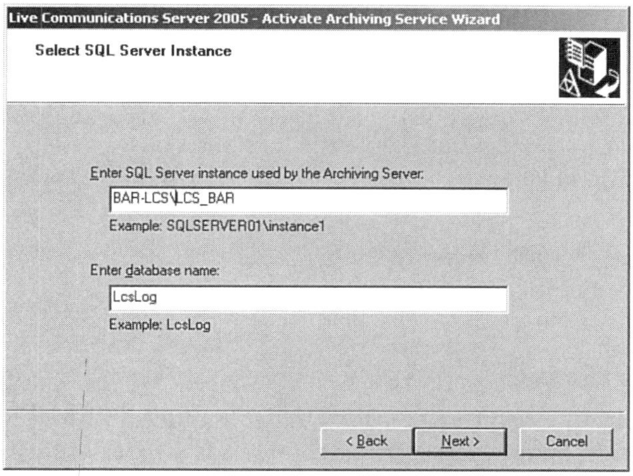

FIGURE 7.16   Enter the SQL server name, SQL server instance, and database name.

The next screen is Option for re-using the database. If you want to use an existing database, make sure the check mark is cleared (because if checked, this process will overwrite any exiting database and the data within).

Next you choose the location of the database files and transaction logs. It is recommended that you place these on separate physical drives. The final screen is the option to start the service after activation. At the completion, click the **View Log** button to check that all actions were successfully completed. Then, click **Finish.**

After successfully installing and activating the Archiving Service, you need to enable it in your LCS environment. To accomplish this, we must open the LCS management tool. Expand the **Forest and Domain** node. Expand **Pools & Servers.** Select the pool you want to enable for archiving and right-click and go to Properties.

On the Archiving tab, click **Activate content archiving.** You will receive a message about the messaging queue not being associated with the archive. Click **OK.**

Select the **Associate** radio button on the Archiving tab and choose a message queue path. (MSMQ should have been installed earlier.)

> **NOTE**
>
> For archiving to function as expected, you must associate a queue for each LCS in the pool. You also need to restart all services on all LCSs in the pool.

After configuring your LCSs for archiving, you need to configure the archiving settings at both the organizational and user level.

> **NOTE**
>
> User-level archiving settings take precedence over organizational-level settings.

Some deployments contain arrays of LCSs, proxies, access proxies, and directors. In such cases, you might want to deploy an IP load balancer to assist with the transport of Layer 4 TCP traffic.

For more information about deploying LCS 2005, refer to the article at www.microsoft.com/technet/prodtechnol/office/livecomm/library/deployment.mspx.

Overview of Federation

Essentially, Federation is the ability of your organization's users to communicate with users in another organization. Federation has already been mentioned a few times in this chapter. By now, you should be asking yourself what exactly it is and how you might use it in your LCS deployment. This is a two-part question with multiple answers, at least on the "how to deploy" side of things. Federation is the ability to connect your organization to external users and allow for IM, presence awareness, and data sharing with users outside your organization. Federated users can collaborate securely and in real time with multiple federated partners across different domains (or even across the Internet with public IM connectivity).

> **NOTE**
>
> By default, federated users cannot see presence information for users in your domain. Users should add the federated partner to their allow list for presence information to be shared with the federated partner. Federation does not support collaboration, audio, or video communications. To share these types of communications outside the domain, you must use third-party products. You can find a list of the relevant products at http://directory.partners.extranet.microsoft.com/searchresults.aspx?i=1&pname=&spec=5&pid=25&vid=0&country=&SearchType=P.

When deploying federation, you must consider several scenarios. We will look at these scenarios and how to configure them. All federation scenarios depend on the deployment of an access proxy configured in your perimeter network to direct all SIP traffic and either Standard or Enterprise Edition of LCS to host users. Federation can be enabled at the user and domain level. Most of the configuration for federation is done at the access proxy, although individual users can have federation enabled using Active Directory Users & Computers.

> **NOTE**
>
> When planning for federation, you should deploy one access proxy server for each federated role you will use in your organization. This will improve security in your perimeter network, while allowing you to manage each federated scenario independently. In smaller environments or where constraints do not allow, you can deploy the same access proxy to handle all scenarios. In such a case, it is important to be sure your server has the capacity to handle multiple federation roles.

The different federation models are as follows:

- ▶ Direct federation or explicit peering
- ▶ Enhanced federation
- ▶ Public IM connectivity (IM service providers)
- ▶ Clearinghouse (default route) federation

Direct Federation

As the name suggests, direct federation refers to a direct connection to an outside partner. Direct federation allows you to choose which partners you want to federate with and requires both the access proxy and SIP domain be specified on both sides of the partnership. All communications to the partner domain are directed to the access proxy of that domain. Direct federation does not require an SRV record for DNS and gives administrators more control and greater security benefits; however, it also requires more administrative attention. Direct federation is deployed in scenarios where the SIP domain you are connecting to is not an LCS 2005 SP1, or where more security over communications is desired.

Enhanced Federation

There are two kinds of enhanced federation: restricted and unrestricted. Enhanced federation requires an SRV record in DNS and valid certificates at both ends. Enhanced federation is new in LCS 2005 SP1 and improves upon direct federation by offering the ability to dynamically connect to other LCS 2005 domains.

Restricted enhanced federation is enabled by default when deployed. Restricted enhanced federation enables the administrator to connect (federate) dynamically to other SIP domains (with a valid certificate) while still maintaining control over which SIP domains can connect (federate) with it. Restricted enhanced federation is much like direct federation, but overall requires less administrative attention to maintain than direct federation. Restricted enhanced federation is the preferable method of connecting to a large number of domains while offering the greatest amount of security.

Unrestricted enhanced federation will allow connections to any SIP domain with a valid certificate. Unrestricted enhanced federation requires the least amount of administrative setup and attention and allows for the greatest amount of collaboration with partners.

> **NOTE**
>
> Undesirable IM partners or domains can still be blocked at the access proxy, either by adding the domain to the Access Proxies Block list or by copying the certificates from domains you want to block to the Untrusted Certificates store on a local machine.

Public IM Connectivity (IM Service Providers)

LCS 2005 SP1 with enhanced federation enables you to connect to three major IM service providers: AIM (AOL), MSN Live Messenger (Microsoft), and Yahoo! Messenger (Yahoo!). IM service providers typically host many SIP domains. To connect to these public IM services, you need a per-user connection license for your LCS. You also need to add the FQDN to the public IM's access proxy or Trusted Servers list into your access proxy.

> **NOTE**
>
> You cannot enable public IM service providers to an access proxy that is acting as a clearinghouse or configured with a default route to a clearinghouse.

To enable public IM connectivity, you also need a dedicated Windows Internet Information Services (IIS) server, with a Web site created for provisioning the exchange of connectivity information with one or more public IM service providers.

> **NOTE**
>
> The connection licenses purchased on a per-user basis cover connectivity to all three IM service providers. The administrator can provision connection to one, two, or all three providers. Although users can be enabled individually for public IM connectivity,

after the number of providers to federate with has been chosen, users with public IM access can connect with any of the public IM services that are specified for the organization. Care should therefore be taken, and it should be determined up front whether all three providers are necessary for provisioning. If it is found that connection to one or more of the public IM service providers is not needed after the initial deployment, these can also be disabled. Then, if needed, they can be reenabled at the proxy server at any time (but you must reprovision the license).

Just as with other types of federation, the organization must present a valid certificate from a public certificate authority (CA) because all traffic is handled via an MTLS encrypted connection. This certificate must be placed in the trusted root of the Windows 2003 server.

Clearinghouse (Default Route)

A clearinghouse route is used in the following scenarios:

▶ When you want to direct all traffic through a single trusted source

▶ When enhanced federation will not be used

▶ When you want to offload administrative tasks from your LCS

Offering the opportunity to simplify a LCS deployment, the clearinghouse can serve as a direct path between enterprises. Traffic is sent to the clearinghouse, and the clearinghouse then routes it to its destination (much like routers today currently handle static routes to a specific location).

NOTE

Access proxies configured for enhanced federation for use with public or private IM providers cannot have a default route specified.

The clearinghouse can be deployed in two ways: restricted or unrestricted.

Restricted Clearinghouse Model

In this model, the clearinghouse can choose which enterprises it will host restricted clearinghouse for. Conversely, the administrator for that enterprise can choose which enterprises will use restricted clearinghouses. This is a good configuration where you have a specific industry or departments that interact directly (and possibly even separately) within an organization. Restricted clearinghouse creates a closed community of users that can directly communicate through a common trusted source.

Un-Restricted Open Clearinghouse Model

This clearinghouse model can be used to direct all traffic not explicitly configured. This model is used where there are no direct partners to connect to. The open clearinghouse trusts all messages that come to the enterprise. The open clearinghouse model also allows for the greatest communication with multiple enterprises with minimal configuration.

Some Final Notes on Federation

Two other considerations for federation are the branch office and the SIP-PSTN gateway. Because branch office traffic must traverse the Internet, even though it might be part of the corporate network, you must establish a proxy server within the branch office network, forwarding all requests to an access proxy within the perimeter network of the home office. The proxy would also in turn handle all traffic coming across the access proxy and into the branch office.

Using a third-party SIP-PSTN gateway, LCS 2005 can support PC phone connectivity. Alternatively, you can use a dedicated LCS to act as a gateway and route all calls through it; this was the only method available in LCS 2003. Because the server must be capable of authentication in either scenario, you cannot use a proxy server as a SIP-PSTN gateway. (Establishing SIP-PSTN gateways goes beyond the scope of this book. To find more information about configuring SIP-PSTN gateways, refer to the article at www.microsoft.com/technet/prodtechnol/office/livecomm/library/pstn/lcspstn_1.mspx.)

Next we take a look at managing an LCS 2005 infrastructure. And, we review the three available clients for use with LCS 2005 SP1. You will also learn how to enable tools from both the domain and user side. To finish up this particular discussion, we take a look at Office Communications Server 2007 (beta).

CHAPTER 8

Live Communications Server 2005/2007: Management of LCS 2005 and Overview of OCS 2007

After your Live Communications Server (LCS) is up and running and you have performed some of the basic configuration you learned in the preceding chapter, it is necessary to understand some of the deeper management issues. These are discussed in the earlier part of this chapter.

And, as a special bonus, we also begin the process of explaining the changes we have to look forward to in the near future as the 2007 Communications Server is released and deployed in the workforce.

Managing a Live Communications Server 2005

There are two main tools for the management of LCS: Active Directory and the LCS management console. While you may be familiar with Active Directory and the management of users, it is still important to discuss how AD and LCS work together. You will also see that AD management tools have been expanded to include LCS configuration options for your users.

In addition, the LCS Management Console, located in Administrative Tools, allows you to manage those aspects of LCS that are outside of the AD management tools.

Active Directory Management Tool

Users can be enabled, configured, moved, and deleted from an LCS deployment at the domain or individual user level within Active Directory. To see these settings, open your Active Directory Users and Computers console from your Administrative Tools and go into the properties of one of your users. The user shown in Figure 8.1 shows the Live Communications tab in the Active Directory User object.

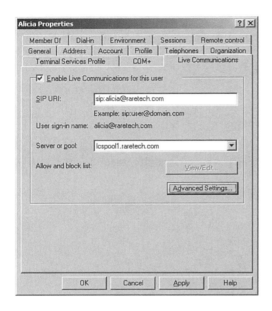

FIGURE 8.1   The Active Directory Live Communications tab.

From here, you can enable LCS for the user and choose the server or pool that will host the user. In fact, Active Directory is the first place for beginning user administration, because the LCS Management Console will not show any user attributes until the user has been enabled for LCS in Active Directory.

Advanced Settings

In addition, you can click the Advanced Settings button, which will take you to the Advanced Settings tab (shown in Figure 8.2), allowing you to configure the following settings for the user:

▶ **Enable Federation.** Allows users to federate with direct partners.

▶ **Enable Public IM Connectivity.** Allows users to connect to public IM service providers.

▶ **Enable Remote User Access.** Allows the user to connect to the LCS from outside the network using an access proxy.

▶ **Enable Remote Call Control.** Used in conjunction with Office Communicator 2005. This allows users to control their phone line from the Communicator client, allowing the user to initiate and receive calls via a Session Initiation Protocol (SIP) or regular telephone.

▶ **Archiving Settings.** For the individual user.

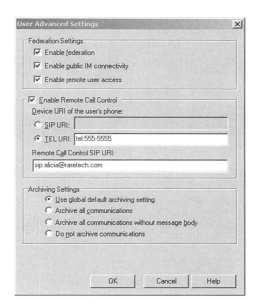

FIGURE 8.2   Advanced configuration settings for your user.

Allow/Block Lists

The Live Communications tab also allows you to configure the Allow/Block list (see Figure 8.3). You can allow users from outside the organization to view your presence information by adding them to the Allowed Users list. You can also deny access for individual users from within the domain or with federated partners. You have three levels of control: All, Domain, User. You also have the option to allow or block, Subscription (the ability to monitor the user's presence information), or Invite (the ability to communicate and collaborate with the user). To perform this task, you need to be a member of the RTCDomainUserAdmins group.

FIGURE 8.3   Examples of allowing/blocking users and domains.

At the domain level, you can bulk configure user settings such as allowing or blocking federation, public IM connectivity, remote access, and archiving settings, as shown in Figure 8.4. To accomplish this, perform the following:

1. From within the Active Directory Users and Computers tool, select the users you want to configure in bulk.

2. Right-click the selection.

3. Select Configure Users, which will start the Configure User Wizard.

4. From the Welcome screen select Next.

5. On the Configure User Settings page, shown in Figure 8.4, enable the Allow Users for the selections you prefer.

6. Once your options are chosen (either allow or block), select Next.

7. Confirm the settings from the Configure Operation Status page. If you want to export the information to an XML file use the Export button.

8. Click Finish.

NOTE

At both the domain and user levels, you can configure archiving by using the following options: Use Default Archive Settings, for the domain; Archive All User Communications; Archive Without Message Content, which will archive communications without the message body; or Do Not Archive User Communications.

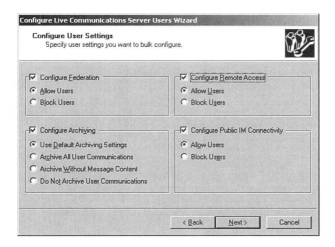

FIGURE 8.4   Bulk user configuration settings.

The LCS Management Console

The LCS management console, which you access through Administrative Tools, enables you to configure and manage settings for your LCS 2005 infrastructure. In a mixed environment, you can also manage LCS 2003 users and settings. This is helpful for a migration or period of coexistence from LCS 2003 to LCS 2005 SP1.

NOTE

For more information about upgrading from LCS 2003 to LCS 2005, refer to the Microsoft article at www.microsoft.com/technet/prodtechnol/office/livecomm/library/upgradefrom2003/lcsupf_1.mspx.

To access the properties of the forest, simply select the Forest level of the folder structure, right-click, and choose Properties. The forest-level properties sheet consists of six tabs, as follows:

▶ **General.** Specify which SIP domains are supported in your organization.

▶ **Search.** Specify how client search queries are handled by LCS. You can specify: Max. Rows returned to the client (the default is 20 contacts per client query, even if Active Directory finds more contacts that match); Max. Rows requested by the server; and Max. (the default is 200 contacts per server query, even if Active Directory finds more contacts that match); and Number of requests per server (the default is 80 queries per server before the requests are denied by the server).

▶ **User.** Specify the maximum number of contacts and devices that can be established for each user in the organization.

▶ **Federation.** Specify whether the forest is established to federate with partners or for public IM connectivity. Here you also specify the fully qualified domain name (FQDN) of the access proxy, proxy, or load balancer.

▶ **Access Proxy.** Specify which access proxies are allowed to communicate with your internal LCSs

▶ **Archiving.** Specify whether to archive communications with internal users or federated partners. You can also specify if you want to archive the message body for either set of users.

The server- or pool-level properties consist of eight tabs, as follows:

▶ **General.** Specify the name of the server or pool, the name of the back-end server, and how many contacts can be listed for that particular server or pool of users.

▶ **Routing.** Used to configure a static route for the URI and next-hop servers in an LCS infrastructure. (For static routes to work, the host address must be added to the Host Authorization tab. This is where you would configure the SIP-PSTN gateway routes.)

▶ **Compression.** Specify outbound server-to-server compression and max number of server-to-server connections. Enable or disable client-to-server compression.

▶ **Authentication.** Specify whether to use NT LAN Manager (NTLM), Kerberos, or both authentication protocols.

▶ **Federation.** Specify the default route or the access, proxy, or load balancer for the particular server or pool.

▶ **Host Authorization.** Specify servers, clients, or gateways that are explicitly trusted by the server or pool.

▶ **Archiving.** Specify archiving options for the server or pool. Microsoft Message Queuing (MSMQ) must be installed and configured for archiving to work. Here you can specify to archive content as well as communications, shutdown the server if archiving fails, or the shut down the server if MSMQ encryption fails. You can also associate LCSs with this archiving service.

▶ **Address Book.** Specify URLs where users on this server or pool can update address book information.

Intelligent Instant Messaging Filter
Building on the Instant Messaging Filter, which already comes with LCS 2005 SP1, is the Intelligent Instant Messaging Filter (IIMF). Installed as a separate package, it provides protection from viruses that can be launched via a URL link or file transfer operation. IIMF is made up of two components: URL filtering and file transfer filtering. The default IMFilter protects you from URLs and file transfers, but the enhanced IIMF is more flexible. With IIMF you can configure when and how protection occurs and it also enables logging functionality.

You can download the IIMFilterInstall.msi file from here:

http://www.microsoft.com/downloads/details.aspx?familyid=
0ED13372-F3D2-40F0-BA5D-C880359A40F5&displaylang=en

The following options are available with URL filtering:

- **Allow hyperlinks to be sent in any conversation.** Hyperlinks are clickable or not depending on the client's settings. (Office Communicator disables links by default.)

- **Allow (local) intranet URLs.** Local intranet URLs are clickable regardless of other filters.

- **Block all hyperlinks defined in the file transfer extension list.** Blocks any URL from the Internet or intranet if the hyperlink contains a blocked file extension type.

- **Block instant messages that contain hyperlinks.** Blocks all hyperlinks and reports an error back to the client.

- **Allow IMs with hyperlinks but convert the link to plain text.** Prefixes the URL with an underscore so that it is not clickable. Instead, users must copy and paste the hyperlink they want to activate.

- **Allow IMs with hyperlinks that contain active hyperlinks.** Allows active hyperlinks to be clicked. This option also enables you to configure a warning message for users before they click the link.

The following options are available with file transfer filtering:

- **Allow all file transfer requests to the server.** Essentially, disables file transfer filtering, allowing all extensions to traverse.

- **Block specific file extensions.** Filters extensions that are defined by the administrator and returns an error message to the client.

- **Block *all* file transfer requests.** Does not allow any file transfers.

IIMF also has logging features to help identify potential dangerous URLs or files that are attempted or that successfully launch in your environment.

Microsoft Office Communicator Clients

All our hard work in planning and deploying an IM server counts for nothing if we don't consider the client side. So, let's take a look at the various clients for LCS 2005 SP1.

Windows Messenger 5.1

Windows Messenger 5.1 allows for basic IM capability and has the ability to create groups and set basic presence information. Messenger allows for real-time communication with other contacts who are using the same IM service. It can include SIP, which is supported by LCS 2005. You can also connect to the Microsoft .NET Messenger services. Figure 8.5 shows the simplicity of Windows Messenger 5.1.

You can download the Windows Messenger 5.1 here:

http://www.microsoft.com/downloads/details.aspx?FamilyID=
a8d9eb73-5f8c-4b9a-940f-9157a3b3d774&displaylang=en.

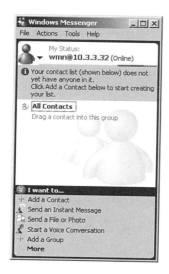

FIGURE 8.5   Windows Messenger 5.1.

Office Communicator 2005

Communicator 2005 allows for secure IM and adds telephony capabilities to create an enterprise-level communications client. Features of Communicator 2005 include public IM connectivity to AOL, Yahoo!, or MSN (If this option is configured on your LCS 2005); the ability to place calls using SIP-PSTN or VoIP; and the ability to share and receive files between uses or collaborate in real time. Communicator 2005 comes in three flavors: the full client, Communicator 2005 Web, and Communicator 2005 Mobile. Communicator 2005 adds the option of sharing applications or conducting video conversations with others. Figure 8.6 shows an example of the look of Communicator 2005.

Office Communicator 2007

Office Communicator 2007 logically builds off the success in the previous IM releases; however, this client product combines with the Communications Server 2007 product to provide for Microsoft's entry into the VoIP world. In addition to IM and presence aware-ness (which is simply the ability to know whether others are online or not, and whether they are busy or available; features we have had for some time), Web conferencing and software-powered VoIP are included. SIP is also supported, and so you can use Communicator with products from industry partners. Figure 8.7 shows the new interface.

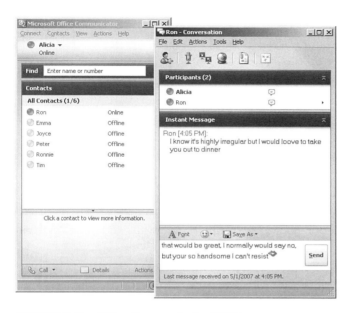

FIGURE 8.6   Office Communicator 2005.

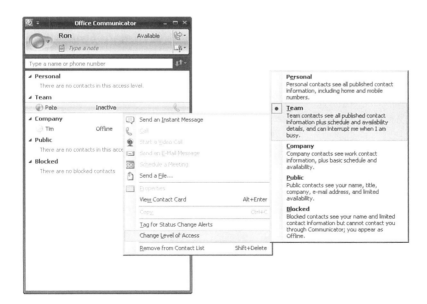

FIGURE 8.7   Office Communicator 2007.

Office Communications Server 2007 Overview

As mentioned earlier, when we began writing this book on the Office 2007 Server suite of products, LCS 2005 was the newest communications server product available, and it still is. However, Microsoft has released its public beta of Office Communications Server (OCS) 2007. To allow greater efficiency in the workplace, this version of the real-time communications/collaborations server builds on the idea of integrating IM, telephony, application and file sharing, and on the idea of supplying real-time presence information.

Microsoft's own developers predict a bold vision: that 100 million users in three years will have access to VoIP through Microsoft Office applications, and that it will cost approximately half of what VoIP implementations do today.

OCS 2007 is one of a suite of programs Microsoft has designed to be part of its unified communications strategy. Used alongside Exchange 2007's Unified Messaging Server role, Communications Server is now poised to become a complete voice, video, and data-collaboration tool. To Enhance OCS 2007, Microsoft has announced the release of several hardware components to complement the features added. Products such as Roundtable and Office Communicator 2007 Phone Edition are meant to add value and build on what the software can do, in effect providing a complete enterprise solution.

Note that although *enterprise class* is a term used a lot with OCS 2007, the Standard Edition of the product holds most of the same features and gives the small to mid-size company access to the same all-encompassing messaging, voice, and data-collaboration tools that the Enterprise Version features.

Again taking a page from the newest architectures at Microsoft Office, Communications Server 2007 is built on the platform of core server functions and server roles. Although there are several server roles in LCS, they have been more clearly defined in this product, and some of these roles (such as the mediation server or Web communications server) cannot coexist with some other server roles.

Because this is essentially an upgrade of LCS 2005, let's look at some new features and some enhancements to a couple of the existing features. Then we take a look at some of the considerations for installation.

Hardware Considerations

As mentioned in the preceding chapter, the ability to bring all these company communication needs under one "umbrella" is a matter of cost. Unless you still work for a company that follows the early 90s dotcom philosophy (team lunches Monday, shiatsu massages Thursday, and IT has no budget limitations), which we assume you are not, you need to take the time to determine the *needs* of your business. Having worked with each of these components, I can "say" I'm going to try to implement all of them for a financial services company I work for. Like most IT professionals, however, I must make my case. To help you make your case, let's consider things from a perspective of needs. The following table shows the physical server requisites to deploy OCS 2007. Microsoft uses the model of minimum and recommended requirements, but for our purposes the recommended requirements really should be considered the minimum (because in most IT environments you are deploying a physical server for approximately three years).

The Microsoft OCS 2007 Planning Guide provided the guidelines listed in Table 8.1.

TABLE 8.1   Deployment Requirements for OCS 2007

Server Role	CPU SPEED	MEMORY	DISK SPACE	NETWORK
Standard Edition servers	2 x 3.2GHz w. HT CPUs	2GB	2 x 18GB SCSI (15K rpm)	1Gb NIC
Enterprise Edition servers	2 x 3.2GHz w. HT CPUs	2GB	2 x 18GB SCSI (15K rpm)	1Gb NIC
Edge servers, with one or more edge server roles	2 x 3.2GHz w. HT CPUs	2GB	2 x 18GB SCSI (15K rpm)	1Gb NIC
A/V conferencing servers and A/V edge	2 x 3.0GHz dual-core CPUs	4GB	2 x 18GB SCSI (15K rpm)	1Gb NIC (A/V) 2Gb NIC (A/V edge)
Mediation server	2 x 3.0GHz dual-core CPUs	2GB	36GB SCSI (15K rpm)	2Gb NIC
Web conferencing server	2 x 3.2GHz w. HT CPUs	2GB	2 x 18GB SCSI (15K rpm)	1Gb NIC
Archiving and CDR server	2.8 GHz quad-core CPU	4GB	5 x 18GB SCSI (15K rpm)	1Gb NIC
Small or medium back-end database	2 x 3.2GHz w. HT CPUs	2GB	2 x 18GB SCSI (15K rpm)	1Gb NIC
Large back-end database	4 x 3.0GHz dual-core CPUs	32GB	4 x 36GB (RAID 1+0)	1Gb NIC

It is important to also consider the software requirements necessary to run OCS 2007. The following list identifies the necessary software to run OCS core components and any server roles you would deploy in your organization:

- Windows Server 2003 SP1.

- Active Directory in Windows 2000 Native mode.

- Windows Internet Information Server (IIS) 6.0 (required by all servers and server roles).

- .NET Framework 2.0.

- SQL Server 2000 SP4.

- 64-bit support for various 32-bit versions of the OCS components can run with 64-bit Windows 2003 SP1 using WOW64.

8

Deployment Considerations

Although it is possible to run most of the server roles on a single server (Standard Server Edition), a few server roles must be separated and require an additional server for the Enterprise Server Edition of OCS 2007. For example, the Archiving Service cannot coexist on the same server as the access edge server. In addition, the Communicator Web Access cannot be deployed on the Standard Edition Server. Although this doesn't mean that Enterprise Edition is needed, a few server roles do require the Enterprise Edition.

So, here's where you must decide which version to choose. Let's take a moment to talk about the core features of both versions. After that, the answer as to which version will suit your organization will become clearer.

Core features of both the Standard and Enterprise Editions include the following:

 ▶ Enhanced IM and enhanced presence

 ▶ Ability to deploy on-premise Web conference and A/V conference servers

 ▶ Ability to create and schedule Web conferences with internal, external, or remote users

Federation

Federation, in 2003, allowed us to securely create partnerships beyond the enterprise to communicate and collaborate. In 2005, enhanced federation was introduced, which enabled us to share presence information, federate with public IM services, and even initiate voice communications.

Enhancements to federation are among the chief upgrades to LCS 2007 SP1. Continuing to build on enhanced federation, Communications Server 2007 now allows federated users to participate in meetings; federated users can attend these meetings as presenters or attendees.

> **NOTE**
>
> The federated user will not have the ability to initiate the meetings; this must be done via invitation from authorized users within the enterprise.

Throttling of traffic from incoming federated domains is another improvement. Throttling can be set based on three criteria: administrative settings, amount of traffic, and the federated partner's trust level. Throttling can be set to limit or completely block incoming traffic.

To support partners with multiple domain names, OCS now uses subject alternate names in certificates, in conjunction with enhanced federation, to ease the process of creating and maintaining partnerships in large organizations.

Enhanced Presence

OCS 2007 now allows client applications to publish and subscribe to enhanced presence information. Enhanced presence is broken down into categories and containers. Categories are information about the user, such as status, location, email address, phone numbers, and so on. Containers are logical ways of publishing categories. Office Communicator 2007 uses enhanced presence to assign contacts to access levels, using the categories and containers. Enhanced presence allows you to set your location information and to create customized locations that can be viewed by members of the team or personal access levels. You can also allow contacts to see as much or as little information as the access level allows. Enhanced presence requires the new client for OCS, Office Communicator 2007. With Communicator, you can set contacts to several defined availability levels called access levels. Depending on where you place the contact, they will be able to view more or less presence information about that user. Although most of the presence information is supplied by OCS, you can set several additional presence attributes in Communicator 2007. Table 8.2 lists access levels and presence information available to these groups (information you can also find on page 15 of the Communicator 2007 Getting Started Guide).

TABLE 8.2   Access Levels and Presence Information

Presence Information	Block	Public	Company	Team	Personal
Offline presence	X				
Presence		X	X	X	X
Display name	X	X	X	X	X
Email address	X	X	X	X	X
Title *		X	X	X	X
Work phone *			X	X	X
Mobile phone *				X	X
Home phone *					X
Other phone *					X
Company		X	X	X	X
Office *	X	X	X	X	X
Work address *	X	X	X	X	X
SharePoint site			X	X	X
Meeting location				X	
Meeting subject				X	
Free busy			X	X	X
Working hours			X	X	X
Endpoint location				X	X
Notes (out-of-office note)			X	X	X
Notes (personal)			X	X	X
Last active				X	X

* These attributes are visible to contacts inside your company with Block and Public access levels if the attributes are displayed by Active Directory. These attributes are not visible to contacts outside your company with Block and Public access levels.

Instant Messaging in Groups

Using Active Directory distribution groups, users can better initiate group IM sessions and can now add voice and video to the group IM session.

Integrated Address Book Server

An address book is now integrated into the installation of either the Standard or Enterprise Edition of OCS 2007. Information about users within the Active Directory is updated dynamically. Part of the core installation of the front-end server, the address book creates a local copy of the contact information for the Communicator client to access. The address book server can also be used for phone number normalization for Communicator, but this is not the preferred method of normalization and should be considered as a last option in deploying telephony phone number normalization.

Management Tool Enhancements

▶ **Deployment tool.** A new deployment tool provides numerous wizards that guide you through the installation, activation, and configuration of all server roles.

▶ **Microsoft Management Console (MMC) improvements.** Along with an easier-to-use interface, the MMC now supports queries to the back-end database pool.

▶ **Support for universal groups.** Placing service and administrative accounts into universal groups allows for ease of administration without the need to perform a cross-domain configuration (to collaborate with users in another domain).

▶ **Delegation of setup tasks.** Now you can delegate certain setup tasks to administrators or even users.

▶ **Global meeting policies.** Meeting policies can be defined on a global level using the MMC.

What's New in OCS 2007?

OCS 2007 includes several new features, such as enterprise voice, on-premise Web conferencing, compliance archiving and CDRs (call detail records), and newer clients.

Enterprise Voice

One new feature of OCS 2007 is enterprise voice. Enterprise voice is technically an improvement, because LCS 2005 had voice capability. In OCS, however, voice communications has been greatly expanded. Enterprise voice is the first of two major initiatives driving this new server build. Voice integration has gone from something available to something to stand up and take notice of—the ability to integrate a corporate PBX and PSTN into OCS 2007 has been made simpler to deploy and has been made enterprise ready in this version. Building on its predecessor, you can now create a unified communications experience using the Office Communicator 2007 client. When used in conjunction with Exchange 2007, enterprise voice enables users to combine IM, voice, email, presence information, and even audio/videoconferencing into a single solution.

Enterprise voice is Microsoft's foray into the enterprise VoIP market, and OCS 2007 (along with Office Communicator 2007) leave no doubt that Microsoft is making a big play to become the all-in-one communications solution for any enterprise. OCS 2007 expands on the type of calls that are now handled in Office Communicator 2007, which are as follows:

- ▶ PC to PC

- ▶ PC to audio conference

- ▶ PC to PBX/PSTN phones

- ▶ Video calls and videoconferencing

In addition, call features such as call forwarding, transfer, hold, and retrieve are available. With Microsoft Communicator Phone Edition, users can work with a physical version of Communicator 2007, by using a SIP-enabled desktop telephone.

As part of Microsoft's unified messaging technologies, OCS 2007 works together with Exchange 2007's unified messaging server role to provide enterprise voice users with the following options:

- ▶ **Call answering.** Basically, this is an integrated voicemail system that resides on your Exchange mailbox server. Call answering enables you to record a personal greeting and have messages or missed-call notifications (if the caller chooses not to leave a message) show up in your inbox.

- ▶ **Outlook voice access.** Enables enterprise voice users to retrieve email, voice messages, the calendar, and contacts from a telephony interface.

- ▶ **Auto attendant.** Provides an interface for external users to navigate a menu system to reach internal users. The list of available users is configured in Exchange 2007.

On-Premise Web Conferencing

The second major initiative in OCS 2007 is Web conferencing. Users can now host, schedule, and present meetings via a Web conference. On-premise Web conferencing enables users to host conferences on internal servers using either Communicator 2007 or the Live Meeting 2007 client. Meetings can include voice, video/audio, presentations, and data collaboration. These on–premise meetings can be either scheduled or unscheduled and can be handled securely and more cost-effectively than off-site alternatives. When we look at server roles, we will consider how you can use your internal network as a Web conferencing center.

NOTE

Microsoft offers a new videoconferencing solution called Microsoft Office Roundtable 2007. Some features include 360-degree views and the ability to record conferences. For more information, refer to the article about unified communications on the Microsoft Web site at www.microsoft.com/uc/Technologies.mspx.

Compliance Archiving and Call Detail Records (CDR)

Compliance archiving and CDR offer a huge benefit to environments where regulation dictates that all communications must be archived and held for a prescribed amount of time. Expanding on archiving features from LCS 2005, this too, is another improvement, but with an addition that makes it a new feature. CDRs enable organizations to capture information such as when meetings start and who joins, when the user signs in and out, IM archiving of peer-to-peer and group IM conversations, usage information about VoIP calls, and more.

New Clients for OCS 2007

With all of these new features come new clients. Many of the enhanced and new features mentioned can only be activated by deploying the new Microsoft client for OCS 2007.

- ▶ **Office Communicator 2007.** The preferred and most robust client for OCS 2007 supports multimode conferencing features such as group IM, audio, video, and data collaboration.

- ▶ **Live Meeting 2007.** Introduced as the client for service-based conferencing, Live Meeting 2007 is now supported for use as a server-based audio-, video-, and data-sharing client in OCS 2007.

- ▶ **Conferencing Add-In for Microsoft Outlook.** Used in Microsoft Outlook 2003 with SP3 or later, users can use this plug-in to schedule conferencing sessions with contacts in their address book. You can use the familiar Outlook calendar to schedule a conference in much the same way as you would schedule an appointment with multiple users in the organization.

- ▶ **Microsoft Office Communicator Phone Edition.** Consisting of a phone-like device, this client is basically a physical version of the Office Communicator 2007 software. Calls can be placed by either dialing from the keypad or by clicking the contact.

NOTE

Windows Messenger 5.1 is no longer supported in OCS 2007. Users can continue to use the Office Communicator 2005 client, but be aware that many of the new features available in Communicator 2007 will not be available in the Communicator 2005 client.

New Server Roles in OCS 2007

Although many of the familiar server roles return in this version, the architecture of OCS 2007 changes the way a few of these servers are viewed. The director and archiving roles have remained, but the access proxy gives way to a series of edge servers. And, mediation servers using media gateways are introduced for enterprise voice. In our review of these roles, we begin with the perimeter roles and then move on to the new server roles on the internal network.

Reverse Proxy Server

Required by the internal Web server, the reverse proxy is used to allow external users access to meeting content from your Web conferencing servers. The reverse proxy also allows remote users access to address books and distribution groups outside of the perimeter network.

Edge Servers

There are several edge servers to choose from, as discussed in the following subsections.

Access Edge Server

Known in LCS 2003 and 2005 as the access proxy, the access edge server is used for the configuration of federation, remote access, and public IM connectivity in the OCS 2007 topology. The access edge server is the first server role deployed in your perimeter network and is necessary to deploy Web conferencing server or audio/videoconferencing server roles.

> **NOTE**
>
> Access to edge server for federated partners using automatic Domain Name System (DNS) discovery is enabled by default during the access edge server configuration. You can change this to *not* allow automatic discovery using DNS.

Each edge server should be deployed on its own physical server. The access edge servers cannot be managed from the OCS 2007 management console. To configure/manage these edge services, use the compmgmt.msc tool or right-click **My Computer** and choose **Manage**, expand the **Services and Applications** tab, and find the OCS 2007 edge server services. You can then reconfigure or deactivate edge server roles. You can also use the OCS 2007 deployment tool to reconfigure edge server roles, as shown in Figure 8.8.

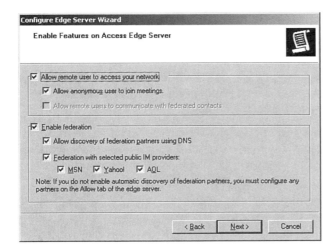

FIGURE 8.8   Access edge server settings.

NOTE

It is important to note here that if you are performing an upgrade from LCS 2005 to OCS 2007, you must first upgrade your perimeter or "edge" servers, deploy all the edge server roles that correspond to the access proxy roles in your perimeter network, and then upgrade your servers or enterprise pools.

Access A/V Edge Server

Acting as a secure media relay server, the access A/V edge server allows external users to participate in audio/video sessions. Deployed within the perimeter network, the A/V edge server can be deployed on the same server as the access edge server or on its own.

NOTE

The A/V access edge server is used in conjunction with the A/V conferencing server to allow external users access to A/V sessions.

Web Conferencing Edge Server

Used to proxy traffic between the Web conferencing server and the external user, the Web conference edge server uses the Persistent Shared Object Model Protocol (PSOM) and requires Transport Layer Security (TLS) connections and a session key from the external client.

From the perimeter, we move to the internal network and look at some new server roles there.

Conferencing Servers

Conferencing servers are part of the front-end server architecture and are part of several conferencing components. The components are as follows:

- ▶ **Focus.** The focus manages the conference state; it also manages all group IM, data collaboration, and A/V sharing for the front-end server.

- ▶ **Focus factory.** The focus factory is simply used to schedule meetings. When a client initiates a meeting, the SIP service sends a scheduling request to the focus factory, which creates an instance on the conferencing database.

- ▶ **Conferencing server factory.** The conferencing server factory serves as the central access point to each of the conferencing roles, determining by means of local policy and server load which conferencing server will receive the meeting request.

- ▶ **Conferencing servers (MCUs).** Conferencing servers, also known as multipoint control units, are used to manage multiple media types.

OCS 2007 has four different conferencing server roles, as discussed in the following subsections.

A/V Conferencing Server

Used to provide multiparty IP A/V mixing and transport for internal users, and available in either the Standard or Enterprise Editions, this server role can be deployed on either the front-end server or on a separate physical server. It works as the back-end A/V server for external users in conjunction with the A/V edge server.

Web Conferencing Server

This server role manages data collaboration for OCS 2007 Web conferences. This server provides native support for Microsoft PowerPoint presentations, application sharing, white boarding, file transfer, and so on. It is used in conjunction with Web conferencing edge server to allow external users to participate in conferences. The Web conferencing server can be deployed on either the front-end server or a stand-alone server.

IM Conferencing Server

The IM conferencing server enables group IM via the MCU. When a third party joins a peer-to-peer IM, the session is moved to an IM MCU, and all messages are routed through that MCU. The IM conferencing server is part of the front-end server installation and cannot be moved to a separate server.

Telephony Conferencing Server

This server role supports the dial-in, dial-out, and third-party call control features. This server is responsible for Audio Conferencing Provider (ACP) integration. ACP integration is required to enable large-scale conferencing or audio conferencing with outside users. The telephony conferencing server role is part of the front-end server installation and cannot be moved to a separate server.

> **NOTE**
>
> The telephony conferencing server cannot support VoIP and PSTN audio mixing in the same call.

8

Archiving Server

Through the archiving server role, OCS 2007 provides a way to archive IM conversations, application sharing, meetings, A/V communications, and so on (with the addition of CDRs). OCS 2007 can now hold more detailed information about conferencing sessions in a SQL Server–based archive.

Mediation Server

This server role, used along with third-party media gateways, creates a logical unit in which to enable enterprise voice users to communicate with PSTNs. The mediation server works with a corresponding media gateway to provide signaling and media transmission. The mediation server also translates SIP over TCP on the gateway side to SIP over Mutual TLS (MTLS) on the enterprise voice side, and encrypts/decrypts Secure Real-time Transport Protocol (SRTP) for OCS 2007. Three kinds of media gateways are available in OCS 2007: basic, advanced, and basic hybrid.

> **NOTE**
>
> The mediation server can be installed only in an Enterprise Edition deployment of OCS. Enterprise voice and telephony are a major component for OCS 2007. It is really a subject all to itself. For more information about configuring mediation server and media gateways, refer to the Microsoft public beta documentation at www.microsoft.com/ downloads/details.aspx?familyid=0A3E2593-5812-4BF5-A554-3215CBBA587A& displaylang=en.

Communicator Web Access

Communicator Web access servers provide users with IM access via a Web browser for those who are not able to install the standard Office Communicator client on their system. This server role enables users with non-Microsoft systems or older Microsoft operating systems (Windows 2000 SP4 and earlier) to communicate with OCS 2007 via a Web browser. A Communicator Web access server is also an ideal solution for remote users who are using publicly available systems (such as at hotels, kiosks, and cafés) or at client sites where the installation of the Communicator client is not an option. Keep in mind that this server role cannot be deployed on the same server as the Standard Edition front-end server components.

Now that you have a fundamental understanding of the changes in OCS 2007, let's walk through an installation and get a look at Microsoft's newest communication and collaboration server.

Installation Walkthrough of Communications Server 2007

Although we do not cover it in great detail here, we do a brief walkthrough of the installation of a Standard Edition of OCS 2007. As you've seen with LCS 2005, much of the deployment process involves preparation and configuration. The OCS 2007 deployment tool has become more intuitive in this version and features wizards that guide you through all aspects of the installation process. At each step, you can now review the prerequisites needed to complete that step. Doing so proves useful in troubleshooting a deployment failure.

To begin, notice in Figure 8.9 that you have several deployment options. The first two choices are considerations for which topology you want to deploy: Consolidated or Expanded. In the consolidated enterprise pool, all conferencing, IM, and presence functions are hosted on the front end (as in the Standard Edition server), but this still connects to a back-end database, which allows for no single point of failure and the ability to scale the environment. A consolidated topology also allows you to deploy multiple front-end servers and to join those to a pool; with the help of the hardware load balancer, you can also provide high availability.

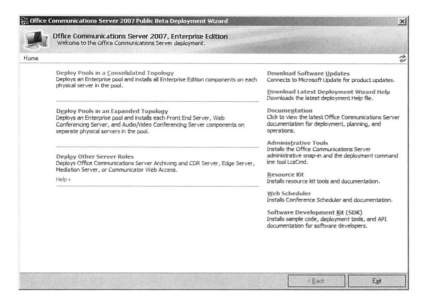

FIGURE 8.9   Deployment choices through the OCS 2007 deployment tool.

NOTE

In the Standard Edition, all front-end server roles are installed to the same physical server. However, the other server roles (edge servers and archiving) can still be deployed on separate physical servers. In an enterprise pool deployment in which two or more front-end servers are deployed, you should deploy a hardware load balancer.

After you have chosen your topology, you can begin the preparation process. Much like you did with LCS 2005, you prep the schema, forest, and domain. However, this is now consolidated into a single wizard in which each step is run and replication of information is verified, as shown in Figure 8.10. So, you can easily see that between the release of LCS 2005 and OCS 2007 changes for the better have been made.

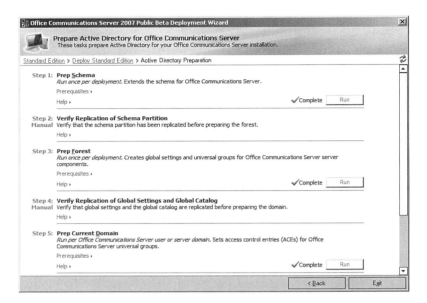

FIGURE 8.10   Preparing your Active Directory, all in one dialog.

After you have completed the Active Directory prep, you can move on to deploying the server. The first portion of the install configures the front-end and conferencing components for OCS. Then you configure your server or pool, which is where you add SIP domains to your environment, choose client logon settings, and configure settings for external access. (You can configure the settings for external access now or return and redeploy the server to configure for external access at a later date.)

After you have configured the server, you must configure certificates. (LCS 2005 enabled you to install and run locally without certificates, but OCS 2007 requires certificates even for local usage.) After you have installed and configured the certificates, you can then start the services.

Finally, and new with the Deployment Wizard, you can verify server functionality. At this point, you verify the previous steps; services will then be started. You are now ready to configure users for OCS 2007. Table 8.3 lists server roles, clients, and additional server roles needed to deploy this function in OCS 2007 (information taken from page 9 of the OCS Planning Guide).

After the initial deployment, you can now install the other server roles to increase the functionality of your server or pool. Figure 8.11 shows the tool you use to deploy other server roles.

TABLE 8.3

Function	Client	Additional Server Role
Instant messaging and presence	Communicator 2005 or 2007 (2007 needed for enhanced presence)	None
On-premise conferencing	Communicator 2007, Live Meeting 2007, Outlook add-in for scheduled conferences	None
Address book server	All available clients	None
Archiving and CDRs	Not required (server-side function)	Archiving and CDR service
External user access	Communicator 2005 or 2007	Access edge server
Federation	Communicator 2005 or 2007	Access edge server
Public IM connectivity	Communicator 2005 or 2007	Access edge server
Web conferencing with external users	Communicator 2007 or Live Meeting 2007	Access edge server and Web conferencing edge server
A/V conferencing with external users	Communicator 2007 or Live Meeting 2007	Access edge server and A/V conferencing edge server
IM and presence through a browser-based client	Communicator Web access	Communicator Web access server
Enterprise voice	Communicator 2007 or Office Communicator 2007 Phone Edition	Mediation server and basic media gateway, collocated media gateway, or advanced media gateway

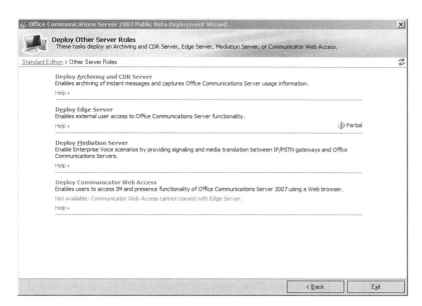

FIGURE 8.11   The tool used to deploy other server roles.

Without going through a step-by-step installation, let's look at an Enterprise consolidated and expanded topology deployment and some of the components and server roles that can be installed. Figure 8.12 shows the Deployment Wizard screen for the consolidated topology.

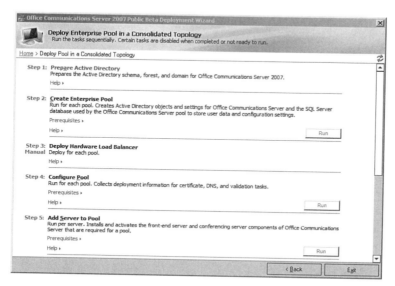

FIGURE 8.12   The Enterprise consolidated topology Deployment Wizard.

To deploy an Enterprise consolidated topology, complete these nine tasks in the wizard:

1. **Prepare Active Directory.** Prepares Active Directory schema, forest, and domain.

2. **Create Enterprise Pool.** Creates Active Directory objects for OCS and the SQL back-end database.

3. **Configure Pool.** Collects deployment information, such as client Logon settings and external user access configuration (see Figures 8.13 and 8.14).

> **NOTE**
>
> If you choose not to configure external user access at this time, you can run the wizard from either the Deployment screen or by using the OCS Administrative snap-in.

4. **Deploy Hardware Load Balancer.** Where two or more OCS 2007s will reside in the same pool, a hardware load balancer must be deployed for each pool.

> **NOTE**
>
> Within the wizard deployment steps, task 4 (Deploy Hardware Load Balancer) is listed before the Configure Pool task (and identified as a manual step). To keep the deployment steps consistent across the different models, however, it appears in this book after the Configure Pool task.

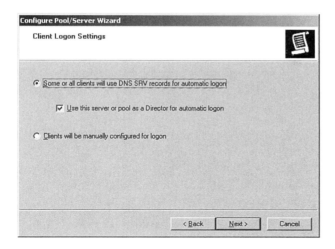

FIGURE 8.13   Configure clients to log on automatically, manually, or define this server/pool as the director role.

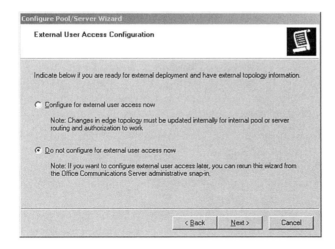

FIGURE 8.14   Indicate whether you will configure your server/pool for external access.

5. **Add Server to Pool.** Installs and activates front-end server(s) in the pool and installs and activates the conferencing components.

6. **Configure Certificates.** Here you create, request, process, and assign certificates for the pool.

7. **Verify Replication.** Confirms the Active Directory changes from the preparation step have been replicated to all domain controllers, before attempting to start the services.

8. **Start Services.** Starts the OCS 2007 services. Some services will not start if Active Directory has not completed its replication or if certificates have not been assigned.

9. **Validate Server and Pool Functionality.** This is a diagnostic to check configuration, connections, and end-user functions. Afterward, it starts the service.

For an Enterprise expanded topology deployment, you must complete a few more tasks, as follows:

1. **Add Front–End Server.** Creates the SIP infrastructure for IM and presences and the multiparty IM functions and telephony conference server role.

2. **Add Web Components.** Enables the uploading of data and presentations via the Web conferencing server, enables group expansion, and installs the address book.

3. **Add Web Conferencing Server.** Enables the hosting of internal and external Web conferences and enables the server for presentation, document, and application sharing.

4. **Add A/V Conferencing Server.** Enables multiparty A/V conferencing for enterprise pools.

Managing OCS 2007

Much like you manage LCS 2005, you can use the Active Directory Users and Computers console to enable, configure, move, and delete users in a domain. The Communications tab in the user object now includes additional user configuration options. For example, there are now meeting and telephony configuration options.

With meetings, you can determine the meeting size, whether to enable Web conferencing, and even the color depth on the desktop sharing. You can determine whether the presenter (or participants) can record the meeting, and you can enable IP audio and video. You can also determine the amount of control non-Active Directory participants within the meeting will have, including the following:

▶ Never allow control of shared programs or desktop

▶ Allow control of shared programs

▶ Allow control of shared programs and desktop

For telephony properties, consider Figure 8.15. You can configure your telephony, federation, and archiving properties from within the Active Directory Users and Computers settings.

The new 2007 management console snap-in supports several new management features, such as managing on-premise conferencing at the global, pool, server, and user level. The snap-in also enables you to configure new server roles (such as the Web conferencing server and A/V server) and includes tools for managing and configuring enterprise voice. With these tools, you can manage both enterprise voice users and users connected to traditional

PSTNs. Figure 8.16 shows the OCS 2007 management console. (Keep in mind that this is taken from the beta, so it's possible things will change a bit with the final release.)

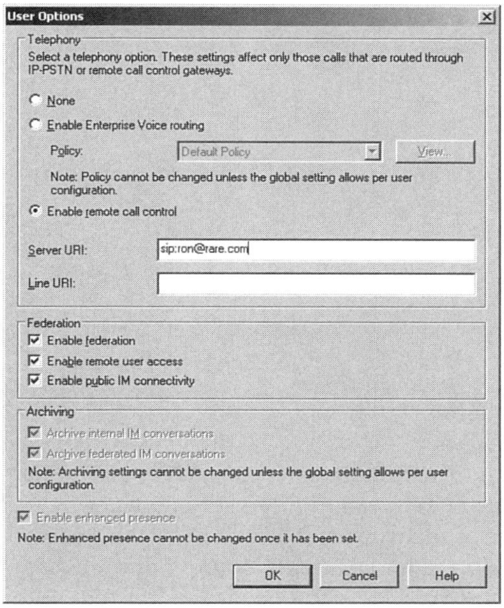

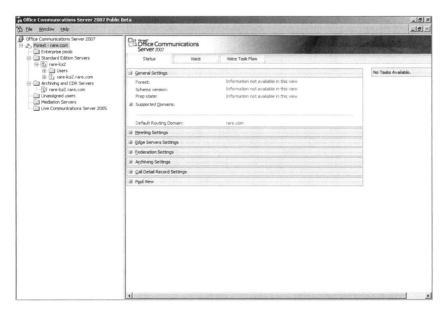

FIGURE 8.15   Configuring telephony settings.

FIGURE 8.16   OCS 2007 management console.

Advanced view settings enable you to view/hide Active Directory domains. You can also use a filter to organize the view by either server role or to show the servers as a list, as shown in Figure 8.17.

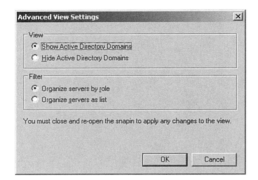

FIGURE 8.17   Advanced view settings in the management console.

Some new management features enable you to set the Intelligent Instant Messaging Filter (separate software install in LCS 2005) and create client-version filters for applications used within Office Communicator 2007. A view of the front-end and conferencing servers allows you to check the service running state, certificate settings, IP address, and media and SIP port ranges. You can also view performance counters and event logs for the conferencing servers, as shown in Figure 8.18.

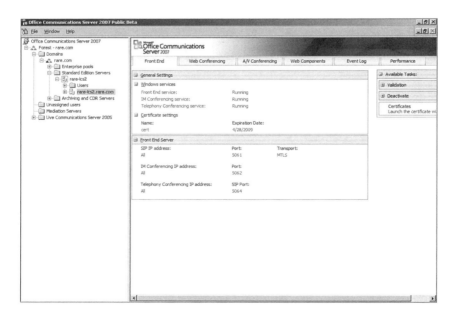

FIGURE 8.18   You can review performance counters and event logs here.

LCS 2005 or OCS 2007? That Is the Question

With all to look forward to in OCS 2007, you might now wonder why you should deploy LCS 2005. Well, to begin with, OCS 2007 is still in beta, and LCS 2005 is ready to be purchased and installed today. Because the upgrade path is easy enough to accomplish, OCS 2007 would then not be a complete new install.

> **NOTE**
>
> Microsoft enables you to migrate the back-end database and archiving database, too, so there is no loss of past communications.

As with LCS 2005, you can host LCS 2005 servers and pools in OCS 2007. Therefore, if you need to retain a specific pool/server or LCS 2005 infrastructure, rest assured; both versions can coexist. Finally, your organization might not need more if you are already using LCS for some IM collaboration, which is fine. Either way we are on the verge of being able to tie in all the ways we communicate and collaborate in a work environment and improve upon that by using a single set of tools. Tools that will allow us to traverse networks, time zones, physical locations, and differing technologies, to make our jobs faster, easier, and more efficient.

8

CHAPTER 9

PerformancePoint Server 2007: Overview and Installation

PerformancePoint Server 2007 (officially labeled Microsoft Office PerformancePoint Server 2007) is part of the next generation of BI tools coming from Microsoft. Following in the footsteps of Business Scorecard Manager, PerformancePoint Server 2007 enables business users to monitor, analyze, and react to organization business data. What does this mean? For years, business analytics was the responsibility of very few. These analysts were entrusted to manually gather data and pass static reports, typically Excel spreadsheets, to corporate executives. This information offered insight into how the organization was performing. Technology has changed this paradigm. It is now much easier to gather, store, and access various types of corporate data. More important, technology has fostered a demand within the business community to provide direct access to this data to form business decisions and initiate process change. PerformancePoint Server 2007 assists in this effort by "bringing business intelligence to the masses." Business users will be both consumers *and* producers of business analytics.

What Is PerformancePoint Server 2007?

PerformancePoint Server 2007 is a server-based product that offers tight integration with other Microsoft server products such as SQL Server and Office SharePoint Server. It offers users a collection of tools for monitoring, analytics, and financial planning. All of this is bundled in a highly secure, easy-to-use interface that allows direct access to business data through a web browser, integration with a corporate portal, or direct access via Office applications. The power of PerformancePoint Server 2007 lies in its ability to present business data to a larger, varied corporate audience with the goal of fostering collaboration, decision making, actionable execution, and measurable improved efficiency.

From a technical perspective, PerformancePoint Server 2007 represents a collection of integrated products. These include the core functionality of Business Scorecard Manager, the core functionality of ProClarity, PerformancePoint Business Modeler, PerformancePoint Server, and a PerformancePoint Excel add-in.

Getting Started with Business Intelligence?

Business intelligence (BI) continues to be a much discussed topic in both corporate boardrooms and in IT server rooms. BI applications offer the Holy Grail of corporate technology usage: the ability to fully understand the strengths, weaknesses, and trends within an organization in such a timely fashion as to allow for real-time course correction. BI, in some ways, is as much a philosophy as anything. It is the belief that if an organization can define and effectively monitor metrics in how it chooses to value success ... and makes the commitment to do so with complete and accurate data ... significant operational efficiencies can be attained and maintained.

BI is not a new topic. For years, corporate analysts have used tools such as Microsoft Excel to gather and analyze business data. This is typically a slow and manually intensive process. The biggest benefits of today's BI tools is the ability to more quickly acquire, analyze, and react to this business data. Think of BI as having two core components:

- ▶ The ability to acquire and analyze business data

- ▶ The ability to communicate the "story" associated with this analysis

Yes, BI is about storytelling—the facility to present with few or no words an indication of how well something or someone is performing (as well as the supporting data to explain why).

Technology advancements have increased the desire for BI tools. Applications such as corporate portals have made it easier to reach all levels of the organization, creating better ways to broadcast announcements and initiate collaboration. An additional byproduct has been the paving of a path of direct access to all business users. This path provides a medium to expose business analytics to a greater audience. A CEO can now use the intranet to access corporate performance metrics, while a salesperson can use the same intranet to analyze personal performance against sales quota.

NOTE

Business intelligence is a business management term, which refers to applications and technologies that are used to gather, provide access to, and analyze data and information about company operations. Business intelligence systems can help companies have a more comprehensive knowledge of the factors affecting their business, such as metrics on sales, production, internal operations, and they can help companies to make better business decisions. Business Intelligence should not be confused with *competitive intelligence*, which is a separate management concept. *Source: http://en.wikipedia.org/wiki/Business_intelligence*

BI projects have been traditionally feared by both IT staff and corporate sponsors. Until recently, BI tools have been perceived as overly complex, requiring significant training and increased business process (to include these tools in day-to-day activities). Next-generation BI tools, such as PerformancePoint Server 2007, look to increase the adoption of BI principles by making it easy for information workers to access data in an environment in which they are already familiar.

Hardware and Software Requirements

PerformancePoint Server 2007 has minimum requirements for both hardware and software. Tables 9.1 and 9.2, taken from the PerformancePoint Server 2007 help files, provides details about the various hardware requirements for both the Planning Server component and the Monitoring Server component.

TABLE 9.1   Minimal Requirements for the PerformancePoint Planning Server

Hardware Requirements	PerformancePoint Planning Servers	File Share Server	PerformancePoint Server Business Modeler	PerformancePoint Server Add-in For Excel
Processor type	Minimum: Pentium 4	Minimum: Pentium 4	Minimum: Pentium 3	Minimum: Pentium 3
	Recommended: Dual Core Pentium x64	Recommended: Dual Core Pentium x64	Recommended: Core 2 Duo	Recommended: Core 2 Duo
Processor speed	Minimum: 2.5GHz	Minimum: 1GHz	Minimum: 1GHz	Minimum: 1GHz
	Recommended: 2.8GHz	Recommended: 2.8GHz	Recommended: 2GHz	Recommended: 2.0GHz
Number of processors	Minimum: 1	Minimum: 1	Minimum: 1	Minimum: 1
	Recommended: 2	Recommended: 2	Recommended: 1	Recommended: 1
Available hard disk space	Minimum: 2GB	Minimum: 40GB	Minimum: 1.5GB	Minimum: 1.5GB
	Recommended: 5GB	Recommended: 500GB	Recommended: 3GB	Recommended: 3GB
RAM	Minimum: 1GB	Minimum: 1GB	Minimum: 512MB	Minimum: 512MB
	Recommended: 2GB	Recommended: 2GB	Recommended: 1GB	Recommended: 1GB

9

TABLE 9.2   Minimal Requirements for the PerformancePoint Monitoring Server

Hardware Requirements	PerformancePoint Monitoring Servers	File Share Server
Processor type	Minimum: Pentium 4 Recommended: Dual Core Pentium x64	Minimum: Pentium 4 Recommended: Dual Core Pentium x64
Processor speed	Minimum: 2.5GHz Recommended: 2.8GHz	Minimum: 1GHz Recommended: 2.8GHz
Number of processors	Minimum: 1 Recommended: 2	Minimum: 1 Recommended: 2
Available hard disk space	Minimum: 2GB Recommended: 5GB	Minimum: 40GB Recommended: 500GB
RAM	Minimum: 1GB Recommended: 2GB	Minimum: 1GB Recommended: 2GB

PerformancePoint Server 2007 is a Microsoft server product and has requirements for additional software availability. The following software is required to begin a PerformancePoint Server 2007 installation:

▶ Windows Server 2003 with Service Pack 1, Standard Edition

▶ Windows Installer 3.1

▶ SQL Server 2005 with Service Pack 2, Enterprise Edition

    Planning Server relational databases can run on a Standard Edition, but Planning Server requires Enterprise Edition for its SQL Server Analysis Services databases.

▶ Cumulative update package (build 3161) for SQL Server 2005 Service Pack 2

▶ Microsoft .NET Framework 2.0

▶ Microsoft Internet Information Services 6.0 (IIS)

▶ Microsoft ASP.NET 2.0

Using the Planning Server SI Account

During Planning Server setup, you must enter the Planning Server Service Identity (SI) account. All Planning Server processes and calls run under the Planning Server SI account. The Planning Server SI account is also used for the IIS application pool account.

Before installing any required software, you must create or select a Windows domain account to act as the SI account for Planning Server. Monitoring Server also requires an SI account. However, that is a separate account, and the Planning Server SI account should not be confused with the Monitoring Server SI account. This account is a service account and should not have administrative permissions on any computer running Planning Server.

Permissions for the Planning Server SI account are set up as follows:

▶ On SQL Server computers that contain relational databases, SQL Server permissions for the Planning Server SI account are configured automatically during installation. The SI account is given db_owner privileges on the PlanningSystem database and PlanningService database.

▶ On SQL Server 2005 Analysis Services servers, permissions for the Planning Server SI account are configured automatically during installation.

▶ On computers that run Planning Web Service, permissions for the Planning Server SI account are configured automatically during installation. The IIS application pool PPSPlanningWebServicesAppPool is created during installation and runs under the SI account identity.

▶ On computers that run the Planning Process Service, permissions for the Planning Server SI account are configured automatically during installation. The Microsoft PerformancePoint Service, a Windows service, is configured to run under the SI account identity.

▶ The IIS application pool PPSPlanningAdminConsoleAppPool is created during installation and runs under the SI account identity.

The SI account may also need db_create privileges when an application is created via the Planning Server Configuration Manager Auto-Create functionality.

The Windows user account used for the Planning Server SI account must have administrator privileges for any SQL Server computer that Planning Server connects to. In addition, the SI account cannot be a group account or the local administrator account on the SQL Server computer. It must be its own distinct account with both local and domain access.

The Planning Server SI account must have the following:

▶ The ability to access computers from the network

▶ The ability to log on to machines as a batch job

▶ The ability to log on to machines as a service

6

The following things are set by the Planning Server Configuration Manager for the SI account:

▶ The SI account is added to the IIS_WPG Windows group.

▶ The SI account is added to a local security policy on the machine.

▶ The SI account is added to the SQL Server Security Logins.

Installations

Although it is not recommended that you install all components of PerformancePoint Server 2007 on a single server, the following instructions walk you through the installation on a standalone machine. This includes Business Modeler, which is intended to be a desktop-based tool. These steps enable you to create an initial test environment. You complete the same steps, across different servers or desktops, in a production deployment. Note the hardware and software requirements mentioned previously.

Installing PerformancePoint Planning Server

1. Double-click **setup.hta**. The PerformancePoint Server 2007 splash screen will display, as shown in Figure 9.1. Click **Install Planning Server**. Prerequisites are assessed, and to proceed, all must be met.

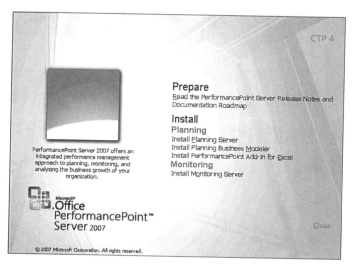

FIGURE 9.1   The PerformancePoint installation splash screen.

2. Accept the licensing terms by selecting the checkbox and then click **Next**.

3. On the Directory Selection page, select the location of the PerformancePoint Server files, as shown in Figure 9.2. You can Browse to a new location or check for available space. Click **Next**.

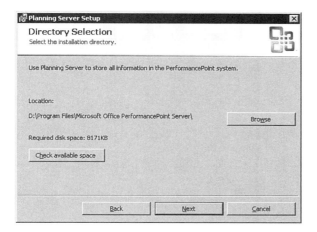

FIGURE 9.2   Choosing the location of server files.

4. On the Install page, click the **Install** button. The installation then extracts all necessary files and places them on the file system. This process takes a few minutes.

5. When installation is complete, the Planning Server Setup page appears. Before clicking Finish, make sure the **Run the Planning Server Configuration Manager** check box is enabled, which says "Run the Planning Server Configuration Manager Wizard. The Installation cannot be completed until the Planning Server is configured." Then click **Finish**.

6. On the "Welcome to the Planning Server Configuration Manager" page, click **Next**.

7. On the Prerequisites page, validate that all prerequisites have been met, as shown in Figure 9.3. Click **Next**.

9

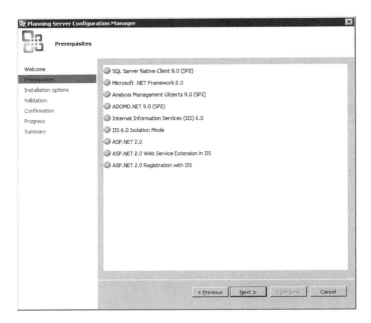

FIGURE 9.3   Ensure your prerequisites are met before moving forward.

8. On the Installation Options page (shown in Figure 9.4), leave the default values (Standalone Configuration) and click **Next**.

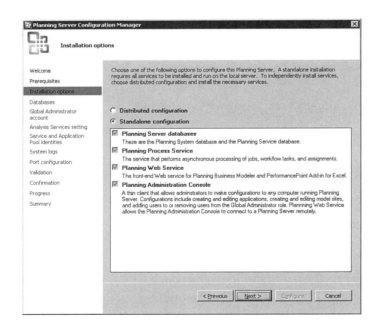

FIGURE 9.4   Installation options for a Distributed or Standalone Configuration.

9. On the Databases page (shown in Figure 9.5), select a SQL Server database. (It defaults to the current server.) Click **Next**.

> **NOTE**
>
> It must be a SQL Server 2005 database with SP2. If your selection is not, the installation will not continue. Also, the database server cannot contain any previously installed PerformancePoint databases. They must be deleted.

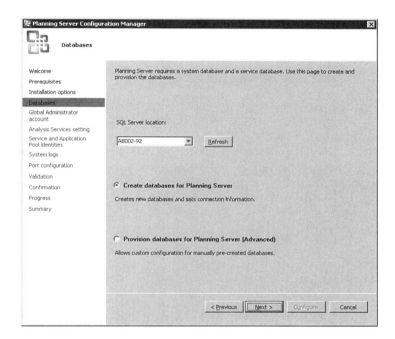

FIGURE 9.5   The Databases page allows you to create databases automatically or manually.

10. On the Global Administrator Account page, validate the account selected for access to the Planning Administrator Console. This is the first member of the Global Administrator role. This user will be able to add other members to the Global Administrator role through the Planning Administration Console and will have administrative permissions in the Planning Server system. Click **Next**.

11. On the Analysis Services Setting page, select the SQL Server Analysis Services server to be used for PerformancePoint cubes. Click **Next**.

12. On the Services and Applications Pool Identities page, enter the domain, user name, and password for the account for the service identity account. This user account will also be used as the Application Pool identity for the Planning Web Site and for the Planning Administration Console. Click **Next**.

13. On the Systems Logs page, leave all defaults for System log location, with auditing and trace logging enabled. Click **Next**.

14. On the Port Configuration page (shown in Figure 9.6), uncheck the **Require SSL connections to all Planning Server Web sites** box. If you want, you can leave this option on, but keep in mind the port numbers for your SSL connections. Otherwise the TCP ports will be necessary for accessing the 'Planning Web Service' and the 'Planning Administration Console'. Click **Next**.

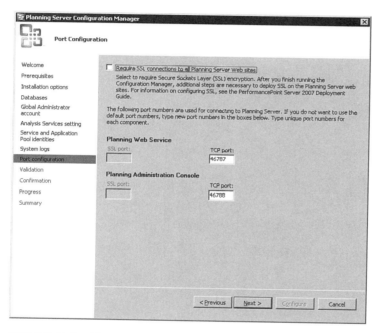

FIGURE 9.6   The Port Configuration page is used to establish your TCP/SSL ports.

15. On the Validation page, make sure your options are all lit up in green and then click **Next** when the installation validation completes.

16. On the Confirmation page (shown in Figure 9.7), review the information, and then click **Configure**.

17. On the Summary page, click **Close** to complete the installation process.

To begin using the PerformancePoint Planning application, open Internet Explorer and navigate to http://localhost:46787.

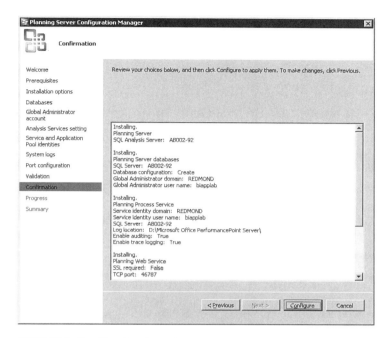

FIGURE 9.7   The Confirmation page allows you to review your choices before you apply them.

Installing PerformancePoint Planning Business Modeler

The next part of the process involves the installation of the PerformancePoint Planning Business Modeler. To do this, begin the installation again and then perform the following tasks:

1. On the installation splash screen, click **Install Planning Business Modeler**.

2. Accept the licensing terms (much like we did before) and click **Next**.

3. On the Directory Selection screen, select the location of the Business Modeler files. You can Browse to a new location or check for available space. Click **Next**.

4. On the Install screen, click the **Install** button. The installation then extracts all necessary files and places them on the file system. This process takes a few minutes.

5. On the Status page, click **Finish** to complete the installation process.

Under **Start > Programs > Microsoft Office PerformancePoint Server 2007**, you should see a link to PerformancePoint Business Modeler. (Remember, this is a desktop tool and would be installed on user machines.)

Installing PerformancePoint Planning Excel Add-In

Your next step is to install the Excel Add-in by performing the following steps:

1. On the installation splash screen, click **Install PerformancePoint Add-in for Excel**.

2. Accept the licensing terms and click **Next**.

3. On the Directory Selection screen, select the location for the Excel Add-in files. You can Browse to a new location or check for available space. Click **Next**.

4. On the Install screen, click the **Install** button. The installation then extracts all necessary files and places them on the file system. This process takes a few minutes.

5. On the Status page, click **Finish** to complete the installation process.

When you open Excel, you will now see a PerformancePoint menu/ribbon tab.

Installing PerformancePoint Monitoring Server

Your next step in the process is to install the PerformancePoint Monitoring Sever by performing the following steps:

1. Double-click **setup.hta**. The PerformancePoint Server 2007 splash screen will display. Click **Install PerformancePoint Monitoring Server**. Prerequisites are assessed. To proceed, all must be met.

2. Accept the licensing terms.

3. On the Directory Selection screen, select the location for the PerformancePoint Server files. You can Browse to a new location or check for available space. Click **Next**.

4. On the Install screen, click the **Install** button. The installation then extracts all necessary files and places them on the file system. This process takes a few minutes.

5. When installation is complete, the Monitoring Server Setup screen appears. Before clicking Finish, make sure the **Run the Monitoring Server Configuration Manager** check box is enabled.

6. On the Welcome screen for the 'Monitoring Server Configuration Manager', click **Next**.

7. On the Prerequisites screen, validate that all prerequisites have been met. Click **Next**.

8. On the Installation Options, make sure all Standalone configuration options are selected. Click Next.

9. On the Database page, select a SQL Server database. (It defaults to the current server.) Click **Next**.

> **NOTE**
>
> It must be a SQL Server 2005 database with SP2. If your selection is not, the installation will not continue. In addition, the database server cannot contain any previously installed PerformancePoint databases. They must be deleted.

10. On the Web Site page, uncheck the **Require SSL connections to Monitoring Web site** check box. Leave the defaults for the remaining fields. Click **Next**.

11. On the Application Pool Identity page (shown in Figure 9.8), leave the defaults. Click **Next**.

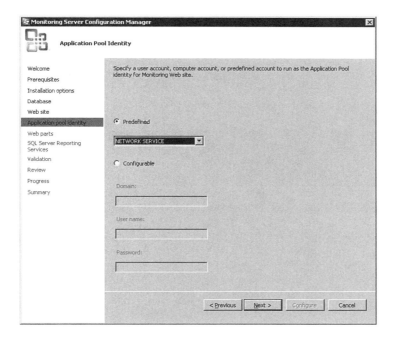

FIGURE 9.8   The Application Pool Identity page allows you to use a predefined or configurable account.

12. On the Web Parts page, select the SharePoint site where you would like to view dashboards. Click **Next**.

13. On the SQL Server Reporting Services page, select the Reporting Services instance on which to deploy the Scorecard Viewer for Reporting Services. Then click **Next**.

14. On the Validation page (shown in Figure 9,9), click **Next**.

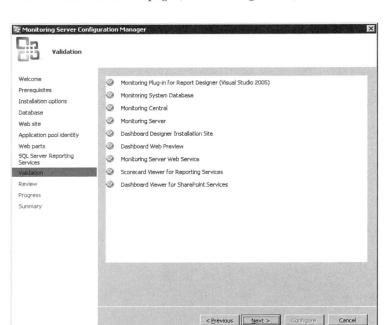

FIGURE 9.9   The Validation page shows you all the features that will be installed.

15. On the Review page, shown in Figure 9.10, you can finalize the options you've chosen, or, if you need to make any corrections, select the 'Previous' button. Click **Configure**.

16. On the Summary page, click **Close** to complete the installation process.

Beyond Installation

Installation of a server or application is just the first step in the process. The server you've installed is a clean slate and will do your business no good unless you move forward and begin the configuration process and, even then, it's not until you have the client-side to the server under your control that you can begin to see the real value in PerformancePoint Server. So, we encourage you to read on and gain the mastery over the Configuration and Client portions of PerformancePoint. Only then will Business Intelligence truly be said to have come to your company.

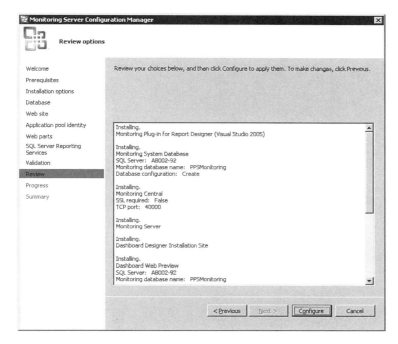

FIGURE 9.10   The Review page shows you the options you have chosen.

CHAPTER 10

PerformancePoint Server 2007: Configuration

This chapter covers the configuration of various components of PerformancePoint Server. Because this is an administrator's guide, you don't have to be an expert in business intelligence (BI) or in analytics. Readers who do have experience with financial analysis and metrics might know a bit more about BI and analytics than the average admin, but for most readers this will be a new experience.

To properly configure PerformancePoint Server tools, you need a somewhat different mindset. To effectively configure the various modules, you might need to collaborate with the departments that will use the tools; but isn't that the direction of the future, from a technology perspective? More collaboration.

Collaboration has become the hottest corporate technology buzzword in the past three years, but in general, the technology-to-business marriage has not in the past been one of voluntary collaboration. Instead, in many environments, it has been one of tolerance. But that line that separates business from technology is becoming less distinct, and PerformancePoint Server certainly blurs the line further. So, embrace it! Those already in a collaborative environment will see those bonds and reliances become stronger. Those who have not forged those kinds of working relationships will be treading new ground. Of course, this calls for flexibility and for doing things you might not be comfortable with. Don't worry; we spend our careers pioneering new technology, and we can now add to that pioneering new ways of working and collaborating within our organizations. Let's begin with the configuration of the Planning Server system via the Planning Administration Console.

Working with the Planning Administration Console

The Planning Administration Console is a Web-based configuration tool used to configure Planning Server. In the current CTP4 version of PerformancePoint Server 2007,
the console is installed as a Web site and is launched from within Windows Internet
Information Services (IIS). You can use the Planning Administration Console to create
and manage various aspects of PerformancePoint Server, such as applications, model
sites, users (users will need to be assigned roles), and data connections.

> **NOTE**
>
> To connect to the Administration Console, the user must be assigned one of the
> following administrative roles on that Planning Server system: Global Administrator,
> User Administrator, Data Administrator, or Modeler.
>
> Options for various tasks in the Administration Console are based on the role's
> permissions. Although permissions are needed to access the Planning Server system,
> the Administration Console can be accessed by all users after installation. Microsoft
> recommends restricting access to the Administration Console by using the security
> permissions within IIS.

To access the Administration Console, open a Web browser and enter the address of the
Planning Administration Console Web page (this is located on the same server on which
Planning Server is installed; for this discussion, however, we'll use http://localhost:xxxxx),
as shown in Figure 10.1.

FIGURE 10.1   The Administration Console for PerformancePoint Server.

Within the Administration Console, we can see the different administrative tasks that we can control in PerformancePoint Server 2007. Let's take a look at those tasks and how to administer them. Table 10.1 shows the links from the left navigation pane.

TABLE 10.1   The Links for Working with the Planning Administration Console (according to the Microsoft Help files for PerformancePoint 2007)

Link	Definition
Connection	Type the path to the computer running Planning Server to which you want to connect.
Applications	Create an application, edit an application, or delete an application.
Model Sites	Create a new model site for a specific application, edit an existing model site, or delete a model site.
Users	Find a user in the Planning Server system by querying on identifying information, add users to or delete users from the Planning Server system, or edit the identifying information for an existing user. You can also import new users into the Planning Server system.
Global Administrator Role	View the current members of this role, and add users to or remove users from the role.
User Administrator Role	View the current members of this role (for a specific application or for a specific model site within an application), and add users to or remove users from the role for a specific application.
Data Administrator Role	View the current members of this role (for a specific application or for a specific model site within an application), and add users to or remove users from the role for a specific application.
Modeler Role	View the current members of this role for a specific application (for a specific application or for a specific model site within an application), and add users to or remove users from the role for a specific application.
Session Settings	Specify Planning Server session limits on a per-user and total-user basis, and specify a chunking size to indicate the number of rows of data to load to the computer running Planning Server on a per-chunk basis. In addition, specify the maximum number of records to return when Planning Business Modeler requests data from the server, and specify the number of seconds before Planning Server times out when requesting data from Microsoft SQL Server.

10

TABLE 10.1   Continued

Link	Definition
Auditing	Specify the maximum size for the audit log file before a new audit log file is created and written to and specify the maximum size of the SQL Server AuditRecords table to determine when Planning Server will stop accepting user requests and processing new work items. In addition, specify the amount of time (in milliseconds) before the queue is checked for new audit entries. You must use the Planning Server Configuration Manager to change the name or location of the audit log file.
Event and Trace Logs	Enable or disable event logging, which writes to the Windows Event Viewer, or enable or disable Planning Server trace logging. Trace logging provides more in-depth and customizable logging than what is written to the Windows Event Viewer.
Planning Process Service	Specify the maximum number of work items allowed in the queue and the amount of time that must elapse before the server checks for new entries on the queue.
Workflow	Enable or disable notifications. When you enable notifications, you must specify the name of the Simple Mail Transfer Protocol (SMTP) server and provide the email address you want to appear in the From line of outgoing notification email messages.
Reporting	Planning Server utilizes SQL Server Reporting Services. Set the location where operational reports are published to and where Planning Server reports are stored.
Cancel Checkout	You can use the Planning Administration Console to reset the check-out status of model site objects.
Data Sources	Specify an external data source to connect to the Planning Server system.
Data Destinations	Specify an external destination to which the Planning Server system will export data.

On the first page, the Connection page, you can see the location of the computer you are connected to (which is running Planning Server). You can change the location and click the Connect button if you need to connect to an alternate Planning Server system.

Applications

Applications in PerformancePoint Server are the database itself and often reflect the structure of your business. Each application you create will define models, reports, and forms. In addition, it will define local and shared dimensions, views, permissions, and process-scheduling metadata associated with the database.

The Applications Page

The Applications page of the Planning Administration Console includes options to create, edit, and initialize applications, and so you use this page to create and edit your Planning Server applications. Application management includes setting the location of forms and templates and provisioning SQL Server application databases and staging databases.

After you have created an application, a process explained later in this chapter, you have the following options from within the console:

- **Take Online.** This setting makes the application available to users with suitable permissions

- **Take Async-Offline.** With this option, you can allow users to interact with the application even while you are turning off the Planning Process Service. (We discuss what the Planning Process Service is and how it is used in the Planning Server system later in this chapter; for now, it is only necessary to know that we must stop this process to prepare the application to go completely offline.) Workflow tasks already in the queue will be processed, but no new tasks will be added to the queue. Applications must be taken to this state before they can be taken offline.

> **NOTE**
>
> To take the application completely offline, all items must be processed and the queue empty.

- **Lock.** This setting locks the application, which can only be done in the async-offline and offline states. While in this state, no new tasks can be added to the application. However, in this state, Data Administrators or Modelers who have permissions to the application can access the application in the Planning Business Modeler.

- **Take Offline.** This setting will make the application unavailable to all users. When an application is in the offline state, a user cannot interact at all with the application (not even within the Planning Business Modeler or within the PerformancePoint Add-in for Excel).

- **Delete.** This option enables you to delete an application that is no longer in use. This setting differs from taking an application offline in that it removes all stored data, not just access to that data.

Figure 10.2 shows the Application portion of the Administration Console, along with various radio buttons for tasks that can be performed.

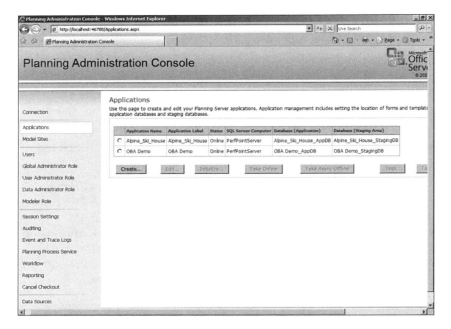

FIGURE 10.2   The Application portion of the Administration Console.

Create a New Application

This section covers how to create a new application. In BI, applications often reflect the organizational entities or needs. For example, the Sales and Marketing department might share resources with the Human Resources and IT departments, but each department might need different things, and so you might want to have an application for each of them.

To create an application, follow these steps:

1. Click the **Create** button to create a new application. The Create an Application dialog will appear, as shown in Figure 10.3. You need to complete this application to create a Planning Server application. Required fields are indicated with an asterisk (*).

    ▶ **Name.** The name of the application. This can be up to 256 alphanumeric characters, but special characters, spaces, and punctuation are not permissible characters in the naming convention of your application. Name is a required field.

    ▶ **Label.** This is case sensitive and must be from 1 to 40 alphanumeric characters long. As with the name, special characters, spaces, and punctuation are not permissible characters in the naming convention, and this is also a required field. Avoid using the underscore in the label (because Planning Server uses the underscore to link objects, and so including an underscore in the label might cause naming conflicts).

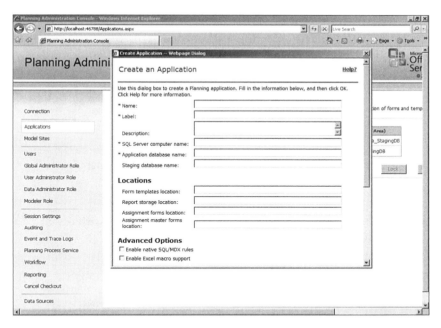

FIGURE 10.3   The Create an Application dialog box (top portion).

> ▶ **Description.** Your description can help define what the application is or the type of data it contains. The description can be 512 characters long, and it is an optional field; however, you should include a description so that you can readily understand the purpose for your application in the future.

> ▶ **SQL Server computer name.** The name of the SQL server and instance name that contains the database; this is a required field. Remember that you must be running SQL Server 2005 for the application to work properly with SQL.

> ▶ **Application database name.** The unique name of the application database. This is a required field.

> ▶ **Staging database name.** Again, this is a unique name for the staging database of the application. It is not necessary to create a staging database when you first create the application. You can go back and add a staging database by editing the application. This is an optional field.

  2. After filling in the fields listed here, scroll down, and then click **OK**.

Technically, you could end the process here (and you would have a new application). However, you might want to consider filling in a few other sections of the application, such as Locations, Advanced Options, Application Scripts, and Default Model Site. Let's consider some of these options in the sections that follow.

Locations

Within the Locations section of the Create an Application dialog box, you can add the locations for supporting documents that are stored within Microsoft SharePoint or on a network share.

> **NOTE**
>
> It is important that permissions be enforced on directories storing these documents. Only the Planning Server system account should be given read, write, and modify permissions to these directories. Except for the reports storage location, Excel Add-in users need read permissions to view reports and to read, write, and modify permissions to create shared reports.

▶ **Form templates location.** Specifies the location of forms associated with assignments. For the Planning Business Modeler to display a list of form templates, a location must be specified.

▶ **Report storage location.** Specifies the location of reports to be distributed to PerformancePoint Add-in for Excel users through assignments. For the Planning Business Modeler to display a list of reports, a location must be specified.

> **NOTE**
>
> If locations are not selected for the form templates and reports storage locations, PerformancePoint for Excel Add-in users might encounter errors and will be able to save form templates and reports to nonstandard locations. Therefore, to keep these items consistent across and organization, it is important to specify a location for these items.

▶ **Assignments forms location.** Specifies the location for assignment instances for the application.

▶ **Assignment master forms location.** Specifies the location of the master forms for the application.

Advanced Options, Application Scripts, and the Default Model Site

Within the Create an Application dialog box, you can scroll down a bit to see some of the other options available, as shown in Figure 10.4.

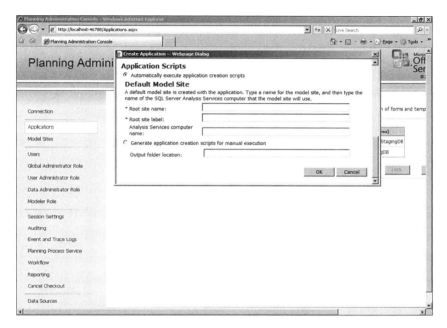

FIGURE 10.4   The Create an Application dialog box (bottom portion).

The following are check boxes under the heading Advanced Options within the Create an Application dialog box:

> **Enable native SQL/MDX rules.** Allows business analysts to use native SQL and Multidimensional Expression (MDX) rules within the Planning Business Modeler.

> **Enable Excel macro support.** Allows PerformancePoint Excel Add-in users to create macros for the Planning Server system.

Under Applications Scripts, you have two options:

> **Automatically execute application creation scripts.** This is the default setting (designed and intended for test deployments, not to be in production environments).

> **Generate application creation scripts for manual execution.** This will allow a database administrator to review and customize scripts before they are run (the application will have to be initialized to be made available to end users). You must supply an Output folder location.

10

When choosing to automatically execute application creation scripts, the default model site is also created. In this case, you must configure the following:

▶ **Root site name.** The name of the root site. This can be composed of up to 256 alphanumeric characters. Special characters, spaces, and punctuation are not permissible characters in the naming convention. This is a required field.

▶ **Root site label.** This is case sensitive and must be from 1 to 40 alphanumeric characters long. As with the root site name, special characters, spaces, and punctuation are not permissible characters in the naming convention, and this is also a required field. Avoid using the underscore in the label (because Planning Server uses the underscore to link objects).

▶ **Analysis Services computer name.** This is the name of the server where the model site data is to be stored; SQL Server Analysis Services must be running on this server.

Model Sites

Model sites organize data in the applications into models and their fundamental parts (these include mapping information and security as well as business process information).

The Planning Administration Console enables you to create, edit, and delete model sites. The process of creating a model site is similar to creating a new application. You supply certain information pertaining to the model, but before that you must choose which application the model site will be associated with, as shown in Figure 10.5

FIGURE 10.5   The Model Sites page from the Planning Administration Console.

Create a Model Site

After we have the application the model site will be associated with, we can begin creating a new model site (a task that can be completed only by a Global Administrator). To create a model site, click **Create**; the Model Site Web dialog box will display, as shown in Figure 10.6. Within this dialog box, you supply the following information:

▶ **Name.** Specify the name of your model site. This is a case-sensitive name and can be up to 256 alphanumeric characters. Special characters, spaces, and punctuation are not permissible characters in the naming convention of your application. Name is a required field.

▶ **Label.** Specify a label for the model site. This is case sensitive and can be composed of 1 to 40 alphanumeric characters. Special characters, spaces, and punctuation are not permissible characters in the naming convention of your application. Label is a required field. Avoid using the underscore in the label (because Planning Server uses the underscore to link objects).

▶ **Description.** A description can help you define the model site or the type of data the site contains. The description can be up to 512 characters long, and it is an optional field.

▶ **SQL FileGroup.** This group should be created before you create the model site; otherwise, the default SQL FileGroup will be used. Here you want to specify the FileGroup data associated with the model site (for example, measure data). For more information about how to create SQL FileGroups, refer to the Microsoft PerformancePoint Server 2007 Deployment Guide.

▶ **Analysis Services computer name.** This is the name of the server where the model site data is to be stored; SQL Server Analysis Services must be running on this server.

After you have entered the required information, click **OK**. You now have a new model site.

> **NOTE**
>
> From the Model Sites page, you can also edit or delete a model site. Keep in mind, however, that you should make sure you have a saved copy of your data before you delete a model site.

10

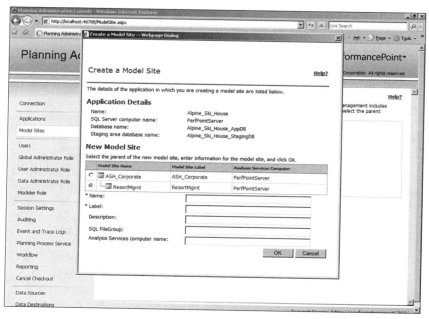

FIGURE 10.6   The Create a Model Site page.

Users and Roles

As mentioned previously in this chapter, all domain users can access the Planning Administration Console by default. Therefore, it is a good idea to alter the IIS settings if you want to prevent users from doing this; however users must be assigned a role if they are to actually administrate any aspect of the Planning Server system.

Create a User

Setting up a user is relatively simple and begins with clicking the **Users** link from the console. Figure 10.7 shows the Planning Administration Console's User page. On this page, click **Add**. The Add a User dialog box will appear and request information about the user (who must already have a valid domain user account). You are then asked to provide the following information:

- ▶ **Display name.** The name that will be displayed in PerformancePoint Server

- ▶ **Used ID (domain name\email alias).** This is the Domain User account type in the following manner: PERFPOINTSERVER\ron.

- ▶ **E-mail Address.** The email address of the user

After you have finished filling in this information, click **Add**.

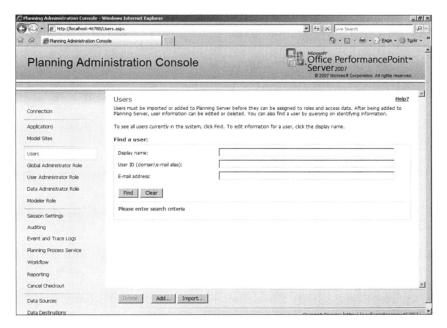

FIGURE 10.7   The Users page from the Planning Administration Console.

Import Users

To import users into the Planning Server system, you use a CSV (comma-separated value) file. The file should be set up for import as shown in the example in Table 10.2. (The email information is optional).

TABLE 10.2   How to Format Your CSV File

Label	Name	Email
PERFPOINTSERVER\ron	Ron Barrett	rbarrett@somedomain.com
PERFPOINTSERVER\tim	Tim Duggan	tduggan@somedomain.com
PERFPOINTSERVER\nick	Nick Saccomanno	nsaccomanno@somedomain.com

When the CSV file is ready, click **Import** on the Users page. Browse to the CSV file you prepared, and then click **OK**.

NOTE

The admin performing the import must have at least read permission to the CSV file being imported.

10

Finding a User

The Users page contains a Find a User section. To locate a user whom you have included in your console, enter one of the properties of a user in the Find a User section (display name, user ID, or email address [which is an optional setting and may or may not work here]), and then click **Find**.

Deleting a User

After locating a user (or users), you might want to delete that user. To do so, on the Users page enable the check box located to the left of the user's information, and then click the **Delete** button.

Roles for Planning Server

At this point, we need to discuss roles and the permissions each has within Planning Server.

Global Administrator Role

This role allows you to change settings on any server in the system that is running Planning Server. The Global Administrator has rights to create, modify, or delete applications and model sites; modify data source and destination connections; add or remove users to the Planning Server system; assign users to the User Administrators or Global Administrators role; and manage server settings such as workflow, auditing, and session settings. Figure 10.8 shows the current Global Administrator in our test domain.

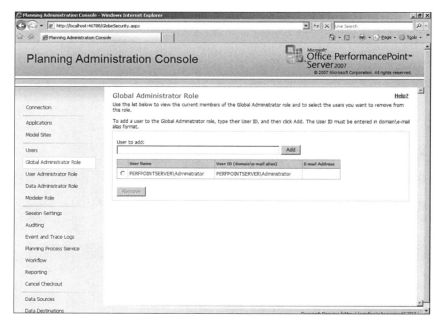

FIGURE 10.8   Global Administrator Role page in the Planning Administration Console.

User Administrator Role

This role allows you to change settings only for the application or model site to which you are assigned.

> **NOTE**
>
> If a user is added to the application, that user automatically has rights to all model sites belonging to that application. For more granular control, you can assign a user to the model site within an application to allow rights only to that model site. Permissions to a model site are not inherited by their subsites, so necessary permissions must be given to each model site and subsite the User Administrator needs to manage.

The User Administrator has permission to manage users in the Modeler, Data Administrator, and User Administrator roles within Planning Server; and can add or remove Planning Server users from business roles in the Planning Business Modeler. As you can see in Figure 10.9, the User Administrator role has more granular assignment ability.

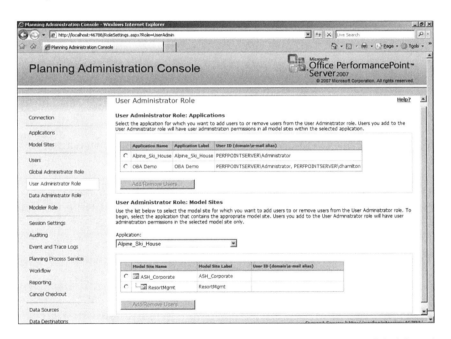

FIGURE 10.9   The User Administrator Role page in the Planning Administration Console.

Data Administrator Role

Like the User Administrator, Data Administrator settings apply only to applications and model sites to which you are assigned. In addition, Data Administrators assigned to a model site do not only have permissions to the application or subsites within that model site. The Data Administrator can create and edit workflow processes, perform data integration tasks, create and configure data, and set up business roles in the Planning Business Modeler. Figure 10.10 shows how Data Administrator roles are assigned.

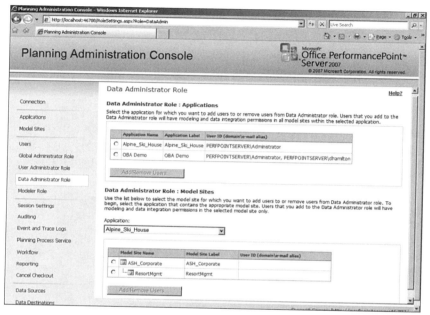

FIGURE 10.10   The Data Administrator Role page in the Planning Administration Console.

> **NOTE**
>
> Users in the Data Administrator role have access to *all* business data within their scope, even if their business role has restricted access. Because these users can browse databases, consider carefully which users you add to this role.

Modeler Role

In the Modeler role, the user can create and configure workflow processes, data, and business roles in the Planning Business Modeler. As with the Data Administrator, these users have access to all data within their scope regardless of the restrictions to their business role. As with the former two roles, the Modeler role allows assignment to either an application overall or to specific model sites. Figure 10.11 shows the role assignments.

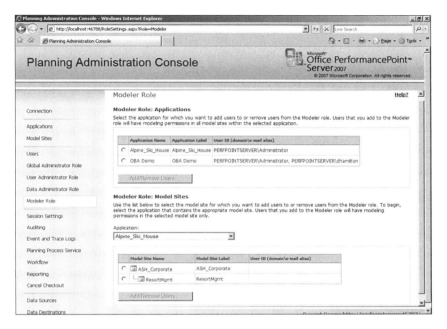

FIGURE 10.11   The Modeler Role page in Planning Administration Console.

PerformancePoint Server Settings

You can configure a variety of settings, and this section walks you through them.

Session Settings

These are preference settings for the Planning Server system. Table 10.3 shows the values that you can set.

TABLE 10.3   Session Settings and Their Defaults

Setting	Default
Session timeout	60 minutes
Maximum sessions per user	128
Maximum total sessions	134,217,728
Chunking size	100,000 rows
Maximum number of query results	1,000
SQL Server timeout	1,200 seconds
Planning Server MDX command timeout	1,800 seconds

10

Auditing Settings

Auditing settings are saved to an XML file that records transactions on the Planning Server system. These transactions might include starting an application, deleting an application, creating a workflow job, creating a recurring workflow job, or adding a user to the Planning Server system. The audit log will help you to identify when a transaction occurred and who invoked that transaction.

There are read-only restrictions on some audit settings (such as "Audit file name" and "Audit writer computer name"), which means you see these items but cannot change them. But, you can change some setting. Table 10.4 shows the settings you can change and their defaults.

TABLE 10.4   Auditing Settings and Their Defaults

Setting	Default
Maximum log size	10MB
Maximum queue size	1,048,576KB
Poll interval	60,000ms

If after making changes to these settings you want to return them to the defaults, just click the **Reset Defaults** option.

> **NOTE**
>
> To make changes to auditing preferences, you must stop and restart the Planning Process Service. In addition, to preserve the integrity of the audit log, it is recommended that you access-protect it.

Events and Trace Logs

Event logging is turned on by default and writes major events to Windows Event Viewer. For an administrator, this is one of the areas of PerformancePoint Server that will seem familiar. The practice of server software logging events is not new in the Microsoft world. However, trace logging is not enabled by default; it has to be enabled by a Global Administrator (shown in Figure 10.12). Trace logs contain standard Windows event messages, along with more specific and detailed information, to help troubleshoot PerformancePoint events. As in the regular event log, trace logs have "levels" of events, as follows:

▶ **Trace error.** Errors that occur within Planning Server and indicate a failure or incorrect configuration, these errors may include application, operation, and user errors. These errors pertain only to Planning Server and can be fixed by a Planning Server administrator.

▶ **Trace warning.** Warnings that indicate a potential failure in Planning Server function; again, these errors pertain to Planning Server only.

▶ **Trace information.** Records events and progress in the Planning Server system, such as the creation or import of a new user(s).

▶ **Trace detail.** As the name suggests, this is the most detailed level of information about events that are taking place in the Planning Server system.

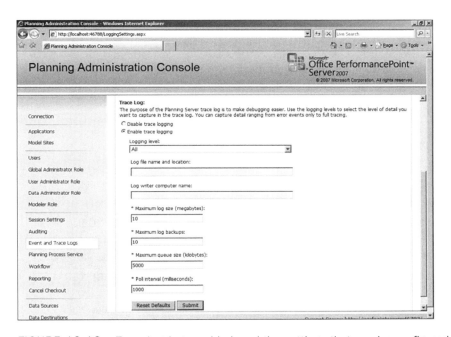

FIGURE 10.12   Trace logging, enabled, and the settings that can be configured.

Planning Process Service

The Planning Process Service is used to control the size and time interval used for the polling of the workflow queues. These workflows use the SSB (SQL Service Broker) to run long or isolated processes asynchronously. Three SSB queues are created by Planning Server for each application. These are the assignment queue, the submission queue, and the job queue. The Planning Process Service ensures that these queues run effectively. Table 10.5 shows the settings and their defaults.

TABLE 10.5   Planning Process Service with Default Settings

Setting	Defaults
Maximum number of queue rows	1,000
Poll interval	60,000 milliseconds

10

Workflow

This creates a notification in the form of an email when a form has been assigned to a user and work needs to begin. Workflow also sends notification when assignments are submitted, approved, reviewed, or rejected. By default, workflow notification is not enabled. When configured, an email notification can be sent. Either the email or a SharePoint Web page can then launch the PerformancePoint Excel Add-in (the Excel Add-in must be installed on the client's computer) with the appropriate assignment.

> **NOTE**
>
> An administrator must install the PerformancePointProtocolHandler.exe file and install it on either the user or machine that will launch the Web link. The following instructions on how to do this are from the Microsoft help file within PerformancePoint Server 2007's Planning Administration Console Help. The Web links use the following syntax:
>
> PerformancePoint:http:\\< *server name* >:< *port number* >&application=
> < *application name* >&assignment=< *assignment number* >
>
> Follow this procedure on each client computer from which users will access assignments. The PerformancePoint Add-in for Excel must be installed on the client computer.
>
> To enable Web links to assignments, follow these steps:
>
> 1. From a command prompt, navigate to *<drive>*:\Program Files\Microsoft Office PerformancePoint Server\3.0\Excel Client.
> 2. To install PerformancePointProtocolHandler.exe, use one of the following options:
>
> To install the feature per user, type **PerformancePointProtocolHandler.exe REGISTER:U**, and then press **Enter**.
>
> To install the feature per computer, type **PerformancePointProtocolHandler.exe –REGISTER:M**, and then press **Enter**.
>
> To uninstall the Web link feature, navigate to the same directory and type **PerformancePointProtocolHandler.exe –UNREGISTER**, and then press **Enter**.
>
> See "Create a Web Link to an Assignment" in the Planning Business Modeler Help for information about creating links in assignment email notifications and on SharePoint Web parts.

Reporting

No system that provides performance and analytic information would be complete without the ability to report on such information. Microsoft no doubt recognized that importance and has provided PerformancePoint Server with reporting capabilities on the Planning Server side. These reports are available not only for the end user, but for the Administrator as well to allow them to see the flow and health of the Planning Server. Planning Server supplies two kinds of reports: operational and business.

Operational Reports

These are reports about the system such as assignments, forms, and cycles. These can be used to monitor the health of the Planning Server system. These reports are produced by using SQL Reporting Services. Planning Server provides eight predefined reports, but these reports are not authored in Planning Server itself. You can use the Excel Add-in to view operational reports (as discussed in more detail in Chapter 11, "PerformancePoint Server 2007: Clients"). Because these reports can be used by several planning applications, it is necessary to configure the operational report location only one time.

> **NOTE**
>
> The predefined reports need to be moved to an accessible share after Planning Server installation. Because the reports are written in Report Definition Language (RDL) format, they must be published to the SQL Reporting Service. You can find instructions for publishing them to the SQL Reporting Service in the PerformancePoint Server 2007 Deployment Guide.

Business Reports

As the name suggests, business reports are directed solely at the business side. Server health and back-end data is not contained in this report. Instead, these reports contain financial information, such as cash flow and balance sheets. The reports are manipulated and reviewed using the Planning Business Modeler and Excel Add-in. These reports are used for viewing financial information and data entry. Configuration consists solely of specifying the reports' locations. And, as with operational reports, these reports are also published to the SQL Reporting Service.

Cancel Checkout

Data Administrators and Modelers can check out models, associations, and dimensions to perform maintenance. When items are checked out, workflow tasks are frozen; other users cannot write data to the object. Canceling checkout frees those objects for editing. Exercise caution when using the Force Cancel Checked Out Objects option; this option will check those items back in and delete any changes made to those objects within the model.

Data Sources

From the Data Sources page, you can add, edit, delete, and activate your source data connections. You can also assign which servers and databases will be used as "sources." Figure 10.13 shows the settings for creating data sources.

Data Destinations

As can be expected the Data Destinations page is the flip side of the coin. All of the functions provided in Data Sources are also provided for the Data Destinations page. You can add, edit, delete, and activate "outbound" data. In contrast to data sources (for which you can assign "sources"), in the Create a Data Destination Connection dialog box, you can assign which servers and databases will be used as "destinations." Figure 10.14 shows an example of this.

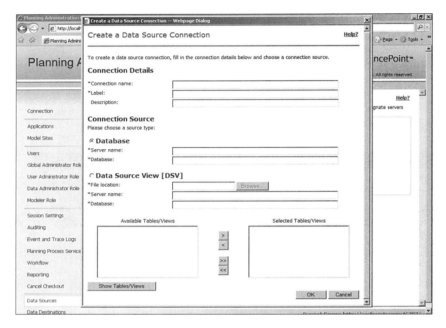

FIGURE 10.13   The Create a Data Source page.

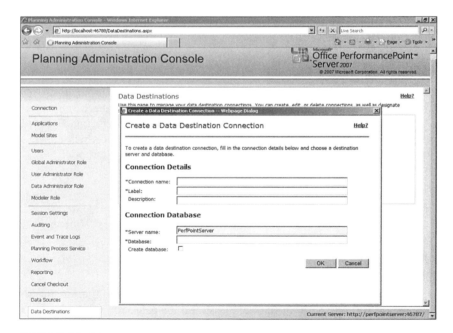

FIGURE 10.14   The Create a Data Destination Connection dialog box.

Configuration for BI

So that covers the configuration portion of PerformancePoint Server. Again for those who have some BI background such as those who have worked with Cognos, OutlookSoft, or SAP, PerformancePoint will still be a new experience for you, because PerformancePoint was built from the ground up unlike many of the newest, purchased and revamped products coming out of Redmond these days. This product was meant to be developed as something different from those products. Although Microsoft intended the configuration of PerformancePoint Server to be logical and easily understandable, the database nature of the product slows down some administrators. It can be daunting if you haven't had prior database, BI, or performance-monitoring experience. One chapter cannot make up for lack of experience; nor can it explain everything. You can, however, find detailed explanations of the topics in this chapter within PerformancePoint Server 2007 help files.

This chapter covered PerformancePoint configuration, but there is still more for you to learn. The next chapter focuses on PerformancePoint client-side configuration. That chapter covers various client concepts, including client types and settings. Even after working through this chapter and the following one, you most likely will still not be an expert BI end user. However, you will find it easier to support PerformancePoint clients.

10

PerformancePoint Server 2007: Clients

Regardless of whether you are an end user of business intelligence (BI) tools in your organization, it is essential that you at least understand what your end users are experiencing. Perhaps you will find that the tools in PerformancePoint Server 2007 can benefit your department, too. This might be particularly so if you have the dual duty of being in charge of budgets. As discussed in Chapter 9, "PerformancePoint Server 2007: Overview and Installation," PerformancePoint Server has several integrated tools on both the server and client side. In this chapter, we focus on the client-side tools.

PerformancePoint Server tools are categorized into three segments: monitoring, analytics, and planning. This chapter examines these tools and explains the installation, configuration, and some basic usage. Remember, however, that this is an administrator's guide, so we are not trying to create BI masters; we just want to make you proficient enough to support the users in your organization.

For those familiar with the previous versions of these products, Business Scorecard Manager 2005 and ProClarity Analytics, you will be pleased by PerformancePoint 2007's integration of the two performance management solutions into one product.

NOTE

With the release of PerformancePoint Server 2007, customers who purchased ProClarity or Business Scorecard Manager (and are current on their software assurance and product maintenance) will receive upgrades to the full version of PerformancePoint Server 2007, including all three capabilities: monitoring, analytics, and planning.

Working with Dashboard Designer

The first client we will look at is the Dashboard Designer. This tool is part of the monitoring category of tools. We will look at how to install the Dashboard Designer, and then take a look around the module. But first, what is a dashboard?

A *dashboard*, or *digital dashboard* as they are more commonly called, is a tool used to establish how a business is doing reaching or maintaining their goals. You could liken it to your car dashboard, which reports to you key performance data at a glance.

The dashboard uses various indicators from different areas of the business and presents it in one (visual) medium, to provide a clear view of businesses "health." Dashboard Designer is Microsoft's tool for creating this visual medium. Those who have worked with Business Scorecard Manager might be familiar with some of the concepts and functionality. Contrary to popular belief, a dashboard is more than "eye candy" for executive managers, more than just a fad; instead, it is a powerful monitoring and analytical set of tools surrounded by a visually appealing (if you are a good designer) wrapper.

Elements

The Dashboard Designer comprises six elements; within these elements, you can create, edit, and delete workspaces. You can also view properties and set permissions, and each element has a Server and Workspace tab. The six elements are as follows:

▶ **Dashboards.** In PerformancePoint 2007, dashboards are a group of scorecards and reports organized into a single view. These may make up a single SharePoint site. Dashboards contain common filters that control which elements are viewed. In this workspace, you can create, delete, and edit items. You can also add and remove additional pages and link reports to a page.

▶ **Key Performance Indicators (KPI).** KPIs are measurements or metrics used to compare actual business performance against the targeted expectations. These indicators can be of both a financial and nonfinancial nature. KPIs will differ depending on the organization, but will ultimately evaluate the present state of your business and prescribe a future course of action.

▶ **Scorecards.** Used to measure multiple areas of business performance. Scorecards may consist of KPIs, metrics, dimensions, and objectives.

▶ **Reports.** In Dashboard Designer, you can create charts, pivot tables, spreadsheets, Web pages, and several other analytical reports.

▶ **Data sources.** Three kinds of data sources are supported in Dashboard Designer: multidimensional connecting, to either SQL Analysis Service or SAP data sources;

standard queries using the ODBC (Open Database Connectivity standard) connection to the data; and tabular lists, which connect to data from Excel, SharePoint lists, and SQL Server tables.

▶ **Indicators.** These are our visual gauges. Dashboard Designer offers several different indicators, including gauges, stoplights, thermometers, progress bars, and other miscellaneous items.

After that brief introduction to the six workspaces in Dashboard Designer, now let's look at how to install the product to the desktop.

> **NOTE**
>
> Obviously, designing dashboards may (or may not) be your forte. However, you are not alone in needing assistance. One of the best sites available for learning more about dashboards and their design, or simply downloading free templates, is the Dashboard Spy (http://dashboardspy.com). And, to see the definitive collection of business dashboards, check out the sister site http://enterprise-dashboards.com/.

Installing Dashboard Designer

Dashboard Designer is installed from the Monitoring Central Web page.

> **NOTE**
>
> You can find the URL for the Monitoring Central Web page in the Microsoft Office PerformancePoint Server 2007 startup menu. For our purposes, we are using a single server to accomplish all our server roles.

When you open the Web page, you will see two radio buttons: Run and View (see Figure 11.1). Clicking the Run button will download the Dashboard Designer to your local machine.

FIGURE 11.1   Monitoring Central Web page shows install and view option for Dashboard Designer.

The dashboard will now download and run from your local machine. After the initial setup has been run, the Dashboard Designer places a shortcut in your Start menu. Because the Dashboard Designer is part of the monitoring tools and is run as an application from within Internet Information Services (IIS), not much is needed from the outset in the way of setup and configuration. So, let's take a deeper look at Dashboard Designer and learn about the interface.

Overview of Dashboard Designer

At first glance, the Dashboard Designer interface might look familiar. Figure 11.2 shows the initial default view of the Dashboard Designer.

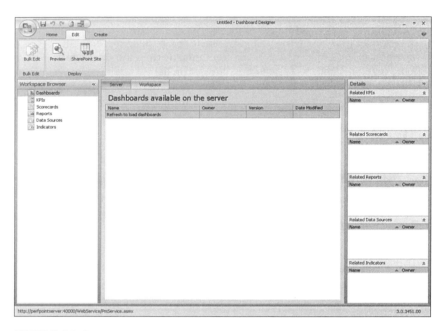

FIGURE 11.2   Dashboard Designer default view.

Yes, the Dashboard Designer is built with the now famous or infamous (depending on your perspective) Office 2007 ribbon. Below the ribbon are three columns: Workspace, Workspace Browser, and Details.

Workspace

This is the center column and the largest area. The workspace has two tabs: Server and Workspace. The Server tab lists the names of dashboards, KPIs, scorecards, reports, data sources, and indicators that are saved on the server. The Workspace tab lists the names of dashboards, KPIs, scorecards, reports, data sources, and indicators that are saved in an individual workspace. The information saved includes the name, modified date, owner, and version.

Workspace Browser

Here you can choose and work within your six elements. In the workspace browser, you can create, copy, paste, delete, and publish your workspaces. When working within an element that has been created, such as a scorecard or KPI, you receive two new tabs, as follows:

▶ **Editor.** Here you actually create the items for your dashboards. These items may be thresholds or actual target information for a KPI or aggregations of KPIs and set formulas within a scorecard.

▶ **Properties.** This tab is composed of General Properties, Custom Properties, and Permissions. Figure 11.3 shows the Properties tab in detail.

General Properties. This section deals with items such as name, description, person responsible, and location of the display folder.

Custom Properties. This section deals with background information, which would only be viewable within Dashboard Designer. It can consist of text, date, numeric values, and hyperlinks. Custom properties are useful for creating remarks about the elements created, such as the source of the statistics, indicators, or research.

Permissions. Here you can add a user and enable the Reader or Editor roles for that element. These permissions apply to users who have rights to use Dashboard Designer.

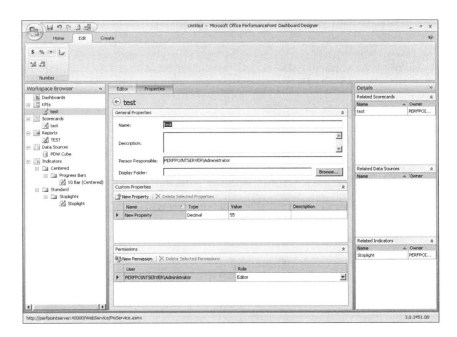

FIGURE 11.3   A view of the Properties tab within the test KPI element.

Details

In the Details pane, you can add more information to your elements and can view the elements related to them. The default view shown in Figure 11.4 shows the related elements for a demo corporate scorecard.

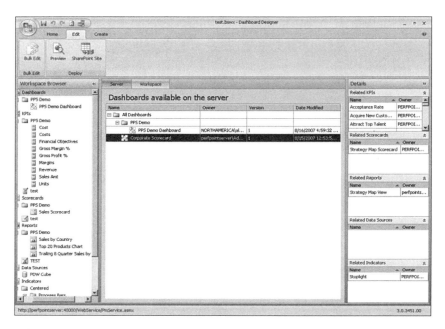

FIGURE 11.4   Demo corporate scorecard shows types of related items that appear in the details pane.

The ribbon is made up of three tabs, as follows:

▶ **Home.** From this tab, you can work with familiar features such as Clipboard functions, actions, and changes. This tab stays consistent regardless of which element you are working within. Here you can publish, copy, and compare data. And you can complete other tasks that are similar to working with Excel.

▶ **Edit.** This tab changes tasks that are available according to which element you are working within. Here you perform functions such as deploying to SharePoint or SQL Reporting Services or using number functions and bulk editing indicators.

▶ **Create.** This tab has two sections: Objects and Reports. The Objects segment launches the templates and wizards to create workspaces in Dashboard Designer. The Reports section launches the wizards to create charts, grids, maps, Web pages, and of course, reports.

Working in Dashboard Designer

Next we look at creating a workspace in Dashboard Designer. This will give us an idea about how to work within each of the elements. Let's start with a new dashboard.

Creating a Dashboard

Open Dashboard Designer and either right-click the dashboard within the workspace browser or click the Dashboard icon under the Create tab. Doing so launches the Dashboard Template window. In this window, you can choose a dashboard layout. You can choose from one to three zones, and can choose rows, columns, or both. As shown in Figure 11.5, the Dashboard Template window displays seven different templates by default.

FIGURE 11.5   Creating a new dashboard.

Next, choose a name for your dashboard and a display folder. After you create a dashboard from the template, you can right-click within the workspace and add more columns and rows (and top or bottom zones) if needed. When you have the initial layout for your dashboard, you can then drag and drop objects into your Dashboard view. These include scorecards, reports, and filters. Let's move on to the KPI workspace.

Creating a KPI

From the Create tab, you can click the KPI icon. You have two options for creating KPIs; you can choose to create either a blank or objective KPI.

NOTE

The objective KPI enables you to add the totals of child KPIs into the KPI you have created.

Once again, choose a name and the display folder. After the new KPI has been created, you can click in the Edit window to change the number format, thresholds (see Figure 11.6), data mappings, and calculation methods.

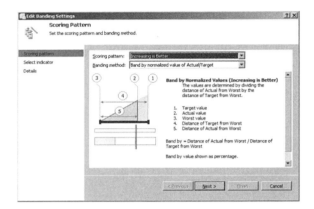

FIGURE 11.6   Setting a new threshold scoring pattern value for a KPI.

Creating a Scorecard

To create a new scorecard, choose **Scorecard** from the Create menu. Then choose which kind of scorecard to create. You can choose from ERP, Microsoft, Standard, and Tabular:

▶ **ERP.** Uses the SAP standard for scorecards and KPIs for PerformancePoint servers that connect to SAP NetWeaver BI data source.

▶ **Microsoft.** Uses a SQL Analysis Services data source to create the scorecard.

▶ **Standard.** Creates either a blank scorecard with no content or data mappings or a fixed-value scorecard that creates a scorecard and KPI with *user-entered* values.

▶ **Tabular.** Uses Excel or Excel services, SharePoint list, or SQL Server tabular data sources to create the scorecard.

Let's take a look at how we create a scorecard in Figure 11.7. For our example, we will choose a Microsoft Analysis Services scorecard.

1. After choosing the scorecard type, click **OK**.

2. Name the scorecard and choose the display folder. (For our example, we will leave this blank.) You can also choose to allow all authenticated users read rights to the scorecard.

3. Select a data source. Now we choose a data source for our scorecard, this can be either a server data source or workspace data source. (We discussed earlier the difference between server and workspace objects).

4. Select a KPI source. Here we choose whether we want to create the KPI source or import it from SQL Analysis Services.

5. Add KPIs to the scorecard. Now we can either select to add a KPI or to select an existing KPI.

6. Add measure filters. We can select measure filters for our scorecard. There are two types of filters we can add: member filters or time filters.

7. Add member columns. In this section, you can add member columns; these columns allow the designer to add dimensions and members to the scorecard.

8. Create the scorecard and confirmation. Next we click Finish and get a detailed view of the indicators and KPIs created; this last step also confirms whether all items were created correctly.

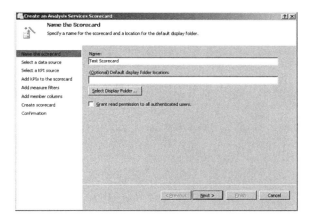

FIGURE 11.7   Creating a scorecard wizard.

After the scorecard has been created, you can drag and drop related items from the Details pane into the workspace, items such as metrics, aggregations, and dimensions. And that completes the preview of scorecard creation. We will skip reports for now because it has its own segment on the Create tab

Data Sources

To add a data source, click the **Data Source** icon in the Create tab. The Data Source Template Wizard will open. You can next choose form three different kinds of data sources, as follows:

▶ **Multidimensional.** Created from SQL 2005 or SQL 2000 Analysis Services or from a SAP NetWeaver connector

▶ **Standard queries.** Created from ODBC sources

▶ **Tabular lists.** Created from Excel workbooks or services, SharePoint lists, or SQL Server tables

Choose your data source type and name your data source. When the data source is completed, you can then choose your SQL Server, database, and role. You can also view related KPIs and scorecards in the workspace.

Indicators

Next we choose our indicators. The Template Wizard can again be launched from the Indicators icon on the Create tab. Figure 11.8 shows the various types of indicators available to PerformancePoint users by default.

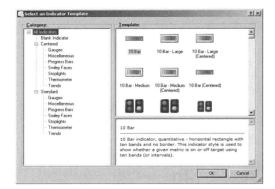

FIGURE 11.8   The Indicators Template Wizard showing the default indicators available.

You have the choice of choosing a blank, centered, or standard indicator. Figure 11.8 shows the various types of indicators that can be used. Indicators can have from 1 to 10 levels of gauges for use in a dashboard.

Reports

The next segment of the Create tab is the Reports section. Users can create several types of reports for use in the Dashboard Designer. Figure 11.9 shows the Template Wizard along with the available reports types.

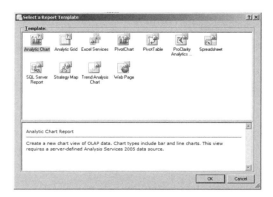

FIGURE 11.9   View of the 11 types of reports available in Dashboard Designer.

For our example, let's create a Trend Analysis report:

1. Choose **Other Reports** from the Create tab, and then choose **Trend Analysis Report**. The wizard will pop up.

2. Name your scorecard and choose the optional display folder. Then click **Next**.

3. Select the scorecard that you want the report to be associated with and click **Next**. You will see the scorecard load. When the scorecard is loaded, you can choose the KPI.

4. Here you can select the KPIs you want to use in your report.

5. Next the report will be created, and confirmation will be given that the report is complete.

After your Trend Analysis report is complete, you can right-click in the workspace area and choose additional menu options to customize your report.

After you have completed your dashboard, you can save and publish your workspace to SQL Reporting Services or to a SharePoint site. This completes our overview of Dashboard Designer. Next we will look at the Excel Add-in.

The PerformancePoint Excel Add-in

Now we will install and look at the functions of the PerformancePoint Excel Add-in. First, though, let's look at what you can do with the PerformancePoint Excel Add-in. To install the PerformancePoint Excel Add-in, run the PerformancePoint Setup file and install the add-in; alternatively, go to a command prompt and navigate to the Excel Add-in folder (by default, this folder is created in *drive*:\Program Files\Microsoft Office PerformancePoint Server\3.0\Excel Client), type **PerformancePointProtocolHandler.exe**, and then type **Register U** to install per user or type **Register M** to install per machine.

Overview of the PerformancePoint Excel Add-in

After the add-in has been installed, it creates a PerformancePoint tab on the Microsoft Office ribbon to begin using the plug-in you need to connect to a Planning Server. Figure 11.10 shows the PerformancePoint tab in Excel and a connection to a Planning Server in process.

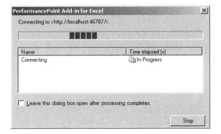

FIGURE 11.10   Excel Add-in connecting to a PerformancePoint Planning Server.

As you can see, there are several new functions added to Excel. Table 11.1 lists the ribbon segments and the function of each item.

TABLE 11.1   The PerformancePoint Excel Add-in Ribbon

Ribbon Segment	Item	Function
Connection	Connect	Opens the Connection dialog box and let's you choose a Planning Server connection.
	Offline	Allows you to take, manage, and work with assignments offline.
	Refresh	Allows you to refresh workbooks, worksheets, and system data or to clear your current changes.
Assignments	Assignments	Links contributors, reviewers, and approvers to their assignments.
	Auto Recalculate	Refreshes the entire form when a change is made to a cell.
Authoring	Reports	Allows you to create, open, edit, publish, import, or export reports. You can also run the Report Wizard.
	Matrix Styles	Allows you to create matrix, row, and column styles.
View	View	Provides three views: Normal, Annotated, and Multidimensional Expressions (MDX).
	Show Action Pane	Let's you see the actions taken on assignments.
Advanced	Jobs	Allows you to launch jobs assigned to you or to check the status of assigned jobs.
	Options	Sets the options for data entry, formatting, and for advanced options such as number of drill-through rows and choices for showing error messages or caching assignments locally.
	Connection Settings	Allows you to test and run diagnostics against various Planning Servers.
Help	Help	Launches the PerformancePoint Excel Add-in Help file.
	About	Shows information about the add-in such as version number of the client and server.

To begin working with assignments, you can either connect to a PerformancePoint Planning Server or users may receive an email with a link that will launch the PerformancePoint Excel Add-in right within your assignment. Users can then work with the assignment online or offline. The beauty of this tool is twofold. First, it is a familiar tool, which means only limited training is necessary. The only thing users have to learn is the new ribbon and what each function of that ribbon is (see Table 11.1). Second, there are some members of an organization who contribute to performance monitoring who do not need to have a host of tools installed on their machines. Again, the simplicity of working with something you are very comfortable with is a great advantage. With the Excel Add-in, you can submit data to the planning server, collaborate, analyze business models, and create reports. The Excel Add-in is also the key component of the workflow model for PerformancePoint Server. Used in conjunction with the Planning Business Modeler, it enables you to provide forms and author reports and to do some analysis using the Office LOB (Line of Business) data.

Because this tool uses Excel, which is already a commonly used product, and because this is only an administrator's guide, it is beyond the scope of this discussion to continue further explanation of this tool. Now it's time to move on to the PerformancePoint Planning Business Modeler.

The Planning Business Modeler

The Planning Business Modeler is the primary client-side application for the Planning Server, which would be considered the back-end infrastructure to PerformancePoint Server 2007 used to create and manage business models. These models take relevant but mostly incongruent data sets and put them into workable views that are used for planning, forecasting, and budgeting. The Planning Business Modeler is installed locally. Unlike the Excel Add-in, however, you must connect and remain connected to a Planning Server. To install the Planning Business Modeler to your local machine, run the setup file for PerformancePoint Server. On the opening splash screen, you have an option to install the Planning Business Modeler. Figure 11.11 shows the user interface for the Planning Business Modeler.

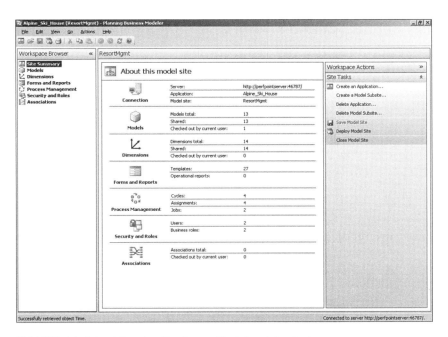

FIGURE 11.11   Planning Business Modeler default view.

Overview of the Planning Business Modeler

The Planning Business Modeler client is divided into three sections, just like the Dashboard Designer: Workspace Browser, Workspace, and Workspace Actions. We start in the site summary state. Here you can see in the workspace statistics information about (among other things) the model site, such as details about the connection, number of models, templates, and total number of users. Let's first look at the workspaces available, and then briefly examine each of the additional pages available in the workspace.

Business Modeler Workspaces

Within each workspace are additional pages with added functionality.

Site Summary

We already discussed this workspace briefly. Table 11.2 lists all items that are summarized in the Planning Business Modeler.

TABLE 11.2   Summary of Items Chart

Item	Summary Information
Connections	Server
	Application
	Model site
	Label
	Description
	Parent model site
Models	Models total
	Shared
	Checked out by current user
Dimensions	Dimensions total
	Shared
	Checked out by current user
Forms & Reports	Templates
	Operational reports
Process Management	Cycles
	Assignments
	Jobs
Security & Roles	Users
	Business roles
Associations	Associations total
	Checked out by current user

Models

This workspace contains both shared models, which belong to parent model sites, and independent models. In this workspace, you can see all the models on that Planning Server. The opening page gives information such as the following:

- ▶ Name of the model

- ▶ Label (for example, Expenditures, Strategic Plan)

- ▶ Model type

- ▶ Parent model site

- ▶ Shared

- ▶ Checked out by

Within a model, you have three additional tabs, as shown if Figure 11.12: Summary, Model Properties, and Business Rules. The Business Rules tab is one of the additional functionality tabs mentioned earlier. Here we can create set business variables for the model site. We can then parse, validate, and run the rule set.

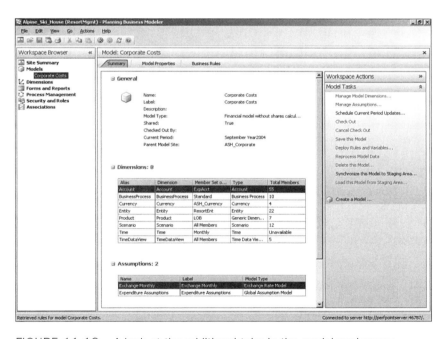

FIGURE 11.12   A look at the additional tabs in the model workspace.

Dimension

Dimensions are organized categories that describe data with similar elements (for example, Assets, Current Assets). The Dimensions workspace includes the General, Member, and Member Sets Maintenance tables. Figure 11.13 shows an example of the member sets.

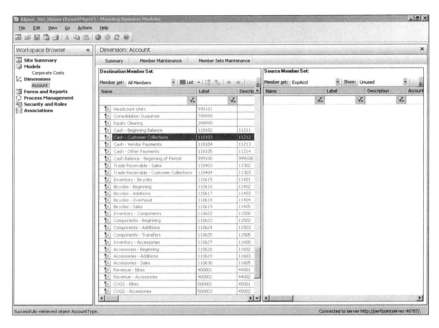

FIGURE 11.13   View of the Dimension Workspace, Destination member set.

Forms and Reports

This section contains forms (Excel spreadsheets) that serve as templates for the model site. This section also holds the operational reports that where discussed in Chapter 10, "PerformancePoint Server 2007: Configuration."

Process Management

Process management provides an area to manage assignments, scheduled jobs, and cycles within a model site. The Process Management workspace is divided into three areas: Cycles (default view), Assignments, and Jobs. You can create a cycle, see available actions, or schedule a job.

11

Security and Roles

Use this area to assign rights to users and roles that are registered to the Planning Server. This workspace has three views, as follows:

- ▶ **Business Users.** Lists all users who are assigned to the business role on the Planning Server

- ▶ **Business Roles.** Lists all the business roles available in a model site

- ▶ **Administrative Roles and Users.** List users who belong to administrative roles (listed by role and divided by application and model site)

Associations

In this workspace, we can create and monitor associations. Associations are relationships between a source and destination model. These associations can be created for the purpose of aggregation of numbers or manipulation of interpretive data.

That concludes the overview of the Planning Business Modeler. Next we look at working with ProClarity.

Working with ProClarity

ProClarity is one of Microsoft's latest acquisitions. Launched in 1995, ProClarity has been a leader in business analytics. Since 1999, ProClarity has been working with Microsoft on their BI strategy. ProClarity is an analytics tool. (And because this is an administrator's guide, you'll find just an overview of the product here.) This section covers the installation, overview, and tour of the user interface. Again, this is not a detailed discussion of ProClarity. ProClarity Professional comes in application (ProClarity Desktop) and Web versions.

Installing ProClarity

ProClarity Professional installs differently depending on what version you are installing. Let's take a look at how we set up each version.

> **NOTE**
>
> You must be logged in with Local Administrator rights to install ProClarity Professional Desktop or Web versions on the user's machine.

Installing ProClarity Desktop Professional

To install ProClarity Desktop, install the product client CD and click **Install Desktop Professional** on the splash screen. You might be required to install or update Microsoft operating system or Office components. (Your system needs a restart before installing Desktop Professional.)

1. Click **Install Desktop Professional**.

2. Click **Next** on the welcome screen.

3. Accept the licensing agreement, and then click **Next**.

4. Input customer information, and then click **Next**.

5. Choose installed features and the installation location, and then click **Next**.

6. Review the installation settings, and then click **Install**.

7. When installation is complete, click **Finish**. Desktop Professional is now ready to run.

Installing ProClarity Web Professional

To install the Web Professional client, follow these steps

1. Add your Analytics Server Web site to your Intranet Security tab in IE.

2. Open your Web browser with the address of your Analytics Server (for instance, http://perfpointserver/PAS/en/src/ProClarity.asp).

3. Click the **Check for Downloads** link, as shown in Figure 11.4

4. Because we are talking about a first-time installation, you will be prompted to install the Download Manager. Click the radio button, when the download pop-up appears, choose **Open**.

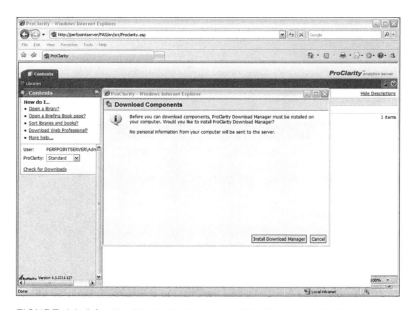

FIGURE 11.14   ProClarity Professional Web Client installation screen.

5. Next you will see the Download Manager dialog box. Select the **ProClarity Web Professional** component and choose **Download Now**.

6. A new download pop up will appear. Click **Run**.

7. The Setup screen will appear. Accept the licensing terms and click **Next**.

8. Click **Finish** when setup is complete, and close the Download Components page.

You are now ready to use ProClarity Web Professional client; no restart of IE is needed. Now that we have installed the clients, let's get an overview of ProClarity and the user interfaces of both the Desktop and Web client.

Overview of ProClarity

To understand what ProClarity does for the end user, it is necessary to explain a few new terms as they apply to ProClarity.

Terminology for ProClarity

▶ **Library.** Files that you have permission to open in ProClarity.

▶ **Briefing books.** A single or collective view created and saved with ProClarity Professional.

▶ **Drill down/up.** A familiar term when working with Pivot tables, here in ProClarity it refers to navigating data from summary *down* to detail, or from detail *up* to summary.

▶ **Cube.** A set of data organized and summarized into a multistructured set of dimensions and measures.

▶ **Decomposition tree.** A view that breaks down a measure to show the raw and percentage data for a component.

User Interface for Desktop Professional

Let's see what the users are looking at when they launch Desktop Professional. Figure 11.15 shows the Desktop Welcome screen.

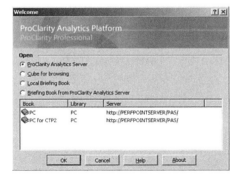

FIGURE 11.15   View of Welcome screen with connection choices.

The default toolbar allows you to navigate and work most functions in Desktop Professional. The toolbar buttons are as follows:

▶ **Back.** To move back to the last view.

▶ **Forward.** To move ahead to the next view.

▶ **Reset.** Resets book to the default view.

▶ **Apply.** Apply changes to your current view.

▶ **Setup.** Shows the setup panel with the data that can be used in cube queries.

▶ **Timeline.** Shows or hides the interactive timeline. Right-clicking the timeline will allow you to choose day, month, quarter, year, or all dates.

▶ **View.** Changes the view type, there are three view types: Advanced Analysis Tools, Business Charts, Grid.

Each of these has views particular to the function, such as performance maps or bar charts:

▶ **Sort.** This has the same features as the Sort function in Office: sort ascending or descending.

▶ **Filter.** Reduces number of visible rows to allow a more concentrated view of the data.

▶ **Wizard.** Launches a wizard to create a new multidimensional view. Based on the measures you choose.

▶ **Decomp.** Opens the Decomposition Tree Wizard, to select data in your book to analyze.

▶ **Analytics Server.** Enables you to retrieve and publish books and files and to manage books and change Analytic Servers.

Once installed, Desktop Professional has a great Getting Started PDF and a Getting Started Help File. Next let's look at the Web Professional client.

User Interface for Web Professional

Now we will look at the ProClarity Web Professional interface. Upon logging in, you will see the library and available briefing books. Open a briefing book to see a list of available folders and briefing book pages. Figure 11.16 shows the opening view of a briefing book page.

The navigation tabs change based on the briefing book page you have opened. The default tabs are as follows:

▶ Contents

▶ Navigation

- ▶ Data Layout

- ▶ View

- ▶ Sort

- ▶ Filter

Opening a page will launch the same interface as the Desktop Professional interface.

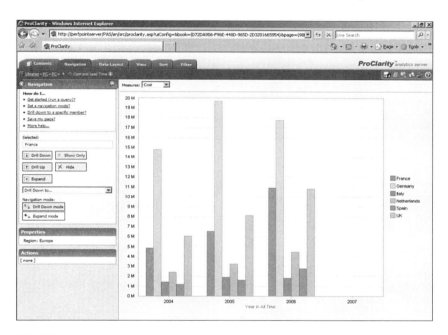

FIGURE 11.16   View of ProClarity Web Professional home page.

Other ProClarity Components

ProClarity also comes with a diagnostic utility, an Analytics Server administration tool, and the ProClarity dashboard tool. That finishes our overview of ProClarity. For more information about ProClarity and Microsoft BI, go to http://www.microsoft.com/bi/products/ProClarity/proclarity-overview.aspx or http://office.microsoft.com/en-us/performancepoint for evaluations, case studies, training, and pricing on PerformancePoint Server 2007.

Closing Words to Administrators

Well, this has certainly been an interesting ride. Performance management and business intelligence are certainly not new subjects to us "technology" guys. Microsoft's leap into this arena is a good thing for us, built upon a familiar Microsoft platform, using familiar

Microsoft back-end products such as SQL Server 2005 and SharePoint Services. In addition to expanding on the capabilities of some of Microsoft's backend system, they have also focused on the front-end applications like Excel and provided us with a Web-based interface. All of these items combined makes PerformancePoint Server 2007 an easy Office server to learn to install and administrate.

Understanding the mechanics of BI and performance management are a bit more difficult, but our hope is that these chapters, along with the many good resources provided by Microsoft and others, can help you to install, navigate, and even support PerformancePoint Server 2007.

NOTE

To stay up-to-date on the latest and greatest of PerformancePoint, visit http://www.microsoft.com/business/performancepoint/.

And if you want to download the RTM software and more technical information, go to http://technet.microsoft.com/en-us/office/performancepoint/default.aspx.

CHAPTER 12

Project Portfolio Server: Overview and Installation

Microsoft Office Project Portfolio Server 2007 is a portfolio management enterprise solution that integrates with other systems, such as Microsoft Office Project Server 2007 and Windows SharePoint Services (WSS) 3.0. This chapter introduces the concept of portfolio management and its evolution over the years, describes how Project Portfolio Server addresses the challenges related to portfolio selection and management, and provides instructions for installing Project Portfolio Server 2007.

Understanding Portfolio Management

The discipline of portfolio management dates back to the late 1970s and early 1980s when the increased use of project management in organizations led to the creation of decision support models to aid in the selection of projects. This came as a result of too many projects that were outside of the strategic objectives of the organization or were too costly given the expected benefits from the project. Organizations began to apply the theories of financial portfolio selection to the selection of projects in an organization. The functional areas of information technology and product development led to the development of frameworks and techniques used to define portfolio management. In both cases, senior leadership teams were forced to decide which products/systems were more important to the organization assuming a limited amount of resources. The process was usually undertaken as part of an annual capital budgeting process. Classic tools included checklists, models for sorting, or mapping projects based on defined attributes and scoring models using financial or nonfinancial measures.

By definition, project selection and prioritization involves assessing individual projects relative to all other projects (and to groups of projects) to determine which ones to implement according to the strategic objectives of the organization and the available resources. In 2006, the Project Management Institute issued its Portfolio Management Standard, which defined the discipline of portfolio management as follows:

> Portfolio management is the centralized management of one or more portfolios in order to achieve specific strategic business objectives. As a process, portfolio management enables organizations to identify, categorize, evaluate, select, prioritize, authorize, terminate, and review various portfolio components to ensure their alignment with current and future business strategy and goals, which in turn helps organization optimize limited resources.
>
> As it is frequently stated, portfolio management deals with "doing the right project(s)" while project management deals with "doing the project right."

In the early 1990s, applications came into the market to support the analytical process for selecting projects in an organization. With the popularity of portfolio management growing, the challenge became one of prioritizing projects for the entire organization, which meant managing large sets of project information with an analytical toolset. In addition, with a new emphasis on governance policies due to Sarbanes-Oxley regulations, increased focus was given to collaboration of participants in the portfolio process that included project data input and signoff of project and portfolio decision making. A third challenge was to make portfolio management systems easy to use for all levels of management. Early models and frameworks were heavily analytical and considered cumbersome by users.

Today, a project portfolio management system collects individual project data from different project stakeholders; performs analysis of all projects based on defined attributes and set criteria; enables reviews by executive management to decide whether to pursue, hold, or kill a specific project; and reports on existing projects through the project life cycle, including the availability of resources to be applied to new projects. The project portfolio management system has become the repository of information on all of the projects in the organization. The use of templates helps to maintain the reliability and accuracy of the project and portfolio information. Sort and filter capabilities by predefined attributes allow for quick analysis of project portfolio data.

Key Differences Between Project and Portfolio Management Systems

Project management and portfolio management systems have gone through significant growth and evolution in the past 10 years as technology has allowed portfolio and project systems to merge while exhibiting capabilities that address each discipline respectively. There are, however, key differences between project and portfolio management capabilities. Although both summarize project-level attributes, a project management system tracks individual project performance against the original project plan. The emphasis is on single project controls and resource task assignments. Updates to the project plan are reflected in the project management system. The availability of resources for project work is known to all project managers through an enterprise resource pool. From a process perspective, a project management system will enable any standard project management methodology such as the initiate-plan-execute-control/monitor-close life cycle from the Project Management Institute.

The summary of all project work in the organization is available for review; however, planned projects in the project management system are assumed to have gone through a selection and prioritization process by the senior leadership team. As a result, the capabilities of a project management system generally do not include the assessment of project opportunities, strategic alignment, and scoring and ranking according to defined prioritization criteria.

The portfolio management system enables the creation of project opportunities, each associated with one or many portfolios in the organization. The project request will follow phases and activities in which different stakeholders provide input on the project request. All requested projects are analyzed against each new and existing project, based on defined criteria to determine whether a project (or sets of projects in the case of a program) is worth executing. Selection, prioritization (or ranking), and optimization of projects and resources are critical components of the portfolio management process. The portfolio management system provides the analytical toolset to achieve this. Once projects are reviewed and approved (or rejected) by the senior leadership, the rest of the organization is then informed, and the assigned project manager continues with the project life cycle. During the project life cycle, the portfolio level data will be synchronized with project information to ensure the accuracy of project- and portfolio-level information.

Introducing the Application Portfolio Management

A variation of the project portfolio management process is application portfolio management. In the case of application portfolio management, an information technology organization defines portfolios according to the major application groups of the enterprise. Similar to the enterprise project portfolio, project request with attributes, governance workflows, and selection and prioritization criteria support the decision-making process. Alignment of projects is not only done by strategic impact but also by processes supported by the applications. The end result is a portfolio of information technology projects catalogued by its perceived value to the organization and by the processes and businesses it supports.

Key Requirements for a Portfolio Management System

To better understand the main attributes of a portfolio management system, listed here are several capabilities that differentiate project portfolio management systems from other project systems:

▶ **Managing demand.** Requests for projects are generated by multiple sources in an organization. All projects, regardless of their size, represent work efforts in the organization that have to be evaluated and, if appropriate, planned and executed. The portfolio management system acts as the repository of all project requests and allows for the standardization of requests for more objective evaluation of projects based on uniform criteria.

▶ **Project topologies.** Within an organization, requests will be generated for different types of projects that vary in size, cost, and deliverables. The portfolio management system permits grouping of projects into multiple portfolios for comparison on an equivalent basis for similar project types.

▶ **Stakeholder involvement.** The importance of portfolio management systems has increased with the focus on corporate governance. Organizationwide decisions with significant impact now require greater oversight. Portfolio management systems now have workflow capabilities out-of-the-box. All stakeholders from the project requestor to the financial managers, project managers, and finally senior leadership can be involved in the creation of a project request, its completion, and signoff by different participants.

▶ **Strategic alignment.** The ability to bridge strategic objectives to projects that will support their achievement continues to be an important capability of portfolio management systems. With the development of more sophisticated strategic planning models, portfolio systems have maintained the ability to define the impact of projects on the organizational strategy.

▶ **Prioritization and optimization.** Together with strategic alignment, prioritization continues to be one of the main objectives of using a portfolio management system. Although Excel is a viable alternative for ranking projects, portfolio management systems now have more sophisticated modeling capabilities for multiple prioritization perspectives and optimization based on different types of constraints.

▶ **Budgeting and cost tracking.** The planning of budgets at a summary level has always been a project attribute taken into consideration in portfolio selection and prioritization. A portfolio management system provides the capability to disaggregate costs by cost types and cost centers. In addition, the tracking of project cost actuals and change requests that can affect the forecast of project costs at completion can also be maintained in the system.

▶ **Executive dashboards.** Reporting of status at the portfolio and individual project level is a requirement for the portfolio manager and the senior leadership involved in the governance process. Because the portfolio management system acts as the central repository of all portfolio information, executive dashboards with summary performance metrics can be produced directly from the portfolio management system.

▶ **Integration.** To enable both inputs and outputs from the portfolio system to other line-of-business systems, integration becomes a key component for leveraging project- and portfolio-level data. Status updates of selected projects in their respective portfolios might come from disparate systems making the need for system interfaces even greater. Therefore, an application programming interface becomes a critical component of any portfolio system.

Project Portfolio Server 2007 Overview

In mid-2006, Microsoft launched Microsoft Office Project Portfolio Server (MOPPS or Project Portfolio Server) as a best breed project portfolio management application. The Microsoft Office Enterprise Project Management (EPM) suite now includes Microsoft Office Project Server (Project Server) and Microsoft Office Project Portfolio Server. While Project Server provides the ability to perform very basic portfolio management tasks, Portfolio Server adds a new set of enterprise-class capabilities to enable an end-to-end project portfolio and application portfolio management process.

Project Portfolio Server is currently sold and implemented as a separate application server from Project Server. Microsoft has announced plans to integrate both Project Server and Portfolio Server capabilities into one EPM application in its future release. Despite being separate, Project Portfolio Server has a gateway for synchronization of project data between Project Portfolio Server and Project Server. For integration with other line-of-business systems, the Project Portfolio Server Interface (PPSI) is the application programming interface (API) that allows other applications to leverage portfolio- and project-level data in Project Portfolio Server.

Project Portfolio Server provides a Web-based client. The Portfolio Web Access (PWA) interface provides access for all users of the application. Server side, Project Portfolio Server requires a single application server to be installed for the system to be operational. However, similar to other Microsoft servers, MOPPS does not come configured out-of-the-box, requiring the support from an experienced Portfolio Server consultant to define the usage and configuration of the tool according to the requirements of the organization.

Project Portfolio Server consists of the three main modules: Builder, Optimizer, and Dashboard, described in more detail in the following sections.

Figure 12.1 shows a map of Project Portfolio Server and Project Server components and at which points of the process they are leveraged.

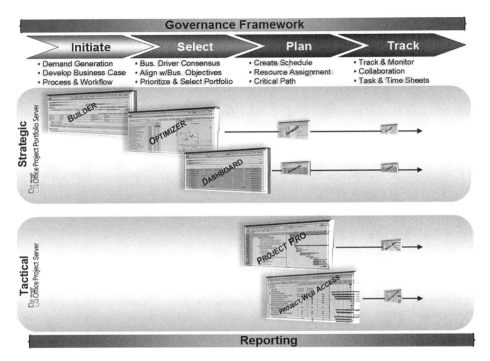

FIGURE 12.1   Project Portfolio Server and Project Server components are utilized during different process phases within the main process.

You can think of an overall project/portfolio life cycle as a four-step process with the following phases:

► **Initiate.** Supports the creation of projects using Project Portfolio Server and the development of detailed business case.

► **Select.** Supports the selection of optimal project portfolio based on the defined business drivers and other metrics.

► **Plan.** Supports creation and planning of projects, including detailed project plan development and resource assignments, and integration with Project Server.

► **Track.** Supports tracking and management of the project to a successful completion within Project Server. The data at this stage is synchronized with Project Portfolio Server.

The Builder

Builder is used during the Initiate governance phase and supports business case development, including resource requirements, cost estimates, benefit forecasts, strategic alignment, risk assessment, and phase and milestone planning.

The Builder module consists of the following functions:

▶ **Settings.** Allows system administrators and other super users to configure and manage Project Portfolio Server options and features.

▶ **My Scorecard.** Displays a portfolio selector with all portfolios and projects currently in the system. Using My Scorecard, users can capture all project requests within a central repository and define business case template to standardize the data collection across the organization. Then, the governance workflow is used to ensure that projects are subject to the appropriate governance controls throughout their life cycle.

▶ **Resource Pool.** Provides access to view various resource information, such as resource original availability, resource requirements, and resource actual availability.

▶ **Preferences.** Allows each user to customize his/her personal settings for specific functions within Project Portfolio Server.

▶ **Reports.** Allows users to view existing reports (public and private), and to create new reports.

The Optimizer

The Optimizer module is used during the Select governance phase and supports portfolio prioritization based on the strategic value, financial value, and risk value analysis and portfolio optimization based on charting analysis, constraint analysis, and advanced portfolio analytics.

In addition, Optimizer facilitates portfolio selection, where the approved portfolios continue to the next governance phase.

The Optimizer module consists of the following menus:

▶ **Edit.** Allows users to edit business drivers and projects within the selected portfolio.

▶ **Analyze.** Allows users to prioritize business drivers, assess the impact of each project request against the prioritized business drivers, prioritize projects, and finally analyze the project portfolio before attempting to make funding decisions.

▶ **Chart.** Allows users to choose a variety of options and chart types for displaying trend, aggregated, or divergence of opinion data in support of portfolio analysis.

▶ **Select.** Supports the portfolio selection process.

The Dashboard

The Dashboard module is used during two different governance phases for different purposes.

The Dashboard is used during the Select phase for the following:

▶ Support of the detailed planning to develop project plan, assign named resources, and define interdependencies

▶ Final approval

▶ Baseline

The Dashboard is used during the manage and track phases to do the following:

▶ Support portfolio tracking using change request management, status reporting, and portfolio reoptimization.

▶ Support project tracking using project tracking, resource management, time reporting, issues and risks management, document management, and team collaboration.

Relationship Between Components

Each of the Project Portfolio components supports different governance phases, and as projects transition from one phase to another, project information is passed from one module to another.

Expected Benefits from Project Portfolio Server

MOPPS offers capabilities that enable you to obtain a number of benefits from its implementation.

Visibility

The term *visibility* is often associated with the purpose of a portfolio management system. By centralizing and standardizing data collection, all present and future project requests can be found in MOPPS. The workflow capability of the system defines the roles of participants in the portfolio process and automates governance while maintaining control of the overall selection and prioritization process.

Objective Analysis

Without a portfolio management system, an organization will tend to rely more heavily on subjective factors to make the selection of projects. Standardization of project requests, governance, and selection and prioritization criteria increase objective factors in the portfolio process. Competing investments are prioritized from multiple dimensions, including business strategy, financial value, risk, or any other set of attributes in the system. The objective analysis of project data is supported by charting and mapping capabilities within the system.

Optimization of Project Portfolios

Prioritization in the context of portfolio management also includes the optimization of the portfolio based on different constraints faced by the organization. The most common constraints are resource constraints, financial, and human. However, MOPPS allows for optimization based on any attributes defined as constraints. The tools within MOPPS support the selection of the portfolio best aligned with strategic and financial goals. Management teams are presented different scenarios through a decision dashboard that displays all the relevant analysis to finalize the portfolio decisions.

Integration

The integration of Project Portfolio Server 2007 with Project Server 2007 occurs through several mechanisms. The Portfolio Server gateway is the automated connector for project data transfer with Project Server. Data is exchanged by running either an import or an export from Project Portfolio Server to Project Server in bulk and typically through a scheduled batch process. For more granular, near-real-time synchronization, the EPMSync Solution Accelerator can be used to synchronize Project Portfolio Server attributes with Project Server custom fields (and a set of project level built-in fields). Finally, the Portfolio Server interface is an API available for developing connectors between MOPSS and other line-of-business systems. Integration ensures data integrity across the Portfolio and Project Servers. For document management, MOPPS can integrate with Windows SharePoint Services and Office SharePoint Server. In addition, MOPPS can integrate multiple Project Server instances, making it possible to consolidate portfolio data at the enterprise level.

Project Portfolio Server 2007 Installation

The recommended deployment of Project Portfolio Server should follow three main phases:

- ▶ **Envisioning.** During this phase, your organization and its key players and decision makers must define the vision and scope for the Project Portfolio deployment. In addition to the solution itself, it is important that the organization is at a maturity level that can support operation of a system such as Project Portfolio Server, and that it has all appropriate processes and metrics defined.

- ▶ **Planning.** During this phase, make sure to define the solution (including the features and processes to be used and the security model) and map requirements and use cases to the configuration settings, its usage, and a rollout roadmap. The more thorough the planning, the easier the implementation is going to be.

- ▶ **Implementation.** Includes the installation, configuration, validation, deployment, and support of the solution.

TIP

Chapters 13 and 14, "Project Portfolio Server 2007: Configuration," and "Project Server 2007: Overview and Installation," respectively, concentrate on the first two parts of the implementation—installation and configuration; but before you move on to installation, make sure other phases' prerequisites have been completed.

This chapter discusses a single-server deployment scenario for Project Portfolio Server 2007 as an example for installation procedures, as shown in Figure 12.2. In this scenario, all components are installed on the same computer. This scenario can be used for small organizations, but the most common use is for testing the deployment.

Single Server

Project Portfolio Server 2007
SQL Server 2005
SQL Reporting Services

FIGURE 12.2   Project Portfolio Server stand-alone deployment.

TIP

For enhanced capabilities, consider installing Project Server 2007 and Windows SharePoint Services 3.0. For additional deployment scenarios, download the Microsoft Office Project Portfolio Server 2007 Deployment Guide from http://office.microsoft.com/portfolioserver.

Before continuing to the installation, review the minimum system requirements from the Deployment Guide, also listed in Table 12.1.

TABLE 12.1   Single-Server Installation Minimum System Requirements

Component	Requirement
Operating system, database, Web server, and utilities	Microsoft Windows Server 2003 SP1 (32-bit)
	Microsoft SQL Server 2005 Standard/Enterprise Edition SP1
	Microsoft Internet Information Services 6.x
	Microsoft .NET 2.0
Processor	2.5GHz
RAM	1GB (2GB recommended)
Hard disk space	1GB

Component	Requirement
Drive	CD-ROM or DVD drive
Display	800×600 (1024×768 recommended)
Browser	IE 6.0 with service packs or IE 7.0, 32-bit browser version
Network connection	100Mbps connection speed
Other requirements	Microsoft .NET Framework 2.0
	IIS 6.0
	ASP .NET 2.0
Additional components	SQL Reporting Services (included with SQL Server 2005), required for reporting
	Project Server 2007, required for Project Server gateway
	Windows SharePoint Services 3.0 (included in Windows Server 2003), required for document management

12

NOTE

System requirements depend on a number of factors that determine the load on the server. Considerations include the number of users and types of users, as well as the number of services on the server.

The following is the order for installing Project Portfolio Server 2007 and its components in a single-server environment running Windows Server 2003:

1. Install .NET Framework 2.0.

2. Install Internet Information Services (IIS).

3. Install SQL Server 2005 SP1.

4. Install Windows SharePoint Services 3.0 (optional for the use of the document management features).

5. Configure the SQL account (required in a distributed workgroup environment).

6. Install Project Portfolio Server 2007.

NOTE

During installation, make sure to use 32-bit Windows Server operating system, 32- or 64-bit SQL Server 2005, and 32-bit Reporting Services.

The following sections provide details about each step of installing Project Portfolio Server 2007 and its components.

.NET Framework 2.0 Installation

The first step is to install .NET Framework 2.0 by downloading it from the Microsoft page: http://www.microsoft.com/downloads/details.aspx?familyid=0856eacb-4362-4b0d-8edd-aab15c5e04f5&displaylang=en.

.NET Framework supports the Web component for Project Portfolio Server 2007 and is required.

Internet Information Services Installation

Project Portfolio Server 2007 and Windows SharePoint Services are Web based and require the installation of IIS. Table 12.2 provides instructions for installing IIS.

TABLE 12.2   IIS Installation

Installation Step	Details
Launch your server.	Click **Start**, **Administrative Tools**, **Manage Your Server**.
Add server role to the application server.	1. On the Manage Your Server page, click **Add** or **Remove Role**. 2. On the Configure Your Server Wizard page, click **Next**. 3. On the Server Role screen, select **Application server (IIS, ASP .NET)** and click **Next**. 4. On the Application Server Options screen, select **Internet Information Services (IIS)**, if not already selected. Do not select Enable ASP .NET because it will install .NET Framework 1.1 (which is unnecessary as you should have already installed .NET Framework 2.0). Click **Next**. 5. On the Summary of Selections screen, click **Next**. 6. Click **Finish**.
Configure IIS to use Secure Sockets Layer (SSL) for optimum security.	For steps on configuring SSL, visit the IIS 6.0 Deployment Guide by going to http://technet2.microsoft.com and searching for "IIS 6.0 Deployment Guide."

SQL Server 2005 SP1 Installation

Install SQL Server 2005 Service Pack 1 by installing SQL Server Database Services, SQL Server Reporting Services, and Workstation components, books online, and development tools.

For detailed installation instructions and other documentation, download SQL Server 2005 Books Online (May 2007) by visiting http://www.microsoft.com/downloads and searching for "SQL Server 2005 Books Online."

When installing SQL Server 2005, you can use either Windows Authentication (recommended) or SQL Authentication mode, however, SQL Authentication mode can be modified at any point after the installation.

> **NOTE**
>
> Project Portfolio Server 2007 is a 32-bit application, and even though all other components of its installation must be 32 bit, SQL Server 2005 can be 32 or 64 bit.

> **TIP**
>
> SQL Server Reporting Services must be running in the native mode.

12

Windows SharePoint Services 3.0 Installation (Optional)

When installing Windows SharePoint Services 3.0 (WSS) on the same computer as the Project Portfolio Server 2007, install WSS first on the default Web site and then create a new Web site to install Project Portfolio Server on. Table 12.3 provides steps for configuring a new Project Portfolio Server 2007 Web site.

> **NOTE**
>
> At the time of writing this book, there was no known way to connect the reporting features of Project Portfolio Server to a SQL Reporting Server running SharePoint Integrated mode.

TABLE 12.3   Windows SharePoint Services Installation

Installation Steps	Details
Create a new directory.	Create a new directory: C:\Inetpub\PortfolioServer2007.
Open IIS Manager.	Select **Start**, **Administrative Tools**, **Internet Information Services (IIS) Manager**.
Create a new Web site.	1. In the IIS Manager, expand the tree, right-click **Web Sites**, and select **New**, **Web Site**. 2. In the Web Site Creation Wizard, click **Next**. 3. Enter **Project Portfolio Server 2007** in the Description box, and click the **Next** button. 4. Create a Web site separate from the default Web site (port 80) by changing one of the following: the IP address, the TCP port number, or the host header. Consider using port 8080 for the Project Portfolio Server site. 5. Click the **Browse** button and browse to the C:\Inetpub\PortfolioServer2007 directory you created, clear the **Allow Anonymous Access to this Web Site** check box, and then click **Next**. 6. Select the **Read** and **Run Scripts** (such as ASP) check boxes, and then click **Next** to close the wizard.

SQL Account Configuration

Before installing Project Portfolio Server 2007, you must first configure SQL Authentication by creating a SQL account. Table 12.4 provides steps for configuring a SQL account.

TABLE 12.4   SQL Account Configuration

Configuration Steps	Details
Ensure SQL Authentication is enabled on the computer running SQL Server 2005.	1. Connect to the computer running SQL Server 2005 using SQL Server 2005 Management Studio. 2. In the Object Explorer window, right-click **SQL Server computer name** and select **Properties**. 3. Access the Security page and ensure that SQL Authentication or Windows Authentication is selected under the **Server Authentication**.
Create a dedicated SQL account for Project Portfolio Server.	The account permissions will depend on whether you will use an existing database or create a new one, such that ▶ If a new database is created, the SQL account will be required to have db_creator and db_securityAdmin permissions. ▶ If an existing database is used, the SQL account will be required to have db_datareader and db_datawriter permissions.
Select the **Database Authentication** option.	On the Database Connection Authentication screen, select **SQL Authentication** from the Database Authentication. The account information is then written to the web.config file and used to allow the Project Portfolio Server application server to communicate with the remote computer running SQL Server 2005.

Project Portfolio Server 2007 Installation

After all the components have been successfully installed, you can install Project Portfolio Server by following the steps in Table 12.5.

NOTE

If you are using a separate reporting server from the server running Project Portfolio Server 2007, you must install the Reporting Services component on that reporting server.

TABLE 12.5   Project Portfolio Server 2007 Installation Instructions

Installation Steps	Details
Set **Allow for IIS Web Server Extensions**.	1. Open IIS Manager by selecting **Start**, **Administrative Tools**, **Internet Information Services (IIS) Manager**. 2. Expand the tree, click **Web Service Extensions**, and set ASP .NET 2.0 to **Allow**.

Installation Steps	Details
Start the PPS.MSI installer.	1. Insert Project Portfolio Server 2007 installation CD and start the PPS.MSI installer. 2. Click **Next** in the wizard. 3. Review the license terms, accept them, and then click **Next**. 4. Enter your 25-character product key and click **Next**.
Select the site to install PPS under.	Select the site under which you would like to install Project Portfolio Server. Type in **PortfolioServer** as the name for the virtual directory that will be created to install Project Portfolio Server, and then click **Next**.

CAUTION

Do not use the default Web site to install Project Portfolio Server if you have installed Windows SharePoint Services on the same server. Refer to the section titled **Windows SharePoint Services 3.0 Installation (Optional)** in this chapter.

Select the features to install.	Select the features to install, and then click **Next**: ▶ **Web Site.** Contains the application part of the PPS. ▶ **Scheduler Service.** PPS scheduler that updates cached values on a regular basis.

NOTE

For security purposes, Scheduler Service should not be installed in the directory accessible through an IIS Web site or virtual directory.

	▶ **Reporting Services configuration.** Includes PPS standard reports and configuration changes. ▶ **Portfolio Component.** Contains the necessary PPS binaries to be installed on a remote reporting server that has SQL Server Reporting services installed on it. Do not select both this and Web site component.

CAUTION

As mentioned in the Deployment Guide, "If you have SQL Server Reporting Services installed on the same computer as Office Project Portfolio Server 2007, set the feature to install and then browse to the SQL Server Reporting Services installation location, typically located under C:\Program Files\Microsoft SQL Server\MSSQL.instance\Reporting Services\ReportServer. Do not select the subcomponent 'Portfolio Component.' Failure to browse to the correct path will result in a failure to install Office Project Portfolio Server 2007."

TABLE 12.5   Continued

Installation Steps	Details
Specify the primary database and create a new database.	1. Specify the primary database server on which PPS database should be installed. 2. Create a new database by selecting the **Create a New Database** check box and use the Integrated Windows Authentication or SQL Authentication to connect to the database server, and then click **Next**. The account used for database authentication must have db_creator and db_securityAdmin permissions on the computer running SQL Server 2005.
Specify Reporting Services URL.	In the Reporting Parameters and SMTP information page, specify the Reporting Services URL. For single-server deployment scenario, the URL is http://localhost/ReportServer/.
Specify the Reports folder.	Specify the Reports folder in which all PPS reports will be saved. The default value is /Reports.
Specify the SMPT server.	Specify the SMPT server used for sending email notifications. This server should be reachable on the default SMTP port 25 from the PPS application server.

NOTE

PPS will not function properly with SMTP servers that require authentication.

Specify the From address.	In the From Address field, specify the email address that will be used to send PPS notifications. Click **Next**.
Install PPS.	Click the **Install** button to install PPS. Click **Finish** to complete the installation.

Configuring Client Settings

In addition to the server configuration, it is important to note client settings that each individual user has to configure on his or her local machine.

TIP

Before individual Windows-authenticated users can use the Project Server gateway, they must first click the Preferences link in the Office Project Portfolio Server 2007 Web interface. This will initialize the user's connection to Office Project Server 2007.

Table 12.6 provides a list of client system requirements, detailed in the Deployment Guide.

TABLE 12.6   Project Portfolio Server Web Access Minimum System Requirements

Component	Requirement
Computer and processor	700MHz processor or higher
Memory	128MB of RAM or more recommended (additional memory might be required depending on the operating system requirements)
Hard disk	40MB of available hard disk space per workstation
Operating system	Windows XP SP2 or later, Windows XP Tablet Edition SP1 or later, Windows Vista
Display	Minimum 800×600; 1024×768 or higher-resolution monitor is recommended
Network connection	Office Excel 2003 or 2007 is required to load the matrix views in the Portfolio Optimizer module and generate reports. Adobe Acrobat 6.0 or higher is required to generate PDF reports.

In addition to the minimum system requirements, each individual workstation user must install appropriate ActiveX controls to ensure all features and views of the Project Portfolio Server are functioning correctly. Review pages 74 through 85 in the Deployment Guide for detailed instructions on configuring your browser settings.

Internet Explorer 7.0 Settings

In addition to the minimum system requirements, each individual workstation user must install appropriate ActiveX controls to ensure all features and views of the Project Portfolio Server 2007 are functioning correctly. Please review pages 74 through 85 in the Deployment Guide for detailed instructions on configuring your browser settings. The list of known ActiveX controls includes the following:

▶ Microsoft Office Project Portfolio Server Chart Display

▶ Microsoft Office Project Portfolio Server Chart Wizard

▶ Microsoft Office Project Portfolio Server Decision Dashboard

▶ Microsoft Office Project Portfolio Server Importance Matrix

▶ Microsoft Office Project Portfolio Server Insight Analysis

▶ Microsoft Office Project Portfolio Server Optimizer Spreadsheet

▶ Microsoft Office Project Portfolio Server Sensitivity Analysis

▶ Microsoft Office Project Portfolio Server Spreadsheet View

Table 12.7 provides steps for configuring IE 7.0.

TABLE 12.7   IE 7.0 Configuration

Configuration Steps	Details
Add Project Portfolio Server to the trusted sites.	1. In the IE 7, select **Tools**, **Internet Options**, **Security** tab. 2. Select **Trusted Sites**, and then click the **Sites** button. 3. Add the PPS URL to your trusted sites by clicking the **Add** button.
Modify security settings for trusted sites.	1. On the Security tab of the Internet Options, click the **Custom Level** button. 2. Scroll down to the ActiveX controls and plug-ins and ensure the following options are selected: ▶ **Download signed ActiveX controls—Enable or Prompt** ▶ **Run ActiveX controls and plug-ins—Enable or Prompt** ▶ **Script ActiveX controls marked safe for scripting— Enable or Prompt** 3. Scroll down to Miscellaneous and ensure the following options are selected: ▶ **Submit non-encrypted form data—Enable or Prompt** ▶ **Scripting—Enable or Prompt** ▶ **Active scripting—Enable or Prompt**
Disable the pop-up blocker.	In the Internet Options window, select the **Privacy** tab and clear the **Turn On Pop-up Blocker** check box.

Microsoft Office Excel 2007 Settings

In addition to the ActiveX controls, Project Portfolio Server takes advantage of Microsoft Visual Basic, which requires additional configuration of the Excel (2003 or 2007). Table 12.8 provides details for configuring Microsoft Office Excel 2007.

TABLE 12.8   Excel 2007 Configuration

Configuration Steps	Details
Modify macro security to trust access for Visual Basic projects and installed add-ins and templates.	1. Open Microsoft Office Excel 2007 and select **Excel Options**. 2. In the Excel Options dialog box, click the **Trust Center** link, and then click the **Trust Center Settings** button. 3. Select **Macro Settings** and select the **Trust Access to the VBA Project Object Model** check box. 4. Click **OK** twice. 5. Close Excel. 6. Restart IE to apply the changes.

Post-Installation Considerations

Once you installed Project Portfolio Server 2007 and all of its components, it is important to consider operational policies and maintenance procedures you will need to follow once the solution is deployed. This section provides high level items that you need to consider.

Validating Your Project Portfolio Server Installation

The first step after installing Project Portfolio Server includes validating your installation. This is an important step prior to configuring the solution as it allows you to discover any potential problems or errors and resolve them.

Perform the following steps to validate your Project Portfolio Server installation:

- ▶ Verify that the World Wide Web Publishing Service and Office Project Portfolio Server Scheduler services are running.

- ▶ Login as a super user (super/pass@word1). This is the default master account that has ability to add organization and the rest of the users. Make sure you change the password for the super user for security purposes.

- ▶ Create an account for your system administrator that will be used to configure the rest of the features and add other users.

- ▶ Validate NT authentication by logging in using the administrator account.

> **TIP**
>
> Download and review Microsoft Office Project Portfolio Server 2007 Deployment Guide for detailed information, tests, and common troubleshooting.

Project Portfolio Server and Its Components Monitoring

Reliability, performance, and security are vital to any organization. A proactive approach to managing your infrastructure requires real-time monitoring. This section outlines several recommendations for monitoring Project Portfolio Server and Windows SharePoint Services (WSS), and their components, and it is intended to complement your existing monitoring processes. As any system administrator knows, the first step in resolving any problem is becoming aware that a problem exists. Waiting for your user base to report an issue is a reactive approach and can result in unnecessary and redundant calls to your help desk.

Monitoring is a proactive way of managing your system, so consider the following procedures as part of your maintenance routine:

- ▶ Windows Server 2003 Log File Monitoring—The Microsoft Windows Server 2003 family provides an extensive mechanism for event log monitoring. If you have administered Windows Servers before, you are no doubt familiar with the Event Log Viewer built into the operating system. To find this valuable tool, select Start, Run, type in eventvwr, and click OK. The Event Viewer window launches.

Another important log to monitor for Project Portfolio Server is the security log. This log contains the successful and, more importantly, the failed attempts to authenticate on the Project Portfolio Server. Monitor this log carefully for potential illegal attempts to access your system.

TIP

Several third-party tools can monitor the event logs in Windows and alert you to potential problems in real time. Do a search online using the keywords: "Event Log Management software" for suggestions and potential software solutions.

▶ IIS Log File Monitoring—Keeping good IIS logging information is important primarily because it assists you in tracking down potential problems and provides a detailed record of transactions for security and monitoring purposes. IIS logs can contain a lot of useful information for recognizing unauthorized entries into Project Portfolio Server and Project Server, including IP addresses, information accessed, logon information, and so on. In addition to the security benefits, these logs contain error entries and time stamps that assist in identifying performance problems and other potential project server issues.

▶ SQL Server 2005 Monitoring—SQL Server usage, performance, database connections, and log files monitoring is an important part of your system maintenance. SQL Server 2005 monitoring consists of two main steps:

▶Establishing a baseline—An important element of monitoring SQL Server is creating a baseline. Over time, performance degrades, and it is difficult to troubleshoot problems without a solid baseline. It is recommended that you use the built-in Windows performance monitoring (PERFMON.EXE) for your baseline.

▶Tracing Events Using SQL Profiler—SQL Server 2000/2005 includes the powerful tracing tool, SQL Profiler. SQL Profiler can monitor the server and databases, providing an effective method of tracking activities and events associated with a SQL instance. SQL 2005 expands on the Profiler tool and offers another excellent tool called the *Database Engine Tuning Advisor*. The Advisor can help you optimize the performance of your SQL server and can further help you analyze the workload and physical implementation of one or more databases.

Project Portfolio Server Database Maintenance

Project Portfolio Server 2007 includes the following database based on your configuration:

▶ PPS2007_AccountIndex—database that includes the index of all organizations you have configured.

▶ PPS2007_AccountData—separate database created for each organization that contains that organization related data.

When maintaining Project Portfolio Server 2007 database, ensure that you address each database, where the total number of databases is equal to 1 index database plus number of organizations configured.

Simple Recovery

The Simple Recovery model is recommended for small implementations where database size and backup capabilities are concerns. Using the Simple Recovery model results in simpler backup and restore procedures. The main disadvantage is that you cannot restore to a specific moment in time but only to the time of the last backup. Organizations that choose this model typically back up nightly and can tolerate some data loss. In this model, when a restore is necessary, data entered since the last backup is lost.

Full Recovery

The Full Recovery method is recommended for larger organizations that can facilitate real-time backups throughout the day. The main advantage to this model is the capability to restore to a specific moment in time, which provides the capability to recover right up to the point of failure. The biggest disadvantages are the large transaction logs generated and the extra resources required to store, maintain, and confirm valid backups throughout the day. This method requires more thoughtful backup and recovery planning, or you will not have what you need when you need it.

Additional Considerations

As part of your Project Portfolio System deployment, it is recommended that you revisit and update accordingly (or define, if not already existing) the following processes:

- ▶ Regular system maintenance—regular, scheduled system maintenance is crucial for the system to continue to function correctly. Review your current system maintenance procedure and make sure that you add items specific to Project Portfolio Server that include:

    - ▶ Regular system monitoring (see Project Portfolio Server and Its Components Monitoring section earlier in this chapter)

    - ▶ Project Portfolio Server database maintenance

- ▶ Disaster recovery requirements—Disaster recovery means being able to recover all the elements of a Project Portfolio Server environment, including re-establishing the farm, the IIS components, any customization—essentially re-creating everything you had before the instance when all parts of your application could be taken down by a disaster. Your organization should have requirements for disaster recovery, and you will need to plan how you will meet those requirements for Project Portfolio Server. Part of the process is making sure that you document all components of your environment.

- ▶ Data Retention Strategies (Archiving)—You might want to create a standard monitoring process to let you know when your Project Portfolio Server databases are getting full. When it attains a certain threshold, you might consider archiving port-folios, projects, and related data. On the other hand, your organization might have an existing definition for when a project should be archived. Archiving is storing project data outside of the current Project Portfolio Server environment. When defining your data retention policies, make sure to consider not only portfolios, projects, programs, and applications, but Windows SharePoint Services artifacts, lists, and sites. Having standards to communicate to your system users help keep the system clean and simplifies future maintenance and performance issues.

▶ Security policy—Strong management oversight is needed to ensure that only autho-rized people can view or change information in the Project Portfolio Server 2007. Therefore, the Project Portfolio Server Web Access security settings must also be managed through change control procedures.

In addition, you will need to plan for Project Portfolio Server to meet the security policies in your organization for continued operations. This means planning for what you will have to do based on firewalls, proxy or alternative access configura-tions, Secure Sockets Layer, virtual private network, or Citrix/Remote Desktop kinds of access.

▶ Change management policy—Make sure that you create and follow a policy around changes to Project Portfolio Server. For instance, if you add a user to Project Portfolio Server, it should be a regular process, but you should have policies around who can be added and processes for how they are added to a groups. You should also have a change policy that includes communication to end users about enter-prise level changes.

▶ Data protection—Significant data protection is performed using the security model, and setting up protections through User Management for Project Server data. You can also set up data protection for portfolio and project documents via Information Rights Management through WSS. You can even set up list item permissions in WSS. Make sure that you plan for how you continue to protect your Project Portfolio Server data throughout the life of your EPM solution.

Summary

Project Portfolio Server 2007 is a complex solution that requires careful planning and deployment. Remember to follow the process of envisioning, planning, and implement-ing the solution to achieve the most success with your deployment.

Once you install Project Portfolio Server 2007, make sure to validate all of its components and access and create the administrator user account that will be used to configure the system.

In addition to the installation and configuration of the system you need to consider maintenance and standard operational polices that will help you manage the system once it is deployed.

CHAPTER 13

Project Portfolio Server 2007: Configuration

The Microsoft Office Project Portfolio Server (MOPPS) application is installed without any configuration default settings and contains an empty database that needs to be fully configured prior to use. It is essentially a blank slate that can be configured with hundreds of potential options to make the system model meet the planning needs of an organization.

Configuration of MOPPS is typically managed by an individual in the role of a business architect. This individual must be able to translate the strategy and intent of the organization into the configuration settings needed to capture the intended workflow and decision support capabilities discussed in the introduction to MOPPS in Chapter 12, "Project Portfolio Server 2007: Overview and Installation."

Although there are hundreds, if not thousands, of potential configuration settings, they can be logically grouped into three primary dimensions:

▶ User group settings that control who is allowed to view and modify the system

▶ Organization and role to control the level of detail and information required or allowed to be used

▶ Project (entity) workflow process management to establish who is involved and what is required as entities move through the system

The workflow, in combination with the organization hierarchy and user roles/permissions, determines what information is available depending on where the project is in the workflow. For example, when the project is first proposed, the detailed financials might not be visible because they have not yet been reviewed or approved. As the project moves through the workflow phases, more detail may be available, depending on the rights of the user. Information fields in the Project Info and Additional Info tabs may be available for editing during a review phase and then may be locked when the review is complete and the project approved. Based on the project (entity) information state, the project tabs might be open for edit, visible in a read-only state, or invisible. It is always important to understand the workflow settings to explain why a user is or is not able to see and edit information.

System Navigation

There are five tabs available on the top menu bar of the initial screen after the system is installed, as shown in Figure 13.1. All five are briefly mentioned here, but the primary focus of this chapter is on the first of the five menu items, Builder, because the configuration is managed there.

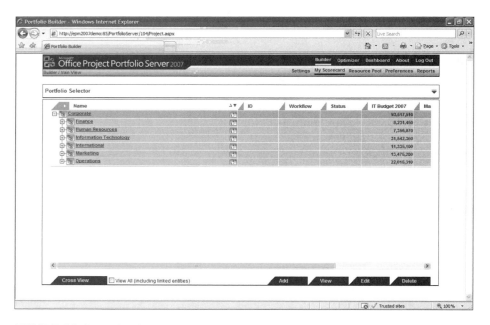

FIGURE 13.1   MOPPS initial screen.

Builder

The vast majority of the configuration requirements are managed within the Builder module. It is also the point where the end users of the system will enter new projects/entities and manage their own preferences and reports. There are five menu items under the Builder module, as shown in Figure 13.1:

▶ **Settings.** Used by the business analyst or application administrator to configure most items within Microsoft Office Project Portfolio Server 2007

▶ **My Scorecard.** Allows the end user to enter application and project information as defined for the role

▶ **Resource Pool.** Contains the availability and requirements for all resources configured in the system

▶ **Preferences.** Allows a user to manage his/her personal settings

▶ **Reports.** Contains portfolio and project-level reports, business cases reports, and other application reports

Optimizer

The Optimizer module is used to provide analysis of the portfolios and projects through a variety of techniques, such as pairwise comparisons and efficient frontier. It is also used to allocate resources and perform what-if analysis to optimize the portfolio of work within the system.

Dashboard

The Dashboard module provides management and tracking and summary reports of portfolios. It also presents an overall health view of all projects and applications.

Help

This menu item provides access to the online user help information.

Settings

As mentioned in the preceding section, the majority of the configuration of the MOPPS application is managed within the Settings tab. Figure 13.2 displays all the configuration main items that are available in this tab.

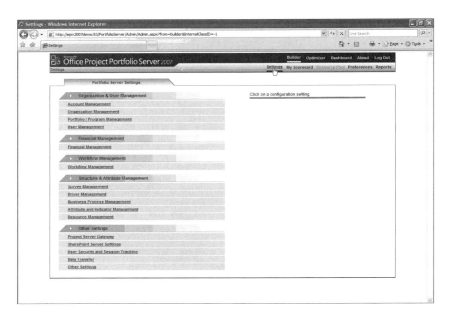

FIGURE 13.2   The Settings tab under the Builder module controls the five administrative setup sections for the solution.

The Settings module is the section of the Portfolio Server tool that allows for configuration of most aspects of the application. It covers global account settings that will be the same for all users and the behavior of specific attributes and indicators for specific types of projects. To navigate to the Settings area after logging in to the tool, select the Builder module in the top navigation menu, and then select **Settings**. The main Settings page consists of the following major sections:

- ▶ **Organization & User Management.** Controls account management (global settings) and organizations, portfolios, programs, and users management.

- ▶ **Financial Management.** Allows you to set up the framework and detailed requirements of financial information contained within projects and applications.

- ▶ **Workflow Management.** Allows you to establish the phase's steps and overall business rules that will make up the workflow for projects managed within the solution.

- ▶ **Structure & Attribute Management.** Controls attributes and indicators that reflect details about planned and actual status of projects and applications.

- ▶ **Other Settings.** This section contains miscellaneous settings that configure other aspects of the tool, including integration with Project Server and SharePoint Server settings.

Privileges are established within the Settings module to control access rights for all users and groups. From the User Group Management section of the tool, user groups may be allowed or denied access to parts of the Settings screen. For users without the rights to access a specific part of the Settings screen, all links appear as grayed-out text.

Account Management Setup

The Account Management screen, shown in Figure 13.3, may only be accessed by a super user, a special kind of user account that exists to configure settings across accounts. Logging in as a super user is done automatically during installation. The super user is the key administrator role in the system and is generally limited to a small group of two or three people. The super user will then establish all further access rights for the system.

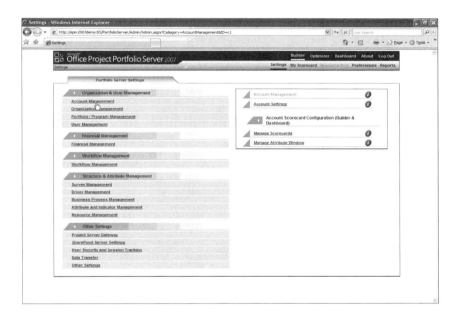

FIGURE 13.3   Configuration begins with account management.

There are four categories of user rights:

▶ **Application settings rights.** These rights apply to settings pages and need to be assigned to a user at the account level, usually the Business Architect or similar role.

▶ **Organization-specific rights.** These rights control data manipulation at an organizational level. User rights are generally limited to data within their own organization and may be even more specifically limited by the user's role or group within the organization. Many of the settings can be used to broadly define a role for the user group so that minimal administration is required at the individual user level.

▶ **Project-specific rights.** Project-specific rights establish the rules within the work-flow and change-request process flow.

▶ **Parts Rights**—Establish access rules for information within projects, programs, portfolios, and applications.

To manage accounts, in the Organization & User Management section of the Portfolio Server Settings tab, click **Account Management**. The Account Management screen consists of four options, described in more detail in the following sections: Account Management, Account Settings, Manage Scorecards, and Manage Attribute Window.

Account Management

Although it is possible to have more than one account, most organizations only set up one so that data can be rolled up to the top level. An account is generally equivalent to an organization or company. However, multiple accounts may be created for distinct organizations with no need for roll-up governance. There is one screen of data to be completed at the account level, as shown in Figure 13.4.

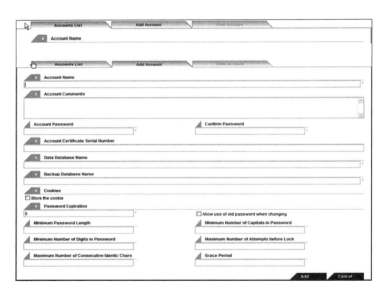

FIGURE 13.4   The Account Management settings establish the controls for the entire organization.

The following items are configured using the Account Management screen:

▶ **Account name.** The name of the new account and is typically the name of the company or organization that is at the top level for rollup purposes. This name is also used for account identification when a dual login procedure is used.

▶ **Account comments.** Optional comments can be added to describe the account's purpose or any other information about the account.

▶ **Account password.** Enter and confirm the account password in these fields.

▶ **Account certificate serial number.** The Account Certificate field is no longer used.

▶ **Data database name.** Enter the name of the database on the database server.

▶ **Backup database name.** Enter the name of the backup database; it may be the same as the active database.

▶ **Cookies.** This field is no longer used.

▶ **Password expiration.** Enter the number of days that a user password is valid. After this number of days, the users must update their passwords. Entry of a 0 in this field means that user passwords do not expire. Choose whether replacement passwords must differ from the previous password. It is recommended to use your organization's security policies when specifying password settings.

▶ **Minimum password length.** The minimum number of characters in all user passwords. It is recommended to use your organization's security policies when specifying password settings.

▶ **Minimum number of capitals in password.** Enter the number of uppercase characters required in user passwords; 0 means that uppercase characters are not required. It is recommended to use your organization's security policies when specifying password settings.

▶ **Minimum number of digits in password.** Enter the minimum number of numeric characters in user passwords; 0 means that numeric characters are not required. It is recommended to use your organization's security policies when specifying password settings.

▶ **Maximum number of attempts before lock.** A user session will be frozen and the user ID locked if the user does not successfully login before the maximum number of times to enter the correct combination of user ID and password is reached. It is recommended to use your organization's security policies when specifying password settings.

▶ **Maximum number of consecutive indent chars.** Enter the maximum number of consecutive identical characters in a user password. It is recommended to use your organization's security policies when specifying password settings.

▶ **Grace period.** The grace period is the maximum number of days users have to reset their password after it expires.

After all the fields have been completed, click **Add** to save the account.

Account Settings

The Account Settings section controls the overall configuration options for each account in a single Portfolio Server environment. These settings apply to all project and portfolio levels within the account. The Account Settings tab displays the following options, as shown in Figure 13.5.

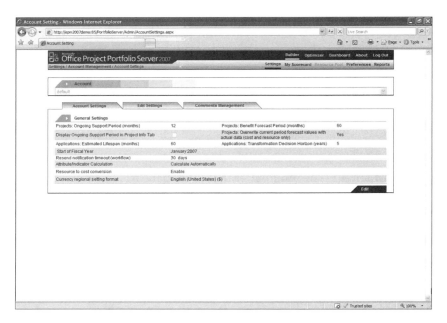

FIGURE 13.5   Establish the account-level settings using the Account Settings screen.

▶ **Projects: Ongoing Support Period (months).** Used to set the standard time period, which starts at a project's benefits start date, for Ongoing Support (capitalization period).

▶ **Projects: Benefit Forecast Period (months).** Used to set how far into the future you would like benefits estimates to be defined.

▶ **Display Ongoing Support Period in Project Info Tab.** Selection of this box shows the Ongoing Support (capitalization period) attribute on the Project Information tab.

▶ **Projects: Overwrite current period forecast values with actual data (cost and resource only).** Allows you to choose whether to replace forecast ongoing values ($ cost and resource levels) with actual values or to retain forecast amounts for historic periods.

> **NOTE**
>
> Resource to Cost Conversion allows you to identify a specific salary for each resource type. If enabled, the cost table is updated for every resource that is added to the project. This will take into consideration the cost of the resources used.

▶ **Applications: Estimated Lifespan (0–60 months).** Allows you to enter the default value to be used for the expected life span (in months) of an application. This attribute is essential for calculating the number of Budget, Forecast, and Actual Cost columns to initially create in the database. It can be overwritten by users.

▶ **Applications: Transformation Decision Horizon (years).** Allows you to set the number of years for the transformation decision horizon for applications. The application transformation decision horizon is the expected life span of the application (set as a maximum of 5 years). This is the time span in which decisions will be made about the action required to be done for the application. Such decisions could be to maintain, enhance, retire, and so on. This is a list of values of the transformation decisions, and the user can run various filters against these values.

▶ **Start of Fiscal Year.** This field *must* be set before any organizations are created for the account. After an organization has been created, it is uneditable.

▶ **Resend notification timeout (workflow).** Allows you to select the number of days to wait before resending workflow notifications (for incomplete tasks) via email.

▶ **Attribute/Indicator Calculation.** Allows you to choose the timing of system recalculation for attributes and indicators. The options are when their tabs are opened, every 30 minutes (automatic), or on demand (manual).

▶ **Resource to cost conversion.** Allows you to specify whether to enable the resource-to-cost conversion feature for the account.

▶ **Currency regional setting format.** Allows you to specify the desired currency to be used in the Budget Cost tab and the U.S. or non-U.S. platform (calendar) for the account.

Manage Scorecards

Figure 13.6 shows a list of all scorecards available in the system. The fields that establish the default views for My Scorecard for all users are displayed once you view the details, as shown in Figure 13.7. Individual users may change their views based on their roles and individual preferences.

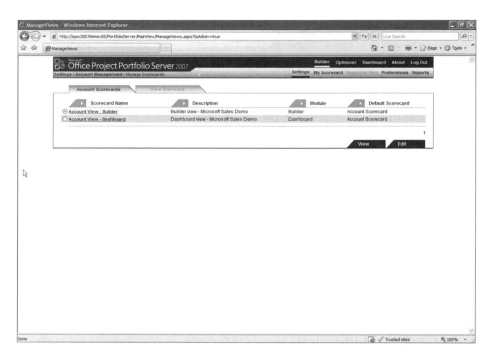

FIGURE 13.6   Set default views for end-user scorecards.

To view the definition fields for each scorecard, select the scorecard and click the **View** button. The View Account Scorecard screen is displayed, showing the scorecard definition fields in a read-only format.

To edit the definition fields for each scorecard, select the scorecard and click the **Edit** button. The Edit Account Scorecard screen is displayed, allowing you to edit any of the scorecard fields, as shown in Figure 13.7.

Manage Attributes Window

The Manage Attributes Window section is used to set default attributes for the views that have been set by default, as shown in Figure 13.8.

To view the currently selected attributes, select the view to configure and click the **View** button. The view attributes are displayed as read-only.

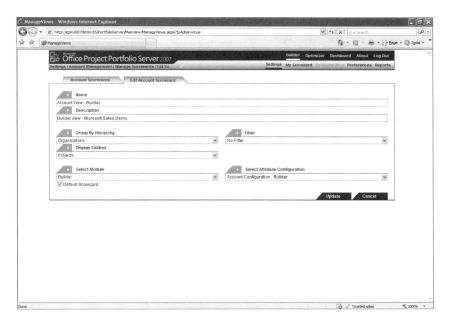

FIGURE 13.7   Set the desired field values for the selected scorecard.

FIGURE 13.8   Select the default view to manage its attributes.

To edit the currently selected attributes, select the view to configure and click the **Edit** button. The View Configuration tab displays all fields and their values for the currently selected view, as shown in Figure 13.9.

FIGURE 13.9   Select the default attributes for the selected view.

User Management Overview

The management of users and groups of users is a key component of configuration for Project Portfolio Server. The proper determination of the roles and the rights and permissions associated with the roles will minimize the amount of management that is required at the individual user level. User groups are a bundle of user rights. Users can be assigned to only one user group for each business unit of the organization tree.

User Group Management

Groups represent the types of roles required. You can establish any number of roles to describe user groups and then assign permissions accordingly. The following examples are just a few of the possible role and permission relationships:

> ► **Account Manager.** A user type with edit rights to all project information, access to all tool modules, and permission to add and delete projects and to change all tool settings.

▶ **Portfolio Manager.** A user type with edit rights to all project information, access to all tool modules, and the permission to add new projects, portfolios, programs, and applications.

▶ **Contributor.** A user type with edit rights to all project information, access to the Builder, and without the permission to add new projects.

Application Managers, Executive Sponsors, Portfolio Analysts, Program Managers, Program Sponsors, Requesters, and Team Members are additional typical roles within an organization. The relationship between the roles in the hierarchy of the organization and the rights associated will establish the actual permissions for each user and user group.

Permissions for each group represent responsibilities and capabilities available within the system. The permissions include Allow, Deny, or None. User rights are inherited from a higher level of the organization hierarchy or they can be specifically set for the lower level, such that:

▶ **Allow** results in allowing the user rights on the assigned level and all lower levels unless overwritten by a Deny on a higher or lower level.

▶ **Deny** results in disallowing the user rights on the assigned level and all lower levels even if it is overwritten on that lower level by an Allow.

▶ **None** results in disallowing the user rights on the assigned level and all lower levels unless overwritten on that lower level by an Allow.

Table 13.1 shows how the permissions will interact based on the relative assignment of the role within the organizational hierarchy.

TABLE 13.1   Permissions Interaction Relative to Role Assignment

Right Assignment on Corporate Level	Right Assignment on Lower Level	Result on Corporate Level	Result on Lower Level
Allow	Allow	Allow	Allow
Allow	Deny	Allow	Deny
Deny	Allow	Deny	Deny
Deny	Allow	Deny	Deny
Deny	Deny	Deny	Deny
Deny	None	Deny	Deny
None	Allow	Deny	Allow
None	Deny	Deny	Deny
None	None	Deny	Deny

Using the information in Table 13.1, the administrator will first establish the user groups from the User Management, User Group Management screen, as shown in Figure 13.10.

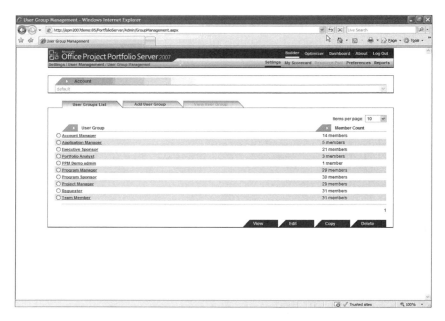

FIGURE 13.10   Select User Group Management to view the list of all user groups and to begin to set up users.

To add a new user group, follow these steps:

1. Select the **Add User Group** tab.

2. In the User Group text box, enter the new user group name.

3. Specify the appropriate rights for that role within the organization by selecting **Allow**, **Deny**, or **None** for each of the items in the category permissions, as shown in Figure 13.11.

4. Click the **Add** button.

5. Repeat this action for every user group that needs to be created.

User rights are specified for each component of the solution. The user group list of rights includes close to 300 different rights. One group of rights relates to the rights to access various settings within the tool. These accesses are referred to as links to the appropriate location or page where settings can be made. Each of the rights is stated as "Access to *xxx* link" and controls access to individual pages in the Settings section.

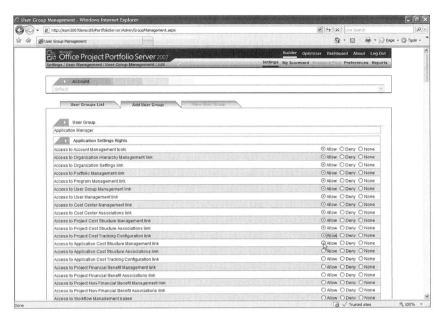

FIGURE 13.11   Assign the appropriate rights for each user group.

To understand the specific rights and restrictions per user, identify the general users'
groups configuration. Use the Configuration Settings file to document the specific category permissions, which include the following:

- **Entity-specific rights.** Project, program, application, organization, and custom
  portfolio specific rights.

- **Project parts rights.** Restriction of data manipulation at project level.

- **Program parts rights.** Restriction of data manipulation at program level.

- **Portfolio parts rights.** Restriction of data manipulation at portfolio level.

- **Application parts rights.** Restriction of data manipulation at application level.

- **The Report permissions** control the user's right to create reports for themselves
  (private) or for the entire tool (public).

User Management

After the user groups have been defined and rights have been set up for the groups, individual users can be added to the system. Their personal information and their user group
assignments within the organization will be managed from the User Management screens.

To add a new user, follow these steps:

1. From the top menu, select **Builder**, and then select **Settings**.

2. Under Organization & User Management, select **User Management**, and then click **User Management** on the right.

3. Click the **Add User** tab.

4. Specify login name, contact details, password, and so on. Use the Organizational Rights Assignment section to specify which user groups the individual is a member of for each organization, as shown in Figure 13.12. Administrators set the initial user passwords and later change it using the User Management section of the Settings page.

FIGURE 13.12   Create users and assign them to user groups.

NOTE

After the administrator sets up the individual user password, it can be changed by the user from the Preferences menu.

A user is "assigned" a specific role (project manager, owner, contributor, and so on) to an entity (project, program, application, or portfolio) if selected under a user group in the Project Information, Additional Information, Program Information, Application Information, or Portfolio Information tab.

Organization Setup

The organization hierarchy is a model of the corporate structure that shows the relationships between the different business units or divisions in an organization. Business units can be represented in a tree with different hierarchies. Higher levels in the tree represent the aggregate of all lower levels.

The Organization Settings section of Project Portfolio Server is used to create the hierarchical structure of the organization. There are two subsections that will be used:

▶ **Organization Hierarchy Management.** Used to model the configuration of the desired hierarchical structure of the organization in the Portfolio Server

▶ **Organization Settings.** Used to capture the configuration of the tool settings linked to each organization level

Organizational Hierarchy Management

Each business unit, division, department, or service unit can be added in this section with its relative level in the organization. As many levels as are appropriate can be added to the mapping.

To add a new level, follow these steps:

1. From the top navigation menu, select **Builder**, and then select **Settings**.

2. Under the Organization & User Management section, select **Organization Management**.

3. Click **Organization Hierarchy Management** on the right.

4. Click the appropriate level in the organization under which to add the new level (use the plus sign to expand the tree to view the lower levels), and click the **Add** button.

5. Fill in the name of the business unit, and select the **Insert Before** level, as shown in Figure 13.13. Click **Update**.

Repeat this process until all business units are entered at the appropriate level and within the appropriate tree structure that correctly represents the organization.

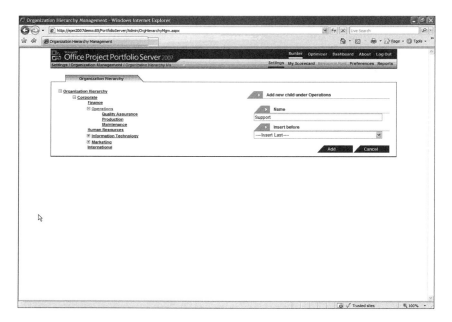

FIGURE 13.13   Add or edit corporate entities from the Organization Hierarchy screen.

Organizational Settings

After the correct organizational tree structure has been defined, it is time to add information about each of the entities included. The information is used throughout the system for naming conventions used in identification, analysis, and reporting of projects and portfolios associated with the entities.

To define new organizational settings, follow these steps:

1. From the top navigation menu, select **Builder** and then **Settings**.

2. Under the Organization & User Management section, select **Organization Management**.

3. Select **Organization Settings** on the right.

4. Use the Organization Hierarchy drop-down to select the organization for which to define settings.

5. Click the **Edit** button to edit the settings or click the **Edit Settings** tab, as shown in Figure 13.14.

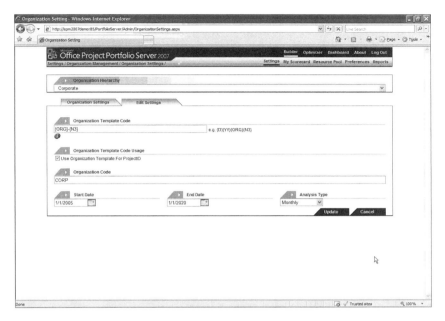

FIGURE 13.14   Enter the data that is appropriate for each business unit.

6. Create the organization template code that will be used for project IDs using the following format:

- ▶ {D}   Current day (1, 2 … 31)

- ▶ {DD}   Current day on 2 characters (01, 02 … 31)

- ▶ {MM}   Current month {1, 2 … 12)

- ▶ {MMM}   Current month abbreviation {Jan, Feb …)

- ▶ {YY}   Current year on 2 characters (for example, 04 represents 2004)

- ▶ {YYYY}   Current year on 4 characters (for example, 2004)

- ▶ {ORG}   Organization code

- ▶ {N}   The project number

- ▶ {Nx} where *x* = 2, 3, 4   Project number on *x* characters

If the template code contains {ORG}, the project number is the current number per project created in the organization; otherwise, the project number is per account.

7. Select the **Use Organization Template for ProjectID** box when using automatic project ID.

8. Specify the organization code.

9. Fill in start date and end date of the business unit. All projects and applications need to have start dates later than the organization start date and end dates before the organization end date. Start date and end date can be extended at a later stage.

10. Choose **Monthly** or **Quarterly** for Analysis Type.

11. Click the **Update** button.

12. Repeat this process for each business unit.

> **NOTE**
>
> Project dates can only be within the start and end dates of the organization they belong to. This must be taken into consideration when selecting the organization start and end dates.

Workflow Management Configuration

Workflow describes how projects will progress through the life cycle from initial concept through completion and closure. Workflow describes both the major phases and the specific steps within each phase along with any business rules regarding notification, review, and approval. The workflow establishes the governance process for the organization and is the primary method used by Project Portfolio Server to move the projects through the system. The following rules have been set within the Project Portfolio Server to manage the workflow:

- ▶ Projects will follow a different workflow based on the value of the Project Class attribute (see the "Workflows Definition" section later in this chapter).

- ▶ Governance phases are common phases that are used to aggregate projects from multiple workflows.

- ▶ A workflow consists of a series of life cycle steps used to subject the project to the appropriate governance controls throughout its life cycle.

- ▶ Life cycle steps are standardized stages in the life of a project in which information about that project is entered or reviewed, and a decision is made to either move the project forward to the next life cycle step, put the project on hold, or cancel it.

- ▶ Every life cycle step has a notification to a certain user group associated to it. Users belonging to this group can move the project forward to the next life cycle step.

- ▶ Every life cycle step can be configured to show cost and resource data (yearly or quarterly/monthly), show or hide certain tabs and make them read-only or writable, advance automatically on approval/rejection or advance manually.

- ▶ Different life cycle steps are linked by transitions.

- ▶ A transition process can send notifications to certain users.

▶ Transition processes can perform actions that are grouped in the associated link process (for example, verification if certain tabs are filled in).

> **NOTE**
>
> Programs and Applications do not follow a workflow.

Figure 13.15 provides an example of a simple workflow composed of 4 major phases and 13 steps within the phases. Progress between the steps and phases is set up within the system to move forward when certain conditions are true. The conditions can include review by the appropriate people, completion of a deliverable, or one of many other conditions.

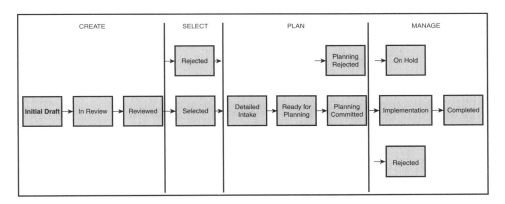

FIGURE 13.15   Example workflow with 4 phases and 13 steps.

Workflow management is composed of six subsections that need to be configured in a specific order. The configuration can be modified at a later date, but it will be much easier to follow the recommended order even if modifications are required:

▶ **Governance phase management.** Configuration of the high-level phases of the portfolio process.

▶ **Workflows management.** Definition of multiple workflows for different project classes in the organization.

▶ **Workflow verification and link process management.** Business rules addition to the workflows.

▶ **Workflow notification management.** Email notifications in the workflow's definition.

▶ **Life cycle step management.** Definition, settings, and transitions between life cycle steps definition.

▶ **Email templates management.** Templates for the email alerts configuration. These templates can also be accessed from the Other Settings screen.

Workflow Management Steps

Configuration of the workflow should be completed after decisions have been made in each of the following steps. The recommendation is to design the workflow phases and steps (for each project class) on paper prior to beginning configuration within the tool. This will eliminate rework because workflow is typically created via an iterative design process.

Follow these steps to define the workflow:

1. Define the governance phases. The phases are created first because they are shared across the entire organization so that project data can be rolled up by phase for analysis and reporting purposes.

2. Create a workflow. Determine the number of different project classes that will be modeled and then add a new list choice to the Project Class attribute. Create a workflow and assign the new list choice to it.

3. Define processes. This is done by creating a menu of business rules that can be applied in different situations. Business rules are applied at points during the work-flow to verify that certain activities have been completed (verification) or to move a project from one point in the process to another (transition).

4. Define notifications. Define the emails (timing, who, and what is needed) and the actual email text of each email type that the tool will be sending. Configuration for this step includes identification of involved user groups (such as reviewers or approvers), creation of email notifications, and templates.

5. Create your life cycle steps. Establish the order in which the actual steps will be performed. Configuration will also include settings, linked business rules, and linked notifications. During this configuration step, you set up default notifications, transi-tions, and other step settings.

Governance Phase Management

Configuration begins with governance phases. When deciding how many phases and the order of phases, consider the planning cycles for the organization. Typical cycles include annual, quarterly, hybrid, and just-in-time. Phases are shared among all different workflows.

To add a new governance phase, follow these steps:

1. From the top navigation menu, select **Builder** and then **Settings**.

2. Under the Workflow Management section, select **Workflow Management**.

3. Select **Governance Phase Management** on the right.

4. Click the **Add Governance Phase** tab.

5. Fill in a name for the phase, such as Create, Select, Plan, or Manage, as shown in Figure 13.16.

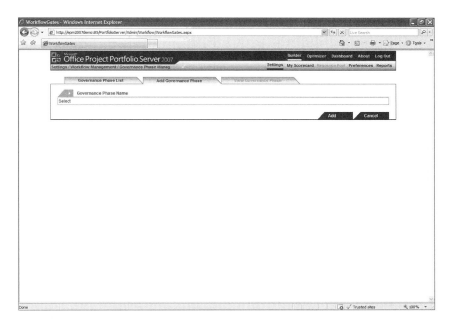

FIGURE 13.16   Create a new governance phase.

6. Click **Add**.

Repeat this process for each of the major phases planned for the organization.

Workflows Definition

As mentioned earlier, the major phases within an organization are kept the same for data rollup and analysis. Within the phases, however, the workflow steps can vary based on the type of work that is being managed. For example, complex projects may require more review and approval steps than simple ones.

Projects can follow a different workflow depending on the value of the Project Class attribute assigned to the project in the Project Information tab. The Attributes and Indicators section is addressed in detail later in this chapter because most of the components deal with project-level capabilities. Project Class is one default attribute that needs to be updated early in the configuration process.

To configure the Project Class attribute, follow these steps:

1. From the top navigation menu, select **Builder** and then **Settings**.

2. Under the Structure and Attribute Management section, select **Attribute and Indicator Management**.

3. Select **Attribute Definition** on the right.

4. On the Attribute Definition screen, click the **Show Default Attributes** button.

5. In the Filter box, type **Project Class** and click **Apply**.

6. Select the **Project Class attribute** and then click **Edit**.

7. Type a new choice in the Instance Name box and click **Add**, as shown in Figure 13.17.

FIGURE 13.17   Add a new choice for the Project Class attribute.

8. Click **Update Attribute** at the bottom of the page.

Each workflow can be associated to only one instance of the Project Class attribute, but you can only have one workflow per project class. When a project is created, the project is automatically routed to the first life cycle step of the workflow associated with the mandatory Project Class value selected in the Project Information tab.

After the workflows have been designed, they are added to the configuration using the Workflow Management, Workflows Management screen, as shown in Figure 13.18.

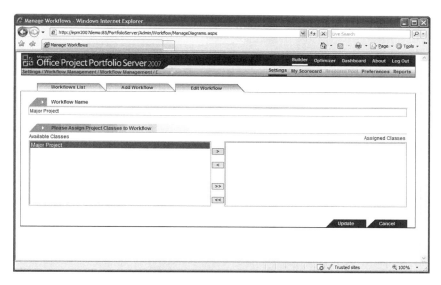

FIGURE 13.18   Add a workflow and associate it with a project class(es).

Workflow Verification & Link Process Management

After the workflows have been created and project classes have been assigned, the steps for each workflow need to be configured. A workflow process is a group of one or more predefined actions that create a flow based on the actions and business rules applied. Processes can be associated to the transition between two life cycle steps or to a life cycle step.

For best graphical results, create life cycle steps beginning from left to right and top to bottom. Figure 13.19 shows the recommended order.

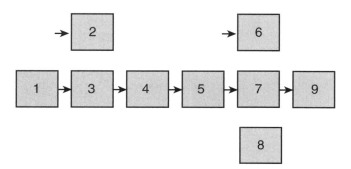

FIGURE 13.19   Enter life cycle steps in the order shown for best graphical results.

When the flow has been decided, the steps can be entered in the solution and eventually will be linked together through the next series of configuration activities.

Begin with the addition of the process names and types, as shown in Figure 13.20 under the Workflow Management, Workflow Verification, and Link Process Management section.

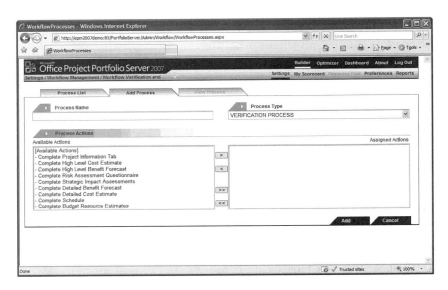

FIGURE 13.20   Choose a process name and a process type.

There are two kinds of process types:

- A **verification process** (or deliverables) is used for a process step where data must be completed before a project can move forward to the next life cycle step. For example, completion of a business case is required before the next step of business case review.

- A **link process** is chosen to execute a specific set of actions when a project is moved from one life cycle step to another.

Next, choose one or more from the available process actions, as shown in Figure 13.20, based on the process type.

Verification process actions include the following:

- Complete Project Information Tab verifies whether all mandatory fields are completed.

- Complete High Level Cost Estimate verifies whether level 1 of the cost structure is completed.

- Complete Detailed Cost Estimate verifies whether lowest level of the cost structure is completed.

▶ Complete Strategic Impact Tab verifies whether strategic impact values are completed.

Link process actions include the following:

▶ A: **Save Requirement Values When Approved.** This action copies all resource requirement values from planned to forecast and computes tracking values. This action should be triggered when the project moves to the first workflow stage where it is considered approved.

▶ B: **Copy Planned Cost to Forecasted.** Copies budget cost values into forecast cost values and computes tracking values. This action should be triggered when the project moves to the first life cycle step where the project is considered approved.

▶ C: **Save Requirement Values When Rejected.** Resets resource tracking and forecast data to zero. This action should be triggered when the project moves from a stage where it is considered approved into a stage where it is considered nonapproved.

▶ D: **Redistribute Budget Cost Data Across Project Period.** Redistributes the annual cost and resource numbers across the months/quarters.

▶ E: **Save Cost Values When Rejected.** Resets tracking and forecast data to zero. This action should be triggered when the project moves from a stage where it is considered approved into a stage where it is considered nonapproved.

NOTE

The proper assignment of link processes can be tricky. Here are a few examples of how they work when properly assigned:

▶ Execute A and B in the list above when you start tracking costs and resources, usually immediately after the final approval life cycle step.

▶ Execute C and E in the list above when a project is rejected.

▶ Execute D in the list above after rescheduling a project.

Workflow Notification Management

Workflow notification management configuration deals with the setup of email and associated feedback requirements to manage responses to process steps in the workflow. Configuration will also be set up for the capture of response data for audit purposes.

Notifications can be sent with feedback or without feedback so the configuration setup will vary based on the type of response required. Feedback notifications are associated to automatic life cycle steps, whereas no-feedback notifications are associated to manual life cycle steps. Proper setup ensures that each life cycle step in the workflow is confirmed by a user.

Notification without feedback is set up so that the recipient of the notice is only informed about the state of the project. This type of notice does not include a response mechanism and comments regarding the notice are not maintained in the audit trail. This notification type can be used on transitions and on manual life cycle steps.

Notification with feedback requires additional configuration settings because the recipient is required to respond to the email with Approval/Rejection or a Yes/No response. Comments are gathered and an audit trail is also kept.

Feedback notifications have two types of response techniques:

▶ **Standard (requires multiple-user signoff).** All users receive notification simultaneously asking them to approve the project.

▶ **Standard (requires single-user signoff).** A single user can sign off to approve or reject the project.

To configure notifications, follow these steps:

1. From the top navigation menu, select **Builder** and then **Settings**.

2. Under the Workflow Management section, select **Workflow Management**.

3. Select **Workflow Notification Management**.

4. Click the **Add Notification** tab, as shown in Figure 13.21.

FIGURE 13.21   Add Notification begins the configuration process for managing workflow notification.

5. Fill in the name, select an email template (described in the "Email Templates Management" section of this chapter), the notification level, user group, feedback check, response technique, and response type, as shown in Figure 13.22.

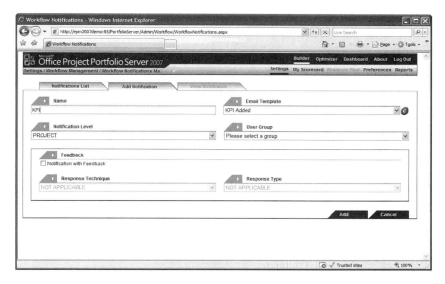

FIGURE 13.22   Use the Workflow Notification Feedback screen to enter the notification parameters.

When the notifications are completed, the steps within the workflow can be connected to each other to complete the workflow management configuration.

Life Cycle Step Definition

To complete the workflow management configuration, the phases, steps, notifications, and responses must be tied together to create a logical flow that reflects the workflow originally designed, as shown previously in the "Workflows Management" section.

To define life cycle steps, follow these steps:

1. From the top navigation menu, select **Builder** and then **Settings**.

2. Under the Workflow Management section, select **Workflow Management**.

3. Select **Lifecycle Step Management** on the right, as shown in Figure 13.23.

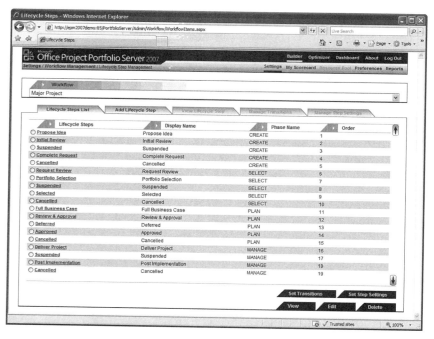

FIGURE 13.23   Lifecycle Step Management is controlled from the Workflow Management, Lifecycle Step Management screen.

Every life cycle step is associated with one of the governance gates and can be configured to display cost and resource data. Additional configuration will provide the ability to show or hide tabs based on progress, advance from one step to another, and be linked with the dashboard.

4. Click the **Add Lifecycle Step** tab and enter the following information, as shown in Figure 13.24:

   ▶ Name (shown as Workflow Status in Builder)

   ▶ Display Name (shown on workflow graph)

   ▶ Governance Phase (corresponding governance phase)

   ▶ Objective (shown in pop-up balloon on workflow graph)

   ▶ Choose whether the life cycle step is an automatic step:

      ▶ Select the default associated notification (users receiving this notification can move the project to the next step in the workflow), or

      ▶ Select a verification process if appropriate. This selection is optional; if not appropriate, the default associated notification should be chosen.

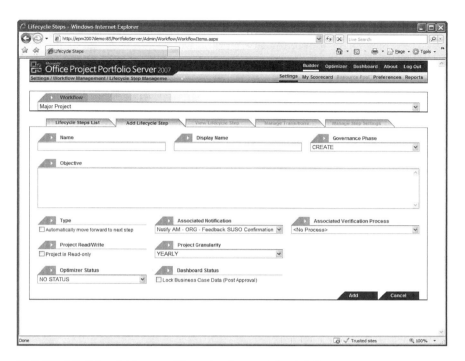

FIGURE 13.24   Add a new life cycle step and its details.

5. Select whether this life cycle step is read-only. If a life cycle step is set to read-only, all tabs will be read-only, including Change Request, Issues & Risks, Status, and so on. Because nothing else can be done with the tabs, this condition is typically only set for post-completion steps.

6. Select the project granularity. The choices are Yearly or Monthly/Quarterly. The granularity of cost and resource data can be set for each step to Yearly or Monthly/Quarterly if allowed by the settings for the Portfolio configuration in the organization. Refer to the organizational settings for details.

7. Select an Optimizer status, if applicable. "No Status" means that there is no relation between the Optimizer and this step. Choose "Project is Selected" or "Project is Rejected" when you want the Optimizer results reflected in this step.

8. Check whether the life cycle step is post-approval or not.

9. Click **Add** to complete the entry of the life cycle step.

Define Transitions Between Life Cycle Steps

After the life cycle steps have been added, the configuration moves to the establishment of the transitions between the steps. There are a few things to keep in mind when setting transitions and linking them to steps:

▸ Every life cycle step has an associated default notification:

    ▸ For an automatic life cycle step, a feedback notification needs to be associated and notified users have to sign off and provide a comment. When this action is completed, the project will move forward to the next life cycle step automatically (the action varies slightly for single-user signoff versus multiuser signoff). The project will move backward to the previous life cycle step if it is rejected by one or more persons.

    ▸ In the case of a manual life cycle step, every notified user can change the workflow stage to the next step (not everybody needs to sign off, only one user is needed). When feedback is required, users must sign off and provide comments. After signoff, links to all the next available life cycle steps will become visible and the project will only move to a following life cycle step after clicking the corresponding link. When feedback is not required (default), no signoff comments are gathered, and the project will move to an available linked life cycle step when the user clicks the corresponding link.

▸ If a life cycle step has a verification process associated, a project cannot move forward unless the data related to that process are completed. If a process without verification is associated (a link process), a notification with feedback is often included with that step, because those users will have to confirm the data entered.

▸ A life cycle step can be linked to the Optimizer. If the project is selected, the Optimizer can automatically move selected projects into this workflow state upon selection. If the project is rejected, the Optimizer can automatically move rejected projects into this workflow state upon rejection. See the Optimizer setting above.

▸ A life cycle step that is set to Post Approval will result in the project being visible in the dashboard. The baseline information will be locked and the project will be ready to show cost and resource tracking information. In a previous transition, the "transition to approved" process should have been executed.

To add a new transition, follow these steps:

1. From the top navigation menu, select **Builder** and then **Settings**.
2. Under the Workflow Management section, select **Workflow Management**.
3. Select **Lifecycle Step Management** on the right.
4. In the Lifecycle Steps list, select the life cycle to define transitions for.

5. Click the **Set Transitions** button.

6. A new screen appears, as shown in Figure 13.25, where you can select the life cycle step to be associated with the transition and also assign notifications as appropriate.

FIGURE 13.25   Transitions between life cycle steps are configured in the Manage Transitions screen.

7. Select the transition to edit and click the **Edit** button or click the **Add** button to add a new transition.

8. Select the end life cycle step and (optionally) a transition process.

9. Assign extra notifications as appropriate for the life cycle step (optional).

10. Click **Update**.

The final piece of establishing the workflow is to configure the tabs that will be visible and available for edit for this transition.

To configure the tabs, follow these steps:

1. Under the Workflow Management section, select **Workflow Management**.

2. Select **Lifecycle Step Management** on the right.

3. Under the Lifecycle Steps section, select the life cycle to define tabs for, and then click the **Set Step Settings** button on the bottom right.

4. A new screen appears, as shown in Figure 13.26, with all the possible tabs that can be configured for the chosen transition.

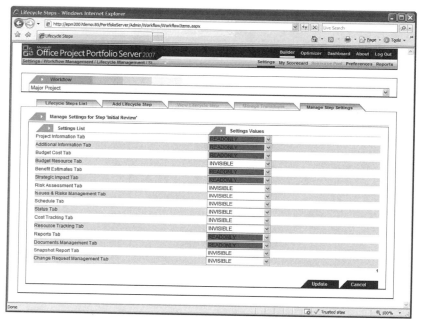

Figure 13.26   Configure each tab with EDITABLE, READONLY, or INVISIBLE values.

5. Select the EDITABLE, READONLY, or INVISIBLE values for each of the settings tabs.

6. Click **Update**.

Email Templates Management

Email templates are customizable emails generated at different points in the workflow. The primary types are as follows:

- ▶ **Notifications.** This type of email notification is pertinent to users at particular points in the workflow. The template can be modified at any time in the process without impacting existing projects.

- ▶ **Alert subscriptions.** This type of email acts primarily as a means for setting auto-respondent emails for users who may not be present at certain points in the process where their attention is required.

Email templates are configured with keywords that will be substituted with the correct value as appropriate for the need (for example, *userName*).

To configure email templates, follow these steps:

1. From the top navigation menu, select **Builder** and then **Settings**.

2. Under the Workflow Management section, select **Workflow Management**.

3. Select **Email Templates Management** on the right.

4. Click the **Add Template** tab, as shown in Figure 13.27.

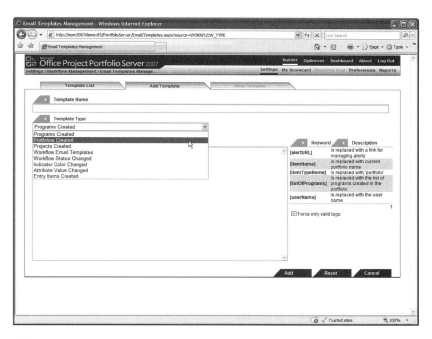

FIGURE 13.27   Create an email template for use in workflow management.

5. Fill in a name for the template, and choose **Template Type: Workflow Email Template**, as shown in Figure 13.27. Create the body of the email and choose the appropriate keywords identified to the right of the body.

6. Click **Add** to complete the email template.

Financial Management Configuration

Financial management is one of the key areas to be configured for Project Portfolio Server. Financial management provides the business users with all the decision support data regarding the costs and benefits of each entity of work that is being considered by the organization. Information regarding specific projects, programs, and applications can be compared to each other for their relative values and their costs. Both planning values and actual values can be tracked by the system after it has been properly configured. There are five primary areas to review for the financial management configuration:

▶ **Cost center management and associations.** Configuration and use of the cost centers of the organization for capturing of financials

▶ **Project cost structure management and associations.** Configuration and use of the project cost structure

▶ **Project cost tracking configuration.** Settings definition for tracking of project's cost post-configuration

▶ **Financial benefit management and associations.** Configuration and use of the project financial benefits structure

▶ **Nonfinancial benefit management and associations.** Configuration and use of the project nonfinancial benefits structure

There are many settings that must be configured for financial management, as shown in Figure 13.28.

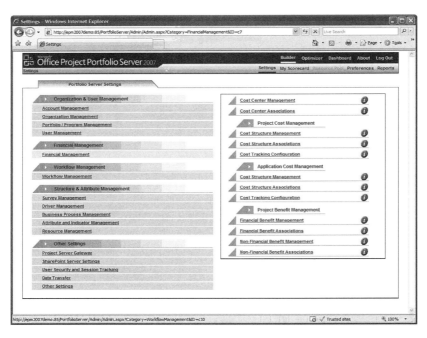

FIGURE 13.28   Project Portfolio Server includes many options for configuring financial management.

Cost Center Management and Associations

Configuration begins with the setup of cost centers. A cost center represents an entity to which costs are assigned. Costs can be associated with human resources and many other elements that must be used to perform work on projects. Each item in the cost tree (yearly or quarterly/monthly) can have as many entries as there are cost centers associated to the organization. At least one cost center needs to be defined and associated to each level in the organizational hierarchy.

To add a cost center, follow these steps:

1. From the top navigation menu, select **Builder** and then **Settings**.

2. Under the Financial Management section, select **Financial Management**.

3. Select **Cost Center Management** on the right.

4. Click the **Add Cost Center** tab.

5. Type in the name to be displayed when entering cost data, as shown in Figure 13.29.

6. Use ID to store any ID data corresponding to the cost center (optional).

FIGURE 13.29   Add a cost center using the Cost Center Management screen.

7. Click the **Add** button.

After the cost centers have been added, add cost center associations by following these steps:

1. Under Settings, select **Financial Management**.

2. Select **Cost Center Associations** on the right.

3. This step will link the cost center to the appropriate level in the organization. Remember, each level in the organizational hierarchy must be associated with at least one cost center. Select the correct organization and portfolio.

4. Select the cost centers you want to associate to this organization level.

5. Click **Update Associations**.

Project Cost Structure Management and Associations

The project cost structure must be configured to report on both one-time costs and recurring costs that can be expected for projects. The data collected can be associated with different levels in the organization and can be rolled up to higher levels as defined in the tree structure.

A cost tree represents the cost structure of an organization and is typically hierarchical. The configuration will define if lower levels of the tree will roll up to a higher level (default). A cost tree can be configured to show yearly or quarterly/monthly data and can be up to five levels deep.

To configure a cost tree, follow these steps:

1. From the top navigation menu, select **Builder** and then **Settings**.

2. Under the Financial Management section, select **Financial Management**.

3. Select **Cost Structure Management** on the right. You can then change a node or add a level as appropriate for your organization.

4. To change a node, select it and then click the **Edit** button, as shown in Figure 13.30. Modify the attributes and click **Update**.

5. To add one or more levels, select the level under which you would like to add more items, and then click the **Add Level** button, as shown in Figure 13.31. Fill out level information, and then click the **Add** button.

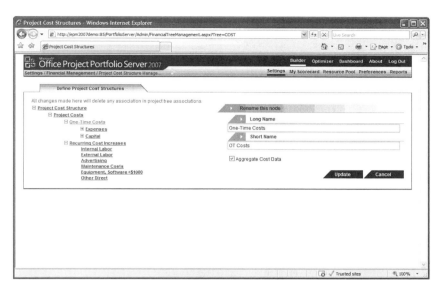

FIGURE 13.30   Change a node on the cost tree.

FIGURE 13.31   Add a level to the cost tree.

After the cost structures have been created, they can be associated with the organizational hierarchy by following these steps:

1. From the top navigation menu, select **Builder** and then **Settings**.

2. Under the Financial Management section, select **Financial Management**.

3. Select **Cost Structure Associations** on the right.

4. Select **Organization Hierarchy and Existing Portfolio**.

5. Select **Cost Structure**.

6. Select **Associations**, as shown in Figure 13.32.

FIGURE 13.32   Associate the cost structure with the appropriate level in the organization.

7. Click **Update Associations**.

8. Repeat for every part of the organization hierarchy.

Project Cost-Tracking Configuration

There are many attributes that can be available for cost-tracking purposes. The items that you want to see must be selected in the menu area. The attributes provide information regarding the original budget, change requests, and revised budgets and actual costs and variance information. Select all columns you want to see in the Cost Tracking tab, as shown in Figure 13.33.

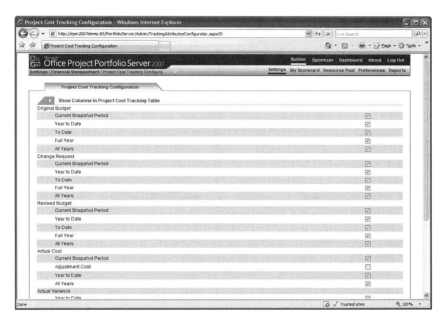

FIGURE 13.33 Select the appropriate attributes for cost tracking.

Financial Benefit Management and Associations

After the cost structures have been configured, the next step is to configure the Financial Benefit Management section. A benefit tree represents the benefit structure for projects (and programs and portfolios) in an organization and is structured in a similar fashion to the cost tree. It can be hierarchical and lower levels of the tree roll up to a higher level. As with the cost tree, a benefit tree can have up to five levels in the hierarchy. A benefit tree can also be shown in a yearly or quarterly/monthly configuration.

Configuration of the financial benefits section requires the following actions:

1. From the top navigation menu, select **Builder** and then **Settings**.

2. Under the Financial Management section, select **Financial Management**.

3. Select **Financial Benefit Management** on the right.

4. Select **Benefit Structure**.

5. Click **Edit**.

6. Change the Long Name and Short Name fields.

7. Select **Propagate Aggregation** if you want benefits to roll up to higher levels automatically (default), as shown in Figure 13.34.

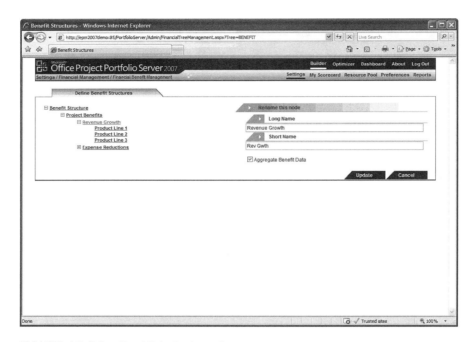

FIGURE 13.34   Establish the benefit tree.

8. Click **Update**.

9. Click **Add Level** to add a new level.

10. Fill in a long name and short name.

11. Select **Propagate Aggregation** if you want costs to roll up to higher levels (default), as shown in Figure 13.35.

12. Click **Add**.

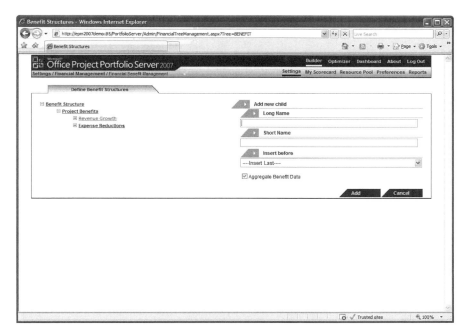

FIGURE 13.35   Add levels to the benefit tree.

After the financial benefit tree has been created, it can be associated with the organization. Different levels of the organization hierarchy can have different parts of the benefit tree assigned to them. The project benefits association section is where this occurs. Whenever possible, based on the organizational process, use the same tree for all organizations. This will provide for a more efficient and complete information rollup. Use the following steps to configure the financial benefit associations:

1. In the top navigation menu, select **Builder** and then **Settings**.

2. Under the Financial Management section, select **Financial Management**.

3. Select **Financial Benefit Association** on the right.

4. Select the organization hierarchy and existing portfolios.

5. Select **Benefit Structure**.

6. Select **Associations**, as shown in Figure 13.36.

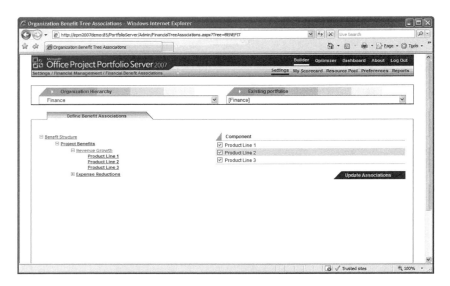

FIGURE 13.36   Associate the benefit structure to the organization.

7. Click **Update Associations**.

8. Repeat for every part of the organization hierarchy.

Nonfinancial Benefit Management and Associations

In addition to financial benefits, nonfinancial benefits can be measured. This type of benefit can often be as important, or more important, in the decision-making process than financial benefits. Examples include compliance with government rulings, audit points addressed, customer-satisfaction scores increase, growth in market share, employee satisfaction, increase in customer-retention rates, technology infrastructure investments, and others. These benefits must be ranked in some manner so that they can be compared to the financial benefits of projects during the optimization and prioritization of project work.

To configure nonfinancial benefits, follow these steps:

1. From the top navigation menu, select **Builder** and then **Settings**.

2. Under the Financial Management section, select **Financial Management**.

3. Select **Non-Financial Benefit Management** on the right.

4. Select **Benefit Structure**.

5. Click **Edit**.

6. Change a long name and short name, and choose a values display format, as shown in Figure 13.37.

FIGURE 13.37   Establish the nonfinancial benefits structure.

7. Select **Propagate Aggregation** if you want benefits to roll up to higher levels automatically (default).

8. Click **Update**.

9. Click **Add Level**.

10. Fill in a long name and short name and choose a values display format type, as shown in Figure 13.38.

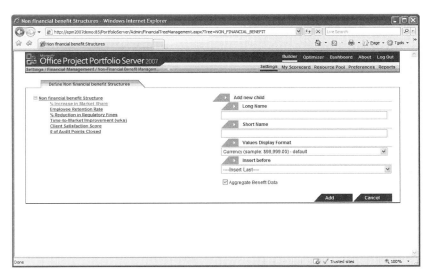

FIGURE 13.38   Add levels to the nonfinancial benefits tree.

11. Select **Propagate Aggregation** if you want costs to roll up to higher levels (default).

12. Click **Add**.

As with the previous cost and benefit structures, nonfinancial benefits need to be associated with the organization. Different levels of the organization hierarchy can have different parts of the nonfinancial benefits assigned. This is defined in the association of the nonfinancial benefits. When nonfinancial benefits are shared across the organization, more efficient rollup of information can occur.

To associate nonfinancial benefits with the organization, follow these steps

1. In the top navigation menu, select **Builder** and then **Settings**.

2. Under the Financial Management section, select **Financial Management**.

3. Select **Non-Financial Benefit Associations** on the right.

4. Select the organization hierarchy and portfolio under Existing Portfolios.

5. Select **Benefit Structure**.

6. Select **Associations**, as shown in Figure 13.39.

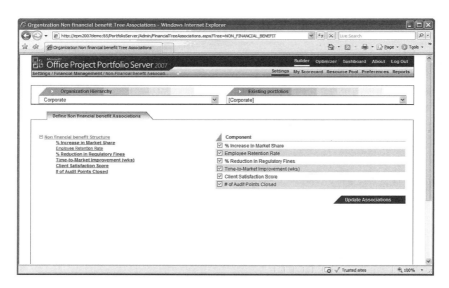

FIGURE 13.39 Associate nonfinancial benefits to the organization.

7. Click **Update Associations**.

8. Repeat for every part of the organization hierarchy.

Survey Management Configuration

Project and program risks can be tracked by the Project Portfolio Server solution after the risk management processes are configured in the Survey Management screens.

Each risk survey has a number of weighted categories. Each category has a number of weighted questions. Each question has a number of weighted answers. The risk surveys are displayed in the Risk tab for each project, program, and application. For each project, program, and application, a score is calculated based on the answers to the questions. Figure 13.40 shows the Survey Management options for Project, Program, Application, and Operational Performance Risk Management.

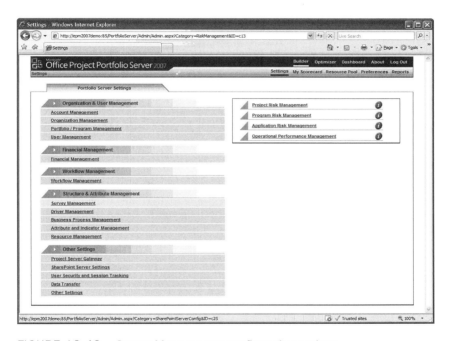

FIGURE 13.40   Survey Management configuration options.

Project Risk Management

To configure the project risk management parameters, select **Survey Management**, and then select **Project Risk Management**. Figure 13.41 shows the screen that will appear to add a risk category.

1. Click **Add Category**.

2. Fill in a category name and a weight assigned to this category.

3. Click **Add**.

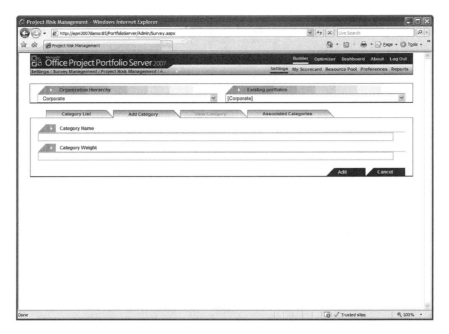

FIGURE 13.41   Add a risk category.

4. After the risk category has been added, select the risk category, and then select **Manage Questions**. The configuration screen shown in Figure 13.42 appears.

5. Click **Add Question**.

6. Fill in a question name, the question, and its weight.

7. Fill in a value and description for the first answer.

8. After adding all answers, click **Add Question**.

9. Click **Add Answer** and repeat for all possible answers.

Repeat this process for all additional questions and answers. When the questions have been completed, they can be associated with categories. Click the **Associated Categories** tab, and then enter the appropriate information, as shown in Figure 13.43.

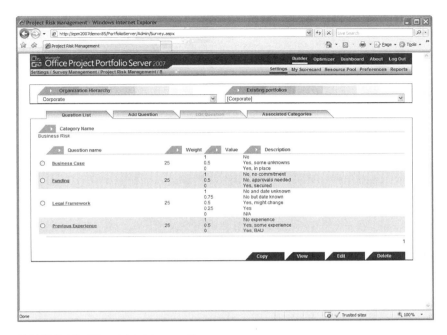

FIGURE 13.42   Add risk questions.

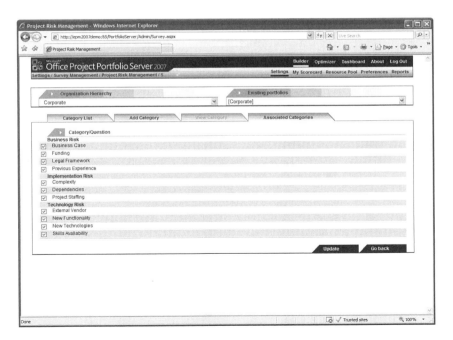

FIGURE 13.43   Associate risk questions with the organization.

1. Select the organization hierarchy and portfolio from the existing portfolios.

2. Select risk questions that should be associated to the selected organization level and/or portfolio, as shown in Figure 13.43.

3. Click **Update**.

Program, Application, and Operational Performance Risk Management

Programs, applications, and operational performance can have their own set of risk analysis questions. The questions are displayed in the Risk tab for each, and a risk score is calculated based on the answers to the questions. These surveys have weighted categories, weighted questions, and weighted answers, which are used to calculate a total risk score for the entity. These scores are then used during the project selection process in the Optimizer. The risk survey can be found in the entity's risk tab.

Structure and Attribute Management Configuration

Introducing Business Cases and Standard Templates

A business case is developed by an organization to gather pertinent information regarding costs and benefits (financial and nonfinancial) and general information for a proposed project or set of projects and programs. Detailed financial analysis is often attached as a separate document with the key financial information entered in one of the tabs of the business case. Business case is a required document within a governance workflow and it must be completed, reviewed, and approved before a project can be considered for addition to a selected portfolio of work.

Modifying Business Case Layout

Select the organization, and the specific project you would like to generate a report on. Select the desired granularity and date range for the report. Choose the options you want displayed in the report. Give the report a name, and choose whether to save or run the report, as shown in Figure 13.44.

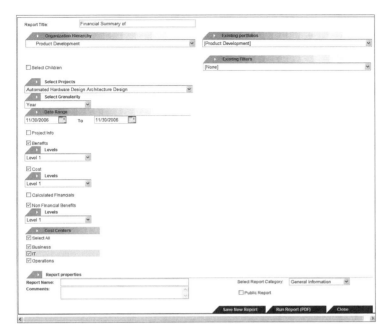

FIGURE 13.44   Modify the business case layout.

Attribute Definition and Association

Attributes provide detailed information about the entities within the Project Portfolio Server including projects, programs, portfolios, and applications. Other types of work may also be included. Attributes can be associated to different levels of the organizational hierarchy.

Attribute functionality is used to capture, report, roll up, calculate, save, and analyze data across the Portfolio Server.

There are two kinds of attributes: default (required by the software such as project class) and custom (defined by the administrator to meet specific organizational requirements).

There are five attribute types, and a wizard is available to help with definition of complex attributes and calculated attributes:

- ▶ **List.** A predefined set of text values shown in a drop-down list
- ▶ **Number.** Numeric value
- ▶ **Date.** Value in a date format
- ▶ **String.** Specific text value
- ▶ **Multiple text.** A predefined list of text values with multiple selections possible

Layout of the attributes in the Project Information tab and Status tab can be customized by editing parts of the project.aspx file. There are separate ASPX files for projects, programs, portfolios, and applications.

Attributes typically are shown on the Project Information tab or the Status tab and can also be associated to different parts of the application:

▶ **Builder.** If the attribute is used in one of the tabs in the Builder

▶ **Dashboard.** If the attribute is shown on the dashboard

▶ **Optimizer.** If the attribute is shown in the Optimizer or is importable

Every attribute will have a custom text label. To begin attribute configuration, select **Attribute and Indicator Management**, **Attribute Definition**, as shown in Figure 13.45.

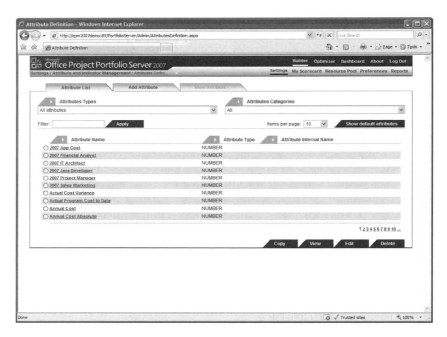

FIGURE 13.45   Attributes list.

You can add a new attribute, search using a text string for a specific attribute, or view the default attributes from the section. Figure 13.46 provides the screen layout to add an attribute:

1. Select the areas where the attribute will be used.

2. Choose the desired attribute type (for example, Change Request, KPI, and so on).

3. Choose a data type and fill in all fields: Name, Attribute Data Type, and so on.

4. Check if the attribute is mandatory.

5. Click **Add Attribute**.

6. Select the **Attribute is calculated based on other attributes (only works for Number data types)** check box.

7. Enter a formula in the pop-up window based on other attributes, cost/benefit numbers, or resource numbers.

8. Click **OK**.

9. When all the parameters are finished, click **Add Attribute**.

FIGURE 13.46   Define and add an attribute.

Project, program, and organization attributes can be calculated based on one of five properties, as shown in Figure 13.47. The properties include the following:

▶ **Project cost.** Broken down by hierarchy level, cost center, time frame, and granularity

▶ **Financial benefit.** Broken down by hierarchy level, cost center, time frame, and granularity

▶ **Nonfinancial benefit.** Broken down by hierarchy level, time frame, and granularity

▶ **Resource.** Broken down by resource type and time frame

▶ **Other attribute.** Calculated based on custom formulas incorporating other attributes

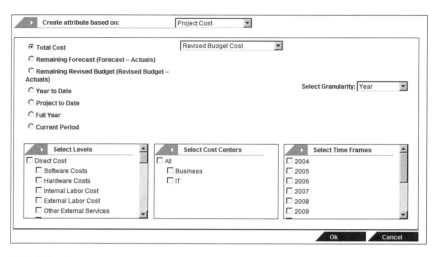

FIGURE 13.47   Attribute properties.

After the attributes have been completely defined, they must be associated. Every level of the organization hierarchy and/or defined portfolio can have different attributes associated to them. Associate the appropriate attributes to each level of the organization hierarchy and portfolio. Use the Attribute and Indicator Management, Attribute Associations screen to complete the appropriate associations.

NOTE

There is no screen available to change the layout of the project info and/or Additional Information tabs. You need to alter a file on the application server:

c:\inetpub\portfolioserver2007\portfolioserver\default\Project.aspx.

There are separate ASPX files for projects, programs, portfolios, and applications. You can format the Info, Additional Information, and Status tabs, depending on the section in the ASPX file. The default layout consists of two columns; possible tags are as follows:

  ▶ attribute = "<default_att>" to add a default attribute.

  ▶ name = "<custom_att>" to add a custom attribute.

  ▶ label = "<label>" to change the label of the field.

  ▶ readonly = "true" to make a field read-only.

  ▶ position = "x" to change the position of the field on the page.

  ▶ colspan = "2" to make a longer field crossing both columns.

  ▶ width = "x" to change the width of a field.

▶ sectionbreak name = "…" to add a header.

▶ sectionbreak to add a separator line.

▶ <allcustomattributes /> to list all new attributes associated to the organization, in alphabetic order.

Indicator Definition and Association

Some characteristics can be reflected on user screens with graphical indicators rather than attributes. Indicators are used in the following:

▶ Status tabs (project, program, portfolio, application)

▶ Dashboards

▶ Reports

Indicators can be manual or can be automatically defined based on a formula. They can be associated to different levels in the organizational hierarchy in a similar fashion as attributes.

Indicators can have four different values: Red, Yellow, Green, Gray (undefined). Every organization level and/or portfolio can have its own indicators defined and associated in a manner similar to the attributes. To minimize confusion regarding the meaning of the indicator color, indicators should be standardized across the entire hierarchy. The thresholds are set by the administrator using the Indicator Management and Indicator Association screens within the Attribute and Indicator Management section. Figure 13.48 shows the details of the Add Indicator tab.

1. Fill in all fields:

    ▶ Indicator Name

    ▶ Order

    ▶ Descriptions for Green, Yellow, and Red status

2. Select **Projects** or **Applications**.

3. Select **Yes** for manual indicators or **No** for automatic indicators.

4. Click **Add**.

After the indicator has been added, set the graphical values. For automatic indicators, specify an absolute or relative formula and the limits between Green, Yellow, and Red. Click **Edit** to define a formula. After the indicators have been defined, they can be associated with the organization and portfolios, as appropriate.

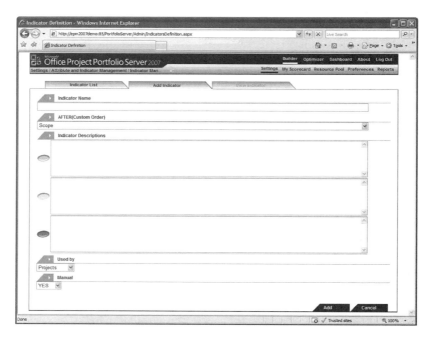

FIGURE 13.48   Add indicator.

Configuring Drivers

Business drivers represent the goals and objectives that an organization establishes to deploy its strategy. They tend to be focused in areas such as growth of the business, financial performance, customer satisfaction, and employee management. All the work of the organization should be related in some way to reaching one or more of the business drivers.

Portfolio Server provides a business driver library capability that contains the business drivers created to assess strategic alignment in the portfolio selection process. Business drivers are associated to an organization or portfolio to be included in the driver set for that organization/portfolio.

Every project/program can have an impact on a certain driver with the impact ranging from low to very high (extreme). Impact definitions should be as quantitative as possible to allow for fair comparison amongst projects and programs. Business drivers can be added to the library by selecting Driver Management, Business Driver Library, as shown in Figure 13.49.

Business Driver Library

To add a new driver, follow these steps:

1. Select **Driver Management**, and then select **Business Driver Library** on the right.

2. Enter the appropriate information in the screen, as shown in Figure 13.50.

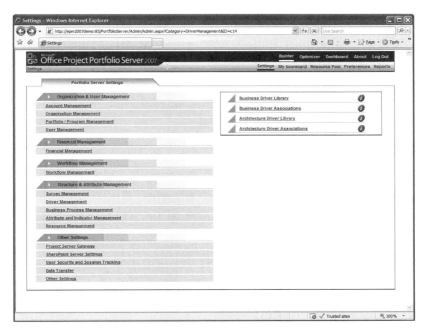

FIGURE 13.49   Add a business driver to the library.

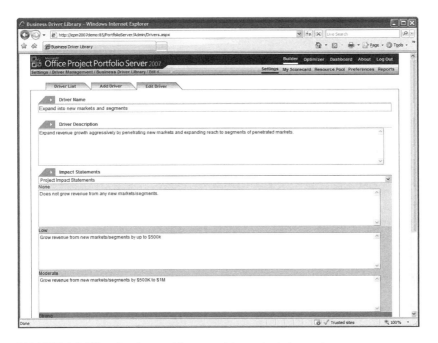

FIGURE 13.50   Business drivers and impact statements.

3. Enter the driver name.

4. Select **Project/Program/Application Impact Statements**.

5. Enter impact statement definitions.

6. Select the appropriate KPIs (optional). At least one KPI attribute must have been added as shown in the section called Attribute Definition and Association.

7. Select **Yes** or **No**. Yes requires one KPI be selected.

8. Click **Add**.

Business Driver Associations

Associate the business drivers to the appropriate organizational and portfolio levels by selecting the Business Driver Associations tab in the Driver Management configuration section. Business drivers and their impacts will be shown on the Strategic Impact tab.

Resource Management and Resource Pool

The Resources Management section of the tool is where competency-level resource portfolio planning occurs. It consists of four subsections:

▶ **Resource Type Management.** This where resource type is added and defined/configured.

▶ **Resource Type Association.** This is where the created and configured resource types are associated to different organizations.

▶ **Resource Tracking Configuration.** This is where the setting up of the resource-tracking functionality occurs.

▶ **Resource to Cost Level/Center Mapping.** This is where resource types are mapped to cost levels and cost centers.

Resources are grouped into high-level competencies or resource types. Projects can capture high-level competency needs in the Budget Resource tab. Competency actual data can be tracked in the Resource Tracking tab, and Forecast Values.

If the organization is using both Project Portfolio Server and Project Server, integration with Microsoft Project Server can define name-level resource assignments. Name-level resources will automatically be rolled up in Portfolio Server into the high-level competencies in the Budget Resource and/or Resource Tracking tabs.

Every organization level and/or portfolio can have its own resource types. Resource values can be defined by the resource type associations. Budgeted and tracked resources can be automatically converted into costs and captured in a defined cost category in the Budget Cost tab:

▶ Resources to cost structure, for example, project manager is mapped to resource cost line item.

▶ Resources to cost center, for example, project manager is mapped to IT cost center.

NOTE

If your organization is using both Microsoft Office Project Portfolio Server 2007 and Microsoft Office Project Server 2007 to manage resources, it will be essential to have the right level of information set up in the two software packages. Named resources should be set up only in Project Server and should be mapped to a specific competency level in Portfolio Server. This can be done in the Named Resource Management link under Project Server Gateway in the Settings page.

Resource Type Management and Association

Click the **Resource Type Management** item under the **Resource Management** tab to begin definition of resources. Select **Add Resource Type**, and then enter the appropriate information for each type as shown in Figure 13.51.

1. Fill in a resource type name and yearly permanent and contractor cost.

2. Depending on the defined resource attributes, fill in the additional fields.

3. Click **Add**.

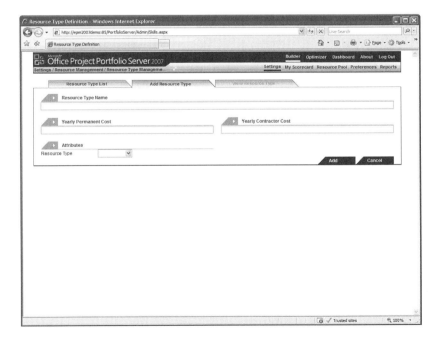

FIGURE 13.51   Human resource management.

After all the resource types have been added, associate them with the appropriate levels in the organizational hierarchy and portfolios using the Resource Management, Resource Type Associations screen.

Resource Tracking Configuration

The Resource Tracking tab shows budget and actual numbers. To configure this component for proper tracking and reporting, select the **Resource Tracking Configuration** screen in the Resource Management Section. Select all columns you want to see in the Resource Tracking tab from the list that appears, as shown in Figure 13.52:

- ▶ Original budgeted resources (pulled from the Budget Resource tab)

- ▶ Approved resources in change requests (pulled from Approved Change Requests)

- ▶ Revised budgeted resources (the sum of original budgeted resources and approved change requests)

- ▶ Actual work done (manually entered or imported from Microsoft Project Server)

- ▶ Actual variance (difference between actual work and revised budgeted work)

- ▶ Forecast work (manually entered or imported from Microsoft Project Server)

- ▶ Forecast variance (difference between forecast work and revised budgeted)

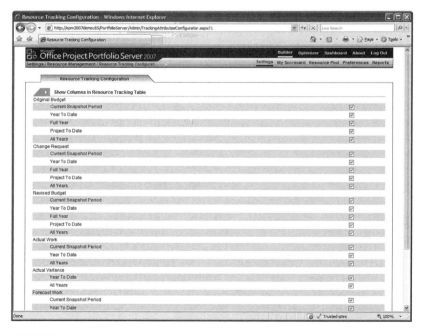

FIGURE 13.52   Select data that will appear in the Resource Tracking tab.

Resource to Cost Level/Center Mapping

When you are using resource to cost level/center mapping, each resource type must be selected as permanent or contractor. Also, you must define where the cost will appear in the cost structure, and to what cost center they should belong. Standards should be defined and followed across the organization to ensure that resource cost is tracking properly.

> **NOTE**
>
> If this functionality is used, it should be used for every resource that is associated to the organization. Otherwise, not all resources entered in the Budget Resource tab will be converted to cost, which can falsely display a project's total resource costs.

1. Select **Organization**.

2. Select **Resource Category**, **Cost Level**, and **Cost Center**.

3. Select specific areas in the application where the mapping defined will be applied, as shown in Figure 13.53. When selected, these options automatically calculate the resource cost, based on resources for all projects in the organization selected. When Convert is selected, this will calculate the cost automatically. Otherwise, the user must manually click **Convert** in the project tabs every time a calculation is desired.

4. Click **Update**.

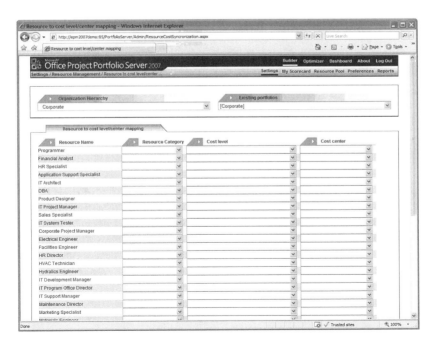

FIGURE 13.53   Map resource to cost levels and centers.

The resource pool allows the user to view resource information for the selected organization. The resource pool functionality enables you to view the following information at the organizational level you have selected in the scorecard:

- **The original availability.** Available resources per resource type for the selected organization

- **Resource requirements.** Total required resources per resource type based on the individual requirements of each project in the selected organization

- **Actual availability.** Original availability minus resource requirements

For the first and last item to display valid information, it is required that your system administrator has updated the original availability data.

Other Settings Configuration

The Other Settings section of the Portfolio Server includes other configuration and usage areas. It includes four subsections applicable to projects.

Project Snapshot Report Management

Project snapshot report management allows you to centrally manage the snapshot reporting process for Projects. Project Portfolio Server captures actual cost numbers, actual resource allocations, and indicators' statuses on a monthly/quarterly/yearly basis. It can also be used to create reports for specific snapshot periods.

When the current month/quarter/year actual numbers are final, a report or snapshot must be archived for the current month to open a snapshot for entering the actual numbers of the following period.

Archiving is the process of creating a snapshot. The projects stay in the same state/life cycle step and actual data is now entered for the following month.

There are two ways to archive a project:

1. Each project manager is responsible for his or her own project(s).

   In this case, all actual data should be entered for the current month, and then the specific project should be archived, allowing data to now be entered for the following month. This is done project by project, and the projects are not necessarily archived at the same time.

2. The administrator creates the snapshots for all projects at the same time.

In this case, the administrator would lock the projects for the month so that users cannot enter data for the following month. If data is currently being entered for January, then by January 31 the administrator would lock the projects, and would only unlock a project if more January data needs to be entered. By February 3, all January data should be in the tool and the administrator can now take a snapshot of January, and unlock the projects for data entry in February.

1. Choose **Organization Hierarchy and Portfolio**.

2. Select the projects you want to archive or lock/unlock. Projects appear in two sections, as shown in Figure 13.54. The first set is in a workflow status that allows for actual data and archiving. Projects in a workflow status that does not allow for actual data and archiving follow the first set and have been grayed out.

3. Click **New Snapshot**, **Lock Snapshot**, or **Unlock Snapshot**. Selection of New Snapshot will open a new reporting period for the selected projects.

4. On the screen that follows, choose a name for the current report that should be archived (for example, June 2005).

5. Choose a name for the new reporting period (for example, July 2005).

6. Click **OK** to close the previous period and to open a new reporting period.

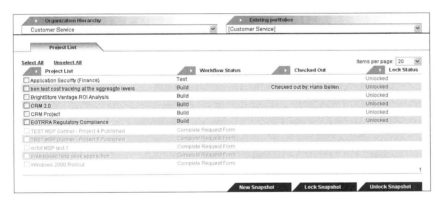

FIGURE 13.54   Project archival.

Application Snapshot Report Management

Application snapshot report management allows you to centrally manage the snapshot reporting process for Applications (this is covered in the APM section).

Filter Management

This function is used to define new and edit existing filters to be used within all modules of Project Portfolio Server. Filters are used to select a bunch of projects, applications, processes, programs, drivers, enterprise drivers, skills, or portfolios, based on the following:

▶ **Entities.** To filter on a list of predefined entities (static)

▶ **Structural attribute.** To filter entities on their value of a certain attribute, for example, cost attribute, workflow status

Different rules and criteria can be combined with and/or statements when you select to use structural attributes to create the filters.

Filter Conditions include the following:

▶ When users filter by structural attributes, the content of the filter is determined by a set of user-defined conditions. These are simple sets of rules that search the attributes of the selected filter type for matching conditions.

▶ Different types of attributes will have different rules for searching. For example, a list attribute such as Workflow Status will only have = (equals), <> (does not equal), Is Empty, and Is Not Empty as rules, whereas an integer attribute will have a range of mathematical operators to use for comparison.

▶ For further precision, use the logical operators OR (any condition true), AND (all conditions true), or END (last condition in the set).

Private versus public filters:

▶ **Private.** Viewable only by the user who created the filters. Ideal for testing filter settings or for highly specialized uses of a filter.

▶ **Public.** Able to be used by any user of the application. Used for common filters shared among several users or groups, especially commonly edited filters.

To add a filter, follow these steps:

1. Select **Add Filter** from the menu options, as shown in Figure 13.55.

2. Select a filter type to see existing filters. Filter types can be projects, applications, business processes, programs, business drivers, architecture drivers, resource types, or portfolios.

3. Choose the filter type and click **Next**.

4. Select the organization hierarchy and/or portfolio.

5. Define the filter. For the filter type projects, programs, and so on, select a static list of entities you want to include in the filter, as shown in Figure 13.56, and then click **Next**.

The final step is to choose a name for the filter and to select **Private** if the filter is only to be used by the current user. If not chosen, this filter will be open for public use.

NOTE

To create a dynamic filter, select the **Structural Attribute** type, and then define the filter rules in the menu.

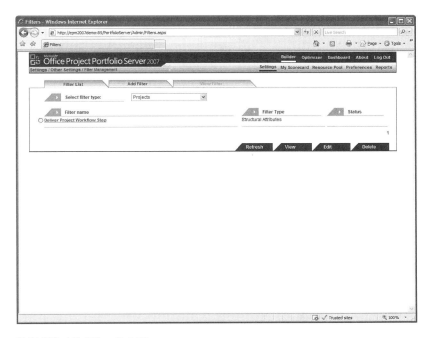

FIGURE 13.55   Set filters.

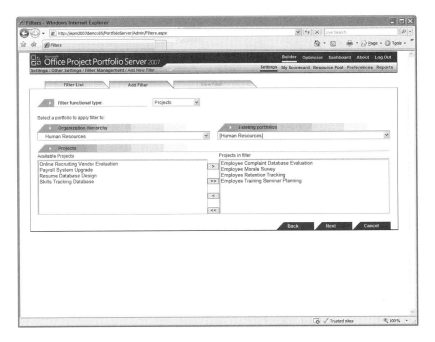

FIGURE 13.56   Filter management.

Email Templates Management

Email templates management: define email templates is used to notify users that an event occurred in Project Portfolio Server.

Email templates are used with notifications (see configurable workflow) and alert subscriptions (for example, when a project is created).

Email templates use certain keywords that will be substituted with the correct value (for example, *userName*).

Email templates can have the following types:

▶ **Programs Created.** Used in alert subscriptions

▶ **Portfolios Created.** Used in alert subscriptions

▶ **Projects Created.** Used in alert subscriptions

▶ **Workflow Email Templates.** Used in the configurable workflow

▶ **Workflow Status Changed.** Used in alert subscriptions

▶ **Indicator Color Changed.** Used in alert subscriptions

▶ **Attribute Value Changed.** Used in alert subscriptions

▶ **Entry Items Created.** Used in alert subscriptions

Email templates have been defined in the "Workflow Management Configuration" section and so are not addressed in detail here.

Configuring Project Server 2007 Gateway

The Project Server gateway allows organizations to perform many tasks, including the following:

▶ Exporting projects created in the Portfolio Server to Project Server by

  ▶ Export dates, numbers, list and text fields

  ▶ Export phases and milestones as an initial project plan

▶ Importing in-flight projects from Project Server into Portfolio Server by

  ▶ Creating mapping templates to allow importing date attributes, numbers, list and text fields

  ▶ Importing selected level of tasks and milestones

  ▶ Rolling up named-level resources assigned to tasks in Project Server into competencies and importing the resource competency assignment to Portfolio Server

▶ Synchronizing the resource availability as defined in Project Server, via the OLAP cube:

   ▶ The rolled-up availability information from the named resources into availability by competency group. It must use the Analysis Servers to be able to automatically generate the OLAP cube.

▶ Setting automatic project info synchronization daily or monthly or manually refreshing between Portfolio Server and Project Server.

▶ Access Project Server screens from within the Project Portfolio Server (for example, Gantt charts and so on) by

   1. Exporting approved Projects from Project Portfolio Server to Project Server (detailed resource planning in Project Server)

   2. Optional: Importing the updated Project Plan in Project Server as the new baseline in Project Portfolio Server

   3. Synchronizing resource actuals, schedule updates, and project attributes from Project Server to Project Portfolio Server

The gateway is used to share information between the servers. New proposals are captured in Project Portfolio Server, and the workflow allows their evolution through the process. Portfolio analysis is used to select projects, and the gateway allows for selected projects to be created in Project Server. Project resources, activities, plans, and so on are managed at the detail level in Project Server. Through implementation, the gateway is used to roll up information to the portfolio level to enable reporting, analysis, and tracking.

> **NOTE**
>
> Before individual Windows-authenticated users can use the Project Server Gateway, they must first access Preferences by clicking the Preferences link. This initializes user's connection to Project Portfolio Server 2007.

Gateway Settings

To establish the gateway between the servers, configuration is managed in Project Portfolio Server.

Project Server Gateway, Project Server Management

To set up a Project Server gateway, follow these steps:

1. Type a name for your Project Server.

2. Choose a description.

3. Type the URL used to access the Project Server Web Service.

4. Type the URL used to access Project Web Access, as shown in Figure 13.57.

5. Click **Update**.

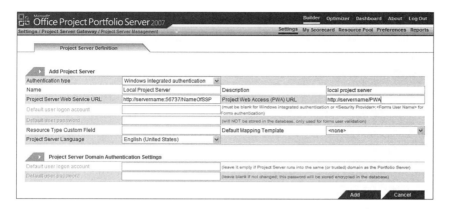

FIGURE 13.57   Establish the Project Server gateway.

Project Server Gateway, Automatic Refresh Settings

Choose the frequency of the refresh (daily, monthly) and the time that the refresh will be run.

Resource Pool Synchronization Settings

To configure the resource pool synchronization settings, follow these steps:

1. Select the organization hierarchy level.

2. Select a Project Server to be linked, as shown in Figure 13.58.

3. Click the **Add** button. Then, repeat Step 2 to link more than one Project Server to the same organization hierarchy level.

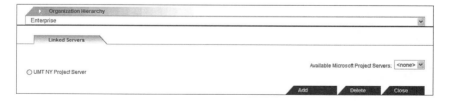

FIGURE 13.58   Establish resource pool synchronization settings.

Synchronization Error Log

The synchronization log should be checked regularly to monitor for errors in the server. There is nothing to configure in this menu item.

Attribute Mapping Template Management

Certain attributes created in Portfolio Server can be mapped to enterprise fields in Project Server for export/import of data.

When creating a custom field in Project Server 2007, choosing the correct "type" is important. When mapping custom fields in Project Server 2007 with custom attributes in Portfolio Server 2007, they must have the same type; for example, text custom fields can only be mapped with text custom attributes.

Select the template to view, edit, or delete, or click **Add** to create a new template. Mapping templates link spreadsheet fields to attributes for faster import of standardized documents.

The following fields can be mapped between Project Server and Portfolio Server:

▶ Project Portfolio Server text and list fields – Project Server text fields

▶ Project Portfolio Server date fields – Project Server date fields

▶ Project Portfolio Server number fields – Project Server number fields

For example, in Figure 13.59, ProjectID is a text attribute in Project Portfolio Server. The drop-down list to the right of this attribute will *only* show Text type fields from Project Server. In this example, a custom text field was created in Project Server called "Free Text Field," and mapped to ProjectID.

Named Resource Management

Creating resources in Project Server 2007 is not described in this chapter. The mapping of the resources to resource competencies in Portfolio Server is done in the Portfolio Server tool.

Figure 13.59 shows the screen where the resources between the two tools are mapped. When adding a named resource in Project Portfolio Server, make sure the resource name matches *exactly* to the name in Project Server.

This is very important because if the name is spelled differently, it will *not* map. Choose what resource competency you want this resource name to be connected with. After this is done, anytime an import of resource is done from Project Server to Portfolio Server, the work needed to be done by John Doe will show up in Project Portfolio Server as work needed to be done by a Developer C++ competency.

FIGURE 13.59   Mapping named resources between the two servers.

Outline-Level Settings

Select the desired task outline level for phase matching, and click **Update** to save the entered value for later use. Milestones do not belong to a level, and will be imported regardless of what level is chosen here. All the tasks in the selected level will be imported, whether they are summary tasks or not. However, *only* the tasks in the level chosen will be imported. For example, if level 2 is chosen, all the tasks at level 2 will be imported as phases into the tool. Level 1 tasks, and the levels below, if any, will *not* be imported.

CAUTION

Mapping at this detailed level between the two systems can be difficult to maintain because of the ability to modify settings in either application. This capability should be tested thoroughly before a decision is made to map at the outline level. In many cases, organizations choose to provide detailed status of progress via the Project Server application instead of the Portfolio Server application.

Configuring SharePoint Integration

Microsoft Office Project Portfolio Server 2007 can be integrated with Windows SharePoint Services 3.0 (refer to the "Account Settings" section earlier in this chapter). The Document Management tab will be linked to a SharePoint site. In the SharePoint Server Settings, you can configure the SharePoint Server that is linked to each level of the organizational structure and each SharePoint site that corresponds to an entity (program, project, or application).

In the Preferences section, each user needs to define the SharePoint user ID and password information.

TIP

It is recommended that Secure Sockets Layer (SSL) be used as username/password is sent over HTTP during this process.

---

1. Type a name for your SharePoint Server.

2. Choose a description.

3. Type the URL used to access your SharePoint Server, as shown in Figure 13.60.

NOTE

This URL should be accessible from the application server. End the URL with a forward slash (/); otherwise, an error message will come up.

---

4. Select the box if this is your default SharePoint Server.

5. Click **Update**.

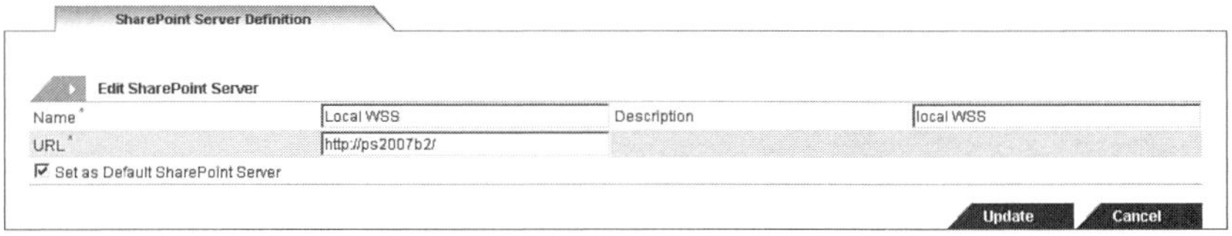

FIGURE 13.60   Integration with SharePoint.

The high-level steps for configuration are as follows:

1. Go to a SharePoint site and create document libraries, folders, and upload templates the way you want them to look like for projects, programs, portfolios, and applications.

2. Save the URL address where you save the selected site templates.

3. Add the URL address to the corresponding field in the SharePoint Server definition within MOPPS and assign a name and description to the documents' site.

Each user will have to set his or her password in the Preferences page, used to access SharePoint. The user must have rights in SharePoint to access (read/write) the linked sites.

> **NOTE**
>
> During the transition of documents to SharePoint, the documents are not encrypted. If the front-end server is moved or the database restored and connected with a different Web front-end server, the cryptographic key will be invalid, and users might get errors depending on the integration features used.

Setting Up User Preferences

The Preferences feature enables the users to set the individual user preferences in the tool. From the Builder main screen, click **Preferences** to get to the Preferences page, where the user can change some personal settings.

Users have the ability to configure the following settings:

▶ **Microsoft Project Preferences.** Allows you to configure Project Server access information, such as Project Server name and user login.

▶ **My Scorecard Configuration.** Allows you to customize My Scorecard views and how you see the initiatives that you are working with. In addition, you can configure your personal Dashboard view and how you view ongoing projects.

▶ **SharePoint Preferences.** Allows you to configure the SharePoint Server information and SharePoint account access.

▶ **User Management.** Allows you to update your personal user information and change your current password.

Microsoft Project Preferences

If allowed by the administrator and available to the user, the user can configure the login information for other tools that work in tandem with the Portfolio Server, such as SharePoint Servers. The Microsoft Project Preferences screen allows you to configure the Project Server access information and to specify Project Server name as well as your login to access Project Server. If needed, your administrator will provide details to fill in this area.

My Scorecard Configuration

The My Scorecard Configuration option allows you to configure My Scorecard views as well as Scorecard attributes. The default view for all users of the My Scorecard and the Dashboard views is fully configurable by the administrator, but you can also select your own personal preferences for this view and set them as the default for your user profile.

Views allow you to define the entity information to be included and the way it is included in the rows of the My Scorecard and Dashboard views.

> **TIP**
>
> Make sure to configure the attributes first prior to defining a view.

Users can customize their own My Scorecard views and how they see all the initiatives they are working with, and their own Dashboard view and how they view ongoing projects. To filter projects differently (rows), click **Configure Scorecard Views**.

Defining Attributes Configurations

Configurations allow you to define different views for the columns displayed in the My Scorecard and Dashboard views. You have to perform this step first prior to defining the view as the attribute configurations you create are required for view creation.

To define a new attribute configuration, follow these steps:

1. From the Preferences page click the **Configure Scorecard Attribute Window** link under the My Scorecard Configuration.

2. To create a new attribute configuration select the **Add Configuration** tab.

3. Provide the configuration information such as the Name, Description, and the Module.

4. In the main area, use the **Insert New Column** link to add new columns.

5. Select the appropriate data category.

6. For each data category select data from set available in that category.

7. Enter column name.

8. Once configuration is complete, click the **Update** button to save your changes.

9. You can revert to the default configuration at any time by clicking the **Restore the default** button.

You can define as many configurations as you would like and then associate them with views you create for the scorecard.

Configuring My Scorecard Views

Once you have created all needed attribute configurations, you can create the My Scorecard views.

To define a new view, follow these steps:

1. From the Preferences page click the **Configure Scorecard Views** link under the My Scorecard Configuration.

2. The My Scorecard List tab displays all views you currently have defined.

3. Add a new view by clicking the **Add Scorecard** tab.

4. Provide all of the general descriptive information for the view, such as Name and Description.

5. You can use one of the several hierarchy groupings to help you organize entities in the system. These are types of categories and subcategories that produce an outline structure on your Scorecard page.

6. Select the types of entities you would like to see, as well as any filter you want to apply. Entity can be organization, portfolio of projects, or program of associated portfolios, projects, or applications.

7. Use the **Select Attribute Configuration** link to select one of the attribute configurations you have already defined.

8. To designate the current view as default, select the **Default Scorecard** checkbox.

9. Click the **Update** button to save changes.

SharePoint Preferences

If allowed by the administrator and available to the user, the user can configure the login information for other tools that work in tandem with the Portfolio Server, such as SharePoint Servers. To do so, from the Preferences page click the **SharePoint Servers** link under the SharePoint Preferences area. If needed, your administrator will provide details to fill in this area.

User Management

If allowed by the administrator and available to the user, the user can change his/her login password and email address. To do so, from the Preferences page click the **Change User Information** link.

The Last Steps

Project Portfolio Server is a complex application that requires not only careful configuration, but definition and existence of necessary processes to support the solution. Once your system is configured, it is important that you validate that the process functions as you defined it and that all user roles have appropriate access.

As a final step after validation, make sure to perform a formal system rollout, including full user training. User training should not only include application training, but also any processes that support the correct operation of the entire solution.

CHAPTER 14

Project Server 2007: Overview and Installation

Here is a simple question to consider: How many companies in the world are you aware of that do not have projects? If you answered more than zero and they are still in business then they will probably have a list of projects real soon.

Given that project management is such a wide open marketplace, it can sometimes be daunting to get your arms around it. You need to consider how projects are selected, who does the projects, how the projects will be managed, and then how everyone on the project team is kept in the loop. Until just recently, the software marketplace took only components of these organizational needs into consideration.

Enter the Microsoft Office Project family of products. Microsoft's 2007 release of the Office Project suite is designed to address all the areas of an organization's Project Management needs. In the previous chapters you looked into the Project Portfolio world, and now we need to go forward into Project Server 2007.

Introduction to Project Server 2007

This third major release of Project Server, Microsoft Project Server 2007, is an entirely new platform from Microsoft development. If you were to ask what's new, the answer would be "everything!" Project Server 2007 is built on the productive, feature-rich code framework and the set of application services in Microsoft .NET Framework 2.0 and Microsoft Windows SharePoint Services (currently in version 3).

Project Server enables a Web-based view of the Project Schedules created with Project Professional. Without Project Server, anyone on a project would have to be very skilled in reading Gantt charts and understanding project management methodologies instead of being able to go online and see their task list. For executives, it provides a dashboard of the current status of projects and how they are progressing.

A primary element of the Microsoft Office Enterprise Project Management Solution, Microsoft Project Server is designed to keep you on the front edge of your program's, project's, and portfolio's schedule. A centralized place to do resource management and resource planning, it also provides a platform for business intelligence against your project program portfolio resource data, designed to provide you with a place to collaborate with all team members, too.

This might all sound quite wonderful, but you may be asking what it actually does. Well, if you have used Microsoft Project in the past, you most likely know the organizing ability this tool has, which can make your project planning and deployment much more proficient. Project Server and Web Access allow you to centralize your project information into a database that allows others to access the project for a variety of reasons—perhaps, in the case of a manager, to drill down and see advanced project details or make alterations; or, as a team member, to see various aspects of the project before them. Access can be controlled quite well to allow different persons the ability to see different portions of the project.

In addition, through the Project Server, you can keep team members informed about important aspects of the project. As a project progresses and you update information, the Project Server can take the input it receives and analyze resources utilized and, through this process, the server can make forecasting requirements to allow for a greater efficiency over project resources.

It's all about communication and collaboration! Microsoft Project Server 2007 is designed to be on the front edge of all your projects: their costs and resource management. Providing a central cache of information, Project Server 2007 will allow you and your organization the visibility and insights needed to evaluate, supervise, and report, as well as standardize and centralize your resource management. Efficiently track and analyze projects with a better understanding of the timetable and impact of changes. Benefit from better economic control and impressive analytics.

You might be wondering whether you need a Project Server to receive these benefits. Not necessarily, and it's important that we mention this at the outset. Various software tools work with Microsoft Office Project 2007, and this family of products supports a variety of approaches to work management, levels of process development, and business goals.

So, for smaller teams (or possibly individuals who are responsible for managing projects, although perhaps not necessarily project managers), there is a product called Microsoft Office Project Standard 2007 that can provide the enhanced desktop tools needed to get the job done. If you lack the job complexity or cannot justify the purchase of Project

Server from a business perspective, Office Project Standard provides the simple, intuitive tools that will enable operational control with minimal overhead.

> **NOTE**
>
> Note that Microsoft Office Project Standard 2007, as with Project Standard 2003 (and Professional 2003, too), cannot be used with Office Project Server 2007. You must use Microsoft Office Project Professional.

If you are working on large teams on critical projects and need to centralize schedules and require a website to share information or ideas, you will want Microsoft Office Project Server 2007. We refer to this product as being an Enterprise Project Management (EPM) solution and will integrate your people and processes with organizational policies and governance.

Microsoft Project Server Family

The Office Project 2007 platform has been extended and has redesigned the Project 2003 client and server applications to take advantage of improvements in the Windows platform. It includes the Project client applications, Project Server, the client and server application programming interfaces (APIs), and the necessary infrastructure, such as Microsoft SQL Server and Microsoft Windows SharePoint Services. Let's consider some of the 2007 family members:

▶ **Microsoft Office Project Professional 2007** is primarily the same as Microsoft Office Project Standard in base functionality. However, it adds more capabilities when extended as the primarily desktop application for use with Office Project Server 2007. Features not provided by the Standard version include active cache for the fast opening and saving of projects over a wide area network; access to a centralized resource pool and the ability to check-in and check-out project plans on Office Project Server 2007.

▶ Microsoft Office **Project Server 2007** is a SharePoint application that manages security access for users and handles all the key functions that enable reporting, email notifications, and upkeep of Project Server 2007 databases.

▶ **Project Web Access** provides access to project information via a browser. All your team members will now be able to access a project's data (whether they have Project installed on that system or not) to see the details of the project or to access timesheet updates or status reports. Project Web Access (or PWA) is fully integrated with Windows SharePoint Services.

▶ **Project Portfolio Server** can be used stand-alone as a ASP.NET 2.0 application for managing your corporate portfolio of projects. However, it has a gateway tool that integrates with Project Server 2007 to allow for bi-directional communications between the two products. A very common scenario here would be to approve a new project in Portfolio Server and have a brand-new project in Project Server get created based on a template.

In addition to these major players in the Project family, two others are considered extensions in the Project world:

- **Windows SharePoint Services (WSS) 3.0** serves as the foundation for Project Server and any collaboration users may wish to have when online. It's easy to see after you install Project Server that the administrative user interface is all based on the WSS infrastructure. In addition, it is through WSS that you have single sign-on, team collaboration features, and reporting features.

- **Microsoft Office SharePoint Server (MOSS) 2007** is not a required component for Project Server 2007 but is worth mentioning here because users may wish to make use of advanced features such as improved search and the ability to create Key Performance Indicators (KPI's) for reporting.

- **SQL Reporting Services** is also not a required component for Project Server 2007 but is typically included in an implementation so an organization can create custom reports that may not be available out-of-the-box with Project Server 2007 or WSS 3.0. Project Server 2007 does offer a denormalized database that is designed specifically to support reporting tools such as SQL Reporting Services.

Installation Prerequisites

You do need to consider some factors for both your server and the clients. You need to be aware of what the hardware and software standards are before even attempting to install. Taking these into consideration beforehand will be helpful in the deployment stage.

Planning an Installation

Before installing Project Server, it is important to note that there are many approaches you can take. For example, if you are just testing out the application, you can install all the software on one computer. For production-level environments you might have a Web server, application server, and a SQL Cluster.

These are all critical choices you will have to make in considering your implementation. Microsoft provides an excellent website with planning and installation documents, which you can access by going to the following address in your Web browser. Go to the "Library" area and find "Project Server".

`http://technical.microsoft.com`

In general, what determines the number of servers, amount of disk space, RAM and other needs is based on usage requirements. For example, if your company has a policy whereby all project updates need to be done by the end of day every Friday and you have two thousand users, then you will want to scale the Web server appropriately. If you have project plans that span many users with hundreds or thousands of resources assigned to them, you will need to size the database appropriately.

Prerequisites for Project Professional 2007

Table 14.1 identifies what you need to operate Microsoft Office Project Standard 2007 or Microsoft Office Project Professional 2007.

TABLE 14.1   The Prerequisites for Project Professional 2007

Component	Requirement
Computer and processor	700 megahertz (MHz) processor or higher
Memory	512MB or higher
Hard disk	1.5GB
Operating system	Microsoft Windows XP with SP2, Windows Vista, Windows Server 2003 with SP1 or later

Prerequisites for Project Server 2007

Table 14.2 identifies what you need to operate Microsoft Office Project Server 2007.

TABLE 14.2   The Prerequisites for Project Server 2007

Component	Requirement
Computer and processor	Server with processor speed of 2.5 gigahertz (GHz) or higher; dual processor, 3GHz or higher recommended
Memory	1GB, 2GB recommended
Hard disk	3GB
Operating system	Microsoft Windows Server 2003 Standard, Enterprise, Datacenter, or Web with service packs
Additional	SharePoint Services 3.0

You might have some additional concerns if you plan to use email notifications or box/forms. For more information, see the deployment documentation Microsoft offers on Project Server 2007.

> **NOTE**
>
> Because an installation of Office Project Server 2007 can range from a single computer (stand-alone installation) to many computers (server farm), the requirements for your installation will depend on the availability and scale requirements for your solution. Microsoft provides minimum requirements, but we recommend you always go beyond the minimum to enhance performance.

During the installation process, you can choose between a Basic install or an install as part of a farm. Keep these recommendation in mind before installation:

▶ Because Office Project Server 2007 is built on Microsoft Windows SharePoint Services 3.0, the requirements that apply to WSS 3.0 also apply to Office Project Server 2007.

▶ We recommend that you perform the installation on a computer that has a new installation of the Microsoft Windows Server 2003 operating system with Service Pack 1 (SP1) or later and all critical updates.

TIP

Because the Office Project Server 2007 Installation and Configuration Wizard marshals many components, if you uninstall Office Project Server 2007, and then later install Office Project Server 2007 on the same computer, the Setup program could fail when creating the configuration database, which would cause the entire installation process to fail. You can prevent this failure by deleting the existing configuration database or by using the **psconfig** command to create a new configuration database.

Some Basic Install Considerations

If you plan to install a Basic version of Project Server 2007, keep the following in mind.

Database

When you perform a Basic installation, SQL Server 2005 Express Edition is automatically installed. When you perform an Advanced installation on a stand-alone computer that already has Microsoft SQL Server installed, ensure that the computer meets the hardware and software requirements for a database server.

Because of Windows licensing restrictions, if you are using Windows Server 2003 Web Edition in a single server environment, you can perform only a Basic installation. This is because the full SQL Server editions cannot be installed on Windows Server 2003 Web Edition. However, you can install SQL Server 2005 Express Edition or SQL Server 2000 Desktop Engine (Windows) (WMSDE).

Operating System

Office Project Server 2007 runs on Windows Server 2003 with SP1 or later. We recommend that you apply all critical updates. You can use the following Windows Server 2003 editions:

▶ Standard Edition

▶ Enterprise Edition

▶ Datacenter Edition

▶ Web Edition

NOTE

The installation of the Web Edition is only used in a Load Balanced environment when the reader has a full version of SQL Server to be used as a backend database. SQL Express and MSDE have imposed limitations that may cause the reader problems down the road.

Office Project Server 2007 administration functions require Microsoft Internet Explorer 6.0 with the most recent service packs or Internet Explorer 7.0.

Windows Components

After you have installed the operating system and applied all critical updates, you must configure the computer to be a Web server by enabling Internet Information Services (IIS) 6.0, including the following:

▶ Common files

▶ WWW

▶ Simple Mail Transfer Protocol (SMTP)

You must configure the server to use IIS 6.0 Worker Process Isolation mode. This is the default setting in new installations. However, if you have upgraded from IIS 5.0 on Windows Server 2000, the Run WWW in IIS 5.0 Isolation Mode option is enabled, and you must change this setting to and enable the IIS 6.0 Worker Process Isolation Mode option.

To enable email notifications, you need to configure incoming and outgoing email settings. To configure sending email alerts and notifications, you must specify an SMTP email server. To configure your installation so that your SharePoint sites can accept and archive incoming email, you must install the IIS SMTP service.

Microsoft .NET Framework 3.0

Before installing Office Project Server 2007, you must install the Microsoft .NET Framework 3.0 and then ensure that ASP.NET 2.0 is enabled.

To enable ASP.NET v2.0.50727, open the Web service extension in the IIS snap-in on the Microsoft Management Console (MMC). If ASP.NET 2.0 is installed on the computer before IIS is enabled, you must enable ASP.NET 2.0 by running the command **aspnet_regiis -i.**

14

Some Server Farm Install Considerations

The primary difference between a single-server and a server farm topology is that you have several server rolls involved, which are based on the three main components of Project Server architecture, as follows:

▶ **Office Project Server 2007 Web tier.** This tier includes two components: Project Web Access and SharePoint Services 3.0. Project Web Access is basically an ASP.NET 2.0 application that is using Project Server Interface (PSI).

> **NOTE**
>
> The PSI is a replacement of the Project Data Service (PDS) in Project 2003. It is a new and complete managed-code API for Project Server 2007. The Project client (Project Professional 2007) and Project Web Access can only interact with the Project Server through PSI Web services.

▶ **Office Project Server 2007 application tier.** This tier includes the PSI, which is the API for the Project Server. It's through this API that Project Professional 2007 and Project Web Access (and other line-of-business and third-party applications) can access the server's databases.

▶ **Office Project Server 2007 database tier.** The Office Project 2007 databases can be built on either Microsoft SQL Server 2000 with the latest service pack or on Microsoft SQL Server 2005. The new security enhancements and improved Analysis Services and Reporting Services that are integrated directly into SQL Server 2005 can be fully taken advantage of by Microsoft Office Project Server 2007.

> **TIP**
>
> Typically, when you have several pieces of an infrastructure (like Groove, with its Manager, Relay, and Data Bridge), they each require a unique set of hardware and software. In this case, the difference between each of the servers in your farm is somewhat minimal. The hardware itself should meet the requirements previously listed for a server. More power is obviously better, so feel free to exceed the recommendations.

For each, keep in mind certain requirements. If you want to install them all on one server, you must meet the minimum recommended system requirements for each server role. If you install more than one role on a single computer, ensure that the computer meets the minimum requirements for all server roles. The server roles include the following:

▶ **Application server.** As for requirements, those previously listed for the Project Server will suffice for the application server. You need to remember to install IIS and configure the components necessary, along with the .NET Framework 3.0.

▶ **Front-end Web server.** With a front-end Web server, you might want to have more than adequate processor speed and memory. You might consider dual processors that are each 3GHz or faster, with more than 2GB of RAM. Because a front-end Web server is a subset of an application server, all features on a front-end Web server are available on an application server. The software requirements for the front-end Web server are the same as the software requirements for the application server before you add specific resources to meet the demands that you forecast as a result of your capacity planning phase.

▶ **Database server.** The computer that hosts the database server role must have SQL Server 2000 with SP3a or later or Microsoft SQL Server 2005 SP1 or later. Some advanced features require SQL Server 2005 Analysis Services SP1 or later. Because of Windows licensing restrictions, if you are using Windows Server 2003 Web Edition in a single-server environment, you can perform only a Basic installation because the full SQL Server editions cannot be installed on Windows Server 2003 Web Edition. However, you can install SQL Server 2005 Express Edition or SQL Server 2000 Desktop Engine (Windows) (WMSDE).

NOTE

A stand-alone installation does not require any database configuration. However, the database tier of a server farm is going to include four databases that we will configure later in this chapter: a Draft database, with tables for saving unpublished projects; a Published database, for all the published projects; an Archive database for backed-up, older versions of projects; and a Reporting database, for the generation of reports.

Deployment Considerations

When planning a Project Server 2007 installation, you must think about several deployment considerations. Your decisions will chiefly be based on whether you are moving to a full or gradual migration. We briefly discuss some of these options, but in short, choosing your best course and then researching is necessary.

When you are taking the full-migration approach, all data (including enterprise global data, resources projects, and so on) will migrate from Project Server 2003 to Project 2007 in one shot. When the migration is complete, users are also moved over.

Because both Project 2003 and 2007 can coexist on the same computer, all the data and the installation from Project 2003 can remain. During the migration process, no information is written to Project 2003's database, and so verification and testing to see that all is functional can be carried out by the administrator before the manual removal of Project 2003. This way, in case of catastrophic failure or if the migration simply fails, it is possible to revert to Project 2003.

It is also recommended that if you are planning on a full migration of projects, you do a full migration of Windows SharePoint Services data, too, so that the data is in sync.

On the other hand, a gradual migration allows for both Project Server 2007 and Project Server 2003 to coexist side by side. You can then migrate a subset of projects from 2003 to 2007. If this is your plan, you should also do a gradual migration of Windows SharePoint Services data, as well, to keep everything in sync.

A gradual-migration approach allows for more control by administrators over the release process. This approach could be used, for instance, when an organization wants a scheduled release to different departments over time. This approach also allows administrators to take the necessary steps if a problem occurs during the first phases of deployment.

Once again, it is highly recommend that you not be in a side-by-side scenario for an extended period of time.

Installing Project Server 2007

After you have considered your deployment scenario, you will move forward to perform the actual installation process. This install can be done as a stand-alone install with all the components on one system, or within a farm environment that can separate the components into its pieces to allow for flexibility and higher availability.

One benefit of the stand-alone install is that you can evaluate the product and test its features before deploying in a larger, farm environment. So, let's begin with an evaluation of the stand-alone method.

Stand-Alone Install

In stand-alone mode, the application server, front-end Web server, and database are all installed to a single computer using default settings. Keep in mind, however, that this mode supports only a single server, precluding your ability to configure redundancy options.

During the install, SQL Server Express 2005 is automatically installed on the server (so that the single system can serve as its own database server for the Project Server). Keep in mind that a farm install requires you to install SQL before the installation. In addition to SQL Server Express 2005, the Project Web Access site, Web applications, and the Shared Services Provider are automatically provisioned. Service account information is not a requirement to perform the installation, which uses Network Service accounts to finish.

After you've installed Windows Server 2003 and configured IIS properly, installed the .NET Framework 3.0 and enabled ASP .NET 2.0.50727, and after you have configured SMTP services (if you plan to use email notifications sent to you regarding your server), you can perform the installation.

To install Project Server 2007 in Stand-Alone mode, follow these steps:

1. Double-click the **Setup.exe** file to begin the setup process.

2. Enter the product key and click **Continue.**

3. Accept the terms of the license agreement by selecting the check box on the End User License Agreement page. Then click **Continue.**

4. You can choose Basic or Advanced installation. Selecting Basic will install Project Server as a stand-alone server in the standard file locations. If you select Advanced, you will be taken to the advanced settings, which will present you with several server types, as shown in Figure 14.1. You will be presented with three radio buttons to choose from:

    a. **Complete.** Install all components (that is, both the front-end Web server and the application server). Can add servers to form a SharePoint farm.

    b. **Web Front End.** Only install components required to render content to users. Can add servers to form a SharePoint farm.

    c. **Stand-alone.** Install all components on a single machine (includes SQL Server 2005 Express Edition). Cannot add servers to create a SharePoint farm.

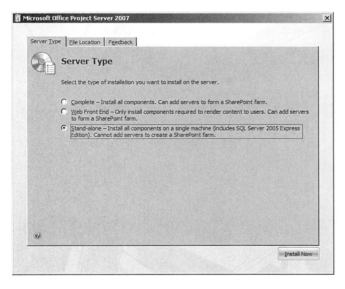

FIGURE 14.1   Choosing a server type.

5. Select your server type, configure your file locations and feedback settings, and then click **Install Now.**

6. When the page appears that says "Run the SharePoint Products and Technologies Configuration Wizard now," select **Close** to begin the wizard.

7. At the Welcome to SharePoint Products and Technologies page, click **Next.**

8. A confirmation dialog message appears, stating that the following services might need to be restarted or reset during the configuration:

    a. Internet Information Services

    b. SharePoint Administration Service

    c. SharePoint Timer Service

9. Click **Yes** to continue. A status bar appears to show the configuration progress.

10. When configuration is complete, the Configuration Successful page will appear. Click **Finish.**

11. The Manage Project Web Access Sites page (as shown in Figure 14.2) will now appear and will list the Project Web Access instance that is being provisioned. Click the **Refresh Status** button from time to time to check whether the Project Web Access instance has been provisioned. When the status appears as provisioned, click the URL to go to the Project Web Access home page.

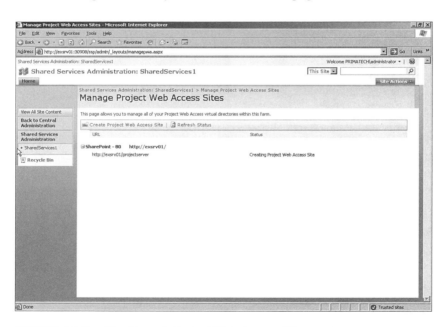

FIGURE 14.2   The Manage Project Web Access Sites page.

NOTE

You might have some difficulty from time to time getting the Project Web Access site to provision. This is usually due to a problem with your SQL services. Generally, they are provisioned using the Network Service account. Check your services and make sure they are all running and that you know the account they are running under.

Installing a Project Server Farm

Extending beyond a single-server approach, the concept of a farm could hold many meanings. We can develop a small, mid-size, or large farm environment. It's important to consider your needs and plan your deployment before taking the steps necessary to implement the farm. Consider the following scenarios and determine for yourself what form of farm you need to implement.

A Small Farm

Implementing Project Server 2007 within a small farm could be as simple as a two-server configuration. Imagine having a front-end Web server with the application server residing on the same system—and a back-end database server residing on a different system (called a two-tiered solution).

When talking about n-tier solutions, the tiers are logical within the application. A two-tier application scenario can include ASP.NET connecting directly to a backend database. The two components (ASP.NET and SQL Server) can reside on the same physical server and still be called 2-tiered solution or you can have it span multiple systems and it would still be considered a 2-tier solution. In a 3-tier solution there is usually a business dll or component introduced. The client, usually ASP.NET in this environment, will talk to the business component and then the business component will talk to the database. I'm not sure that there is a one-tiered solution. I believe it would require the consumer of the application to work directly with the database but that usually requires some type of tool (Query Analyzer or Management Studio), which itself would then be a tier, thus creating a 2-tiered solution.

Some may decide to install a one-server farm if you plan to grow in the future and know you will need to expand the farm. However, this is not recommended. If you can afford the extra server, it is better to begin the process by, at least, separating your database server back end from the front-end Web services. It really is better if you install a 2-node farm upfront. Complications can be introduced by adding a second node to an already existing production cluster. Session state is the biggest issue that won't show up in a "single node farm." Introducing the second node might make the application unavailable. Additionally if the user has gone through the trouble of installing a farm you might also want to suggest installing a separate SQL Server. By running the SQL Server on one of the farm nodes you drop the level of fault tolerance you were trying to accomplish in the first place. You should not imply that it would be OK to have a node in the front-end farm running the database.

To actually install the farm on a single server, you begin the process, much like for a stand-alone install, but you select the Advanced installation. You want to select the Complete installation, which will then install the binary files and bring you to the SharePoint Products and Technologies Configuration Wizard. At this point, you have to make a few different decisions.

14

NOTE

Remember, unlike the stand-alone install, which installs and configures SQL Express for you, you need to make sure your SQL installation is complete before you perform the farm installation. Otherwise, you cannot provide the information during the install for the database. We discuss in greater detail the SQL installation procedure later in this chapter.

For starters, you are asked whether you want to connect to a server farm. Obviously, your answer is either yes or no (see Figure 14.3).

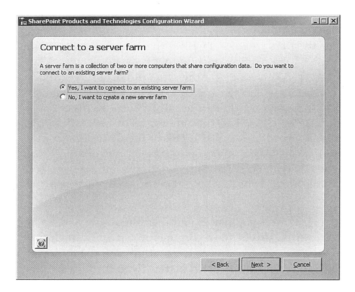

FIGURE 14.3   Connecting to a server farm.

In either case, you need to supply database configuration settings. If you want to connect to a server farm, you must supply the name of the database server and the database name (and a username and password). If you choose to create a new farm, you are asked to provide the same information, as shown in Figure 14.4, although in this case you can provide a database name that, if it doesn't exist already, will be created within your SQL Server. The default is SharePoint_Config. (If you are connecting to an existing farm, you can click the Retrieve Database Names button, to initiate a search for the databases that are already configured on the SQL Server.)

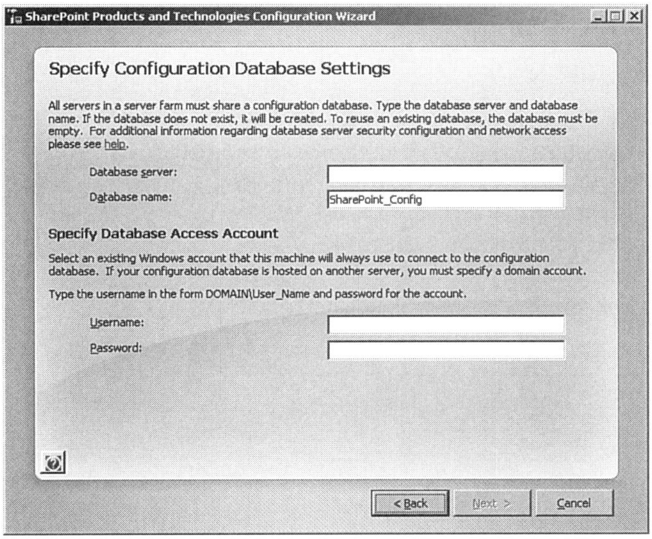

FIGURE 14.4   Configuring your database settings.

Next, you will reach the SharePoint Central Administration Web Application page, shown in Figure 14.5. From here, you are told "A SharePoint Central Administration Web Application allows you to manage configuration settings for a server farm. The first server added to a server farm must host this Web application. To specify a port number for the Web application hosted on this machine, check the box below and type a number between 1 and 65535. If you do not specify a port number, a random one will be chosen."

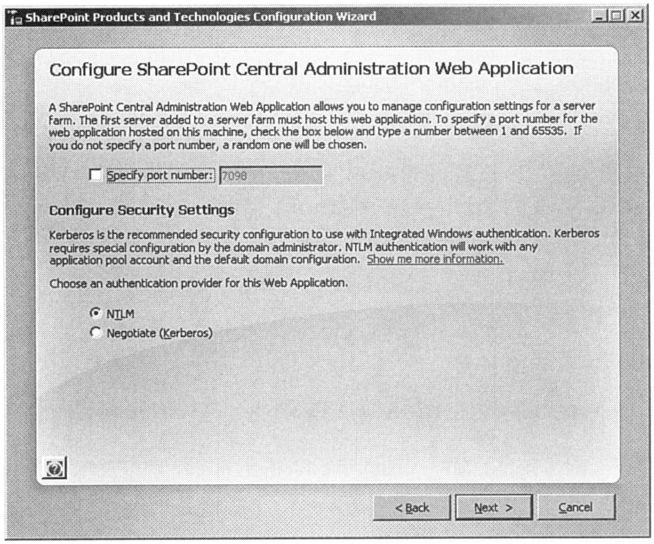

FIGURE 14.5   Port selection and security options.

The security options ask whether you want to use the default setting of NTLM or change to Kerberos. Generally, you should leave the default unless you have a Kerberos-supported environment. To configure Kerberos with SharePoint Services, see the Knowledge Base article KB 832769.

After you have set your options, a summary page of your choices displays. Moving forward, the installation will proceed. When the installation completes, you are taken to the Central Administration page (as with other servers that use WSS as their base), where you are shown your tasks to complete, as shown in Figure 14.6.

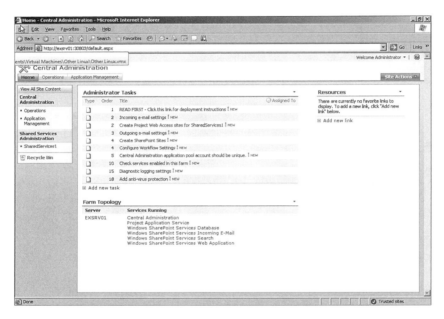

FIGURE 14.6   The Central Administration page, with a view of your server farm and administrator tasks.

You might have some difficulties accessing the Central Administration site initially, because of the strict settings of your Internet Explorer in relation to sites you trust. To change this, follow these steps:

1. In Internet Explorer, from the Tools menu, select **Internet Options.**

2. From the Security tab, in the Select a Web Content Zone to Specify Its Security Settings dialog, select **Trusted Sites**, and then select **Sites.**

3. Make sure to clear the **Require Server Verification (HTTPS:) for All Sites in This Zone** check box.

4. From the Add This website to The Zone textbox, enter the URL for Central Administration, and then select **Add.**

5. Select the **Require Server Verification (HTTPS:) for All Sites in This Zone** check box. (Note, you can leave this checkbox unchecked if you don't want to re-apply the security verification.)

6. Click **Close** to close the Trusted Sites dialog box.

7. Click **OK** to close the Internet Options dialog box.

You might also have to configure the proxy server settings to bypass the proxy server for local addresses. This setting is also found in the Internet Explorer Internet Options. From the Connections tab, under the Local Area Network (LAN) Settings section, select **LAN Settings.** From the Proxy Server section, select the **Bypass Proxy Server for Local Addresses** check box.

Unlike the stand-alone installation, you must do a few things manually on your farm after it has finished installing, including the following:

▶ Configure farm services for the application server.

▶ Start the Project Application service.

▶ Create a Web application.

▶ Create a site collection for that Web application.

▶ Create a Web application for the Shared Service Provider and the Share Services Provider.

Those concepts might be new to you. We explain what they are here, however, because you will see these terms again when working with other Office 2007 servers. Creating a Web application simply means telling your SharePoint Services (the underlying force behind your Project Server) that you need certain work to be accomplished through that application. When you create a site collection, which is just a Web site that you will use to connect to and project items to, the site will use that Web application to manage it. The Shared Services Provider (SSP) was designed as a replacement for the Shared Services infrastructure of SharePoint 2003, especially with regard to deployment and configuration. Each Web application in a MOSS farm and site is associated with one SSP. However, you can configure different SSPs and then break up each Web application to use the different SSPs.

A Mid-Sized Farm

Obviously, we are looking at a larger configuration here, one that might include three servers (possibly a three-tiered solution) to accommodate a larger organization. With each tier, we place a different portion of the Project Server solution (the Web, application, and database portions) on a different system.

The mid-size, or medium, farm installation has flexibility in its design. You might decide to add a secondary front-end Web server and perhaps include a secondary database server. You might load balance the front-end servers, and cluster the back-end ones to provide for a higher level of availability and failover.

To establish the mid-size solution, you should start with your database server already installed and waiting. Next, you want to install the Project Server as the application server using the Advanced installation and select the Complete installation type, creating a new farm and a new configuration database. This is logical because this is the first server in the farm.

When the application server is prepared, you can install the front-end Web server role. To do this, choose the **Advanced** installation option and select the **Web Front End** option. Provide the credentials necessary for the database server, which you already established for the application server. Now, when asked whether you want to create a new farm, or connect to an existing one, remember to connect to the existing farm.

A Large Farm

Larger farms follow the same pattern as the mid-sized but with an increase in Web front end and SQL database back ends. The larger farms might also be integrated with SharePoint Server 2007 servers to allow for some of the other features available (such as Search and Index tools or Excel Calculation Services).

Adding more front-end servers is somewhat easy. You just have to select the Web Front End option during the installation and provide information for your existing farm, and it will then connect into the farm, and all the existing websites will be replicated to the new server automatically.

You can increase the application servers you have to distribute the load on those systems. To do this, select the **Complete** option during the install and connect it to the existing farm. (Do not create a new farm.) The benefit of doing this is that incoming requests can be handled in a round-robin manner. So, the first request might go to Application Server 1, and the second request would be routed to Application Server 2 (thus distributing the load on this server).

Preparing SQL Server Settings

We wanted to walk you through the Project Server installation first, but remember, you must have the SQL Server configured before you do an install for a Project Server farm. Let's walk through this procedure. (Make sure to note your configuration choices and password settings.)

For one thing, the Project Server 2007 install automatically creates the databases for your back end, after you provide the information on the server name and provide the credentials needed. However, you can create these databases ahead of time if your environment calls for it.

The databases you would create include the following:

ProjectServer_Published

ProjectServer_Working

ProjectServer_Archive

ProjectServer_Reporting

Use the same Setup user account for all databases. From the SQL Server Management Studio (Enterprise Manager and/or Query Analyzer for the readers using SQL Server 2000), add the SSP account and the database owner roles to the Users group of each database. When you create these databases, you need to adhere to SQL Server collation requirements. The configuration direction given through TechNet states, "The SQL Server collation must be configured as case-insensitive. The SQL Server database collation must be configured as case-insensitive, accent-sensitive, Kana-sensitive, and width-sensitive. This configuration ensures filename uniqueness consistent with the Windows operating system." You can research these options further online.

You want to keep track of several accounts when installing SQL and configuring Project Server, including the following:

▶ **SQL Server service account.** The SQL Server will request this account during the setup process. It will be used as the service account for both the MSSQLSERVER and the SQLSERVERAGENT services.

▶ **Setup user account.** This is the account used to run setup on each server.

▶ **Server farm account.** Also known as the Database access account, this is used to access the SharePoint Central Administration website.

Completing the Installation Process

Whereas the stand-alone install quickly handles most configuration issues, this isn't the case with a farm install, even a small one. One primary reason for this is because you need to purposely address the final administrative tasks, including starting the services. To begin with, select the server that appears on your Home page for the Central Administration site, as was shown previously in Figure 14.6. By selecting the name, you will be taken to the Operations tab, under Services on Server (as shown in Figure 14.7). At any time, you can also go to the Operations page and under the Topology and Services section click the Services on Server Link. From here, you need to turn on certain services. Which ones? Well, that depends on the server role you select on the page.

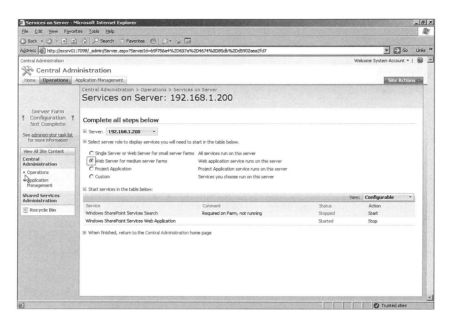

FIGURE 14.7   Services to start for your Project Server 2007.

Your options include the following server roles and the corresponding services:

▶ Single server or Web server for small server farms (All services run on this server.)

▶ Web server for medium server farms (Web application service runs on this server.)

▶ Project Application (Project Application service runs on this server.)

▶ Custom (Services you choose run on this server.)

Now, we cannot tell you which one to choose. Based on what you already know from our discussion of different farm deployments, you know whether this server should be configured for a small, mid-sized, or large farm. Based on that decision, you will see that certain services may already be started, and others are noted in the Status column as Stopped. For whichever selection you make, you need to start the services for that server role by selecting Start from the Action menu.

When configuring a service to start, you may have to provide credentials for that service. It is recommended that you create a specific account for services with the proper credentials on your server.

Your next step is to create Web applications, as mentioned previously. You need to create a Web application for two different sites:

▶ The Project Web Access site

▶ The SSP home site

Afterward, you need to create a site collection for the Web application that is hosting the Project Web Access site.

Create a Web Application

Exactly what are you creating when you create a Web application? You are creating an application that can be accessed through a Web browser. However, no one is saying that you have to be a programming genius to configure Project Server. The process of creating a Web application to connect to your Project Web Access site is more of a step-by-step (paint-by-the-numbers) approach to getting that application in place for your site to function with.

To create the application, follow these steps:

1. From the top pane of the Central Administration page, select **Application Management.**

2. From the Application Management page, in the SharePoint Web Application Management portion, select **Create or Extend Web Application.**

3. From the Create or Extend Web Application page, in the Adding a SharePoint Web Application portion, select **Create a New Web Application.**

4. From the Create New Web Application page, perform the following tasks:

   a. Within the IIS Web Site section, select either **Use an Existing IIS Web Site** or **Create a New IIS Web Site.** Note that it is recommended that you use port 80 if you are creating or using an existing site, because this will eliminate the need for host headers for users who need to access the site, and users won't need to remember a port number to access the site.

   b. Within the Security Configuration portion, you have several decisions to make. Under Authentication Provider, select either **Negotiate (Kerberos)** or **NTLM.** Your answer will depend on your network. If you aren't sure, use NTLM. You can also allow anonymous (although that isn't recommended) access, and you can choose to use Secure Sockets Layer (SSL).

   c. Within the Load Balanced URL portion, enter the URL that will be used for access to the Web application, or leave the default entry of http://*servername*:80. The URL should be in the format http://*servername*:*port*. If you are using multiple zones on the server, you can select another zone in the Zone list.

   d. From the Application Pool portion, select **Create New Application Pool.** This will define the account and credentials used by this service.

   e. From the Application Pool Name box, a unique name is generated automatically based on the extended Web site you selected. You can continue with this entry or you can type another unique name.

   f. Select **Configurable**, and then, in the User Name box, enter the Windows account of the farm administrator. In the **Password** box, enter the password for the account.

14

g. The Reset Internet Information Services portion allows you to restart IIS automatically or manually.

h. The Database Name and Authentication portion has a default database server and database name. It is recommended that you leave the defaults. The same is true for database authentication, the default setting as Windows authentication, as opposed to SQL authentication.

i. Finally, you can configure a search server to associate a content database with a specific server that is running Windows SharePoint Services search service.

5. Click **OK.**

What you have just done is establish a Web application that is going to be the basis, the launching pad, for your site collection. So, let's proceed on to the site collection portion.

Create the Site Collection

A site collection is a fancy way of saying "a Web site that becomes your connecting point to your Web application." The Web application we created in the preceding section will do us no good unless we associate a site collection to work with. To create a site collection, follow these steps:

1. From the Application Created page that appears, select **Create a New Windows SharePoint Services Site Collection.** Note that the creation of this site collection will allow the configuration of a top-level site for the Web application.

2. From the Create Site Collection page, do the following:

   a. In the Title and Description portion, in Title, enter a title for the new site.

   b. In Description, enter a description of the site collection.

   c. In the Web Site Address portion, specify the URL name and path to create new sites. In the URL list, select a managed path to append to the URL under which new sites will be created. Note that if you want to add new paths to the list, click the Define Managed Paths link and enter the information in the Add a New Path portion.

   d. In the Primary Site Collection Administrator portion, enter the username of the site collection administrator in the corresponding field. (You can do this for the secondary site administrator, too.) Note that you can use the Windows SharePoint Services service account as the username.

   e. The Quota Template portion is used to limit the amount of storage available on the site. The default template is No Quota. You can keep this option or choose from any additional quota templates you have created. Note that you can create additional quota templates and change this setting later through the SharePoint Central Administration site in the SharePoint Site Management portion of Application Management.

     f. In the Template Selection portion, in the Select a Template list, select the template you want to use when the top-level site of the site collection is created, and then select **OK.**

3. On the Top-Level Site Successfully Created page, the URL for the new, empty top-level site is displayed. Select **OK** to return to Central Administration.

Creating the Shared Service Provider

Before you can create the Shared Service Provider, you need to know what an SSP is, and then you need to create another Web application to host the SSP. SSPs are part of the SharePoint Services design, and these are created and used within SharePoint to establish boundaries between content. So, you might have, for example, one set of services running under one SSP, and another running under a separate SSP.

So, to begin with, follow the procedure discussed previously to create the Web application you will use for the SSP. When establishing the IIS website portion, remember the port number you used because you will need this later when configuring the SSP portion.

To create the SSP, follow these steps:

1. From the top portion of the Central Administration page, select **Application Management.**

2. From the Application Management page, in the Office SharePoint Server Shared Services section, select **Create or Configure this Farm's Shared Services.**

3. From the Manage This Farm's Shared Services page, select **New SSP.**

4. From the New Shared Services Provider page, do the following:

     a. In the SSP Name section, in the Web Application list, select the Web application created when you created the Web application to host the SSP.

     b. In the SSP Service Credentials section, enter the name and password for a Windows user who is the SSP administrator.

     c. SSPs require a database for each SSP to store service-specific data. In the SSP Database section, the database server name by default will list the one hosting the configuration database. The database name will also be automatically generated for you. You can keep the default settings or can change them if you prefer.

5. Select **OK.**

6. After you have successfully create the SSP, the Success page displays. Select **OK** to go to the Manage This Farm's Shared Services page.

14

Provision the Site on the Farm

Your final configuration settings involve creating the Project Server instance on the farm. Here is where you configure the Administrator account for the Project Server, and direct Project Server to the database server for the databases that you may, or may not have already created.

To provision the site, follow these steps:

1. From the Manage this Farm's Shared Services page, located in the SSP and Associated Web Applications list, select the SSP you just created. Make sure to select the SSP and not a Web application listed under the Shared Services Provider.

2. From the home page for this SSP, in the Project Server section, select **Project Web Access Sites.**

3. From the Manage Project Web Access page, select **Create Project Web Access Site.**

4. From the Create a New Project Web Access page, do the following:

    a. In the Project Web Access Site Location section, from the SharePoint Web Application to Host PWA list, select the name of the extended website. Do not select the Web site being used for the SSP.

    b. In the Project Web Access Path box, the default name of the Project Web Access path appears. You can continue with this name or type in another.

    c. In the Administrator Account section, enter the Windows user account that will be given administrative credentials to the Project Server instance.

    d. In the Primary Database section, in the Primary Database Server field, enter the name of the computer running SQL Server on which the Publish, Draft, and Archive databases will be located. In the Published, Draft, and Archived database name fields, enter unique names for each Office Project Server 2007 database. You can use the default database names. However, make sure they do not already exist on the SQL Server.

5. In the Reporting Database section, if the computer running SQL Server that is hosting the Reporting database is the same as the primary database server that you specified, select **Use the Primary Database Server.** If it exists on a different SQL Server, clear this option and then enter the name of the SQL Server in the Reporting Database Server field. In the Reporting Database Name field, enter a unique name for the Reporting database. You can use the default database name. However, as before, make sure it does not already exist on the SQL Server.

6. Select **OK.**

7. You will return to the Manage Project Web Access page. Click the **Refresh Status** button to update the status of the provisioning process. When provisioning is complete, an entry in the Status column will say Provisioned. When that happens, you can select the URL to go to the Project Web Access site.

Configure Client Connectivity

It is a fine thing to plan and deploy with success your Project Server 2007. However, unless clients can connect up and start using it, it isn't much more than a lot of hard work. So, let's finish this chapter with a discussion about how you can connect your Project Professional 2007 client to your Project Server 2007.

Keeping in mind that you need to install Project Professional 2007 (knowing as you do that previous version do not have the ability to connect, nor does Project Standard 2007), we want to install the application and then create an account profile so that the client can connect to the server.

To configure the account profile, follow these steps:

1. Start Office Project Professional 2007.

2. From the Tools menu, point to **Enterprise Options,** and then select **Microsoft Office Project Server accounts,** as shown in Figure 14.8.

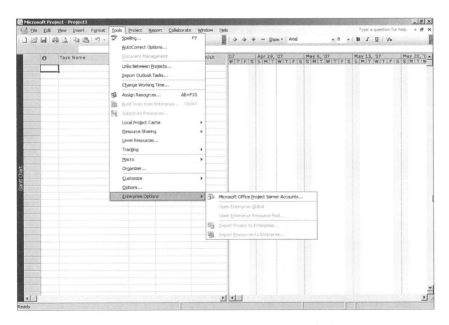

FIGURE 14.8   Configuring your Project Professional 2007 accounts.

3. From the Project Server Accounts window, select **Add.**

4. From within the Account Properties dialog (shown in Figure 14.9), complete the following:

    a. Enter a unique name in the Account Name box.

    b. Enter the URL of the Project Server instance in the Project Server URL box.

c. From within the When Connecting section, you can keep the default Use Windows User Account option or you can use a Forms-authenticated account, which is new for Project Server 2007. You provide a username here, but provide the password when you make the connection.

d. Select Set as Default Account if you want to use this profile as the default profile.

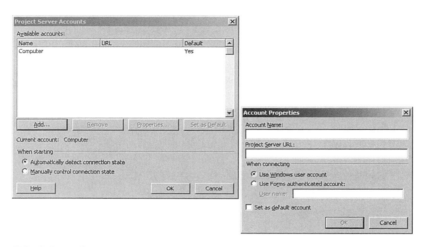

FIGURE 14.9   Project Server accounts and account properties.

5. After you select OK, your account will show in the Project Server Accounts window.

6. In the Project Server Accounts window, you can configure your preference on how you connect to Office Project Server 2007 in the When Starting section:

a. Select **Automatically Detect Connection State** if you want Project to automatically detect and make a connection to the specified default server. If a default server is not specified, Project will open offline with no server connections.

b. Select **Manually Control Connection State** if you prefer to select a server to connect to each time that you open Project. Use this option if you have multiple servers you frequently access, or if you sometimes prefer to use Project offline.

NOTE

You might also want to connect to Project Server 2007 through the Office Project Web Access. To accomplish this, open your Web browser and enter the Project Server URL. Office Project Web Access will use Windows authentication by default, so you want to verify you are logged in with the account with which you installed Office Project Server 2007. After you log on, you can create additional accounts with which to access the server.

CHAPTER 15

Project Server 2007: Administrating Your Project Server

The preceding chapter covered the purpose of using a Project Server, and you learned how to set up Project Server with Microsoft SharePoint services. At this point, we need to look into the administrative side of that server. After loading Project Server, you should have the administrative Web-based tools supported by SharePoint services. By default, Microsoft Project will set up the Web page under PWA (which stands for Project Web Access, and you might note has a familiar feel if you have ever worked with Exchange Server, because in Exchange you have OWA, for Outlook Web Access).

Be careful to follow the recommended installation steps mentioned in the preceding chapter, and have your prerequisites in place. Without those, many encounter problems accessing and administrating their Project Server through the Web Access tools.

Office Project Web Access

Now that your site has been established and you have signed in for the first time, you will notice from Figure 15.1 that the default PWA site displays. You'll see a Reminders section in the middle of the Site Actions area that indicates Tasks, Timesheets, Approvals, Status Reports, and Issues and

Risks. You'll also have your Project Workspaces at the bottom of the page. The left column offers you several subheadings that will take you to other portions of the administrative site.

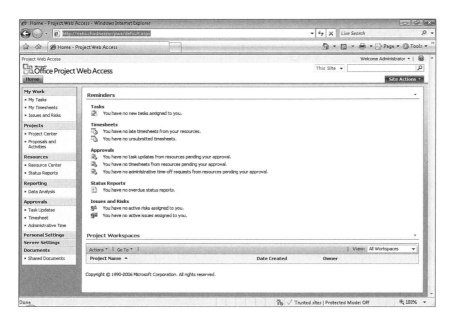

FIGURE 15.1   The PWA administrative home site.

Down the left side on the menu, you will see Server Settings. This is where we are going to spend our time now. Only those with the proper administrative permissions can enter and make changes to these settings.

When you select Server Settings, the Server Settings page will open with the following headings and suboptions from which to choose:

▶ Security

   Manage Users

   Manage Groups

   Manage Categories

   Security Templates

   Project Web Access Permissions

▶ Enterprise Data

Enterprise Custom Field Definition

Enterprise Global

Enterprise Calendars

Resource Center

About Project Server

▶ Database Administration

Delete Enterprise Objects

Force Check-in Enterprise Objects

Schedule Backup

Administrative Backup

Administrative Restore

▶ Look and Feel

Manage Views

Grouping Formats

Gantt Chart Formats

Quick Launch

▶ Cube

Build Settings

Configuration

Build Status

▶ Time and Task Management

Financial Periods

Timesheet Periods

Timesheet Classifications

Timesheet Settings and Defaults

Administrative Time

Task Settings and Display

Close Tasks to Update

15

▶ Queue

Manage Queue

Queue Settings

▶ Operation Policies

Alerts and Reminders

Additional Server Settings

Server-Side Event Handler Configuration

Active Directory Resource Pool Synchronization

Project Workspaces

Project Workspace Provisioning Settings

Configuring Security Settings

Obviously, the Security heading has a variety of options to control users and groups and the level of access they have with the Project Server. Project Server security is actually based on users and groups.

Managing Users and Groups

Let's look at the first heading, Security, under Manage Users (shown in Figure 15.2). Here, you can search for any user by either dropping down the list and locating or searching by email address. If you check the box beside the user, you have the option to deactivate the user. You can also select Add User to configure security settings for more users. Every user who wants to access the Project Server must have an account that allows the user to interact with the Project Server. You can use domain accounts or create Project Server users specifically. You can also deactivate and reactivate user accounts or merge two user accounts that apply to a single user.

When you create a new user, you can choose the groups they belong to and establish the categories and global permissions for that user.

You can use the Groups page to create, modify, and delete security groups; identify the users and categories associated with the groups; and configure Active Directory synchronization (see Figure 15.3).

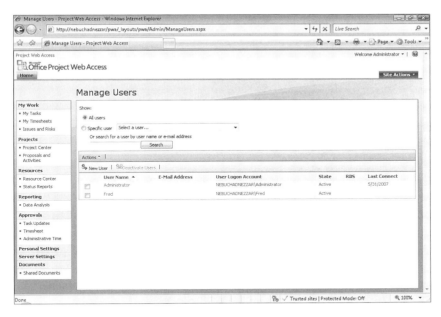

FIGURE 15.2   Managing users through the Security options.

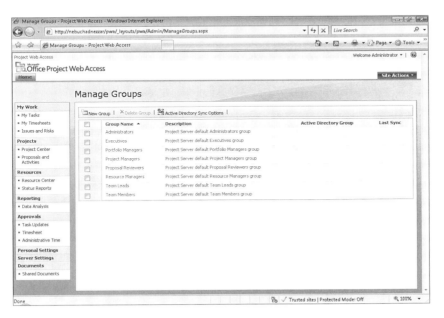

FIGURE 15.3   Managing groups.

You can see that there are eight default groups at your disposal that you can organize your users into:

▶ Administrators

▶ Executives

▶ Portfolio Managers

▶ Project Managers

▶ Proposal Reviewers

▶ Resource Managers

▶ Team Leads

▶ Team Members

It's recommended that you use groups to establish permissions for various users. Usually users need to access the same data in the same way, and placing them within a group will make the management of those users easier for you as an administrator.

Configuring Categories Manually or with Security Templates

After a group has been created, you can then use security categories to provide your users and groups with access to specific parts of your Project Server. So, you want to define your groups according to the needs of your users to access areas of Project Server.

Six default categories are created:

▶ My Direct Reports

▶ My Organization

▶ My Personal Projects

▶ My Projects

▶ My Resources

▶ My Tasks

Each of these categories can be selected and edited to suit your needs (as shown in Figure 15.4), and new ones can be added. Categories allow you to define the projects and views to which a user or group may have access.

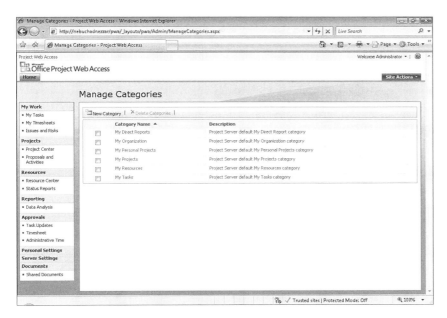

FIGURE 15.4   Using default categories to manage users.

NOTE

To see a list of the many different permission settings and their corresponding actions, refer to http://office.microsoft.com/en-us/projservadmin/HA011642791033.aspx.

For each of these categories, you can manually configure a list of permissions or can apply a security template to them. If you want to manually configure these settings, select the category, and then select either **Allow** or **Deny** for each activity in the Permissions list that appears. It's important to understand the way permissions work before you select options manually. You can choose Allow, Deny, or nothing for a particular permission set:

▶ **Allow.** Gives permission for a user/group to perform the actions being defined.

▶ **Deny.** Explicitly denies permission for a user/group to perform the actions being defined. If a user is part of a group that has the Deny permission established on an action, and is part of a group that has Allow permission on that action setting, the Deny takes precedence. For that reason, you want to use Deny settings sparingly because you never know how that might affect you later on.

▶ **Nothing.** If you have neither one selected for a particular action, users are implicitly denied that action, meaning they will not be allowed to perform the task. However, if they belong to another group that does have Allow enabled on that action, that permission allows them to perform the tasks because an explicit Deny hasn't been established.

NOTE

If you are going to adjust permission settings, it is recommended this be done on the group level rather than the individual user level. This will make administration of your users and groups easier and less time-consuming.

You can automatically configure permissions for your categories by using security templates. Eight default templates have been created, and they align with the predefined groups mentioned previously, as shown in Figure 15.5.

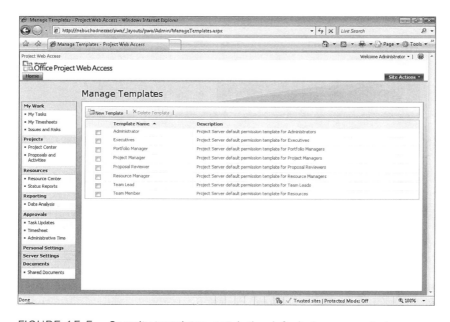

FIGURE 15.5   Security templates match the default groups created.

Security templates provide a way to assign multiple permissions to categories, groups, and users. If you create a new template or edit one of the default ones, the permissions will be set to the categories, groups, or users as they are applied. You can customize your templates or create new ones to apply, depending on your specific needs.

The permissions you configure through these templates, when they are applied, will allow or deny the access to Project Server security objects.

Project Web Access Permissions

The control of the global and category permissions that are enabled on the Project Server can be set in the Project Web Access Permissions. If you have the Administrator permission, you can allow, restrict, or deny to anyone any particular feature in Project Professional or Project Web Access. If a Project Web Access permission is turned on (as shown in Figure 15.6), the same permission will then be available for users and those with permissions either globally or on certain categories.

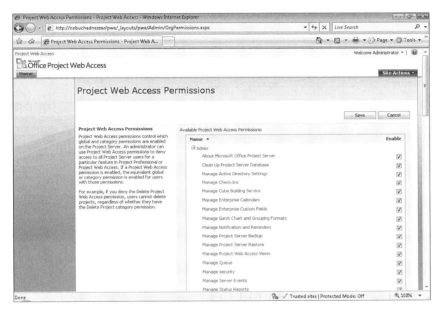

FIGURE 15.6   Project Web Access Permissions.

To illustrate, when you deny Delete in Project Web Access Permission, users will be unable to delete projects, even if they have the Delete Project category permission.

Configuring Enterprise Data Settings

When considering the various configuration options under Enterprise Data, keep in mind that these changes will relate to all organizational projects. In other words, the changes you make here will enable you to establish consistency through all of your organizations projects.

Enterprise Custom Field Definition

Enterprise Custom Field Definitions, shown in Figure 15.7, enable you to edit and add to fields that are part of the Enterprise Global template. They apply only to projects that are saved to the Project Server from Project Professional. The fields you create are available to all the users in your organization, and they enable you to configure operations through a standard set of fields.

Keep in mind that much of the information for custom field definitions relates to developers, not administrators. But, you might be asked as an administrator to add the fields that your developers are using.

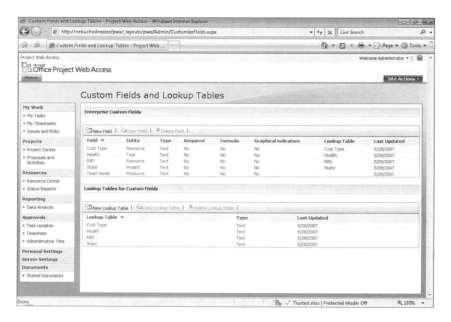

FIGURE 15.7   Custom field definitions.

NOTE

Keep in mind that there are Local and Enterprise custom fields. Local fields exist on each system that has Project Standard or Professional installed, and they can extend the attributes of tasks, resources, or projects. Local fields are limited in number, and they apply only to the scope of a single project, whereas Enterprise customer fields are unlimited in their number and in who they can apply to. You define them in Project Web Access, and they are used for all projects within an organization.

You can edit the five default fields listed here to suit your needs, or you can add new fields as required:

- ▶ Cost Type
- ▶ Health
- ▶ RBS (Resource Breakdown Structure)
- ▶ State
- ▶ Team Name

In addition, as you can see in Figure 15.7, there are Lookup Tables for Custom Fields settings, which again can be edited or added to. Here, you can create or modify custom fields within Microsoft Project Web Access and add these fields to your projects. You can also apply lists (or attributes) to custom fields that help create the values that team members will see and use. These attributes come from the following:

▶ **Lookup tables.** These are the values that, after being created, team members can pick from a list when adding a custom field to their Project plans.

▶ **Formulas.** Formulas are used to generate field values by calculating multiple fields and functions.

NOTE

To understand more about how custom fields and lookup tables work (for both Project Server 2003 and 2007), refer to the article at http://msdn2.microsoft.com/en-us/library/ms447495.aspx.

Enterprise Global

Certain Enterprise customizations are made from within the Project Professional desktop client by checking out the Enterprise Global template. In this setting, you have the option to set your Microsoft Project Professional's customization settings. Setting changes made in this way will affect all users who connect to your Project Server. Even if users make changes locally to their settings, if those settings are defined in the Enterprise Global template, those settings will be applied when the user saves the project back to the server.

The customizations can be made on the following areas:

▶ Grouping

▶ Toolbars

▶ Maps

▶ Forms

▶ Tables

▶ Filters

▶ Views

▶ Reports

▶ Modules

If you want to check out the Enterprise Global template, click the only button on the Configure Project Professional page. Only one user can work with the Enterprise Global template at a time, and that user must have the permissions to make changes on the template (the Save Enterprise Global permission). (Note that another way for users with permissions to open the Global template is through Project Professional directly. They don't have to go through PWA. They can just open the Tools menu, point to Enterprise

Options, and then select Open Enterprise Global.) A blank project will display, in which you can configure all the customization options mentioned previously and then save.

Enterprise Calendars

You use your calendars to schedule your working time so that resources and tasks are structured. Under Enterprise Calendars, you will see a list of calendars based on the ongoing projects. You have the option here to check out or edit, copy, delete, and create a new calendar.

You will see a Standard default calendar to begin with, but you can customize the calendars used, and it will be reflected in the Enterprise template for scheduling consistency throughout your organization.

Resource Center and About Project Server Pages

The final two Enterprise Data settings available are the Resource Center and the About Project Server pages.

Resource Center

As suggested by the heading of this section, this is the area where you can see a list and add new resources. By selecting one in the list, you can edit details about that resource. You can also do a bulk edit on a group of resources or view assignments and availability. Under the Actions menu, you can again open a resource, select all resources, and clear the selected resource list. You can also export the grid to Excel or print the Grid. See Figure 15.8.

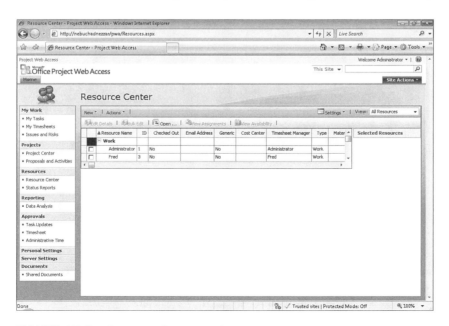

FIGURE 15.8   Resource Center settings.

About Project Server

When you click this link, a page will display with a Number of Active Project Server Users list and a Number of Project Professional Users list. There are no configuration options available here, just an OK button that you can click.

Database Administration

One of the most important aspects of an administrator's job is backup and recovery. All applications that utilize databases require various administration tasks that, for Project Server 2007, fall under the purview of database administration, including the following:

Delete Enterprise Objects

On occasion, you might want or need to create more working space within your Microsoft Office Project Server 2007 database. You can do so from the Delete Enterprise Objects page, shown in Figure 15.9. From here, you can delete old data about projects, resources, tasks and assignments, task updates, status reports, and timesheets.

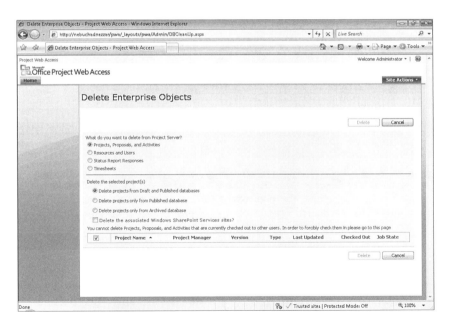

FIGURE 15.9   Deleting enterprise objects to make room in your database.

As you can see, you can select all the projects or individual ones and choose to perform the following:

▶ Delete projects from Draft and Published databases

▶ Delete projects only from Published database

▶ Delete projects only from Archived database

A Delete the Associated Windows SharePoint Services Sites? check box is also available. You select this check box if you want to remove those sites.

The items that you delete from the database can be restored. On the Quick Launch, just select **Server Settings, Administrative Restore**. Be aware, however, that any changes that were made from the time the item was deleted and restored cannot be restored.

Force Check-In Enterprise Objects

When a team member leaves an enterprise object in a state in which it cannot be checked in to Microsoft Office Project Server 2007, an administrator can force a check-in. These enterprise objects may include projects, resources fields, calendars, lookup tables, and resource plans.

To force a check-in, follow these steps:

1. Under Quick Launch (menu on left side of the home page), select **Server Settings**.

2. Under Server Settings, select **Force Check-in Enterprise Objects**.

3. Under Select the Type of Object You Want to Force to Check-In list, select the type of objects that you want to display in the table.

4. Select the object and click **Check In**.

NOTE

After you complete the preceding steps, the user who had the object checked out can now only save the changes to the object if he saves it as a new object. The alternative is to check the object out again, make the changes, and then save it.

Schedule Backup

The Daily Backup Schedule page, shown in Figure 15.10, allows for a scheduled backup of certain components of Microsoft Project. This backup will support item-level backup/restore, which is designed to work in conjunction with a SQL backup, not in place of one.

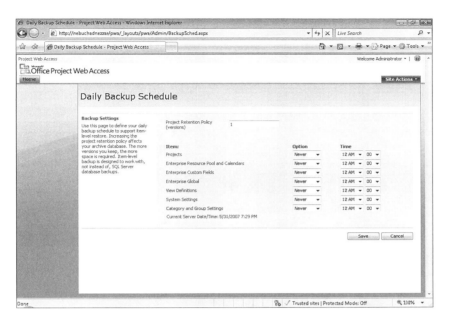

FIGURE 15.10   The Daily Backup Schedule settings.

You can change the project retention policy (versions) to include more versions, although this will directly affect your archive database size; the more versions you keep, the more space required.

You can back up the following items:

▶ Projects

▶ Enterprise resource pool and calendars

▶ Enterprise custom fields

▶ Enterprise Global template

▶ View definitions

▶ System settings

▶ Category and group settings

Then, determine the schedule for your backup.

Administrative Backup and Restore

Similar to the daily backup, the administrative backup stores the information in the Microsoft Office Project Server 2007 database. An automatic backup can be created based on your schedule, or you can choose to back up manually. As the administrator, you can also do a restore of items that may have been accidentally deleted.

The structure for this backup is a bit different. You select with check boxes the different items (the same items as a daily backup), and you then click the Backup button to immediately perform the backup.

If you want to restore any of the items you have backed up, you just go to the Administrative Restore page and select the item (projects, for example) and then select all projects to restore, or select individual ones that you might need to restore.

Changing the Look and Feel of Project

Formatting certain aspects of Project can be done from within the Look and Feel settings presented through your Server Settings page. You can add new views, change the formatting of grouping and Gantt charts, and alter Quick Launch settings.

Manage Views

At first glance, the Manage Views options show you a list of all the views that are possible for the users to see in their client (see Figure 15.11). As an administrator, you can edit or add the needed changes in each view or make the program more applicable to the specific needs for your organization.

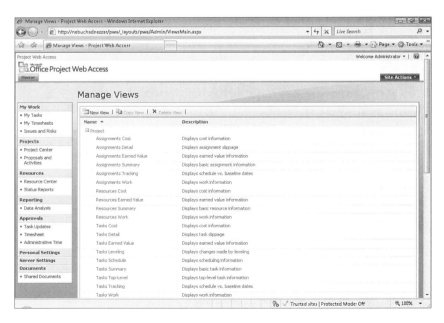

FIGURE 15.11   Managing the views your client can see.

If you select the New View option, you can select a type of view to add. Nine different views are available:

- ▶ **Project.** This view relates to the task, assignment, or resource details of a particular project.

- ▶ **Project Center.** This view relates to a review of information about all the projects that are in the Project Center.

- ▶ **Resource Assignments.** This view relates to a review of specific resource assignment details.

- ▶ **Resource Center.** This view relates to a review and comparison of all the resources within the Resource Center.

- ▶ **Data Analysis.** This view relates to a review of all the project and resource information through PivotTable and PivotChart reports.

- ▶ **My Work.** This view is used by team members to review their task assignments.

- ▶ **Resource Plan.** The view is used by managers to create resource plans for their projects.

- ▶ **Team Tasks.** This view is used by team members to reviews tasks that are assigned to their team as a resource.

- ▶ **Team Builder.** This view is used by managers to create a team for their project

- ▶ **Timesheet.** This view is used by team members to report time in connection with the projects to which they are assigned.

When a type is chosen, you can provide a name and description and then begin the process of selecting tables and fields for the new view you are trying to define. When your new view is complete, remember to save it.

Grouping Formats

On the Grouping Formats page, you can select a grouping format for the Tasks section and up to ten grouping formats for views (see Figure 15.12). These formats will apply to the Project Center, the Resource Center, and Project and Assignment views.

You can alter the various level colors for the groupings and the patterns that are associated with these levels, and you can see this reflected back in the client when you open different views.

Gantt Chart Formats

Project Web Access can display a personal Gantt chart on the Tasks page and can display up to 19 different types of Gantt chart views in the Views section. You can use the Gantt Chart Formats page to select a chart and alter the formatting for how the Gantt chart is displayed, as shown in Figure 15.13. You can format the color, shape, and pattern of the Gantt chart bars.

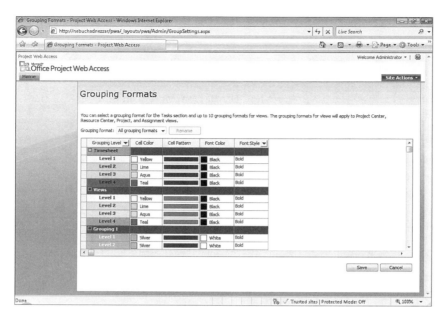

FIGURE 15.12   The Grouping Formats settings.

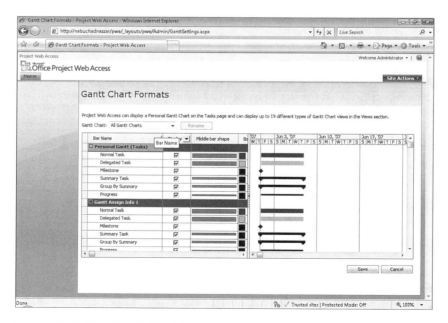

FIGURE 15.13   Gantt Chart Formats.

Quick Launch

The Quick Launch, which we have referred to several times, is the menu that is available on the home page on the left side of the page (see Figure 15.14). It contains links to pages, lists, and libraries in Microsoft Project Web Access. By adjusting the Quick Launch to reflect the links needed for your organization, you will simplify and make it easier for your users.

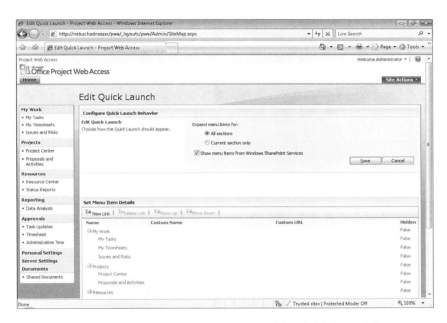

FIGURE 15.14   Editing the "Look and Feel" of the Quick Launch bar.

The Quick Launch editor enables you to change names and headings for your sections and the URLs to which they link. You can also create a parent/child setting for additional pages to be added into the Quick Launch area with new links you may find helpful.

Cube Configuration

Cubes have been mentioned in other parts of this book and discussed at length in the PerformancePoint 2007 chapters. Cubes are the heart of the analytic approach or online analytical processing (OLAP) approach to multidimensional queries, which can often occur in project management.

Build Settings

The Build Settings page, shown in Figure 15.15, allows you to schedule when the cube should be built and the data ranges used in creating the cube. These date ranges are important because they impact on the time the cube takes to be built and the amount of data you want to analyze.

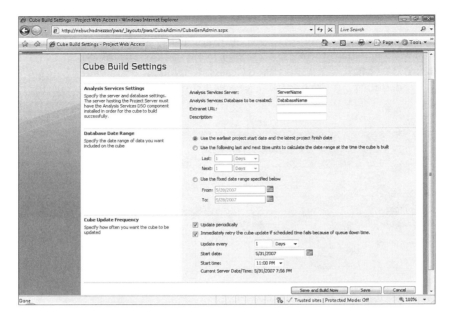

FIGURE 15.15   Changing your cube build settings.

There are three areas where settings can be made under this section: Analysis Services Settings, Database Date Range, and Cube Update Frequency.

Under Analysis Services Settings

▶ You need to specify the server and the database settings.

▶ The Analysis Services DSO component needs to be installed on the server hosting Project Server, for the cube to build successfully.

NOTE

You must have a server in place to handle the Analysis Services. You can use SQL Server 2000 Analysis Services or you can use SQL Server 2005 Analysis Services for cube building. You have to meet specific requirements to use either one, but keep in mind that the latest version of SQL includes major changes to the business intelligence features, as discussed by Mark Frawley in his article "Analysis Services Comparison: SQL 2000 vs. SQL 2005" (www.devx.com/dbzone/Article/21539). Regardless of which version you decide to use, you need to keep in mind certain requirements. For a list of those requirements, refer to the article "SQL Server 2000 Analysis Services" (http://technet2.microsoft.com/Office/en-us/library/5d90076f-bbcc-48c1-a569-bd236862d47c1033.mspx?mfr=true) and "SQL Server 2005 Analysis Services" (http://technet2.microsoft.com/Office/en-us/library/86910044-701c-4b02-89d7-e094e9cb7dcd1033.mspx?mfr=true).

Under Database Date Range

▶ Specify the date range of the data you want included on your cube.

Under Cube Update Frequency

▶ Set how often you want the cube to be updated.

Your options at the bottom of the page then are Save and Build Now, Save, and Cancel.

Configuration

On the Configuration page, you can customize the Project Server OLAP cubes by adding custom fields as dimensions or measures to the cubes associated with the selected entity and by adding calculated measures (see Figure 15.16). Any selected custom field will appear only after its data has been published.

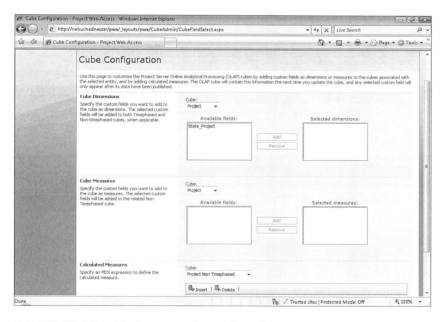

FIGURE 15.16   Altering your cube configuration.

There are three areas for these settings:

▶ **Cube Dimensions.** Specify the custom fields you want to add to the cube as dimensions. The selected custom fields will be added to both Timephase and Nontimephased cubes, when applicable.

▶ **Cube Measures.** Select the custom fields you want to add as cube measures. The customs fields will be added to the related Nontimephased cube.

▶ **Calculated Measures.** Here you need to specify a Multidimensional Expressions (MDX) expression to define the calculated measure.

Build Status

The Cube Build Status page is essentially a reporting page. It provides information about cubes that have been created and their status. Questions are answered: Did it build successfully? When did it build? How long did it take to build? You can see the various stages of your cube as it is being built and view detailed logging of the cube building process.

Time and Task Management

Projects are easy to create, but planning them out by time and task is another story. Working with timesheets isn't as automatic as it might seem. You might want to pool a variety of opinions to configure your timesheet management properly, including those of your accounting department and various managers.

> **NOTE**
>
> There are some changes in Project 2007 (as compared to Project 2003) with regard to how timesheets are handled. For example, now every timesheet entry is represented by a row in a database table, meaning the data will be precise and accessible through the Project Server Interface (PSI). In addition, anyone who can access timesheets through Project Web Access (which means they are members of the Viewers security group) can make entries. To learn more about the Timesheet Web Service, refer to the Project 2007 Software Development Kit (SDK).

Management of timesheets is handled through the Time and Task Management page through Project Web Access using a variety of options, considered one at a time in the following sections.

Financial Periods

Financial or fiscal periods are primarily for use in cube reporting, where there are two time dimensions (one being calendar, the other fiscal). The fiscal periods are also available as a timescale in resource plans and as a filter condition in timesheet approvals. The definition of fiscal periods drives these timescales, and as you can see each is a total of 52 weeks, which is a year on any calendar. Fiscal periods can be defined only for the years 1984 to 2049.

- ▶ **Manage Fiscal Period.** Select the year you want to define, delete, or edit. If you select the Define option, you need to be ready to enter a prefix, numbering sequence, and suffix.

- ▶ **Adjust Fiscal Months.** You can change the end dates of any fiscal month. The system automatically adjusts the start date of the next month to one day after the end of the previous month until the last month. Adjustments between fiscal years are not automated.

Timesheet Periods

To make changes in the timesheet periods, shown in Figure 15.17, you need to know the number of periods, the length of each period, and the starting date for the first period. The default settings are 52 periods with a length of 7 days starting on today's date, but all of this is configurable through the Define Bulk Period Parameters.

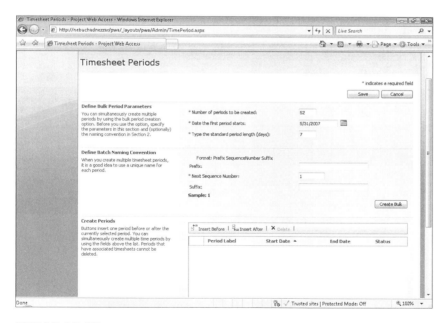

FIGURE 15.17   Changing timesheet periods.

After you have the period configuration set, you must create a bulk grouping of these periods by configuring settings in the Define Batch Naming Convention portion of the page. Create the prefix (for example, period_num), a next sequence number (for example, 1), and then a suffix (which is optional). Click the **Create Bulk** button, and they will appear in the Create Periods portion of the page. You can use the Create Periods portion to add periods before or after a selected period, which gives you some flexibility to change what you need for your timesheet periods. When you have finished configuring these, select **Save**.

Timesheet Classifications

You can duplicate/edit your timesheet to reflect the requirements for business or accounting reasons. To accomplish this, define timesheet line classifications, which will become the unique identifier for a timesheet line.

There are many reasons for doing this. Here are a couple of examples.

▶ You have a task that is common throughout your project. It is done many times. The reasons for doing the task can be different. In some instances, the task is done as a matter of standard maintenance, and in other instances it is done to satisfy warranty requirements. You want to track why the work was performed. Creating a timesheet line classification would allow you to track this distinction.

▶ Your organization supports three types of overtime: 150%, 200%, and flex time. You want to be able to differentiate between these types of overtime. Creating a timesheet line classification would allow you to track these overtime differences.

Timesheet Settings and Defaults

This page contains quite a bit of information for you to choose from, as shown in Table 15.1. We need to look at each option and the settings available within each one.

TABLE 15.1   Timesheet Settings and Defaults

Option	Definition	Settings
Outlook Display	Timesheets can display planned work, overtime, and nonbillable time. Choose the option from the right that best meets your business needs.	Timesheet in Outlook will display the following time types (radio buttons): Actual Hours and Scheduled Hours Actual, Overtime, and Scheduled Hours Billable, Nonbillable, Overtime, and Schedule Hours (default)
Project Web Access Display	Timesheets can display planned work, overtime, and nonbillable time. To disable the overtime and nonbillable timesheet types, clear the check box to the right.	(Check box) The timesheet will use standard Overtime and Nonbillable time tracking.
Default Timesheet Creation Mode	Users can enter data on their timesheets against projects or current assignments. This setting allows site-level consistency for the type of default timesheet users will see.	By default, timesheets will be created by using one of the following (radio buttons): Current task assignments (default) Current projects No prepopulation

Option	Definition	Settings
Timesheet Grid Column Units	Timesheets support weekly or daily tracking. When Weekly is specified, each column in the timesheet represents seven days, and the date in the column displays the first day of the week.	The default timesheet tracking units are as follows (radio buttons): Days (default) Weeks
Default Reporting Units	Timesheets support viewing and reporting in either hours or parts of a day. You can specify here which units are used.	The default timesheet units will be as follows (radio buttons): Hours (default) Days The number of hours in a standard timesheet work week is 40 (default).
Hourly Reporting Limits	Accounting systems, customers, or internal business policies might restrict how time can be entered. If you use team resources, be sure to consider such restrictions when you set these values.	Time tracking data entry limits are as follows: Maximum hours per Timesheet 999 (default) Minimum Hours per Timesheet 0 (default) Maximum Hours per Day 999 (default)
Timesheet Policies	You can use settings in this section to help you comply with accounting and regulatory policies. You can restrict users from reporting time in future timesheet periods. You can restrict users from specifying timesheet lines that cannot be verified against Project Server items.	(Check boxes) Allow future time reporting (default) Allow unverified timesheet line items (default)
Auditing	You can use timesheet auditing to record changes saved to timesheets during creation, approval, and later adjustments.	(Check box) Enable Timesheet Auditing (default: off) Purge Log button
Approval Routing	Fixed-approval routing will disable the ability to change the next approver during timesheet submission. The transaction comment will also be disabled for timesheet submitting, therefore, users should use the timesheet header comment instead.	(Check box) Fixed Approval Routing

15

> **NOTE**
>
> If you want to practice making changes to the settings within Project Web Access, you can access an excellent set of test labs at www.informationworker.co.za/EPM/Documents/Contoso%20Project%202007%20Test%20Plan%20Sample.doc.

Administrative Time

Here, you can track the exception time (nonworking and nonproject time such as administrative, vacation, and sick) and any other categorized nonproject time spent by users and requiring tracking.

It can be set so that managerial approvals are required before employees are allowed to actually commit the time. You can ensure that all users' timesheets have a line for the category by selecting the Always Display option. To add more categories, click the **New Category** button and configure the settings.

Task Settings and Display

This page has a variety of settings you can choose from, as shown in Table 15.2.

TABLE 15.2   Task Settings and Display

Option	Description	Settings
Tracking Method	Specify the default method for reporting progress or tasks, and whether the Tracking mode should be enforced on all projects.	(Radio buttons) **Percent of work complete.** Resources report the percent of work they have completed, from 0 through 100% (default). **Actual work done and work remaining.** Resources report the actual work done and the work remaining to be done on each task. **Hours of work done per period.** Resources report their hours worked on each task per period. (Check box) Force project managers to use the progress reporting method specified above for all projects (default: on)
Reporting Display	Specify how you want resources to report their hours.	(Radio buttons) Resources should report their hours worked every day (default). Resources should report their total hours worked for a week. Week starts on: Monday (default)

Option	Description	Settings
Protect User Updates	Select the Restrict Updates to Project Web Access check box if your business requires that the project manager not be able to change actual time worked. Select the Time Entry by Timesheet Only check box if you want to ensure that your users always report the same timesheet hours as task progress. Users must then import from timesheet to update task progress and submit.	(Check boxes) Restrict updates to Project Web Access (default: off). Time entry by Timesheet only. Users will sync to update tasks (default: off).
Define Current Tasks	When viewing their current tasks, resources will see all tasks that are currently in progress in addition to tasks that are scheduled to start within a certain number of days from the current date or those that have completed within the same number of days in the past.	Current tasks are those tasks that … Have started but not yet finished Or have been rejected and not yet resubmitted Or are not older than or further in the future more than ten days (default)
Enable Team Member Gantt view	If your organization allows team members to download ActiveX controls, the Gantt Chart view will be available to team members, accessible from the Go To menu on the main task grid page. To enable this, select the check box on the right.	(Check box) Enable ActiveX Gantt view for all users.

15

After establishing all settings, click the **Save** button to save them and put them into effect.

Close Tasks to Update

The purpose of these settings is to lock down the tasks within specific projects. Under this view, you must first select the project that you want to lock down the tasks in. This will not take effect until the next time the Project file is opened. When you select the project, the task list will be populated, and you can select the tasks that you want to lock. When you have finished, click the **Submit** button to complete the process.

Queue Management Settings

A queue is another word for a line—not like one you draw, but a waiting line; for example, when you go to the bank and wait in the line, you are in a queue. No matter how fast computers have become, sometimes processes or requests are held in a queue. Imagine a situation in which it's the end of the day on Friday and all 1,000 of your employees attempt to submit their timesheets in Project. That is going to cause a queue that your Project Server needs to handle.

> **NOTE**
>
> The Project 2007 Queuing System is a new, key feature that you can learn all about (from architecture to administration) from the TechNet article at http://technet2.microsoft.com/Office/en-us/library/348d1f05-5cc6-41bb-be2c-ea28bbf1c3421033.mspx?mfr=true.

Queue management can be handled from within the Server Settings through either the Manage Queue or Queue Settings tab.

Manage Queue

The Manage Queue page, shown in Figure 15.18, looks something like a printer administration tool. The current status of jobs shows, and you can take administrative action on them if necessary.

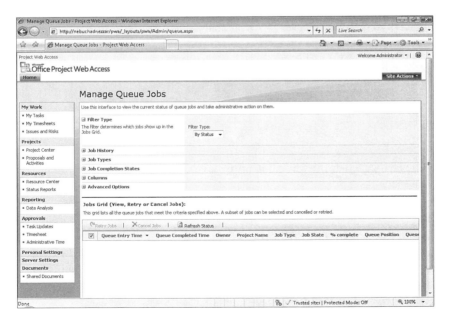

FIGURE 15.18   Manage queue jobs.

You can filter the jobs by status, jobs, projects, or ID. You can also narrow down your results by using the following parameters:

► **Length of History.** You can specify a certain number of days, or you can view a history of jobs that meet the criteria you establish in Choose Job Type and Choose Job Completion States.

► **Choose Job Type.** Let's you choose a job type to look for.

► **Choose Job Completion States.** Let's you choose a job completion state to look for.

► **Choose Columns.** Select the columns you want to appear in the Jobs Grid section.

► **Advanced Options.** Allows you to cancel jobs getting enqueued and subsequent jobs in correlation.

The settings you configure will be shown in the Jobs Grid section of the page. From here, you can retry a job or cancel a job. You'll notice that there is a Refresh button within the Job Grid settings. This button is there because you have to manually refresh the list to update the page.

Queue Settings

These settings are per Project Web Access, per queue type, and do not require restarting the queue NT service to refresh. Even across multiple queue services (as in a load-balanced environment) they will all refresh. There are the following sections:

► **Queue Type.** These include either the Project Queue (the default setting) or the Timesheet Queue.

NOTE

There two separate queues:

► **Project queue.** Used for Project messages related to saving, publishing, reporting, and cube building. The information is stored in the Office Project Server 2007 Working database.

► **Timesheet queue.** Used for the timesheet messages related to saving and submitting a timesheet. The information is stored in the Office Project Server in the Published database.

► **Maximum Number of Job Processor Threads.** Enables multiple jobs to be processed at the same time. The default is 4 threads, with a minimum of 1 and a maximum of 20.

► **Polling Interval** (in milliseconds). This is the time interval at which the queue polls the database for new jobs, again allowing a setting from a minimum of 500 (.5 second) to a maximum of 300,000 (5 minutes) with the default at 1,000 (1 second).

▶ **Retry Interval** (in milliseconds). If there is a job processing failure due to transient issues (such as a SQL deadlock), instead of failing the job this setting can adjust the retry time. They are a minimum of 0 (immediate retry) to a maximum of 300,000 (5 minutes) with the default at 1,000 (1 second).

▶ **Retry Limit.** Here you can set the number of retries each time it retries with the time specified above. Minimum is 0 (no retries) to maximum 100 and a default of 5.

▶ **SQL Retry Interval** (in milliseconds). The queue will poll the database to retrieve jobs that need to be processed. Again, if it fails, this sets the time between retries. Again, the minimum is 0 (immediate retry) to maximum 60,000 (1 minute); the default is 1,000 (1 second).

▶ **SQL Retry Limit.** This provides the settings for the number of retries. The default is 5.

▶ **SQL Timeout.** The queue makes calls for executing jobs. This setting is the timeout value for these calls. The default is 1,800 (30 minutes) with a minimum of 30 and a maximum of 86,400 (1 day).

▶ **Cleanup Interval** (in hours). This determines the frequency with which the queue cleanup job runs. The default is 24 (1 day) with a minimum of 1 and a maximum of 100,000.

▶ **Cleanup Interval Offset** (in minutes). The time of day at which to run is set here. The default is 0 (or 12:00 a.m.), with a minimum of 0 and a maximum of 1,439 (which is 11:59 pm).

▶ **Cleanup Age Limit for Successful Jobs** (in hours). This is the age threshold at which successful jobs can be purged when the Queue Cleanup job runs. The default is 24 (1 day), with a minimum of 1 and a maximum of 100,000.

▶ **Cleanup Age Limit For Non-Successful Jobs** (in hours). This sets the age threshold at which any job in a completed nonsuccessful state can be purged when the Queue Cleanup job runs. The default is 168 (7 days), with a minimum of 1 and a maximum of 100,000.

▶ **Bookkeeping Interval** (in milliseconds). Starting up jobs that have been in a "sleeping state," updating the heartbeat timestamp, or checking whether Queue Cleanup needs to be executed. The default is 10,000 (10 seconds), with a minimum of 500 (0.5 second) and a maximum of 300,000 (5 minutes).

▶ **Queue Timeout** (in minutes). This is part of the failover system. If the farm contains multiple servers, the Queue Service fails on one server, and the jobs are automatically distributed to the other servers. The default is 3, with a minimum of 2 and a maximum of 20.

▶ **Fast Polling.** If for some reason the server becomes overwhelmed by the jobs queued, you can switch off Fast Polling, which is on by default. This will then have the queue check for empty threads, load them, and then wait for the whole job to be completed before moving on.

Setting Operation Policies

Most settings fit within their own category. The following settings are the "leftovers" of the Project configuration settings. One of the section headings is literally "Additional Server Settings," which is just another way of saying "and everything else." So, let's look into this cornucopia of leftover settings.

Alerts and Reminders

Settings for email notification are set here. Complete the settings for the default sender email address and email message to be broadcast. You need to know the SMTP mail server address. Here is where you also schedule the service for sending reminders to users for upcoming or overdue tasks and status reports. See Figure 15.19.

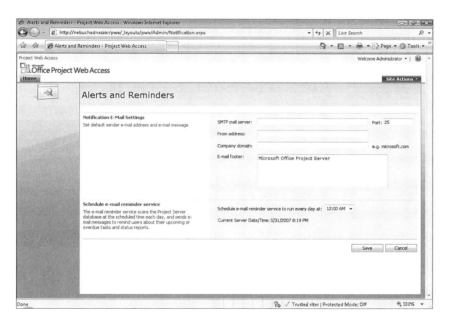

FIGURE 15.19   Configuring alerts and reminders.

Additional Server Settings

There are five additional server settings, as shown in Figure 15.20:

▶ **Enterprise Settings.** Here you set whether master projects and projects containing local base calendars are going to be published to the server.

▶ **Currency Settings.** Set the default currency and whether projects can be published only in that currency.

▶ **Resource Capacity Settings.** Set the months ahead and behind of capacity data that the report database maintains for resources.

▶ **Resources Plan Work Day.** This is for entering the average length of day for all resources in a resource plan.

▶ **Project State Field.** This controls the behavior of the State field in Project Web Access.

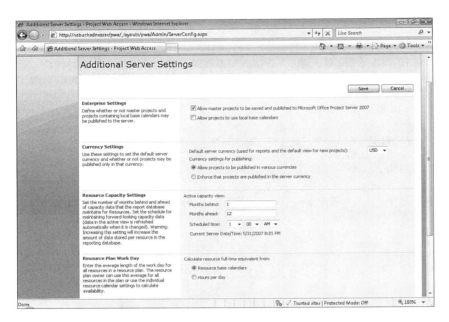

FIGURE 15.20   Additional server settings.

Server-Side Event Handler Configuration

This page is used to manage custom server event handlers. You are shown a variety of standard events that happen on the server automatically.

Active Directory Resource Pool Synchronization

As suggested by the heading, the settings in this section apply to Active Directory enterprise resource pool synchronization. Included in the settings are Active Directory Group, Synchronization Status, Scheduling Options, and Resource Options.

Project Workspaces and Provisioning Settings

There are four settings in this section:

▶ **Site URL.** You can select the default Web application and site URL here.

▶ **Default Workspace Properties.** You can set the default language and default workspace template here.

▶ **Automatic Provisioning.** You can set either automatic or manual provisioning here.

▶ **Workspace Permissions.** You can choose how the Project Server grants access to project workspaces here.

Installed and Configured: What's Your Next Step?

At this point, we have covered all the settings that are available in the Project Web Access site. Many administrators stop here with their understanding of the subject. But, the next chapter takes you through the use of the Project Professional client. In the chapter, you learn how to put a project together and see how Project Server provides the means to collaborate as never before.

You will see, as you no doubt have already with other subjects you've explored in this book, that a modern administrator can function better in our world today by knowing the concepts behind some of the more intense applications that are being developed to handle communication, collaboration, project management, and business intelligence.

15

CHAPTER 16

Project Server 2007: Working with Project Professional

Well, we've gone through all the effort of setting up Microsoft Project Server, and you've installed Project Professional as the client program. This chapter we're going to have some fun with Project. It's hard to imagine that working with a project can be considered fun, but the ability to be more productive is certainly going to increase the joy of your office. In this chapter, we spend some time looking at the objectives and approaches that you can use to make project work best for you and your needs.

We're assuming that most of you reading this have had at least some exposure to the previous releases of Microsoft Project and have a good idea about why you would use it in the first place.

Project is just a tool. It's not the process. To use Project properly, you need to understand what project management is. You won't instantly have a successful management scheme just by installing Microsoft Project. Project is an essential tool to help you implement what you already know about project management.

What Is Project Management?

Project management has been defined by the experts as the application of knowledge, tools, skills, and methods (learned through both study and experience) to achieve projects that are on time, on budget, and according to specification. A project is a temporary undertaken venture to accomplish a specific goal. Project management know-how and practices are best described in terms of its components. These components can be grouped into five Process Areas: Initiating, Planning, Executing, Controlling, and Closing—with nine Knowledge Areas: Integration Management, Scope Management, Time Management, Cost Management, Quality Management, Human Resource Management, Communications Management, Risk Management, and Procurement Management.

We manage projects daily. We all have the ability to do this without ever stepping foot in a class. For example, consider the simple "project" we undertake each morning: getting to work on time. To manage this project, you formulate a project plan. Sure, we don't call it that, but that is what it is. For starters, your plan includes setting an alarm for a time early enough so that you can prepare, leave, and arrive at work on time (or early). Even though you usually don't think of this as a project plan, consider what your mind tells you if you are running late. You know you have to tweak prep time, commute time, or something else to still arrive at the office on schedule.

Within your project of getting to work, you might have side tasks that you need to complete (tasks that might not necessarily relate to the project at hand, but that might be part of your overall "highest priority" projects). For example, you might need to prepare lunch for the kids before they leave for school. Although this task has nothing to do with getting to work on time, it is an essential part of your main project: life.

Project plans can be changed on-the-fly, but there is always the danger that this will alter the completion of the project on time. So, if you adjust one portion, you have to see where you can pull time from another. So, going back to our illustration of getting to work on time, if you hit the snooze button too many times, you might have to skip breakfast. The project is still on time, but you have suffered a personal loss due not to poor planning, but to poor delivery. You move forward with your modified plan.

In addition, modifications are necessary when an unforeseen occurrence comes your way. You never know when something might hit. What happens when you start to make that lunch for your kids and you find there is no more jelly for their sandwiches? You modify the plan a bit more and give them each enough money for lunch (which is great to them because it's pizza day at school), and you navigate through that disaster to successfully arrive at work on time.

Is your project a success now? Not quite. You are, in fact, on time, but you had to spend more money than planned, so you are not on budget. Were you to specification? Well, that depends on the purpose of your project. If the goal is just to get to work on time, then yes, you met specifications. If your true goal is to perform each of the tasks along the way, then no, you have failed to meet specification.

Projects within a work environment are going to involve the same concerns but at a higher level, with many tasks and a higher budget, but … it's the same line of thinking you use in simple miniprojects. The difference is the magnitude (and the PhD vocabulary often used to describe the process of project management).

Successful Project Management Thinking

Consider another everyday scenario: recording your favorite TV show. Depending on your age, this scenario might involve a VCR or a DVR (Tivo or other type). Let's use the VCR approach. You have your project plan. Right before you leave for soccer practice, you are going to toss a tape in, set the time, and record that show for later. When the time comes to put the tape in, you find that you have no more blank tapes. You are frantically looking for another tape. The kids are in the car screaming, it's time to go, something has to give! You are no longer managing a project; instead, you are now managing a crisis.

You need to think through various ramifications and assess what can be changed. Do you use a tape with another show on it? Do you skip the taping and just leave? Do you call a friend and entrust the project into her hands?

Analyzing the situation at hand and determining what can be altered in the plan is part of good project management. You have to assess the impact of project reality (the reality being that you don't have a blank tape and are running out of time) to succeed. Negative project management is getting fed up and just walking out, or losing site of the ultimate, more important goal (which might be getting your kids to practice).

Phase Management

When you start a project, you need to have an end date. Projects *must* end. However, sometimes certain aspects change within our projects. Suppose, for example, that a builder is hired to build 24 homes over a 6-month period. This is the project. But suppose there is a change in the plan, and now there is a request for 48 homes. The project has changed. These types of changes occur all the time. Projects can change, and it might seem like we never achieve anything, even though the reality is that we are accomplishing quite a bit.

One idea, when a project changes, is to establish phases. So, the original plan of 24 homes to be completed in 6 months is called Phase 1, and future homes are placed into Phase 2. At the completion of Phase 1, you can rejoice in the delivery of the project structure. It gives you closure and provides the perception to all involved that there are results, that benefits have been realized.

What you don't want to deal with is the project that never, ever ends. So, create phases for your project.

Projects Require People and Resources

Depending on the type of project you are managing, you might be dealing with different teams and pulling from a variety of resources. For example, a large building project might involve several different construction teams (one for the foundation, one for framing, one for electrical, one for plumbing, and so on) and the use of different resources (company tools, perhaps large equipment such as backhoes and bobcats).

Those people and resources need to be managed within a project. So, if you manage projects poorly, you might have the electricians coming in before the roofers, which means you wire a home before it is protected from the elements. Or, you might have the backhoe on another job on the week you need to break ground in a new development. So, not only do you need to manage the project, you also have to be in sync with the people and resources it will take to complete that project. Remember, a project manager doesn't get the project done, he/she is only one key player in the process. You *must* manage people and resources!

Where Does Microsoft Project Assist?

Microsoft Project 2007 offers a rich toolset, which can be very helpful to you, but it can also be so complex to some that it can feel overwhelming. Project 2007 helps us to completely map out our work breakdown structure (WBS), which is the entire scope of a project.

NOTE

The WBS is a technique for defining the full scope of a project under a hierarchical structure. Wikipedia, the free encyclopedia, describes a WBS as follows:

"The first two levels of the WBS (the root node and Level 2) define a set of *planned outcomes* that collectively and exclusively represent 100% of the project scope. At each subsequent level, the children of a parent node collectively and exclusively represent 100% of the scope of their parent node. A well-designed WBS describes planned outcomes instead of planned actions. Outcomes are the desired ends of the project, and can be predicted accurately; actions comprise the project plan and may be difficult to predict accurately. A well-designed WBS makes it easy to assign any project activity to one and only one terminal element of the WBS.

One of the most important WBS design principles is called the 100% Rule. The *Practice Standard for Work Breakdown Structures (Second Edition)*, published by the Project Management Institute (PMI) defines the 100% Rule as follows:

The 100% Rule ... states that the WBS includes 100% of the work defined by the project scope and captures ALL deliverables—internal, external, interim—in terms of the work to be completed, including project management. The 100% rule is one of the most important principles guiding the development, decomposition and evaluation of the WBS. The rule applies at all levels within the hierarchy: the sum of the work at the 'child' level must equal 100% of the work represented by the 'parent' and the WBS should not include any work that falls outside the actual scope of the project, that is, it cannot include more than 100% of the work ... It is important to remember that the 100% rule also applies to the activity level. The work represented by the activities in each work package must add up to 100% of the work necessary to complete the work package." (p. 8)

Microsoft Project allows us to allocate resources to the project. It also allows us to estimate various parts of the project. For example, we might estimate that it will take two weeks for the plumbing team to complete the project for their portion. It also lets us establish dependencies between tasks, so that we have a good idea of what needs to be done before another portion. So, for example, we realize that the roof needs to be on before the carpeting is installed.

In addition, Project helps us calculate our costs (for the project, for the materials, and so forth) and the budget for our project. Project is also an excellent tool for daily monitoring and management of your project. It is flexible enough to handle the ongoing changes that occur within a project. It's more than a planning tool, but it can be used to schedule (with its automatic scheduling tool), budget, and analyze your project. There are terrific tools to help you "what if" your project plan.

Getting Started with Project Objectives

At this point, several steps need to be considered to fully benefit from the program's features. Regardless of the size or complexity of the project, you need to take advantage of an organizing stage. This gives you the opportunity to define your goals.

Your project's success will be measured by how closely you are able to meet the expectations or original objectives. Mark Twain said it best: "The secret of getting ahead is getting started." The secret of getting started is breaking your complex, overwhelming tasks into small, manageable tasks and then starting on the first one.

Being able to adjust for the unknown as your project ages is an absolute must. Information such as the availability of certain resources, timing on deliverables, and even just time scheduling—these are things you must consider ahead of time.

The flexibility in Project allows for the project manager (or team, in the case of Project Server–based instances) to plot out the course of the job, keeping in mind the constraints that might be placed on the project, such as job completion dates, cost of resources, or budgets.

After we have these steps identified, the next is to put together the objectives, tasks, and work involved to get it done and create a document that describes the scope of the project and how it will be managed and adjusted as needed. Easier said than done, right? So, where does one begin the task of building a project from the ground up? With data entry!

Building Your Project

Now is the time to start plugging the information into Microsoft Project. Now you can attach the documents that you created earlier. (If they were created in Microsoft Word, or if it is a workflow chart that was made with Microsoft Visio, PowerPoint, or Office OneNote 2007, they can be inserted.) You will see later how with Project Server these documents will then become available for all project management team members involved.

You can create your new project in the usual way, just opening Project as New Project. Or, if similarities exist in the project, team, or resources, you can opt to work with an existing project as a template. Project also includes templates that can help you get you started.

Depending on whether you are using Project Server, saving your work will be somewhat different. Saving it locally or offline will, of course, allow you to continue to make changes to the project while not connected to Project Server. You can also import an in-progress file to an existing file that resides elsewhere on another server. In the case of an enterprise project, for which you're using Project Server and the file resides on that server, you need the proper permissions to sign the file in and out as you work and save your contribution to the file.

At this point, if you've outlined your objectives properly, you have a good understanding about what you're trying to accomplish, and so you can start creating your task list in Project. This is really the foundation, or root, of any project, and the success of your project may depend a great deal on the organized structure of that list. Whether your project will take years to complete or weeks, the care you take now in methodically laying out the task list will make a difference.

If you have already created your task list in another form or program, you can either import the data or embed the data. Whether it's an Excel worksheet, another database, or tab-delimited or comma-separated text format files, the data can be imported into Project. Many use Microsoft Outlook to help organize day to day, but did you know you can also easily import whatever tasks that you have in Outlook straight into Project?

To import tasks from Outlook into Project, follow these steps:

1. From the menu bar, select **Tools, Import Outlook Tasks.**

2. From the dialog box that displays, you can pick the tasks that you want to import. (Note that you need to have Outlook open, toggle to Project, and click the command; you are be asked by Outlook to allow the connection.)

> **NOTE**
>
> You can manipulate the task(s) in Project as needed. The tasks that you import will be appended to your existing task list. When no tasks have yet been created, the imported information from Outlook will constitute your first tasks on the list.

Now that we've tried importing, it's time we create a new task directly in Project. Here is where the detail that might be needed to make sure no part of the project is missed becomes evident (as you can see by how much we break down any given part of the project). The number of steps or substeps required to complete a task determines the task's sensitivity/complexity.

Breaking projects into shorter tasks (as far as completion times) will facilitate the scheduling of your resources/people required to complete the task.

> **NOTE**
>
> Here is where you might need to fine-tune your project. The default setting for working hours is 8 a.m. to 5 p.m., Monday to Friday, with an hour for lunch. These can and should be adjusted at this point as needed. You can also slot in any holidays and vacations.

Okay, let's look again at our software and begin the process of creating a new task. You can choose from many different views. You will probably spend a great deal of your time in the Gantt view; but if you select the View menu, you can click through the different views, which will offer you different pieces of information. For example, you can see the Calendar view or the Resource Sheet, and so forth. There is a lot of information held within Project, and the views present that information to us in various ways that allow us to be most effective, depending on what job we are seeking to do.

To start creating tasks, follow these steps:

1. Select **Gantt Chart** from the View menu.

2. Choose Split from the Window menu.

3. Select the first empty row in the task list and name the task. You can also set the duration of the task (how many days).

4. Notice the box Effort Driven. If you check this box, you fix the task duration time without consideration to any outside influences.

5. The form columns allow you to add resources and predecessor tasks and any other necessary details. Add the resources and predecessor tasks you need.

6. When you're ready to move on, click **Next.**

NOTE

You might be wondering what a Gantt Chart view is. This is a bar chart that shows a project schedule, with emphasis on the start and finish dates. It includes terminal elements and summary elements of a project. Those are the WBS of a project. In addition, through Project, you can see the dependency relationships of certain activities. The Gantt view is one of the more popular views in Project.

TIP

If you need to create subtasks (an extra step necessary to meet your project goal), you can insert a new task. Just click the far left of the screen, open the Insert menu, and select **New Task.** After you have added the information by right-clicking, you can indent the task, making it a subtask. You can manipulate this later by highlighting and clicking **Outdent** (thus making it a main task).

16

Now that you have added and inserted a single task, let's try adding recurring tasks. Suppose that you have a project during which three days of the week you have a certain resource or group performing something repetitive. To configure this within Project, follow these steps:

1. Select **Gantt Chart** from the View menu.

2. Click the row in the chart that you want to add these tasks to.

3. From the Insert menu, select **Recurring Task.**

4. As you did with the single task, you need to name the task.

5. In the Duration box, identify the amount of time each occurrence of the task will take each time it is performed.

6. Under Recurrence pattern, select how often the task will occur: daily, weekly, monthly, or yearly. Check the box.

7. Select either End after (the number of times you want the task to recur) or End by (calendar date).

At the bottom of the form is a calendar for scheduling this task. Your options are Standard, Nightshift, and 24 Hours. If you don't want to apply a calendar, be sure to leave it at None. There is a "Scheduling Ignores resource calendars" check box, and it does just that, allowing you to put time frames to resources regardless of the main tasks' calendar restraints.

As you add these tasks, when you select time frames outside your preselected time range a dialog box asks you if you want to reschedule to fix the problem, as you can see in Figure 16.1. This occurs when you set your calendar to a time outside of your preselected time range.

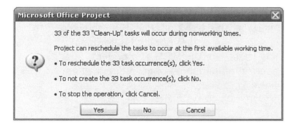

FIGURE 16.1   The request to reschedule.

TIP

To properly assign your resources to recurring tasks, be certain to use the method suggested. If you directly add them to a recurring summary task by typing them in the Resource Names field, they will be assigned to the total work on the recurring task rather than to the desired individual recurring task.

Creating Budgets

Part of reaching your goals in any project will require knowing and remaining within your budgetary limitations. And, so now let's take a look at Project and see how we can make this happen.

You must do a few things to create your budget before we actually get started:

▶ Create budget resources, which are basically the total amount available for the project, including project management costs, actual work on the project costs, and the material costs.

▶ Apply the budget resources that you create to the entire project to the project summary task.

▶ Track any and all resources in your project against the budget of the project by grouping them according to the budget type they are being tracked.

▶ After you have identified your budget resources, grouping them so that you can see how they compare to your projected budget, you can proceed with the budget.

We're going to create a few budgets for our project. Let's name them Budget-Accommodation, Budget-Rentals, Budget-Supplies, and Budget-Travel. Using this type of nomenclature will allow you later to easily identify what is what.

So, to get started, let's go to the Resource sheet and add our budget:

1. From the View menu, select **Resource Sheet.**

2. Double-click one of the empty rows; it will open the Resource Information dialog.

3. Enter the resource name (as shown in Figure 16.2), and then select the type of budget from the Type drop-down list.

4. Check the box Budget, and then click **OK.**

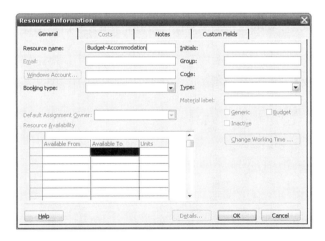

FIGURE 16.2   Establishing your budgets.

The next step in the process is connecting the budget resources to the project task summary:

1. From the View menu, select **Gannt Chart.**

2. From the Tools menu, select **Options**, then open the **View** tab.

3. Notice Outline Options. Select the **Show Project Summary** task, and then click **OK.**

4. Now you need to assign resources, which can be located on the toolbar or under the Tools menu.

5. In the Resource Name field, select the budgets that we created and click **Assign.**

6. You can now close that window.

Your next step is entering values for the resources that you have created as your budgets:

1. From the View menu, select **Resource Usage.**

2. You are going to insert two columns so that you can enter the values for your budgets. They could be Budget Cost and Budget Work.

3. From the Insert menu, select **Column.** In the Field name box, select **Budget Cost,** and then click **OK.** Do the same for the other column you created, Budget Work.

4. On the project summary task row, enter the cost and work budgets.

5. Now you need to get those two columns in the view of your project. To do so, select **Detail Styles** from the Format menu. Notice in Figure 16.3 that you need to select from the Available Fields window your new created Budget Cost and Budget Work and select Show to move them to the Show These Fields window. You must do this one at a time. Then click **OK.**

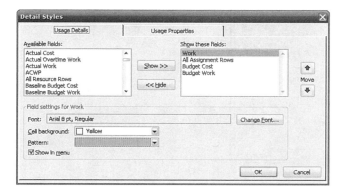

FIGURE 16.3   Setting up the fields you need to see.

Now in (and only in) the project summary task, you can enter your budget values for each time period.

We're getting near the end now. We still have to group or categorize our budget resources by again creating a custom field and using a naming structure that will be easily understood and identifiable. To do so, follow these steps:

1. From the View menu, select **Resource Usage.**

2. To group, go to Group by, which is under Project, off the main menu and select **Customized Group By.**

3. Using the custom resource text fields that you created in the preceding step, highlight the name in the Field Name and click **OK.**

You have learned all of this relatively quickly, so let's briefly review what we've done. We've taken some time to look at the client and see how we can practically start a project and get it underway.

Monitoring

When collaborating on a task, one of the driving forces will be monitoring a critical path. I say *monitoring* because, as is true in real life, each additional task and viable resource can shift the timeline and easily put you off course. As a user of Project, you realize that any task on the critical path becomes a critical task and, as mentioned previously, any shift of those tasks will change the path's final and ongoing projected finish dates.

It is easier to monitor if you alter the view you are working with. To do that, follow these steps:

1. From the View menu, select **More Views.**

2. Select **Detail Gantt**, and then click **Apply.**

Alternatively, you can use the Gantt Chart Wizard. To locate this wizard, first make sure that you're in the Gantt Chart view, and then select **Gantt Chart Wizard** from the Format menu.

The wizard's first dialog box asks what kind of information you want to display in your Gantt chart. Make your choices, and then click **Next.** You are then asked what task information you want to display with your Gantt bars. This information would include dates, resources, or both, or you can select to customize. The next dialog box asks about link lines between dependent tasks and whether you want this. And then, that's it. Just click **Format** (or **Back** if you want to change anything).

As you work more with this, and especially when we start talking about connecting and utilizing Project Server, you will see not only the importance of highlighting your critical path, but also how you can include multiple projects and then choose how to show interconnecting multiple critical paths.

16

Linking Tasks

Another important step to information management within Project is linking the various tasks that might exist across multiple projects (and even within the project file that you might be using). In other words, although there may be multiple projects, there might be commonalities and convergent tasks across the projects; by linking those tasks, those factors are projected in.

In a single project, not looking for external linkages, you link tasks that have a dependency or relationship. For instance, one group or resource is responsible for installing the servers, and the other task and resource may revolve around the cabling needed. Although either one would work independently, to meet the critical path or "project end," they would need to respectively finish within a given time to meet the goal test and commission, for instance. Therefore, we have linked tasks.

You can accomplish linking in either the Gantt Chart view, Network Diagram view, or Calendar view. This is simply done in the Gantt Chart view by selecting two tasks (use Ctrl if they are not side by side, or Shift or drag if they are next to each other). By default, Project will use Finish to Start as the type of dependency. However, you can double-click the link in the Gantt chart; a dialog box will open where you can drop down and choose Start to Start, Finish to Finish, or Start to Finish (see Figure 16.4).

FIGURE 16.4   Changing dependency settings.

In the Network Diagram view, it is even easier. Just click and drag the task you want to link to the other task. That's it! Follow the previous instructions to change the type of dependency you need to have.

Let's look at the last one, the Calendar view. Similar to the Network Diagram view, just click and drag the tasks that need to be linked and follow the previous instructions for the type of dependency.

We should mention one more linking process before looking at how to link across project files. Project is designed by default to autolink tasks if, for instance, you insert a task between two others. If this feature is not desirable, select **Options** under the Tools menu, and then open the **Schedule** tab. Remove the check from the Autolink inserted or moved tasks check box.

Now let's move on to linking between two separate projects or project files. To accomplish this, follow these steps:

Here's how you may do that:

1. Open two different project files, and then select **Show Windows Stacked** or **Arrange All.**

2. In Gantt Chart view, select the task with which you want to create the dependency.

3. Click the **Task Information** icon and open the **Predecessors** tab.

4. Enter the project name and the ID number (separated by a backslash) in the ID column (for example, Project1\1).

As mentioned previously, when an external dependency is part of your project you need to update those dependencies regularly to be certain of their effect on your critical path. To do that, follow these steps:

1. Make sure that you are in Gantt Chart view.

2. Note, whether **AutoFilters** is turned on. (It is turned off by default.) If it is, turn it off; with it off you will see all tasks displayed. Simply select the **AutoFilter** button to turn it off.

3. From the Tools menu, select **Links Between Projects,** and then open either the **External Successors** tab or the **External Predecessors** tab.

4. You can view the differences in the Differences column, and this will display the changes, which might include start or finish date changes.

5. At this point, you can either accept all the changes or review and select them individually. After you accept those changes, however, you can't go back; although you will be updated, you cannot change the records at that point.

By default, you will be notified in the event an externally linked task is changed. When you open a plan with external links, you are given the opportunity to accept any and all changes. However, if you would prefer not to be notified of those changes, you can select **Tools menu, Options,** and the **Views** tab. Go to the **Cross project linking options for** selection and clear the checkbox labeled **Show Links Between Projects dialog on open.** You can also accept changes automatically by selecting the checkbox to automatically accept new external data.

We can also add a filter that will enable us to see only the tasks that have external dependencies. To do so, follow these steps:

1. Once again, make sure that you are in Gantt Chart view.

2. Turn off your AutoFilters.

3. Under the Project menu, select **Filtered for**, and then select **More Filters.** This will open up the More Filters dialog.

4. Select **Task, New,** and then enter the name you want for your filter.

5. Select **Predecessors** in the first row of the Field Name column.

6. In the Values column, remember that you have to put a backslash to show that the information is coming from an external source.

You can now test your filters by doing the following:

1. Select **Or** in the second row of the And/Or column.

2. Select **Successors** in the second row of the Field Name column.

3. Under the second row of the Test column select **contains** and then type the backslash in the second row of the Values column.

4. After clicking **OK** on the Filter Definition, click **Apply.**

Of course, much more can be said about Project Professional, but as mentioned at the outset, we assume that you have a pretty good knowledge of the product and how it works. So now, we turn our attention toward the collaboration part of this program and take a more detailed look at the connection we need to make with Microsoft Project Server.

Interaction Between Client and Server

Given that the last couple of chapters explained a couple of ways to set up Project Server, at this point we're going to look at connecting your Project Professional client to Project Server. Although the steps are simple, getting everything to work takes a bit of effort.

We'll mention a couple of the problems you might see and what you can do to get around them. The first thing you need to do to connect is to set up an account. To do this, you have to have the settings on Project Professional set at stand-alone.

Then, follow these steps:

1. From the Tools menu, select **Enterprise Options, Microsoft Office Project Server Accounts.** The Project Server Accounts dialog will appear, as shown in Figure 16.5.

2. Click **Add,** and then enter a name for the account.

3. In the URL box, use the complete name of the Project server (for example, http://*servername/pagename*). By default, the Web page is named PWA.

4. You need to fill in how it will authenticate, whether it is a Project Server account or whether you are using Windows authentication. Then, select whether you want this to be the default connection.

You can add as many of these servers as you need by following these instructions.

FIGURE 16.5   The Project Server Accounts dialog.

What you need to understand here is that the SharePoint site that is created at installation provides a centralized depository, so to speak, for individuals to manage and track their connected and supporting files. With the right setup, you can store and use those files and be notified of updates and changes on those files. Microsoft Office 2007 is especially designed to take advantage of this technology; other Microsoft programs save to the library in the same manner as you would save in any other area other than your local disk (just pointing as you would to a network drive or Web site and then saving).

Part of the setup is, of course, to include the permissions to be able to access those areas. If you plan for those in your group to be able to contribute to your file, you need to be sure they have the required permissions, too. The terminology for this permission is the ability to contribute to the SharePoint site library. If you are the administrator of that site, you might want to enforce additional information to be added when a file is being saved to the library (information such as what department that you are part of or what type of information is included in the file).

Just like a literal library, your checking out a book removes it from circulation and makes it impossible for others to access the file. To make this work, therefore, after you have made your contribution to the file, it needs to be saved back on the SharePoint Server site and file library to make it both available and able to provide the update notification to team members. Depending on how you have your library set to track files, you have differing results. For instance, if you have it set to notify on only major versions, a notification will be sent only on significant content changes. Minor versions, however, notify when something as simple as spelling changes are made.

16

As mentioned earlier, many additional setup settings are available to you. These change the way files are received, seen, or made visible on the server. This becomes useful for group managers, making it possible to review as necessary any contributions to the project first before making it available to other team members. As with any application, you can do a local hard drive save of the file that you're working on and upload it at another time.

So, how is it done? Let's just quickly go over the steps. Remember, however, that the steps are generalized. As mentioned previously, the settings on your server might differ and require additional or different steps.

1. If this is the first file that you have saved to the server, you can simply select **File, Save.**

2. If you saved a file already but in a different location, select **Save As.** When the Save In choice appears, select **Network.**

3. If the server or site is located there in that window, just select it and click **Open.** If it's not there, you have to enter the URL of your server in the File Name box.

4. With the proper server selected, select the location to which you are saving your files and click **Open.**

5. Enter the name of the file in the File Name box and click **Save.**

> **NOTE**
>
> If the file you are saving was checked out, be certain that you check in the file to make it available. Be certain at this time that you are following the procedure that has been set up on your server. As mentioned previously, this could include listing what type of information is on the file. This could also include the information about your department and the project number.

As mentioned previously, Microsoft Office 2007 has provided for a simpler interface for this operation with the following programs: Microsoft Word, Excel, and PowerPoint. With these programs, just click the **Microsoft Office** button, select **Publish,** and pick **Document Management Server.** When providing your information for your team's dissemination, remember that you have to publish your file. Creating and saving an enterprise project does not make it automatically available to your team members. Again, you might need to create a workspace for this project (a task easily completed by just selecting that command). After you have saved the plan, which is necessary to allow you to publish, click **Publish** and save the project in the created space.

Updating an Enterprise Project

To update an enterprise project, the project file that you're working on must be an enterprise project and you must have connectivity to a Microsoft Office Project Server 2007.

To check the progress or changes submitted by team members, follow these steps:

1. From the menu bar, select **Collaborate and Update Project Progress**.

2. A New Requests page will open. On this page, you can view whatever changes have been made. From that information, you can determine the need to log on to the server through the Project client and accept or reject the changes. Note that you can also gain access to New Requests through the Microsoft Office Project Web Access.

3. You can accept or reject in the following manner:

   a. On the list of updates, to the left of each task, you can check the box whether you want to accept or reject that update.

   b. If you have created rules that will automatically carry this out, select **Actions, Manage Rules**. Select the rule that you want to run, and then select **Run Rule** (or **Run All Rules** if you have multiple rules).

One operation possible here is to preview. That is, before actually approving or rejecting an update, you can take a look and see how it works out. Also note the command Administrative Time Requests. This is designed for the review of such requests as sick leave, vacation, and other company-specific categories.

Sharing an Enterprise Project

Here is another scenario. You have a project that you need to share with someone who is vital to the actual project in the tasks that he has, but he's not part of your networked group or just doesn't have access to your resources. What now?

One thing that is a must if you are going to send your project for review to someone, that person must have either Microsoft Project Professional 2007 or Project Standard 2007 to view the file.

To share a project file with someone who you need to send it to, follow these steps:

1. After connecting to Project Server where your file resides, select **Open, Enterprise Projects.**

2. To open your file, double-click the file you're looking for, or select **Retrieve the list of all projects from Project Server.**

3. When the file opens, look in the File menu for Save for Sharing. Then, in the Save in box, select where you want the file to be saved.

4. Save the file by entering the filename you want to call the shared project and click Save.

5. You can now send off the shared file.

> **TIP**
>
> As in other places where you may customize or add things to your project, it is a good idea to use something in the naming structure that indicates that it is a shared file.

The next step is to check in the file after the changes have been made by others. Save the returned and modified file to your local computer first, and then connect to Project Server 2007. After you have saved the file (by selecting File, Save As, Save), the file again becomes available in more than a read-only format.

Handling Risks and Issues

What is a risk? Like in other parts of life, a risk is anything that can come between you and your goal and typically not be beneficial. Notice that I wrote *can*. Why? If what we feel is a risk actually happens, it escalates to an issue; now it's something that we have to deal with. What this means therefore, is although you might and should realize that you will have risks to meeting the challenge of your project's completion, knowing what those risks are and addressing them will make for a successful project.

For us to be able to view and work with this information you need to be connected from your client, Microsoft Project Professional 2007, to your Microsoft Project Server 2007, with a workspace for your site setup.

To view issues and risks

1. Select either **Risks** or **Issues** from the Collaborate menu to view what a certain risk or issue concerns, about its name.

If you need to modify or create a new risk, follow these steps:

1. Select **Risks** from the Collaborate menu.

2. While on the Risk page, either

   a. Select **New, New Item**

   b. Or, if modifying, select the risk and pick **Edit Item**

3. Create a new name for the risk in the Title area.

4. Now you Browse to find a user within your company who can manage that risk for you, who will be the owner, or you can enter a name and check names as you would in other Microsoft software.

5. Now you need to actually assign the responsibility by entering your choice in Assigned To.

6. In the Status section click the status for the issue. In the Category section click a category number to group similar risks.

7. Under the **Due Date** section, enter the date and time by which the risk should be resolved. Under the Probability section, choose a percentage value to represent how likely that risk is.

8. With 10 representing the highest impact that the risk could have on your project, select a value. (This can become a filter later for identifying problems by severity.)

9. In the Cost area, insert an amount that correlates to the financial impact.

10. Enter a description of the risk.

11. In the Mitigation Plan area, you have the opportunity to include a plan that the project manager might use to change or prevent the impact of a certain risk.

12. In the Contingency Plan section, describe how you could minimize the effect of the risk, by another plan.

13. Describe in the Trigger Description area the condition(s) that will generate the event.

14. And for the trigger itself, pick the circumstance that activates the trigger. There are three values from which to select. Alternatively, you can designate your own value.

15. Click **OK**, and it will be saved and connected to your project.

Now that you understand the risks, it's time to look at the issues. To do so, follow these steps

1. Under the Collaborate menu, select **Issues**.

2. As you did with risks, you can either create a new issue by selecting New or highlight an existing issue from the drop-down window and select Edit Item.

3. Create a title and, once again, assign an owner from within your company by either entering a name and selecting **Check Name** or selecting **Browse** and searching.

4. In the Assigned To section, type a name or search for a person who should be responsible to resolve this particular issue.

5. Select **Status**, and if desired group your issue under Category.

6. Selecting a priority in the Priority area will allow you later to weigh the issue against others in the project.

7. Via the pop-up calendar, select your due date.

8. In the Discussion area, you can elaborate on the issue and the possible resolutions.

9. As suggested by its name, in the Resolution area you can identify what should be done to fix this issue.

10. Click **OK**. The issue will be added to the project and to any other issues that have been created.

Establishing a Workspace Site

We're going to interject here with a topic that is an important part of Microsoft Project Server and is integral to the collaborative capabilities of the program. You learned earlier how to upload your project that you created in a Project Professional client to Project Server 2007. As you will see, there will be times when supportive additional information might be required to help you successfully manage your project. These can take various forms, from a simple note or document to any one of a number of Microsoft Office files.

Before they can be added to the Project Server document library, however, the library or workspace site needs to be created. Generally, with SharePoint Server 3.0 already installed, when you add Project Server 2007 to your Windows server a site is created. However, at times this might not be created successfully, possibly because of a failure to meet the prerequisites or possibly by choice of the system administrator. In any event, after that site has been created, you can begin to upload any documents that you need to have available, with the proper permissions.

Here are the steps:

1. Under the Collaborate menu, select **Documents**, which will open the All Site Content page (which lists the document libraries).

2. Project, when it loads, creates a directory called Project; if it's not there, however, it could be for the reasons mentioned previously.

3. If you have Microsoft Office 2007, you have the option to create a new document directly under the Project Documents page.

4. If you do not have Office 2007, you need to create the document, select **Save As**, navigate to the folder through the network, and click **Save.** The first time you save a document you might be prompted for more information, such as owner and status of the document.

If you have a document already created, you upload this way:

1. From the Upload menu, select **Upload Document.** On this page, browse to find the file you're adding, and then click **Open.**

2. As with other areas of Windows, if you choose to replace a file that is already in the directory, select **Overwrite Existing File.** That will add the document library.

3. If you're adding multiple files, do the same as above, but select all the files you want to add from that directory and click **OK.**

As mentioned previously, there can be supporting documents, graphs, tasks, or whatever that can become part of or need to be considered in any given risk or issue that is part of the project. To make this information available across the team, we need to link that information.

To link information, follow these steps:

1. Once again, because this information resides on Project Server, you need to go in your client to the Collaborate menu and select either **Risks** or **Issues.**

2. After selecting either Risks or Issues, click the drop-down arrow and select **Edit Item.**

3. Select **Link Items.**

4. In that dialog box, select what you want to link to. (Selecting something in this dialog box will open the next one, where you can link to what you need.)

Attaching a Note

At times you may want to add supporting information, such as a note to a task, resources or assignment. You can even add a note to an entire project. Along with a simple note you might include a document that goes along with the note, for further supporting documentation.

To accomplish this for a task, resource, or assignment, perform the following. (Note, this information is for including a note in tasks, however the same method would apply from resources or assignments):

1. From the View menu, click a task from the Task Name field of a task view and then select, **Task Notes.** You can also double-click the task; the same action will become available, as shown in Figure 16.6.

2. From the **Notes** box, type the message you want in the note and click **OK.**

3. You can format the text by selecting it and changing the font, alignment, or making bulleted or numbered lists. You can even include a graphic by selecting the **Insert Object** button.

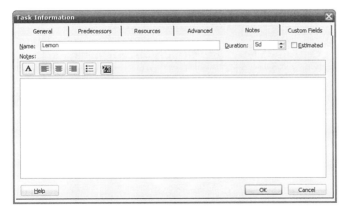

FIGURE 16.6   The Task Information Notes tab.

You can also add a note directly pertaining to the project as a whole. The simplest way to create a limited size note is to add it to the comments of the Properties tab of the project. To do so, follow these steps:

1. Without anything selected in the project file, select **File**, and then choose **Properties.**

2. Open the **Summary** tab. Notice the Comments dialog box in Figure 16.7. Add your information within that dialog.

FIGURE 16.7   Adding comments into the properties.

If you need to add more information than that small area will allow for, just follow these steps:

1. Under the Tools menu, select **Options, View, Outline Options** and make sure that the Show project summary task is selected, as shown in Figure 16.8.

2. From the Project menu, select **Task Notes.** You can now enter your information in the Notes box, as shown in Figure 16.9.

3. You can format the font, alignment, and list view. You can also insert an image if needed by selecting Insert Object from the available tools.

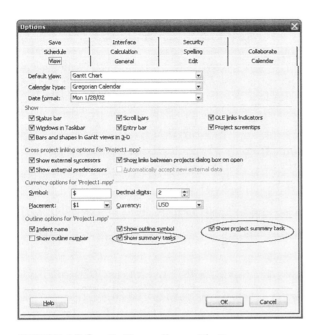

FIGURE 16.8   Outline option settings.

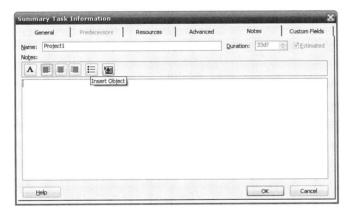

FIGURE 16.9   Summary Task Information pane.

File Import and Export

Sometimes your project information might have to be distributed to others in your organization via another file format. Again, this is possible with Microsoft Project Professional 2007. To simplify both the import and export processes, there is a wizard that will help make this happen. The wizard helps to automatically map the information and direct it to the proper fields and format.

Let's first look at adding, or importing, information. You can do this from Microsoft products such as Access and Excel, or it can come from a tab-delimited or comma-separated text file along with Extensible Markup Language (XML).

1. Select **Open** (or **Open from File** if you're connected to Project Server 2007).

2. Pick the file type that you are going to import the data from.

3. Locate the folder in the typical manner through the Look in box, and then click **Open.**

4. Select the data that you want to import. This will kick off the Import Wizard.

5. First you are asked whether you want to create a new map or use an existing one. Choose **New Map** to create your data settings from scratch. Choose **Use Existing Map** to see the ready-made maps available to you. Then click **Next.**

6. You are offered three options for importing the data. Make your choice from the following, and then click **Next:**

    a. As a new project

    b. Append the data to the active project

    c. Merge the data into the active project

7. Notice the options of whether the information will be added as a task resource or assignment mapping, and then adjust that information as needed. If you are importing an Excel file, you can choose to include the headers or not. Click **Next.**

8. You are now taken to the Resource Mapping dialog box, shown in Figure 16.10. You can change field names by clicking in the To column and entering what you want:

    a. Deleting a row can be done by highlighting in the From column and selecting Delete Row.

    b. Inserting a new field is done by selecting the From column and selecting Insert Row.

    c. Use Clear All if you need to remove all tasks, resources, or assignment fields. To add all, select Add All.

9. Click **Finish** to complete the wizard.

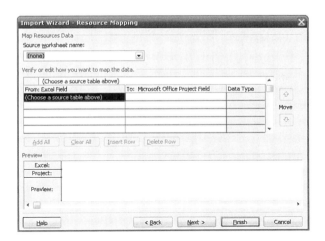

FIGURE 16.10   The Resource Mapping dialog box.

The Use of Calendars in Project

We haven't yet discussed the use of calendars in Project. Because Project is a tasking and scheduling program, however, this is essential. Therefore, let's take a few moments and take a look. There are four different types of calendars: base calendars, project calendars, resource calendars, and task calendars. Each offers a different level of management for the scheduling of your project. You can modify the calendars to establish the working structure of the project itself, for groups or individual resources, or for specific tasks—all help keep your project on time.

Let's take a closer look at the base calendar of Project, which can be broken down into three basic types:

▶ **Standard.** This represents the normal workweek, Monday through Friday, 8 a.m. to 5 p.m., with an hour for lunch, as shown in Figure 16.11.

▶ **24 Hours.** As it suggests, this one is "on the clock" all the time. This calendar could be used for equipment or material resources that are available around the clock, or resources available on a shift-work basis.

▶ **Night Shift.** This is specifically designed for the 11 p.m. to 8 a.m., Monday through Saturday, shift.

In addition, you can create and add your own calendar to suit your project's base calendar needs.

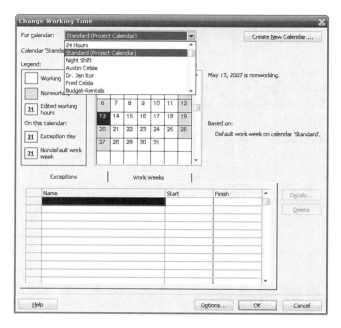

FIGURE 16.11   The Standard calendar.

The base calendar represents your company's working time schedule. This calendar is used primarily for tasks that have a fixed duration. However, you can also create alternative calendars to suit your needs.

On the other hand, a resource calendar is designed to reflect the schedules of either people or equipment that make up the resources in any given project. Whereas for the most part the resource calendar can be much like the project calendar, the schedule can be adjusted to reflect anything from a leave of absence to vacations to equipment downtime.

To illustrate how this can be used, consider this scenario. Suppose you have a certain group of people or trade that works specific times. To reflect that accurately in the project, you need to customize the calendar by selecting Changing Working Time in the Resource Information dialog box and editing the calendar to reflect your needs. You can also assign an entirely different base calendar to display the specific working times of the resources.

The resource calendar is used by default whenever a resource that is not on a fixed calendar is applied to the project. This way, when a resource has on its calendar a vacation or leave time during the period of the task, the project will not schedule the task for that time period.

A task calendar allows for tasks that need to be scheduled for what are atypical time periods. Again, you can create your own calendar. You can see in Figure 7.11 how to do this. If you have a conflict between a resource calendar and a task calendar, open the **Advanced** tab in the Task Information dialog box and click **Scheduling ignores resource calendars.**

Whereas the calendar setting in Tools, Options Calendar (as seen previously) set the general time settings that the project uses (for instance, the start day of the week, number of days part of the workweek, and number of hours a day that comprise a workday), if you create a calendar that differs from that baseline calendar, your Duration field might not reflect what you expect. In such a case, you need to adjust your calendars to match work time settings.

Milestones

We've talked about calendars in our scheduling process, but there is also another means by which we can mark our progress through our project. These markers are referred to as milestones.

These milestones can be set to help determine the progress of your project. They can be represented by any task you decide to mark as such. Project will automatically mark any task that has a zero duration as a milestone. If you have tasks included that are external tasks—that is, tasks that are performed by others but are integral to the project—these can be marked as milestones by marking them with a zero duration (because the time spent is outside your concerns). Marking this way and setting the date of completion creates that milestone.

To create the milestone, follow these steps:

1. From the View menu, select **Gantt Chart.**

2. If you are creating a new milestone, pick the first empty row and enter a name for the task.

3. Under the Duration column, enter **0**; this will automatically place the milestone mark on the Gantt chart.

If your milestone does require a duration time, follow these steps:

1. From the View menu, select **Gantt Chart.**

2. If you're creating a new milestone task, just pick the first available task row and enter the name or select the task you want to associate the milestone to.

3. From the Project menu, select **Task Information.**

4. Open the **Advanced** tab (shown in Figure 16.12), enter the duration, select the **Mark task as milestone** check box, and then click **OK.**

16

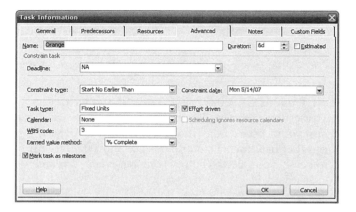

FIGURE 16.12   Making your tasks into milestones.

Where to Go from Here?

Let's take just a little more time to talk about the features of Microsoft Project Server 2007 that are going to make a difference for you. Looking at it from the administrator side for a bit, let's look at the features that will make it better for you and help you do your job of maintaining the project environment.

As with any new software, the dreaded learning curve can eat into your time ... time that is often hard to come by. However, Microsoft Project 2007 management functions have been refined. This has been accomplished by a single Web interface called Server Settings and synchronization with Active Directory, which facilitates easier access to the resources that will be needed, simplifying your work of managing your directory services.

In addition, the client Microsoft Project Professional can open Project file formats created in Project 2003, 2002, and even 2000. Project 2007 can save files to XML, CSV (comma-separated values), text (tab delimited), Microsoft Excel PivotTable, and a workbook Web page.

Note that although both Project Server 2007 and Microsoft Project Professional can migrate several file formats, as mentioned previously, there is no interoperability between the older versions. In other words, the connections between Project Professional 2007 and Project Server 2007 are new, and earlier versions must be migrated.

A smoother, more robust connection between the client, Microsoft Project Professional, and Microsoft Project Server 2007 ensures the information that you need for you and your team will be available and accessible anywhere you go. As you have seen, whether it is the management of resources or the budgeting of finances, Project 2007 will help you by collaboration and communication from the start through to the completion of your project.

CHAPTER 17

SharePoint Server for Search 2007: Overview, Installation, and Administration

Microsoft Office SharePoint Server for Search has been added to the Office servers list to provide for the business needs for both intranet (enterprise) and Internet search. With regard to infrastructures, Microsoft Office SharePoint Server (MOSS) for Search has various deployment options that can fit into different scenarios, depending on both infrastructure and organizational needs.

Enterprise search is in many cases an important aspect within organizations. Search is one of the few options to make large amounts of content findable by users. Together with Internet and desktop search, enterprise search is essential for information workers.

Looking at the other MOSS 2007 products (MOSS 2007 and MOSS 2007 for Internet Sites), MOSS 2007 for Search is very interesting for organizations that want to implement enterprise search and want the option to upgrade to a portal later, without changing its infrastructure and search implementation. It provides the ability to search file shares, SharePoint sites, Web sites, Exchange public folders, Lotus Notes databases, and customer repositories via protocol handlers.

An Overview of Microsoft Search Technologies

One study by IDC (www.idc.com) claims that up to $14,000 annual opportunity cost per user is lost due to inefficient data search. Opportunity cost, as defined in economics, is the most valuable forgone alternative to a decision. For example, if you have a piece of property and build a park for children on it, you have given up the opportunity to build homes or businesses on that property, which is your opportunity cost.

Enterprise search. It's one of the latest catchphrases in the industry. Being that we are all connected in the modern world, we know that information is out there. It is scattered, however, across the world, across the Internet, located on servers, in intranets, within databases ... we just need to get at it. Microsoft is working hard to increase our ability to find and use that information. They have focused in three main areas: desktop, intranet, and Internet search. Here are some of the products they have developed to enhance our search abilities.

Desktop

Windows Desktop Search (WDS) is a feature that is built in to Windows Vista and can be downloaded for Windows XP SP2 and Windows Server 2003 SP1 at www.microsoft.com/windows/desktopsearch/default.mspx. It can search through more than 200 common file types, including emails, documents, images, music, and videos. There is an excellent Preview pane that offers you clear previews of your content, along with a summary of information. Because of its design, other partners can develop applications that build upon it. For example, if you have had the opportunity to work with Outlook 2007 or Windows Live Search Center, these are two products that build upon the technology in WDS. Outlook 2007 can provide inline quick search, with query-hit highlighting. Windows Live Search Center aggregates search results of the desktop, intranet, and Internet. The end result is a single index on the system, rather than multiple indexes.

Intranet

The primary solution for finding content within the enterprise (and it is important to note that when we say intranet, we mean enterprise) is Office SharePoint Server. There have been several flavors of SharePoint Server, with the 2003 version getting excellent reviews. More recently, we have the 2007 version that builds upon the success of its predecessor and offers us a few more options in terms of use.

What can SharePoint Server offer us? It crawls through our office world—our files and databases—and includes a new feature called the Business Data Catalog (BDC), which can search structure line-of-business (LOB) databases such as SAP, Siebel, and so forth. And, because it is based on the same technology as WDS, the same extensibility components written for WDS can be used.

The purpose of this chapter is not to provide a full discussion of each flavor of Microsoft Office SharePoint Server. Suffice it to say that the full Enterprise Version contains more features, including the BDC. However, our goal in this book is to discuss the SharePoint

Server for Search version, which provides most of the functionality we've discussed and can be upgraded to the other versions if necessary.

Internet

To see what Microsoft is offering in the way of Internet search, check out Live Search at www.live.com. What you will find, visually, is a site that looks just like Google. But, you might appreciate some of the cool enhancements. Just check out the Images link on the Live page to see the improvements.

NOTE

If you want to know more about the world of enterprise search, check out the main site from Microsoft located at www.microsoft.com/livesearch/default.mspx. In addition, one of the leading developers at Microsoft is also a great blogger of what his team is doing to enhance search functionality; his name is Arpan Shah, and his blog is located at http://blogs.msdn.com/arpans/.

Which Flavor of MOSS 2007 Is for You?

Logically, functionality is often mitigated by cost. The new Lexus LS 460L is an excellent example. It can parallel park itself … but can you afford that? Well, before you decide on which version of MOSS you want, you need to understand the functionality offered, and then the price for that functionality.

Table 17.1 shows the various features of search that apply to the different versions of SharePoint (source: http://office.microsoft.com/en-us/sharepointsearch/ FX102063541033.aspx). For example, notice that only the MOSS 2007 Enterprise CAL Version includes the BDC mentioned earlier. If you absolutely require indexing of your SAP (or other) database, you need to look at pricing for MOSS 2007 Enterprise. If you do not require this functionality, however, you might consider going with a cheaper version of SharePoint (perhaps one of the two versions of SharePoint Server for Search).

TABLE 17.1   Search Feature Comparison for MOSS 2007 Versions

	MOSS 2007 for Search (Standard Edition)	MOSS 2007 for Search (Enterprise Edition)	MOSS 2007 (Standard CAL)	MOSS (Standard plus Enterprise CAL)
File shares	X	X	X	X
Web sites	X	X	X	X
SharePoint sites	X	X	X	X
Microsoft Exchange Server public folders	X	X	X	X
Lotus Notes databases	X	X	X	X

TABLE 17.1   Continued

	MOSS 2007 for Search (Standard Edition)	MOSS 2007 for Search (Enterprise Edition)	MOSS 2007 (Standard CAL)	MOSS (Standard plus Enterprise CAL)
Third-party document repositories	X	X	X	X
Secure content access control	X	X	X	X
Enhanced search center user interface			X	X
Search for people and expertise			X	X
BDC				X
Search structured data sources				X
Document limit	500,000	No limit	No limit	No limit

Licensing

Before installing MOSS for Search, you need to plan the deployment scenario and understand the licensing model. Which version is needed and what will the infrastructure look like? For MOSS for Search only, the licensing model basically has two different options:

▶ MOSS for Search Standard Edition

▶ MOSS for Search Enterprise Edition

Basically, the only difference between the two versions, as you saw in Table 17.1, is the number of documents the index can contain. The Standard Edition is limited to 500,000 documents, whereas the Enterprise Edition can have an unlimited amount of documents.

Microsoft foresees upgrading MOSS for Search to MOSS 2007 (Standard or Enterprise) later on.

Licensing costs are always an important factor in IT investment choices. Although prices always strongly depend on licensing agreements, Table 17.2 indicates the financial investments required for MOSS for Search (source: http://office.microsoft.com/en-us/sharepointserver/FX102176831033.aspx).

As noted in Table 17.2, MOSS 2007 for Search only needs a server license with no additional client access licenses (CALs). When upgrading to MOSS 2007, you should obtain the relevant CAL (Standard or Enterprise).

TABLE 17.2   Estimated Licensing Costs Per Server Version (U.S. Dollars)

Servers	Estimated Price
Office SharePoint Server 2007	$4,424
Office SharePoint Server 2007 for Search Standard	$8,213
Office SharePoint Server 2007 for Search Enterprise	$57,670
Client Access Licenses	**Estimated Price**
Office SharePoint Server 2007 Standard CAL	$94
Office SharePoint Server 2007 Enterprise CAL	$75

Price Versus Functionality

So, in analyzing the different functionality and considering the pricing, we can see two things:

▶ MOSS for Search is aimed at the midmarket (midsized firms and departments in large companies).

▶ To determine the full cost of each offering, you need to remember that the Standard and Enterprise Versions of MOSS for Search are for the server. For the full versions of SharePoint 2007 (both Standard and Enterprise), you have to figure in the CALs. You don't want to forget the CALs when determining cost.

Okay, so let's suppose you have thought it through and know you need a SharePoint Server for Search 2007 implementation in your company or within your department. What is your next step?

System Requirements and Planning

Planning for your deployment is one of the most important aspects of MOSS for Search. The reason deployment planning is so crucial is because each day your environment will change, more content will be created, your needs will grow, and current solutions will shrink. Good planning can make the difference between your being boxed in or prepared to grow with your data.

With proper planning, you can start small and build up. Staged deployment is a wise way to implement a search structure if one is not in place. This section first discusses the hardware and software needs of your servers, and then it maps out what you need to do in the planning stages.

Hardware and Software Requirements

Table 17.3 lists the hardware prerequisites for MOSS for Search 2007, and Table 17.4 lists the software prerequisites for MOSS for Search 2007.

17

TABLE 17.3   The Hardware Prerequisites for MOSS for Search 2007

Component	Requirement
Computer and processor	A server with processor speed of 2.5GHz or higher (3GHz recommended)
Memory	1GB RAM minimum, 2GB recommended
Hard disk	3GB available space
Drive	CD-ROM/DVD drive

TABLE 17.4   The Software Prerequisites for MOSS for Search 2007

Component	Requirement
Operating system	Microsoft Windows Server 2003 Standard or Enterprise Edition. You can also use the Datacenter Edition or the Web Edition.
Other software installed	Windows SharePoint Services 3.0.
	Microsoft Internet Information Services (IIS) 6.0 (with Common Files, WWW, and Simple Mail Transfer Protocol [SMTP] enabled).
	Microsoft .NET Framework 3.0. (After the installation, you need to enable ASP.NET 2.0.50727 from the IIS Manager.)
Browser needed	Level 1 browsers offer full functionality and include IE6 or IE7. Level 2 browsers offer basic functionality and include Firefox 1.5 and later, Netscape 8.1 and later, and so forth.

Other considerations will depend on your planning and design. For example, if you decide to deploy SharePoint as a farm, you must install SQL Server 2000 SP3a or later for the primary features, and you must install SQL 2005 SP1 and SQL 2005 Analysis Services SP1 or later for some of the advanced features. To clarify, you don't need two versions of SQL for a server farm, you just need to know what features will require the SQL 2005 Analysis Services SP1 update.

It's recommended, if you decide to install MOSS for Search in a server farm, that you install each server role (application server, front-end Web server, back-end database server) on its own system, although you could technically include more than one role on a system.

Planning

Before installing MOSS for Search, it is important to plan a few things:

▶ Identify the people involved.

▶ Plan to crawl content.

▶ Plan for user experience.

Identify the People Involved

It is good to know which people are involved when implementing search. First of all, the maintenance and installation of the server farm is performed by an IT professional. This person basically provides the infrastructure and software, without the need to know the actual search implementation. You can find more about installing MOSS for Search later in the chapter.

Second, three types of administrators have influence on the search implementation:

▶ The shared service provider administrator is responsible for the shared services used in the server farm. The global search settings are administrated here.

▶ The site administrator is responsible for the search settings on the (search) site(s).

   Administrative tasks for both preceding roles are described later in this chapter.

▶ The application administrators can use the search service within their (custom) applications and can index content in the application.

Plan to Crawl Content

Next you must plan the content sources that need to be crawled. For MOSS for Search, the content sources can be of several different types:

▶ **SharePoint content.** This contains all the SharePoint sites, lists, list items, documents stored in libraries, people, and so on.

▶ **Network shares.** The SharePoint indexer can also index file shares, including its documents. Not only the content of the documents will be indexed, but also the user rights will remain when searching. This means that only the documents a user has rights on will be returned as results by MOSS.

▶ **Exchange public folders.** MOSS for Search can access and index Exchange public folders.

▶ **External content sources.** External Web sites can also be indexed by MOSS for Search. Therefore, you can search through external Web sites, too (depending on the number of hops or levels deep the indexer will go). This also means that MOSS for Search can be used as an indexer and search engine for external Web sites or other applications. The search Web service that comes with MOSS can be integrated into these applications.

It is also useful to determine the content types (for example, which type of documents will be indexed). By default, MOSS for Search has the option to index a lot of different file types. Basically, most of the Microsoft file types are supported (Office file types, HTML, and so on). For the file types that are not supported by default, IFilters are available in many cases for download. For example, PDF is not supported by default, but can be downloaded for free from the Adobe Web site.

Although not every third-party IFilter is free to download, most common file types are available.

> **NOTE**
>
> Windows Desktop Search uses IFilters to enable it to index new file types. You can find out which ones are already installed on your system by downloading the IFilter Explorer tool from www.citeknet.com, and you can download most IFilters from the several standard links, including http://addins.msn.com (from the MSN team), www.citeknet.com, and www.ifiltershop.com. To learn more about IFilters and how you can find others or make your own, check out the Channel9 article "Desktop Search IFilters" at http://channel9.msdn.com/wiki/default.aspx/Channel9.DesktopSearchIFilters.

Plan for User Experience

MOSS for Search has several options to change the user interface for searching:

▶ **Search Interface.** MOSS for Search contains only one template, which is the Search Center. This Search Center provides a page with a search box and the result pages. The result pages contain many different Web parts that can be configured depending on the user's needs.

▶ **Search Scopes.** Within MOSS itself, it is possible to define different scopes that use the content sources. For example, it is possible to make a scope that searches through an external Web site, but only a specified part of it.

▶ **Keywords and Best Bets.** It is possible to influence the search results with keywords and best bets. Best bets are basically the results that you want a user to see when searching on a particular keyword or its synonym. It is good to make an inventory of the most important searches with the appropriate results.

▶ **Relevance.** The relevance of search results can also be influenced based on the URL of the result. Results from particular domains can be influenced using the Authoritative Pages settings.

You can use the preceding options to influence the user experience in a positive way. Although it is important to plan them, you can easily adjust them later after receiving feedback from users.

Installing MOSS for Search 2007

After you ensure that you meet hardware and software prerequisites, and have considered the potential use of your MOSS for Search server, you can consider the installation. Before installing MOSS for Search, make sure you have decided which license (Standard or Enterprise) you want to use for the installation. When running setup, you are asked to provide the key.

Just like the other installation options you have seen in the Office 2007 servers collection, the installation begins with a request for the product key and your agreement to Microsoft Software License Terms. After these have been configured, you click **Next.** At that point, you choose between the Basic or Advanced installation:

- ▶ **Basic.** Installs MOSS for Search with some default settings and uses SQL Server Express Edition for the databases. You should only choose this option when you want to install an environment for testing of development and do not need to have specific settings.

- ▶ **Advanced.** Enables you to manage all the settings, databases, and user accounts when installing MOSS for Search.

For the installation walkthrough that follows, we selected the Advanced installation.

After you have answered the standard questions, a new screen asks you to select a server type, as shown in Figure 17.1. Basically, you can make the choice you need. The SQL Server Express Edition, when you choose Standalone, is free to use, so you don't need an additional SQL Server license to run it. Note that only for search purposes, this could be a good option; keep in mind, however, that when you want to upgrade later to MOSS 2007 (portal), the Express Edition can have some shortcomings compared to the full version of SQL Server 2005.

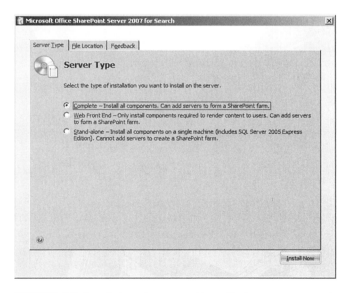

17

FIGURE 17.1   Select the type of installation you want to install on the server.

In addition, you have the option to choose a file location for the installation, and you have some feedback options in the other tabs on this screen. In this case, we chose Complete, to show the options you have for configuration. Click the **Install Now** button to start the actual installation of MOSS for Search. After you have installed it, you are asked to finish the installation and start the Configuration Wizard.

The Configuration Wizard is made to run one time to set all the configuration options (such as the database that should be used, the Central Administration configuration, and the access accounts).

Now it's time to work with the Configuration Wizard:

1. After the start screen, click **Next.** You will be notified that when continuing, the IIS and some SharePoint services will be stopped during the configuration. If your other (Web) applications cannot be stopped at this moment, cancel the configuration and continue later on.

2. Click **Yes.** A screen appears enabling you to choose whether to connect to an existing server farm or create a new one. If you plan this installation to be an installation for another server in an existing farm, you can choose the option to connect to an existing farm. It will add the server to the configuration database, and the server will become available in the farm.

3. (Because we want to show you the more complicated scenario, so that you can gain the fullest level of knowledge, we choose to install in a new server farm.) In this case, a page opens upon which you can configure the new server farm settings, as shown in Figure 17.2.

   This screen contains several options; we chose the database server. This server must run SQL Server 2005 or SQL Server 2000 (SP4). The SQL 2005 server version is highly recommended. You can also provide an instance of a database server (that is, [DBSERVERNAME]\[INSTANCE]).

   Choose a database name for the configuration database. By default, this is SharePoint_Config. If you plan to host more than one SharePoint farm on the same database server, you should give it a more descriptive name. Then, provide a database account and password for the database access. This account should have the security admin and database creation roles in SQL Server. After providing these settings, click **Next** to continue.

4. Your next screen is the Configure SharePoint Central Administration Web Application, as shown in Figure 17.3. The Central Administration is a Web site that can be used to configure the SharePoint settings. By default, the port number is randomly generated by SharePoint. You can also manually specify this port number under which the Central Administration will be available. You can also choose the authentication provider for the Central Administration site. Based on the infrastructure settings and your needs, you can choose NT LAN Manager (NTLM) or Kerberos authentication. Note, in this example, you will see in the next screen that we will chose NTLM. Click **Next.**

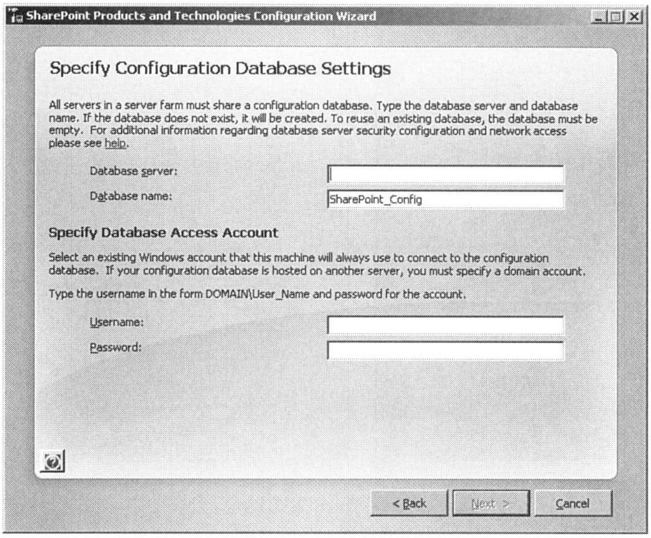

FIGURE 17.2   Specify configuration database settings.

FIGURE 17.3   Configuring the SharePoint Central Administration Web application.

5. Now the Completing the SharePoint Products and Technologies Configuration Wizard opens, enabling you to see a configuration summary. View the summary of settings, shown in Figure 17.4, and click **Next** again to start the configuration.

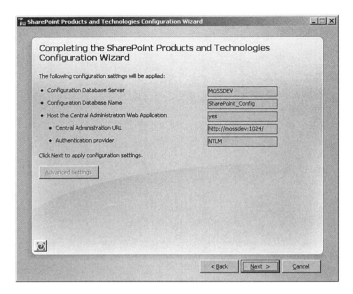

FIGURE 17.4   Finalizing the configuration summary.

6. During the configuration, you will perform nine tasks. (The Central Administration Web site will be created, and you will set the databases, security settings, and so forth.) This process can take a while; but when you have completed these tasks, a success page opens. You can click Cancel at any time to cancel the process.

7. Upon successful configuration, a message tells you that your settings were successfully applied. After you finish the configuration, the Configuration Wizard will be closed, and the Central Administration application site will be opened in a browser. The installation is complete!

After completing your configuration, you must begin administration of your new SharePoint Server for Search 2007 site.

Configuring Your MOSS for Search

After installing and configuring MOSS for Search, you have a Web site available to assist you in administration of your MOSS for Search server; it's called the Central Administration site, as shown in Figure 17.5. You can use this to configure options for your standalone MOSS for Search server, or the SharePoint farm administrators can use this site to configure global farm settings for the MOSS for Search installation.

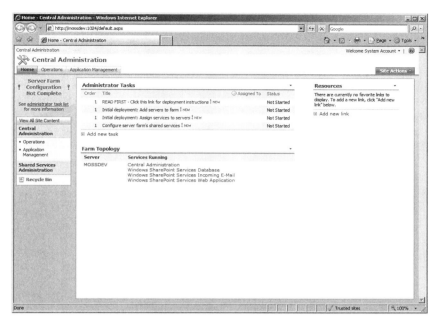

FIGURE 17.5   The MOSS for Search Central Administration site.

The Central Administration consists of three parts, accessible through the global site navigation:

▶ A home page contains the administrator tasks and the farm topology overview. You can see from Figure 17.5 that you are presented with administrator tasks to perform. You are also shown your server and what services are running.

▶ On the Operations tab, you configure operational tasks, such as services on the farm, the servers in the farm and access accounts, and so forth.

▶ On the Application Management tab, you configure and create specific applications, such as a search center application.

Besides these options, you also have the option to go to the Shared Services Administration, where the shared service providers (SSPs) can be managed or created. Shared services are the services within MOSS 2007 that can be used across different (SharePoint) Web applications. Services such as the BDC, user profiles (MOSS 2007), reports, and search can be managed from these SSPs. You have these "shared" services because the same search settings can be used within different site collections, which makes MOSS very flexible and efficient.

17

Configure Operations

Before implementing search, you first configure the server farm in the Operations tab. Open the **Operations** tab, and you will be shown the various links in Figure 17.6.

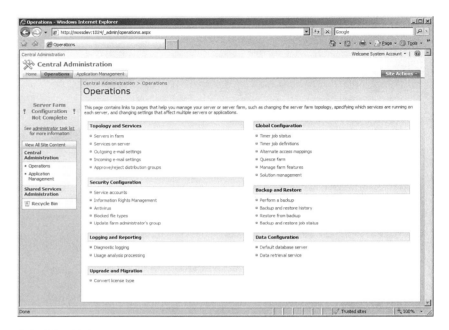

FIGURE 17.6   Configuring operations.

First you need to enable the services on this server. Under the Topology and Services heading, click **Services on server** to go to the Services page, as shown in Figure 17.7.

From this administration page, you can start and stop the available services in the MOSS farm. We want to start the Office SharePoint Server Search services. To do so, click **Start** under the Action column in the list.

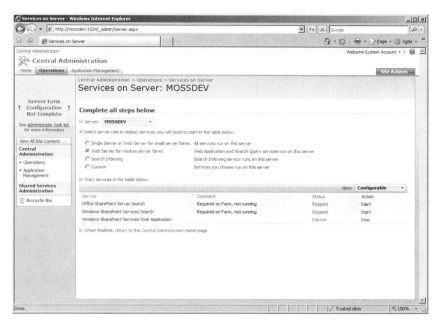

FIGURE 17.7   Starting services on our SharePoint Server for Search server.

When you attempt to begin the services, you will have to set the properties for the search service. Depending on the topology, you can specify the search tasks for this server. We want to check both options: Use this server for indexing content, and Use this server for serving search queries. This way, we let this server index the content and perform the queries. Of course, it is possible to divide those tasks over different servers, but keep in mind that there can only be one indexing server per farm.

After you select the check boxes, some more options will appear:

▶ **The index server file location.** This is the location for the index.

▶ **The indexer performance settings.** It is possible to improve or reduce the performance of the indexer. This way, you basically give to or take priority from other processes on the server (for example, the front-end Web sites).

▶ **The web front-end and crawling property.** Here you can set the server(s) that will crawl content.

In the same screen, shown in Figure 17.8, you also set an email address and the account that runs the service. When you click **Start**, the Office SharePoint Server Search service begins.

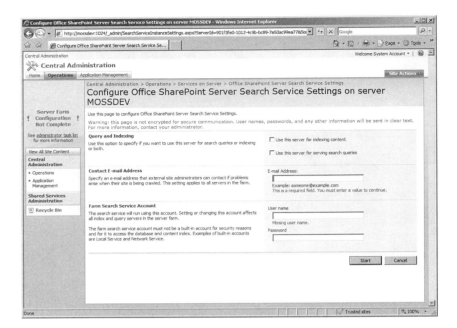

FIGURE 17.8   Configuring search server settings.

Next, we want to start the Windows SharePoint Search Service. Back on the Services page, we notice the Action setting on which we can select Start. By clicking Start, we are directed to the page where we can configure these settings.

NOTE

One question you might be asking is why there are two search services you have to start. It's a valid question, and Microsoft provides a full answer on their TechNet site at http://technet2.microsoft.com/Office/en-us/library/e8c0fccd-8364-4352-8778-c9c46a668b701033.mspx?mfr=true.

The basic answer is that the Office SharePoint Server Search service is based on the service provided with earlier versions of SharePoint (although improved for the 2007 version) and can be used to crawl and index all content you want searchable, with the exception of the Help system. The Help system is cared for by the Windows SharePoint Service Help Search service (and is the same as provided by Windows SharePoint Services 3.0); and this can index site content, index Help content, and server queries. They each have separate indexes and function independently; so when users make queries in the Search box for the Help system, the returned results only include Help content. You are not required to use this service, but for the sake of configuring all aspects of MOSS for Search 2007, we are going to enable it.

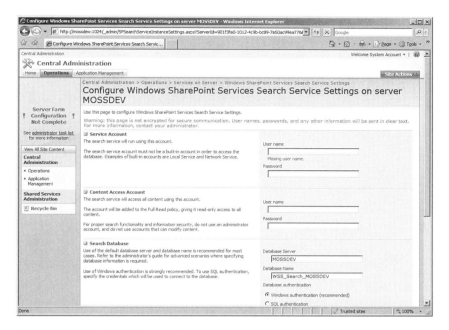

FIGURE 17.9   WSS Search Service settings.

Notice in Figure 17.9 that we provide two accounts in order to configure the Windows SharePoint Services Search Service Settings on our server. One for the service account, the account the service will run under; and one for the content access account, which will be used to access the content to be indexed. We also need a new database for the search settings, which can be provided under Search Database. The last part is the indexing scheduling, to schedule the updates of the search. Click **Start** to start the service.

Create the Search Interface

For searching, we need an interface that provides a Search box and a search results page. MOSS for Search provides a user interface that should be created from the Central Administration pages. To do so, go to the Application Management part of the Central Administration tabs, and click **Create or Extend Web Application**, which will take you to the Create or Extend Web Application screen, shown in Figure 17.10. Click the link **Create a new Web application.**

When you click Create a new Web application, you are redirected to the Create New Web Application page, shown in Figure 17.11.

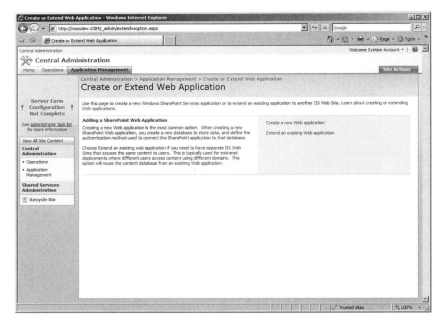

FIGURE 17.10   Creating a new Web application.

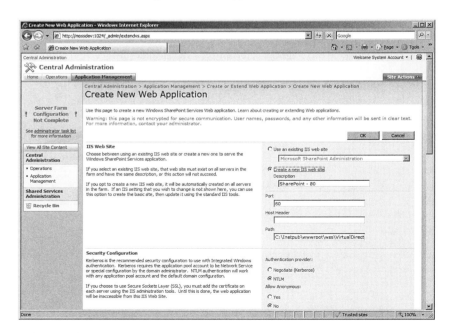

FIGURE 17.11   The Create New Web Application screen.

On this page, you can fill in the application settings and let MOSS create a new application in IIS. You can provide the following settings:

▶ **Create new application or use an existing one.** In most cases (unless you have already created one before), select to create a new one. You can specify the host header or port number and the path to the file location here.

▶ **The security settings** (such as the authentication providers and access). Depending on the infrastructure, you can choose either NTLM or Kerberos authentication. You can also specify to enable anonymous access to the search interface.

▶ **Load balancing settings.** The settings are relevant when you are using more than one front-end Web server.

▶ **The application pool settings.** These are the settings under which the application will run.

▶ **The content database settings.** These are the settings that determine how all the site content will be stored.

To start the application creation process, click **OK.** When the application creation is complete, you will receive a message that says the following:

The Windows SharePoint Services Web application has been created.

If this is the first time that you have used this application pool with a SharePoint Web application, you must wait until the Internet Information Services (IIS) Web site has been created on all servers. By default, no new SharePoint site collections are created with the Web application. To create a new site collection, go to the Create Site Collection page.

To finish creating the new IIS Web site, you must run "iisreset/noforce" on each Web server.

Create the Site Collection

Now that the application has been created, you can create the site collection, which is the (SharePoint) site that will be used as a search interface. To do so, click the **Create Site Collection** link on the application creation results page (or under the Application Management section in the Central Administration). You will be redirected to the Create Site Collection page, shown in Figure 17.12.

17

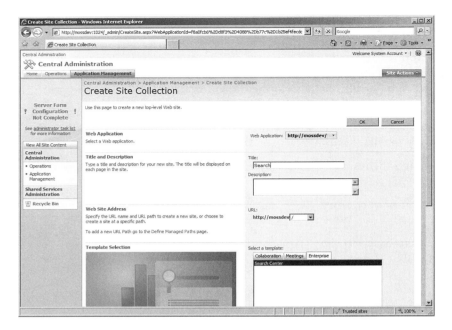

FIGURE 17.12   The Create Site Collection page.

To create a new site, you use the following settings:

▶ **The title.** Choose an appropriate title for the search interface.

▶ **The URL.** By default, the URL is the host header of the application.

▶ **The template.** Because Windows SharePoint Services 3.0 (WSS 3.0) is installed automatically when installing MOSS 2007 for Search, some collaboration templates are available by default. These templates are grouped under Collaboration and Meetings. To create a search interface for MOSS, we selected the Search Center template under the Enterprise tab.

▶ **The site collection owner.** The person who has control over the user interface site.

▶ **The site quota.** The amount of data this site may have.

Now click **OK** to create the interface. After it has been created, follow the link to the site, as shown in Figure 17.13.

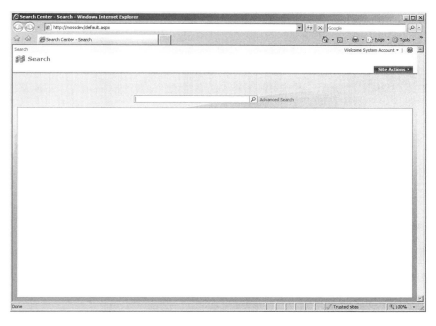

FIGURE 17.13   Your search site.

The Shared Service Provider

So far, you probably have had little difficulty understanding the process for installing and configuring your MOSS for Search server. We installed and then went to the administrative site. We configured the services to run. We then created an application that would handle the site. Then, we just created a site. It doesn't seem like there is much left to do. In a basic stand-alone install, there wouldn't be much else left to do; you could jump to the administration portion of this chapter. However, when working with a farm, you might want to know a little bit about SSPs.

SSP was designed as a replacement for the Shared Services infrastructure of SharePoint 2003, especially with regard to deployment and configuration. Each Web application in a MOSS farm and site is associated with one SSP. However, you can configure different SSPs, and then break up each Web application to use the different SSPs. By doing this, you can have different search results from different portal sites.

All of this might sound confusing. To bring it into the more realistic realm, imagine setting up a search server for a team called Research. They crawl through all their content, and it's a huge hit. But now, the Management team also wants to use this server. You could simply direct them to the same site and crawl their content, but now you don't have the content broken down by team; it's all one big search. You can create a second SSP and assign a second Web application and portal site to that SSP. Then, the persons in Management would be able to search only their content.

17

In addition, this is a great way to use other features such as Excel services and the BDC, although these features are not part of MOSS for Search. They are included in MOSS 2007, however.

Because most of the search settings are done in the SSP, it is recommended to first create a new SSP. Let's walk through the creation of an SSP:

1. In the Office SharePoint Server Shared Services section, under Application Manage-ment, click **Create or configure this farm's shared services.** Doing so will take you to where you can create a new SSP, as shown in Figure 17.14.

FIGURE 17.14   Creating a new SSP.

2. Click **New SSP** on the toolbar to create a new SSP. Now you can enter the SSP configuration settings, as shown in Figure 17.15. You have several options to create the SSP. If you have already created one or more site collections, the option is there to create the SSP under the URL of the Web application that already exists. In this case, we chose to do this. You also need to set an account under which the SSP server will run, the SSP database (which contains the settings of the SSP), the search database for the SSP, and the indexing server (which you've already specified before in the Central Administration). You can also choose to let the Web services (which is one of the ways to use the search) run under Secure Sockets Layer (SSL) so that data will be encrypted.

3. Click **OK** to create the SSP. A success page will acknowledge successful creation and indicate the location of the shared services administration site.

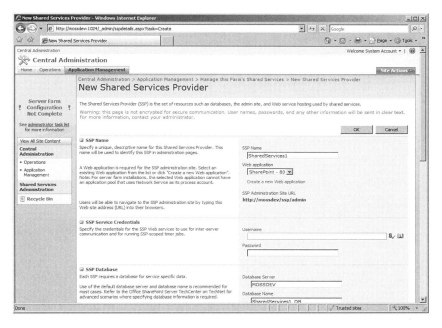

FIGURE 17.15   Configuring SSP settings.

Administrate SSP: Crawling

You can now administrate the SSP search settings by going to the SSP you just created. You can access it later, too, by clicking SharedService1 (or the name you provided) in the left site navigation. When you go to the home page for the administration, you might be disappointed by the immediate lack of options. On this page, you can configure two things:

▶ The search settings for the sites that use this SSP

▶ Usage reporting, for statistics on site usage for this SSP

You can enter the search settings by clicking the link. This link takes you to the Configure Search Settings page, shown in Figure 17.16. On this page, you can manage the crawl settings, the SSP search scopes, and the authoritative pages. This is the starting point for creating new indexes, search scopes, scheduling, and other search settings.

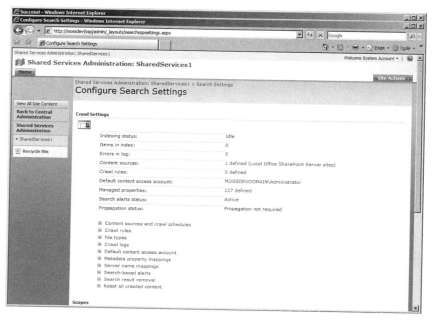

FIGURE 17.16   Configure Search Settings page.

Content Sources and Crawl Schedules

On the Configure Search Settings page, click the **Content sources and crawl schedules** link to open that page. Upon entering the page, you have the option to manage and create content sources and the update scheduling. By default, the content source Local Office SharePoint Server sites is created, which is the container of the SharePoint content. When you hover your cursor over this item, a context menu will expand, on which we can select the options for this content source. If you choose Edit, you are redirected to the page on which to edit the source, as shown in Figure 17.17.

Because we created the SSP under the host header for the search interface, this host header is added as a starting point for the indexer. You can add URLs for the search system to crawl. On this page, you can set several settings such as crawl settings and the crawl schedule. There are two options for crawling content:

▶ **Full crawl.** Full crawl lets the indexer crawl all the content and replaces the old index with the new crawled content. This crawl type takes a lot of resources and is basically only needed when you create a new content source.

▶ **Incremental crawl.** Incremental crawl only adds or updates content that is new in the content source. In most cases, this is the schedule that is set to run multiple times a day, to keep the index current.

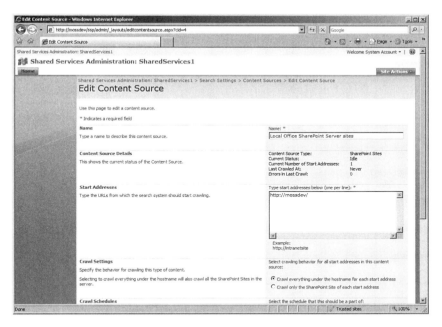

FIGURE 17.17   The Edit Content Source page.

On this page, you can also choose to start a new full crawl. If you do so, or start the update from the context menu, the status of the content source changes to Crawling Full.

The Crawl Log

When the crawling has been completed, you can access the Crawl Log by hovering your cursor over the content source and selecting **Crawl Log** in the context menu. The Crawl Log, as shown in Figure 17.18, provides an overview of all the crawled content and its status. This log is very useful to see which errors occurred during the crawling process and why those happened. From this page, you can select different (filter) views, based on status, time, URL, and content sources.

Create a New Content Source

From the Content Sources page, you can create new content sources. Click **New Content Source** on the toolbar to do so. The Add Content Source page will appear, as shown in Figure 17.19. First of all, you choose a title for the new content source.

17

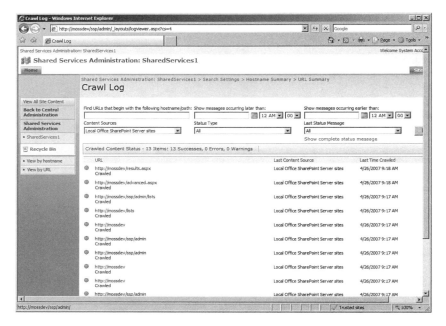

FIGURE 17.18   The Crawl Log.

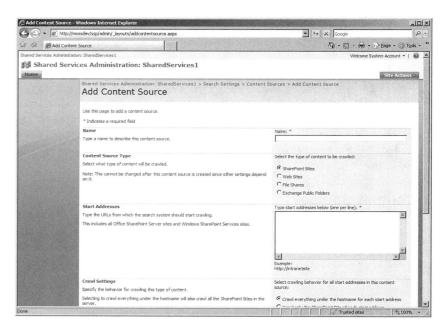

FIGURE 17.19   Adding more content to crawl.

You can choose from a few options for the content source type:

▶ **SharePoint Sites** (for indexing SharePoint sites). By default, the local SharePoint sites are crawled, but it is possible to also add other SharePoint sites to this list.

▶ **Web Sites.** If you choose this option, you can specify the URL, but also other crawling options such as whether you want to only crawl the start page, the page depth, and the number of server hops during the crawl.

▶ **File Shares** (to index network shares, for example). You can specify whether you also want to crawl subfolders.

▶ **Exchange Public Folders.** As with the network share, you can specify whether you want to index subfolders, too.

If you've created a new content source, you need to start a full crawl to start populating the index.

Crawl Rules

In some cases, it is not preferred to have all the content of a content source available. For example, Web forms, or content based on different parameters in the URL, have no use in searches. In these cases, you can administrate crawl rules, as shown in Figure 17.20. Based on a URL and wildcards, it is possible to include or exclude URLs. You also have the option to specify certain rules based on the URL parameters, such as crawling complex URLs (that contain a question mark). You can specify more than one rule, and the rules are applied by the order in which they are set.

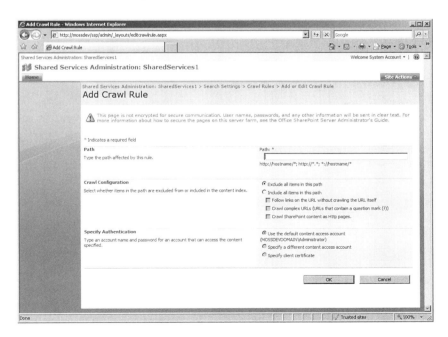

FIGURE 17.20   Adding crawl rules.

File Types

As mentioned previously, MOSS for Search can index a lot of different file types. MOSS recognizes many (Microsoft) file types, but you can also add third-party file types, such as PDF or AutoCAD. To have those file types indexed, you should install IFilters. It is also possible to let MOSS be aware of those other file types. From the Manage File Types page, you can manage those other file types, as shown in Figure 17.21.

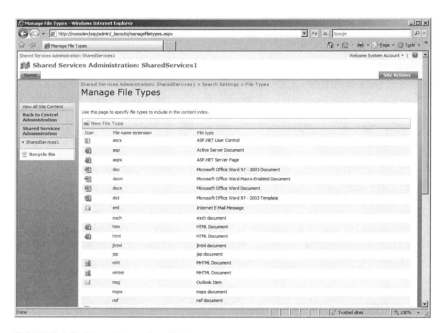

FIGURE 17.21   Managing file types.

To add a new file type, just click **New File Type** and enter the extension. To connect an icon to the file type, you should make changes to the file system on the SharePoint server. By editing the file DOCICON.XML in the folder [drive]:\Program Files\Common Files\ Microsoft Shared\web server extensions\12\TEMPLATE\XML, you can add icons to the file type. Just add a new entry in the XML with the right file extension and a mapping to the icon, and the icon will be available in MOSS, as shown in Figure 17.22.

Metadata Property Mappings

MOSS for Search can use metadata of documents and content to find content. Authors, the title, or filename of the content items can be used to retrieve the content when searching. These metadata properties can also be managed or expanded in the Metadata Property Mappings page, shown in Figure 17.23.

When adding new properties, you must configure some server options, such as property name, property type (text, integer, Boolean, date, and so forth), and the mappings to the property, based on the content type.

```
DOCICON.XML - Notepad
File  Edit  Format  View  Help
<?xml version="1.0" encoding="utf-8"?>
<DocIcons>
    <ByProgID>
        <Mapping Key="Excel.Sheet" Value="ichtmxls.gif" EditText="Microsoft Office Excel" Op
        <Mapping Key="FrontPage.Editor.Document" Value="ichtmfp.gif" EditText="Microsoft off
        <Mapping Key="InfoPath.Document" Value="icxddoc.gif" EditText="Microsoft Office Infor
        <Mapping Key="InfoPath.Document.2" Value="icxddoc.gif" EditText="Microsoft Office In
        <Mapping Key="InfoPath.Document.3" Value="icxddoc.gif" EditText="Microsoft Office In
        <Mapping Key="InfoPath.Document.4" Value="icxddoc.gif" EditText="Microsoft Office In
        <Mapping Key="ODC.Cube" Value="icodcc.gif" EditText="Microsoft Office Excel" OpenCon
        <Mapping Key="ODC.Database" Value="icodcd.gif" EditText="Microsoft Office Excel" Ope
        <Mapping Key="ODC.Table" Value="icodct.gif" EditText="Microsoft Office Excel" OpenCon
        <Mapping Key="PowerPoint.Slide" Value="ichtmppt.gif" EditText="Microsoft Office Power
        <Mapping Key="Publisher.Document" Value="ichtmpub.gif" EditText="Microsoft Office Pu
        <Mapping Key="SharePoint.WebPartPage.Document" Value="icsmrtpg.gif" EditText="Micros
        <Mapping Key="Word.Document" Value="ichtmdoc.gif" EditText="Microsoft Office Word" O
        <Mapping Key="XDocs.Document" Value="icxddoc.gif" EditText="Microsoft Office InfoPat
        <Mapping Key="SharePoint.Link" Value="DOCLINK.GIF"/>
    </ByProgID>
    <ByExtension>
        <Mapping Key="accdb" Value="icaccdb.gif" EditText="Microsoft Office Access" OpenCon
        <Mapping Key="accdt" Value="icaccdb.gif"/>
        <Mapping Key="accdc" Value="icaccdb.gif"/>
        <Mapping Key="accde" Value="icaccde.gif" EditText="Microsoft Office Access" OpenCon
        <Mapping Key="accdr" Value="icaccde.gif" EditText="Microsoft Office Access" OpenCon
        <Mapping Key="asax" Value="icasax.gif" OpenControl=""/>
        <Mapping Key="ascx" Value="icascx.gif" EditText="Microsoft Office SharePoint Designe
        <Mapping Key="asmx" Value="icasmx.gif" OpenControl=""/>
        <Mapping Key="asp" Value="ichtm.gif" OpenControl=""/>
        <Mapping Key="aspx" Value="ichtm.gif" EditText="Microsoft Office SharePoint Designer
        <Mapping Key="bmp" Value="icbmp.gif"/>
        <Mapping Key="cat" Value="iccat.gif" OpenControl=""/>
        <Mapping Key="chm" Value="icchm.gif" OpenControl=""/>
        <Mapping Key="config" Value="icconfig.gif" OpenControl=""/>
        <Mapping Key="css" Value="iccss.gif" OpenControl=""/>
        <Mapping Key="db" Value="icdb.gif" OpenControl=""/>
```

FIGURE 17.22   Connecting an icon to the file type you include.

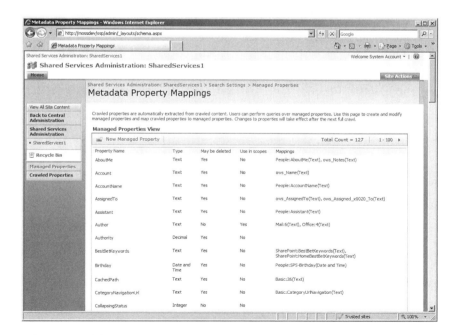

FIGURE 17.23   Metadata Property Mappings page.

Server Name Mapping

Sometimes content is accessed from different locations. For example, the document can be accessed via one URL from inside the domain and another URL from outside. In these cases, a problem may occur: When searching for a document, the result can contain the wrong URL.

In this case, it is possible to add server name mappings, whereby the address in the index can be transformed into an alternative URL.

Search-Based Alerts

In MOSS 2007, you can set user alerts, also based on search queries. When the result of the search query changes, the user who has set the alert receives a notification of the change. On the Search Based Alerts page, you can configure whether users are allowed to set alerts on search queries.

Search Result Removal

In MOSS for Search, you can influence the search results for the user. One of the options is to remove URLs from the search results; you set this option on the Remove URLs from Search Results page. On this page, it is possible to remove URLs instantly from the index.

Scopes

For the SSP, administrators can define a set of search scopes that site administrators can use in their interface. On the Scopes part of the Search Settings page, it is possible to manage the scopes.

To configure a scope, follow these steps:

1. On the Search Settings page, click the **View Scopes** link.

2. From this page that displays, you can create a new shared scope, where you can enter a tile, description, and a customized URL for the results page, if needed. After adding the new scope, you must configure the rules that apply to this scope. From the overview site, click **Add Rules.**

3. Now you can add the rules based on different properties:

   a. Web address (only return results from a specific Web address, based on the folder, host name, or domain)

   b. Property query (only return results that meet the property criteria you specified; for example, only return documents of a specified user)

   c. Content source (only include results that are stored in a content source)

   d. All content

Of course, it is possible to apply more than one rule per scope. You have to apply at least one rule to connect content to a new scope. In the scope overview, you can see how many documents a scope contains.

Authoritative Pages

The last option in the SSP is to define authoritative pages. Authoritative pages are basically a list of pages ordered by importance. The search results will use this list to order the result relevance. With this useful option, you can fine-tune the result set based on the user experience.

Using Search

After you've configured all the search settings and server settings on the Central Administration pages and the SSP pages, you can configure the front end to use the search in the user interface. To do so, follow these steps:

1. Go to the SharePoint site where the search center was created. When entering a search query, we get back a result from the available content sources.

    Note that it is possible to do some actions on this result. It is possible to set an alert (if it is active in the SSP) or subscribe to the RRS feed that contains the result set.

2. Because this site uses the SSP, you can manage the search scopes for this site. In the Actions menu, click **Site Settings**; the page shown in Figure 17.24 will open. Under Site Collection Administration, you have a few search settings available. To manage the scopes, click **Search Scopes.**

FIGURE 17.24   The Site Settings page.

3. This page shows all the available scopes. These are the scopes that come from the SSP, and site-specified scopes that are created in this site collection. Here you can specify which scopes are displayed in what group. The groups can be used either in the Search box (Search drop-down), so that you can choose a scope when searching; or on the Advanced Search page, an alternative page where a user can set more search properties to refine the search.

4. In the site collection, there is another option to influence the search results. One option is to use keywords. Keywords can be manually created, as shown in Figure 17.25, including synonyms, definitions, contact details, and expiring date. After a keyword has been created, best bets can be connected to this keyword. The best bests are the results that the search should return when searching on that keyword or one of its synonyms. After the keyword has been created, the best bet will return in the search results with a star, at the right side of the search results page.

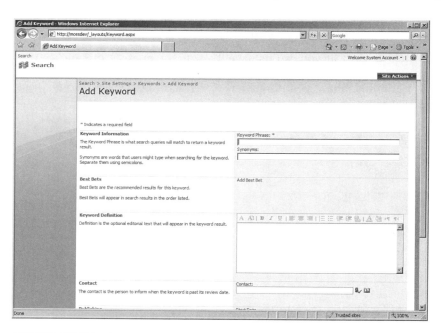

FIGURE 17.25   Keywords and best bets.

Customizing the Results Page

On the default search results page, you can configure the search Web parts to meet business needs. By clicking Site Actions and then Edit Page on the search results page, you are redirected to the Design view of the search results page, as shown in Figure 17.26. This view contains all the search Web parts that are available on this site. Now you can change the properties of each Web part by expanding the Edit button on each Web part.

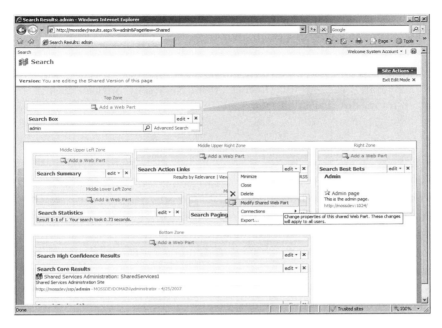

FIGURE 17.26   Customizing the results page.

When the Edit button is expanded, select **Modify Shared Web Part** to change the properties. For each Web part, you have a large number of settings to configure. All the settings are not described in this chapter, but a brief overview here can help you configure your results page as wanted:

▶ **Search box.** The box where a user can enter the search keywords. This Web part can be configured to show the Search Scope drop-down box, too.

▶ **Search core results.** This Web part displays the results. The results are displayed using Extensible Stylesheet Language Transformations (XSLT), a way to transform XML data to a readable layout. This XSLT can be edited so that the results display as you want them to. When users are searching products, for example, you might want to show a picture in the result set of the product.

▶ **Search statistics.** This Web part displays the number of results and the search time.

▶ **Search summary.** Displays a summary of the search query.

▶ **Search action links.** The actions that can be performed on the results, such as settings alerts or subscribe to RSS feed.

▶ **Search best bets.** Displays the best bets of the search query.

▶ **Search paging.** When the number of results exceeds the specified number of results per page, paging will automatically be set.

▶ **Search high-confidence results.** Displays keywords, best bets, and high-confidence results.

Note that the search Web parts differ from other Web parts. From a developer's perspective, it is not possible to create your own search Web parts. Documentation is not available and hard to obtain.

Microsoft's vision is that this set of Web parts, including the properties, can meet the needs of enterprise search in organizations. However, third-party solutions based on the MOSS for Search technology are available that extend the search user experience and options.

Conclusion

Microsoft Office SharePoint Server for Search 2007 is a welcome addition to the Office server group. For organizations that want to implement enterprise search, or use search for external-facing Web sites, MOSS for Search 2007 is a competitive solution.

The extensibility to a corporate intranet, for example, is just a matter of upgrading the license key, which makes MOSS for Search a good starting point for many organizations.

The configurable options and the scalability of the product enable administrators to fine-tune the solution for the user experience. And, third-party solutions on top of MOSS 2007 can be a good addition to the standard functionality.

CHAPTER 18

The Future of Collaboration with Office 2007

We've seen it all now as we've walked together through these seven servers and their various features: online forms, anywhere/anytime collaboration, advanced presence detection and Voice over IP (VoIP) technology, project management solutions, business intelligence with digital dashboards, and high-caliber search abilities. What more could we discuss? Let's explore the future—not necessarily a future as it will be, but one that we might like to see in terms of advancement made on these existing technologies.

The Final Frontier

In the world of collaboration and communication, will we ever reach a final frontier? We now have technology that enables us to see every part of the globe. For a while, I was living in a small town in South America, and a friend sent me a picture of the roof of my home. That amazed me at the time ... briefly. We are always impressed by something cool when it comes out, especially if we can see the value in it, where it makes our life easier or more productive or simply more enjoyable. Hopefully, you've seen that in the new Office servers we've discussed within this book. So what might be the next generation for the software or hardware world that can assist us in collaborating or communicating?

Let's consider what we have as the base.

Forms Server

Just as a quick review, Microsoft InfoPath Forms Services allows InfoPath forms to be accessed and filled out using any browser, including mobile phone browsers. InfoPath Forms Services also supports using a database or other data source as the back end for the form. In addition, it allows centralized deployment and management of forms. InfoPath Forms Services–hosted forms also support data validation and conditional formatting, as does their InfoPath counterpart. It also supports advanced controls (such as Repeating section and Repeating table). In a world that uses more and more electronic forms, having a way to host them for a variety of clients is essential.

The price for a Forms Server comes in at just less than $5,000, which is certainly cheaper than an entire SharePoint server but still a pricy option. Perhaps a future version of Forms Server could offer a Forms Express that isn't so expensive but allows for a few forms to be hosted by a server. This might be added directly into a future Windows 2008 Server service pack release. We have Internet Information Services included for free, why not a mini Forms Server to work along with the free SharePoint Services download?

Forms Server is only marginally cheaper than the full Microsoft Office SharePoint Server 2007 (MOSS) and lacks functionality important to forms solutions, such as workflow, single sign-on, data connection libraries, and others. MOSS provides all the functionality required for moving an electronic form to a solution that actually connects the form to back-end systems and workflows. That is why we prefer to talk about InfoPath Forms Services rather than the Forms Server, which only enables rendering of InfoPath design forms in the browser.

However, some InfoPath controls cannot be used if they have to be hosted on InfoPath Forms Services. Let's hope for that in a future release of the product. Getting support for all InfoPath features would be a nice step. It would make it easier for developers to design forms without the worry that certain aspects won't work.

Christian Stark, the Senior Product Manager for InfoPath Forms Services within Office, said, "It is unlikely that we will support all InfoPath controls in the browser. With the browser, we try to reach more users with the most common forms (85 percent to 90 percent of all forms today can be built for the browser)."

Also, developers today don't have to worry about which features are available or not when they work in "enabler browser form" mode because the UI doesn't show any features not available in the browser.

We appreciate these thoughts, and it is true for the majority of forms created, although we should point out that more advanced forms will still require the InfoPath client.

Groove Server

So, just to recap the world of Groove: It's an amazing software that provides anywhere, anytime, with anyone collaboration. You might recall from Chapter 4, "Groove Server 2007: Overview and Installation," that the Groove client can connect to servers that either Microsoft hosts (either through Live Groove for individuals, or through Groove

Enterprise Services) or you host in-house. The future of this product is almost certain considering the amount of time, money, and effort Microsoft is putting into it.

So, what can we hope to see from a future release of Groove? Well, you might have noticed in the discussions that Groove has its own directory, although it can connect up with Active Directory. This might remind us of Exchange 5.5 days. When Windows 2000 was released (with Active Directory in its first release), the product that had a directory already was Exchange 5.5. You had to work with the Active Directory Connector to get these two directory services to communicate with each other and keep one updated with the other. In a similar sense, we see Groove's directory evolving in the next version so that it is completely Active Directory integrated.

We would love to see a few other features in Groove, but this might not happen. For example, it would be great if Groove were to combine efforts a bit with MOSS and offer a Web-based collaborative workspace. Some have said this is not quite what Groove was designed for. It is entirely client based. Because there is no centralized data store (the data is all on clients, with the exception of when data is en route to the client and the client is offline temporarily), and so there is nowhere to hit with a Web browser. That is all well and good, but it would be nice to be able to offer some Web capabilities for clients that do not use the Groove client. We've discussed this with InfoPath. InfoPath 2003 required the client, 2007 doesn't; it's obvious this is a concern, so why not offer some options that the workspace creator can select so that certain clients can at least participate in the workspace without the Groove client?

The need for three Groove servers is a bit overkill considering what it provides. Considering the fact that Exchange 2007 can be installed on a single server, it is hard to convince me there is a need to configure two or even three for Groove. I envision one server for the future that handles all your Groove needs, and then the data bridge (which is really just a connecting piece) would either be an installable connector for certain back-end applications or would be included automatically with certain applications (such as SharePoint or SQL).

On the client side, Groove can be enhanced in many ways to offer integration with many more programs and games. One personal feature I would love to see is Groove integrated with the MSN Game Zone. I hate having several different logins and programs to do the same thing. If Groove could be Game Zone integrated, I could play my game of chess on the network but not have to open yet another tool. I would also like to see it open up to more applications that are not necessarily owned by Microsoft, such as Skype and other VoIP tools. Most likely, Microsoft wouldn't develop these tools anyway. It would be nice to see a more Groove-oriented world in the future so developers can add functionality to their own software within the Groove environment.

Communications Server 2007

Although the 2007 version is just getting started, we can still see the future possibilities here. Just to review what you have with Communications Server 2007 … we are looking at Microsoft's move to a "unified communications" dream. We are looking at a server that provides presence-based VoIP call management, audio/video/Web conferencing, and instant messaging. In conjunction with the Office Communicator 2007, we have a strong server for the back end with a streamlined tool for the front end. In working with the two, it's almost like the first time we saw *Star Trek: The Next Generation* for the first time, when we realized that communicators were no longer those handheld flip-phone devices, but now you simply touched the triangle on your shirt! Communicator 2007 provides a VoIP softphone, with secure IM, audio/video/Web conference capabilities, and more.

So, what do we see for the future?

Well, hopefully a new look at the concept of "presence awareness." To be honest, this feature is only as honest or aware as the humans behind the scenes choose to be. When the icon tells us they are not at their desk, is that true? Or are they just avoiding calls. If we call them, or check in with their secretary, or walk over to their desk, will that give us the truth? So, tracking down individuals becomes a different game. What could be done? For starters, admit that this feature isn't accurate and stop trying to track down people. Instead, there should be a greater focus on persistent conversations.

> **NOTE**
>
> Persistent conversation refers to interactions carried out using chat, instant messaging, text messaging, email, blogs, wikis, mailing lists, newsgroups, textual and graphical virtual worlds, and so on. The persistence of such conversations gives them the potential to be searched, browsed, replayed, annotated, visualized, restructured, and recontextualized, thus opening the door to a variety of new uses and practices.

Bob Serr, the Parlano CTO (www.parlano.com), wrote the following, which can be found at http://bobserr.typepad.com/so/2006/07/office_communic.html:

> While it is interesting to be people-centric and presence-based, these two components alone are not enough. Specifically, sometimes you don't even know who to contact, let alone whether or not they are available. In this case, you are better-off looking for a topic. You don't need to know *who* you need to know; instead you are only interested in *what* you need to know. This concept is only possible if you organize people naturally around groups which are organized around the topics of your business. While presence and IM are a good start, it is topic-based, group messaging that will be the primary launch-pad for other, higher fidelity modes of communication. This launch-pad will be a major contributor in making Unified Communications successful.

So, we can look for some exciting things in the future with regard to communications—perhaps even one of those triangle things on our shirts (or an injected chip in our shoulder ... or is that too *1984* for us?).

To me, perhaps the single most important thing about unified communications is that thanks to the development of products such as Office Communications Server, Live Meeting, Communicator 2007, Exchange 2007, and SharePoint Server 2007, to name a few, it is now possible to create an enterprise-level communications solution on a small to medium business (SMB) budget. For years, the idea of videoconferencing meant you needed to be either a major corporation or willing to spend like one; this is no longer the case. Besides enhancing technological capabilities, these solutions have leveled the playing field a bit. IT professionals can now offer integrated communications solutions to their company without breaking the budget, which means they can come out looking like stars. And although IT budgets have been on the rebound in the post-dotcom era, we still have yet to see (nor do I believe we will ever again see) the open-wallet policy in our organizations.

Hardware will also play a factor, and Microsoft knows this. Therefore, Microsoft will soon release Microsoft Roundtable, which is meant to specifically complement Office Communications Server 2007. Roundtable combines 360-degree views along with audio and software to create truly interactive Web conferences. Also soon to hit the scene, as mentioned earlier, is the Office Communicator Phone Edition. We have already seen the integration of Communicator on Windows Mobile devices, and it doesn't stop there. Microsoft has partnered with several telecom companies to create a product that goes beyond the Windows Mobile–powered devices and includes direct integration with Exchange 2007, Office Communications Server, and the more traditional private branch exchange (PBX) corporate phone systems. The idea is to move voice communications off of the phone and onto the PC or otherwise integrated mobile devices, which will give you one point of presence regardless of how you interface via your desktop, mobile device, or a Web browser. You can learn quite a bit from Microsoft about new developments at their unified communications site at www.microsoft.com/uc/default.mspx.

Not to be forgotten in this discussion of the future of communications is the move to integrate Microsoft Speech Server into Communication Server 2007. This integration will create even more interesting scenarios for communicating with an IM user via the telephone, collaborating via cell phone, and actually being able to make changes to a document using speech-recognition systems built into Communications Server. Of course, this probably means we'll all start getting just three hours of sleep each night (because we will be so readily accessible). But hey, now your boss can give you a wakeup call on your PC. And, you can IM him by just speaking into your phone (or that injected chip).

While the world keeps getting smaller and smaller, we keep finding more new and creative ways to be "in touch." The idea of collaboration and unification is to create intertwined secure working environments. This idea should lead us down some interesting new technology "roads," and Communications Server 2007 certainly has taken a big step on that road. The journey should prove interesting; and thanks to the technologies we have discussed, more technologists will be a part of that movement.

PerformancePoint Server

PerformancePoint Server 2007 was still incubating through the beta process when we wrote this book, but we need not shy away from discussing its future. You recall that PerformancePoint (with its business intelligence concepts) is Microsoft's entry into the performance management arena. According to Gartner (www.gartner.com), performance management is a "combination of management methodologies, metrics, and IT (applications, tools, and infrastructure) that enables users to define, monitor, and optimize results and outcomes to personal or departmental objectives while enabling alignment with strategic objectives across multiple organizational levels (personal, process, group, departmental, corporate, or business ecosystem)."

To make this move, Microsoft purchased ProClarity in April 2006, and has been actively converting all of ProClarity's analytic, dashboard, and data-visualization capabilities in to the PerformancePoint product. That is not to say that Microsoft developers haven't created much of the product themselves; they have … but they have borrowed where needed.

Michael Smith, Director of Marketing for the Microsoft Office Business Applications Group, said, "The product has been under development for a number of years. Really, it's an application to help you improve the business process of performance management. Analyzing that performance, that's where the ProClarity acquisition came in. We've been building out the underlying platform that those features sit in or hang off of. So, we've incorporated the server-side aspects of ProClarity into PerformancePoint."

So, first of all, what does PerformancePoint do to enhance our business intelligence world? It attempts to address the following weaknesses, according to Zlatan Dzinic, a database developer from South Africa who discussed the subject on his blog (http://dotnet.org.za/zlatan/archive/2007/05/09/philosophy-behind-performancepoint-server-2007.aspx). Zlatan credits David A. J. Axson, author of the book *Best Practices in Planning and Management Reporting,* for his references:

▶ **Limited integration.** Only 26 percent of companies have tightly integrated planning and reporting processes. Logically, a high degree of integration would be expected between the business strategy, the operational and financial plans, and what is then reporting and forecast. The whole objective of the process is to translate strategies into results.

▶ **Lack of consistency.** Only 56 percent of the financial measures are reporting during the planning process—no wonder many organizations complain of the lack of accountability for results.

▶ **Poor understanding and communication of strategy.** Only 25 percent of organizations freely share strategy plans, whereas 60 percent of world-class companies do so.

▶ **Too financially focused.** Nearly half of all companies view the planning process as financial and annual. Financial plans and budgets cannot be linked directly to the strategy they support.

▶ **Costly.** The average billion-dollar company devotes 23,000 to 25,000 person-days each year to planning and management reporting. A best practice company can produce more effective plans and reports in about half the time (11 to 13 full-time people).

▶ **Slow and tedious.** Much of the time dedicated to planning and reporting is wasted. On average, more than 50 percent of professional staff time is spent collecting and validating data rather than analyzing and planning. At best practice companies, 88 percent of time is spent performing analysis.

▶ **Calendar-driven reports that prevent flexibility.** The ability of an organization to get the right information at the right time in order to make timely decisions should be an indicator of the company's flexibility. However, 92 percent of all management reporting is available only on a predetermined calendar basis, typically monthly, whereas only 8 percent of management reporting is available on demand.

▶ **Too detailed.** The average company financial plan is 372 line items. Best practice companies operate with at least a third of that. There is no evidence that more details provide better accuracy.

▶ **Isolated performance management makes analysts slaves to their spreadsheets.** Spreadsheets' greatest strengths are also their greatest weaknesses: great independence and flexibility, but issues with basic quality assurance and control processes. Other issues include backup, accuracy of the calculation routines, security, and data integrity. On average, 30 percent of end users have access to online applications for ad-hoc reporting (compared to almost all for best practices companies).

PerformancePoint was designed to assist in each of these areas. So, a future release could only improve upon them further. Areas in which PerformancePoint shines include monitoring, analytics, planning (including budgeting and forecasting) and reporting, and consolidation.

One of the biggest factors with PerformancePoint is the pricing. As a BI solution that comes in at around $20,000, we are looking at a very compelling solution here for companies.

Where do we see future improvements for PerformancePoint?

Being that PerformancePoint is the newcomer on the market (although it has a history in ProClarity), the key to predicting its future features is to examine the current leaders in the market. For example, consider Actuate (www.actuate.com), which is touted as the world leader in enterprise reporting and performance management applications. For a review of some of the newest features of their products, check out www.actuate.com/company/news/press-releases-resources.asp?ArticleId=9913.

One positive side to PerformancePoint for users is the fact that the front-end key tool is Excel, which business users are quite comfortable with. Excel will continue to evolve to fit in with the PerformancePoint features, starting with an add-in for Excel to help users to connect into the database for budget forms and templates. However, SQL is going to play an even bigger role on the back end. Michael Smith, quoted earlier, says, "Microsoft has been making significant investments in its business intelligence product stack. The base of that stack is really SQL Server, which for us is our business intelligence platform. We also have another set of capabilities in the Office and the end-user platform, in Excel 2007 and SharePoint." He continued, "What we're doing with PerformancePoint is taking those two platforms and building on them a set of applications that are geared toward solving a business problem. We use SQL Server in the back end, we use Office in the front end, and

18

PerformancePoint has specific business logic around things like budgeting and planning performance and score-carding."

Here is where it finally gets interesting. If Excel is the front end, and PerformancePoint acts as the middle … SQL as the back end becomes a whole lot more interesting. The next flavor of SQL (codenamed Katmai, which is a volcano in southwest Alaska and was, incidentally, also used as the codename for the Pentium III) will be released in 2008 and promises to "bring powerful BI capabilities and valuable data even closer to every user." Some of the promises made in the May 9, 2007, press release (www.microsoft.com/presspass/press/2007/may07/05-09KatmaiPR.mspx) include the following:

▶ Empowers users to easily consume information due to increased integration with front-end tools in the 2007 Microsoft Office system, including Office Excel 2007, Excel Services, Office SharePoint Server, and Office PerformancePoint Server 2007

▶ Provides reports of any size or complexity internally within organizations and externally to partners and suppliers

▶ Aligns corporate decision making by collaborating on key analysis and reports within Microsoft Office SharePoint Server

▶ Integrates all relevant data within the enterprise into a scalable and comprehensive data warehouse platform

So, the next vision of SQL (possible name being SQL Server 2008 if it stays on projected schedule) is the key to increased capabilities in PerformancePoint. Between now and then, Microsoft developers can fine-tune the product they have and add to it. And, who knows, perhaps some other features already exist that Microsoft will copy (or purchase). However, this is a really nice product for Microsoft and a great move in entering the business intelligence game. Usually, the complaint with Microsoft products is that they are very pricey compared to other competitive products (or open source solutions). In this case, however, PerformancePoint is considered a great product at a much cheaper price than offered by competitors. We have much to look forward to here.

Project Portfolio Server

Project Portfolio Server lets you create project portfolios for single or multiple projects. Through the portfolio, you have centrally hosted workflows you can connect to from anywhere through your browser. Portfolios can also help with centralized data aggregation, with regard to project planning and implementation.

Microsoft didn't quite create Project Portfolio Server, but began by purchasing UMT Portfolio Manager 3.3 Server on January 19, 2006 (not that long ago). The first release was the 2006 version, which became an add-on to the Project Server 2003 product. So, this is the second version since Microsoft purchased and revamped it. UMT continues to provide consulting services, a much-needed field considering the complexity of Project Portfolio Server.

Due to a lack of understanding regarding the various features of Project Portfolio Management (PPM), some have questions about the future of this product in its entirety. However, UMT, the company that designed it in the first place, is pretty convinced of its value. On their Web site (www.umt.com), they write, "Research has shown that organizations that have implemented PPM as a core management discipline routinely outperform organizations with no or low PPM maturity—having a portfolio perspective that ensures alignment is no longer a 'nice to have' but a business necessity."

Whereas Project Professional allows persons to manage their own projects, and Project Server goes to the next level and allows a projects management to be visible and collaborated upon, Project Portfolio Server is for enterprise project management (EPM) and manages projects throughout a company, alerting managers when they fall behind schedule or fail to meet requirements, and keeping track of resources needed to keep projects moving forward.

What we would like to see out of this product for the future is for it to be integrated with Project Server as a complete package. These two belong together. However, to minimize the confusion that already exists in the marketplace, the next idea is to market Project Server as different flavors: Project MidRange and Project Enterprise. (Of course, we will leave the naming convention up to the wiz kids in marketing.)

We will need to see more feedback from users on this product, but it appears as if specialized dashboards and a variety of other requests are already coming in. Increased analyzing and visualization abilities are no doubt coming in future releases. And, with the ability to access your project information through browsers, the tablet PC market might find a friend in Project Portfolio–based offerings.

Project Server

Project Server takes Project to the next level by storing project information in a centralized database that can be configured to allow a variety of access levels to different members of a project. Project administrators control the security for their projects. Persons can access the project they are working on through Web access capabilities—to see calendars, tables, projected dates, graphical analysis of resource workloads, and more.

What do we see as the next level for this server? Well, that all depends on whether Microsoft takes the suggestion to combine its features with Project Portfolio. Aside from that, the real expansion of Project Server will come from the client side. Microsoft Project is an excellent tool that has been around in various forms for 20 years. While Project Server takes the application into the world of EPM, its value continues to grow for companies who see the need to keep track of every pencil these days.

What we hope to see is Project becoming more visible and made a little more friendly. A Chinese proverb says, "Tell me and I'll forget, show me and I may remember, but involve me and I'll understand." People need to grasp the concepts behind project management a bit more to fully appreciate all that these tools already offer.

18

One of the finest capabilities in Project 2007 is the Cube Building Service, which can truly provide business intelligence and insight through the new reporting infrastructure that connects into a dedicated reporting SQL database. The various cubes (and virtual cubes) offered are helpful (including Project Non Timephased, EPM Timesheet, Issues, Risks, and so forth), but we see additional cubes coming in the future, too.

SharePoint Server for Search

SharePoint for Search has very little room to evolve, unless Microsoft decides to enhance the functionality that currently exists. As you might recall, SharePoint Server for Search enables clients to index common data sources (file shares, Web sites, SharePoint sites, Microsoft Exchange public folders, Lotus Notes databases, third-party document repositories). We discussed two different flavors: the Standard Edition, which can handle 500,000 documents; and the Enterprise Edition, which is almost limitless.

So, what can be added here? It's a simple product that does its job. What more do we need?

Perhaps a future version would do well to include the Business Data Catalog (BDC), which can search structure line-of-business (LOB) databases (such as SAP, Siebel, and so forth). This is a great feature, but only included in the MOSS editions. It would be great if this could be added in. Microsoft isn't interested in giving away their software, so they insist on the purchase of the MOSS server for that functionality; but, it seems odd to provide pieces of the features. First you hack off a piece of your server, form it into a new product with a new price, but then keep important pieces out of it? That doesn't quite make sense. Either keep your MOSS product together and say, "Nope, you have to buy the whole thing," or sell the pieces in complete packages.

So, we'd like to see more flexibility here. We want, in at least the Enterprise Edition, to have the enhanced search center user interface, we want the search for people and expertise feature, the BDC, and the ability to search structured data sources.

What might drive the future of the search world (be it SharePoint Server for Search or the search features in general in MOSS)? Well, the competition perhaps. There are, in fact, competitors in the world of enterprise search, with Google being a big player.

Google is offering its search algorithms in servers that companies can install themselves. Google offers the Google OneBox for Enterprise solution. According to Google, "Google OneBox for Enterprise delivers relevant, real-time information from enterprise sources, such as CRM, ERP, and business intelligence systems, based on a user's search query. Google OneBox for Enterprise can provide users with secure access to everything from simple phone book listings to graphs of inventory levels and sales trends. Current OneBox partners include Cisco, Cognos, Employease, Netsuite, Oracle, Salesforce.com, and SAS—and the list keeps growing." For more information about Google enterprise solutions, check out www.google.com/enterprise/index.html.

In addition IBM has thrown its hat into the search ring by teaming up with Yahoo! and releasing a software product called OmniFind Yahoo! Edition (which is *free*). It's an enterprise search solution that offers support for up to 500,000 documents per server, more than 200 file types, and documents in more than 30 languages. OmniFind Yahoo! Edition also uses the open source Lucene indexing library to provide cross-platform full text indexing. In addition, it is fully integrated with Yahoo! Search, providing one-click access to send queries to Yahoo! Web, image, video, audio, directory, local, and news search services. You can download this from http://omnifind.ibm.yahoo.com/.

The primary focus of this book is Microsoft technology, so why are we showing the competition? Well, we fully expect Microsoft to come out on top of the "search solution war." However, during that battle, it's looking at the competition that is going to give us a possible idea of what might be coming from Microsoft in the months and years ahead.

The Continuing Voyages

The Office 2007 Server technologies have begun their maiden voyage. True, certain pieces have existed for a time, and we see an evolution of their framework in the 2007 release, but it's this first release under the 2007 banner that places them into the public eye in such a unified manner. They will grow and develop. Prices and licensing will change. Pieces will be snapped in or pulled out. We might even see one of these products cut from the lineup if there isn't enough demand for it, or if Microsoft yields to a competitor's strong grip. (Fat chance that will happen; Microsoft is quite the bulldog with show-downs.) But, it is an exciting thing to see so much new technology all in one year.

"May you live in interesting times" is an oft-quoted phrase that seems to have disputed origins and various meanings. Some say it is a blessing, others claim it is a curse. You might have noticed already that the interesting times we are living in might be considered both. The blessing of new technology … the curse of having to learn and implement it. It is our hope that you have found this *Administrator's Guide* guide a key toward unlocking the blessings of the new Office 2007 servers.

18

Index

Numerics

A

E

F

G

N

O

S

How can we make this index more useful? Email us at indexes@samspublishing.com

BOOKS ONLINE
ENABLED

THIS BOOK IS SAFARI ENABLED

INCLUDES FREE 45-DAY ACCESS TO THE ONLINE EDITION

The Safari® Enabled icon on the cover of your favorite technology book means the book is available through Safari Bookshelf. When you buy this book, you get free access to the online edition for 45 days.

Safari Bookshelf is an electronic reference library that lets you easily search thousands of technical books, find code samples, download chapters, and access technical information whenever and wherever you need it.

TO GAIN 45-DAY SAFARI ENABLED ACCESS TO THIS BOOK:

- Go to **http://www.samspublishing.com/safarienabled**
- Complete the brief registration form
- Enter the coupon code found in the front of this book on the "Copyright" page

If you have difficulty registering on Safari Bookshelf or accessing the online edition, please e-mail customer-service@safaribooksonline.com.

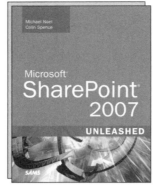
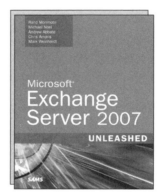